THE GERMAN DISCOVERY OF THE WORLD

STUDIES IN EARLY MODERN GERMAN HISTORY

H. C. Erik Midelfort, Editor

THE

German Discovery of the World

RENAISSANCE ENCOUNTERS
WITH THE STRANGE AND MARVELOUS

Christine R. Johnson

UNIVERSITY OF VIRGINIA PRESS
Charlottesville and London

University of Virginia Press
© 2008 by the Rector and Visitors of the University of Virginia
All rights reserved
Printed in the United States of America on acid-free paper

First published 2008
First paperback edition published 2009
ISBN 978-0-8139-2734-3 (paper)

1 3 5 7 9 8 6 4 2

The Library of Congress has cataloged the hardcover edition as follows:

Library of Congress Cataloging-in-Publication Data
Johnson, Christine R., 1971–
The German discovery of the world : renaissance encounters with the strange
and marvelous / Christine R. Johnson.
    p.   cm. — (Studies in early modern German history)
Based on the author's thesis (doctoral)—Johns Hopkins University.
Includes bibliographical references and index.
ISBN 978-0-8139-2712-1 (alk. paper)
    1. Germany—Intellectual life. 2. America—Discovery and exploration—
Public opinion. 3. Public opinion—Germany. I. Title.
DD65.J64 2008
970.01072043—dc22

2007040673

To my parents

Contents

Acknowledgments

THIS BOOK was made possible only through the financial and intellectual support of numerous institutions and individuals. Initial research for this project was funded by a grant from the Deutscher Akademischer Austauschdienst (DAAD), a Short-Term Fellowship from the Newberry Library, a Helen Watson Buckner Memorial Fellowship from the John Carter Brown Library, and a fellowship from the Dr.-Günther-Findel-Stiftung at the Herzog-August-Bibliothek. Subsequent research support was provided by Washington University, including a Faculty Summer Research Grant.

From its beginnings as a dissertation, this book has been shaped by my advisor at Johns Hopkins University, Mack Walker, whose insight, guidance, and patience I once again have cause to acknowledge. My colleagues in the History Department at Washington University in Saint Louis have followed the book's progress with interest, and I would particularly like to thank Iver Bernstein, Howard Brick, Derek Hirst, and Hillel Kieval for their advice and encouragement at crucial points. My editors at the University of Virginia Press, Dick Holway and Erik Midelfort, expertly helped me realize the potential of the manuscript, which also (in whole or in part) received constructive scrutiny from Pia Cuneo, Anthony Grafton, Christian Kiening, Mark Pegg, Sarah Rivett, Corinna Treitel, and Bethany Wiggin. Much of their advice was put to good use, and all of it probably should have been. Carol

Sickman-Garner prevented many infelicitous phrases and obscure references from reaching the published page.

The chance to think about things other than this book made writing it possible. For different perspectives, I would like to thank the members of the Augsburg Mafia, especially Hans-Jörg Künast, Stephanie Leitch, Beth Plummer, and Ann Tlusty, for reminding me of everything else that was happening in early modern Germany, and Jenny Abel, Dirk Bönker, Elaine McGirr, Jeri McIntosh, Juliana Swiney, and Natalie Zacek, for keeping me in touch with the wider world. In Saint Louis, Sharon Marsh, Jenny Heim, and Lilla Vekerdy have provided invaluable excuses to close up the laptop entirely. My parents, Robert and Judith Johnson, and my sisters, Jennifer and Catherine, have been a source of support (technical, intellectual, and emotional) throughout, and to them go my final thanks.

THE GERMAN DISCOVERY OF THE WORLD

Introduction

I N 1492, CHRISTOPHER COLUMBUS discovered islands in the Western Atlantic, the first of what subsequent expeditions would reveal to be a vast collection of new islands and mainlands. In 1497, Vasco da Gama established a new sea route to India by circumnavigating Africa around the Cape of Good Hope and then crossing the Indian Ocean to the great spice emporium of Calicut. In their wakes, soldiers and settlers streamed west to the vast New World, while Portuguese armadas set sail yearly along the Cape route to gain mastery of the seas and access to the tropical goods of the African and Indian coasts. These voyages of exploration and conquest, along with later ones by the English, French, and Dutch, would reconfigure maps; introduce new trade routes and trade goods; strengthen European states; confront Christianity with new converts and new challenges; and unleash slavery, political domination, and terrifying new diseases on native populations. The transformation of the globe, scholars have long held, also produced a transformation in European knowledge, because reports of the newly discovered lands and peoples challenged the sterile categories and the obsession with the classical past that characterized Renaissance thought. Only through abandoning the limited horizons of inherited knowledge could Europeans properly understand the significance of the discoveries.[1] The Renaissance and the European expansion have been portrayed as separate, even contradictory, historical developments.

The present work, however, uses the case of Germany—the source of both significant works of Renaissance learning and some of the earliest and most important texts and maps explaining the newly discovered territories to European audiences—to demonstrate the vital connections between these two historical developments. Although distant from the political and administrative exigencies of colonization, Germany was well positioned to generate knowledge about places most of its inhabitants would never see. Its wealthy cities, new universities, and numerous elites supported the most exuberant publishing industry in Europe. These same factors, as well as close connections with Italian centers of learning, also put Germany at the forefront of new forms of humanist and scientific inquiry that, while not first and foremost concerned with explicating the overseas expansion, did provide obvious and fruitful venues for discussing the significance of the discoveries. German scholars generated maps displaying the East and West Indies, botanical handbooks describing maize and chili peppers, and polemics on the moral problems posed by luxury and foreign goods. Meanwhile, Germany's extensive diplomatic and mercantile connections linked German elites to the courts and ports of Europe, and German observers monitored, discussed, and even occasionally acted on the new opportunities for political and commercial gain. The prompt and substantial German involvement was predicated on their participation in the intellectual, economic, and cultural developments that characterized the Renaissance in Europe.[2] German responses to the Spanish and Portuguese voyages of discovery and conquest demonstrate the compatibility between Renaissance categories and the overseas expansion of Europe.

On the basis of this compatibility, Renaissance Germans responded early and often to the widening of European horizons. The new worlds of the Iberian empires were incorporated into ongoing discussions about the nature of God's creation, the proper ordering of society, and the ambitious entrepreneurship of German merchants. Because they served as immediate and powerful examples of issues confronting Renaissance culture as a whole, the Portuguese and Spanish expeditions appeared in an extraordinary array of scholarly writings, maps, prints, collections, chronicles, and letters.

The German Discovery of the World analyzes the paths by which Germans received news of the discoveries, the cultural resources they could bring to bear on understanding these discoveries and appropriating them for their own purposes, and the perceptions of the newly discovered lands and peoples that resulted. I argue that Renaissance Germans persistently and successfully used existing techniques of knowledge and established areas of expertise to make sense of the overseas world. To achieve this result, German authors worked long and hard to wrestle incomplete information obtained through imperfect methods into an ordered and convincing form, a process aided by the flexibility of available structures of thought and by carefully crafted strategies for preserving credibility. German participants and observers chose to stress their ability to understand and control the overseas environment, not out of fear or anxiety about the unknown, but because it was intellectually and financially rewarding to do so. Molded and then explained by German cultural arbiters, the East and West Indies became familiar and comprehensible places, susceptible to the extension of European control.

EXPLAINING THE EXPANSION

"Familiar" and "comprehensible" are not terms usually used by scholars to describe the lands that appeared on the European horizon at the end of the fifteenth century. Instead, as will be shown in more detail in the following chapters, "newness" and "difference" have long been considered the defining qualities of the territories and cultures reached by the Spanish and Portuguese expeditions. Members of these expeditions in fact frequently commented on the number of previously unknown things they had encountered and the strangeness of the people and the places. Because these remarks supposedly made inescapable the incompatibility of the discoveries with existing conceptions and ancient authorities, scholars have credited such declarations of the new lands' novelty and alterity with exposing the limitations of a static, closed Renaissance intellectual world, in the thrall of ancient epistemologies, thereby preparing the way for the new, modern philosophy based on experience and experiment. The travelers and new philosophers, joined in their appreciation of the challenges posed by the newly discovered lands and peoples, have thus traditionally been the protagonists of scholarly accounts.

Other sixteenth-century attempts to make sense of the discoveries have neither met with similar approval nor been accorded equal intellectual significance. In analyses particularly well developed for the case of America, scholars have identified and simultaneously criticized two ways in which "old" European categories were extended to cover the "New" World in the opening stages of exploration and conquest. First, through what Anthony Pagden has labeled the "principle of attachment," certain acts and accounts were "intended to shrink the distance between Europe and America, between [the European] and the geographical and cultural 'Other.'" The principle of attachment "allowed for the creation of an initial (if also sometimes troubling) familiarity" and "allowed the discoverer to make some measure of classification."[3] The veneer of familiarity, in this analysis, was an illusion that momentarily concealed the fundamental incommensurability between the Old and New Worlds. Because the principle of attachment did not acknowledge the ways in which these new sights and sounds blew apart the comfortable conceptions of an insular European civilization, it delayed the necessary removal of intellectual barriers.

Graver consequences, though, are said to proceed from the second way in which sixteenth-century Europeans thoughtlessly attached familiar terms to the newly discovered lands and peoples. In these instances, although a particular aspect of the discoveries may have been correctly viewed as "different," this aspect was associated with an image of difference, of "Otherness," already carved out in the European imagination. Such images could be pleasant, as in the association of the tropical lands with the Earthly Paradise, or the native cultures with the Golden Age of mankind. More often, however, they were used to demonize the natives, through inverting the image that Europeans held of themselves. Therefore, the natives were barbarians, devil worshippers, sexual deviants, and cannibals. These associations had devastating consequences for the lands and peoples assigned the label of "Other." While the positive images, for example, incited dreams of inexpressible pleasures and immeasurable wealth, available for the taking, the negative images were used to justify ever-increasing control of the natives' beliefs, practices, and labor, a process most fully developed in the Spanish Indies.[4] Unlike the unimaginative and temporary principle of attachment, therefore, the process of "Othering" carries the heavy burden of the oppressions of European imperialism.

If the principle of attachment and the processes of Othering were self-serving misreadings of the novelty and alterity of the New World, the labels "new" and "strange," so frequently applied to these lands and peoples by contemporaries and modern scholars alike, seem to be straightforward acknowledgments that the discoveries escaped comprehension within European categories. Yet closer inspection reveals that identifying the New World as new or strange likewise required the imposition of European categories on an indeterminate reality. Both new and strange things are characterized by being "unfamiliar," that is, outside previous knowledge or common experience. This definition, however, needs as a base either "previous" or "common" things and therefore makes sense only within the context of prior knowledge and shared experience. In other words, *different* can only be defined relative to *same*. Tying the "new" and the "strange" even more tightly to European concepts is the fact that the unfamiliarity of the new and the strange was often only partial. The strange is not necessarily new, for example, in the case of the "Other," in which the strange is absolutely typical. The reverse is also true: the new is not necessarily strange. New stars, which the Europeans saw for the first time when they entered the southern hemisphere, looked exactly the same as their northern counterparts and could easily be fitted into the European heavenly structure as part of the fixed-stars sphere. In order to have an impact, the elements of the encounter had to be identified and connected with meaningful terms. "New" and "strange" were meaningful terms in Renaissance Europe: the categories themselves were familiar, however much unfamiliarity defined what was included in them. When Renaissance authors described lands and peoples as new or strange, they were not recognizing qualities intrinsic to peoples, cultures, landscapes, flora, or fauna; they were making an interpretive choice that fit the discoveries into existing frameworks.

If novelty and alterity cannot be privileged as labels free from interpretive frameworks, neither can they necessarily be privileged as more accurate interpretations of the realities of the new lands. The case for distinctiveness is not unassailable, even for the Americas. The signs of difference and newness are many: the lack of the expected Asiatic landmarks, the unintelligible languages, the brilliantly colored flowers and birds, not to mention unusual natural phenomena like the Sargasso Sea. These characteristics have prompted one scholar to comment that "the New World and its peoples were so totally unfamiliar and unexpected to their first discoverers" that reaching it was almost like setting foot on "another planet."[5] Yet observers could and did notice similarities that they found helpful and plausible. While modern naturalists consider pumas and lions to be members of different species (albeit members of the same family), in a practical sense, a puma is a lion to the extent that both are furry, fast-moving quadrupeds with sharp claws and a taste for meat.[6] And, in many cases, this information would have been sufficient for a successful encounter with a puma (i.e., an escape without serious bodily harm). The principle of attachment, then, was often enough to enable a useful (in European terms) transaction. This reassessment does not mean that invalid comparisons were impossible. To continue the above example, while their joint characteristics made possible the equation of pumas and lions, the same standard for comparison made it impossible to legitimately claim that parrots were lions. The parameters for what counts as a valid classification, however, should be set by Renaissance, not modern, systems of classification. That modern observers have decided (not recognized) that pumas and lions are different further illustrates the social basis and historical specificity of processes for generating and assessing knowledge.[7]

Renaissance European systems of classification made it legitimate to categorize the newly discovered lands and peoples on the basis of either difference or similarity. If "new" and "strange" were legitimate labels, so was "just another": just another example of human behavior, just another island, just another plant, just another opportunity for commercial profit or corruption. Emphasizing difference was merely one of a broad array of valid interpretive choices. In so roping claims of difference back into the milling herd of interpretative possibilities, I do not wish to assert that it did not matter whether the discoveries were classified as different from or similar to previous knowledge and common experience. The first approach made the newly discovered lands and peoples significant by heightening their distinctiveness; the second made them significant by minimizing it. However, the problem to be investigated is not why some participants and observers correctly perceived the new territories as different and others blindly persisted in their assertions of similarity, but why some chose to interpret the new territories as different and others chose to interpret them as similar.

The case of Renaissance Germany throws this problem into sharp relief, because the responses its inhabitants generated to the Spanish and Portuguese voyages most often reduced the discoveries to a series of "just anothers." Part of my analysis in the present work is devoted to explaining why this emphasis on similarity and familiarity was convincing, and another part to explaining why this emphasis was desirable. Immediate political, commercial, intellectual, and moral concerns usually made it more rewarding to incorporate the European expansion as seamlessly as possible into existing structures of knowledge. To stress the limits of knowledge and proclaim the fundamentally different nature of the overseas territories would have undermined the claims of expertise and practical usefulness that fueled the production of maps that showed, texts that discussed, and ships that sailed to these new worlds. However, German commentators, when it suited their needs, were also capable of making the kinds of statements about new and strange lands that have attracted so much scholarly attention. The range, extent, and sophistication of German responses reveal the adaptive possibilities of Renaissance culture and the importance of context for determining how the discoveries would be interpreted.

All of these choices exerted some form of intellectual control over the discoveries. This claim is obvious when similarity is asserted, but it also holds true for the case of difference. In his seminal *Orientalism* Edward Said argued that representations of "Otherness" evidence "a certain *will* or *intention* to understand, in some cases to control, manipulate, even to incorporate, what is a manifestly different (or alternative and novel) world." [8] The first part of this statement is fundamental for my understanding of Renaissance representations as well. However, I would modify the second part: such representations understood, controlled, manipulated, and even incorporated these territories *through interpreting them* as manifestly different, alternative, and novel. Discussions of novelty and alterity are therefore integral to my argument that German commentators made the East and West Indies into familiar and comprehensible places, and thus susceptible to the extension of European control.

The German preference for connecting the Old World and the New is clearly displayed in the consistency with which Germans considered the fifteenth- and sixteenth-century Spanish and Portuguese expeditions as part of the same event. The joint characteristics that made such a classification possible included the near simultaneity of the voyages of Columbus and da Gama, along with a number of other substantial similarities that diminished the distinctiveness of the discovery of America. Expeditions both east and west sailed from the same peninsula, using the techniques of deep-sea navigation, to reach places and peoples that shared a remarkable number of characteristics—from warm breezes, green trees, and parrots, to precious metals, sweet-smelling spices, and naked, man-eating natives. [9] Rather than viewing the discovery of America as a unique event, this study takes as its starting point the Renaissance German concept of a worldwide Iberian expansion and uses it to analyze how Germans understood the discoveries and why they understood them in the ways they did.

THE RENOVATION OF EUROPE

Important new scholarship on the Renaissance provides insight into the European intellectual, commercial, and political developments that paved the way for this successful incorporation of the newly discovered lands and peoples. The supposed limitations of Renaissance culture have long been used to explain why the reports of the discoveries did not immediately produce a wholesale reevaluation of knowledge in Europe. In the conventional narrative, at the same time that sailors were seeing new sights that shattered the comfortable confines of knowledge, the rise of humanism as the dominant form of scholarly investigation turned the attention of European elites into an unproductive obsession with the past. Humanists' emphasis on classical forms and interest in recuperating the glories of Greek and Roman civilization delayed the inevitable recognition of the novelty of America and in other ways blinded European observers to the challenge posed by the discoveries to previous ways of understanding the world. Recently, however, new interpretations of the Renaissance, particularly the work of Anthony Grafton, have demolished the image of humanism as an intellectual restraint that kept its practitioners from engaging with the changing world around them or acknowledging the cracks in the foundation of ancient knowledge. Humanist refurbishing was responsible for bringing many of the errors, uncertainties, and obscurities of ancient texts to the surface, and even if humanists did not originally intend to uncover these differences and difficulties, they nevertheless developed techniques to deal with them, techniques that would then serve them well in relating ancient material to the new discoveries of the Spanish and Portuguese. This type of innovation was not just required of humanists; the entire European intellectual inheritance available to German commentators was rife with disagreements, inconsistencies, and open questions. Creative reinterpretation and reinvention were endemic in German scholarly, commercial, and political endeavors prior to and apart from the Iberian discoveries. The European expansion simply extended these practices to new parts of the world.

8

Recent scholarship has also shown the importance of extra-European contacts for the creation of the intellectual and material climate of the Renaissance, a pattern of international interaction that was already vital and routine by the time of the voyages of Columbus and da Gama. Mediterranean powers, such as the Byzantine Empire and the various Islamic kingdoms up to and including the Ottoman Empire, had preserved and enhanced the Greek and Roman heritage, while the development of economic exchange and economic practices was fostered by desire for and access to the goods of the East through the Mediterranean routes.[10] The discovery of America and the sea route to India did not bring an isolated Europe for the first time into contact with the wider world, but instead formed part of a continuing process of exchange, negotiation, and warfare.

The expansion of trade also produced new practical instruments and techniques that both reflected and furthered the dynamism of the Renaissance. While Atlantic seamen learned the finer points of deep-sea navigation through the use of instruments like the astrolabe, Italian merchants developed new financial practices, like transferable bills of exchange, and new accounting practices, like double-entry bookkeeping. Methods of production also took on new forms, whether through technical innovations in mining or through the introduction of the putting-out system. The novelty of the Renaissance was generated within the context of the familiar, and the overseas expansion of Europe then provided opportunities for reaffirming what Europeans had already learned through interactions closer to home.

This new understanding of the ways in which innovation and cultural transformation were integral to Renaissance culture is vital for explaining how that culture could adapt to the discovery of new lands and peoples. Along with flexibility, however, prevailing intellectual trends encouraged a stability of form that required disparate experiences to be integrated into the same framework. While scholarship on Renaissance humanism has largely focused on the genres based in the *trivium* of grammar, logic, and rhetoric, the Renaissance also experienced a revival in the mathematical *quadrivium* of arithmetic, geometry, astronomy, and music. Renaissance intellectuals considered these subjects an integral part of a humanist education, and a variety of ancient works on the subject, including Euclid's *Elements of Geometry* and Ptolemy's *Almagest,* underwent the typical philological scrutiny and textual commentary. The revival of mathematics provided a contrast to the sense of historicity and change accompanying the scholarship of the *trivium.*

The goal was to restore and then resume the search for perfectibility and certainty believed possible through the sciences of measurement and calculation, whose concepts and relations remained immutably valid, allowing disputes to be resolved through appeals to the truths of mathematical demonstration. Mathematics provided a universally applicable armature.

The use of established genres, another hallmark of the Renaissance, aided in the presentation of new knowledge by providing clear criteria for what counted as significant knowledge and clear rules for the proper presentation of knowledge. German commentators used genre conventions to communicate with audiences that, in turn, expected the use of such organizing principles to define what information should be presented, how, and to whom. These conventions, whether scholarly forms such as cosmographies and botanical herbals or commercial accounting practices, meant that initial responses to the news from abroad were shaped according to the past training and current professional position of German observers. The information about the newly discovered lands and people was recognized as valuable only through being incorporated into existing patterns of knowledge. Renaissance scholarship had thus developed techniques for recognizing change and containing its implications; the Spanish and Portuguese expeditions were simply another manifestation of this familiar process. The dynamism and flexibility that characterized the Renaissance gave German participants and observers the ability and confidence to incorporate new information and new opportunities into existing frameworks.

The existence of a relationship between the Renaissance and the Reformation is as clear as its specifics are contested. The relationship between the Reformation and the developments I examine in the following chapters is more marginal. Luther's (initially hesitant) challenge to the Catholic Church began twenty-five years after Columbus set sail, so that considerable momentum in interpreting the discoveries had been generated well before Luther raised his first doubts about indulgences. Although the appearance of fierce polemics and stern official measures soon made clear to many that Christians were now faced with wrenching choices, these were choices whose implications could be (and often were) restricted or delayed in areas not connected with the immortal soul. The shifting nature of the debate and the hopes for an eventual reconciliation, not dashed until the failure of the Regensburg Colloquy and the start of the Council of Trent in the 1540s, seem to have limited the extension of the religious discussion into the texts discussed in this book. By 1580 the confessional lines between Lutherans, Calvinists, and Catholics were unavoidably part of the scholarly and political landscape, but before then it would be premature to assume Protestant or Catholic identities as analytical principles. The implications of the Reformation for European history, like those of the overseas expansion, did not emerge fully fledged, but were instead subject to contestation and negotiation as people struggled to understand their world.

GERMANY

"German" as a word and as a concept referred, at the end of the fifteenth century, to several characteristics unifying a part of Europe that stretched from the Baltic Sea to the Alps, and from the west bank of the Rhine River to the Slavic regions in the east. Like all concepts of national belonging, "Germany" and its variants were constructs, but this "imagined community" was forged from patterns of communication, political circumstances, and shared cultural forms that make it a useful organizing principle for this study.[11] At its broadest, the term referred to the German-speaking areas of Central Europe, a definition that sets the outer limits of the "Germany" discussed here. This linguistic unity made possible the seamless transmission of texts through sale and republication. Latin, of course, was the language of the universities and scholarly endeavor, but Latin literacy did not break the linguistic attachment to German. The discussion of individual texts throughout the present work will show that there was a great deal of cross-fertilization across the language divide as German texts, such as Sebastian Brant's *Narrenschiff,* were classicized, and Latin texts, such as scientific treatises, were popularized. Because the results of scholarly investigations were not only translated into the vernacular but explicitly related to the concerns of their linguistically defined German readership, the international world of knowledge to which scholars had access was used to fuse a closer relationship with domestic audiences. The material examined here thus consists of sources that had a defined audience within these linguistic confines: texts published in German; texts published in Latin in the German-speaking areas; manuscript narratives, correspondence, and images produced for an audience within these boundaries; and activities undertaken as a result of the arrival of this information within the German-speaking areas.[12]

Within the limits of the linguistic unity that determines the boundaries of this inquiry, sixteenth-century German writers overlaid other features that defined their nation.[13] Because these points of identification were available only to select groups or regions within the German-speaking areas, the "Germany" that participated in the European expansion shifted in keeping with Germany's patchwork political, economic, and cultural development. The understanding of what being "German" meant also shifted, from a civilization to rival that of ancient Rome, to an elaborate web of business associates and economic opportunities, to an embattled bastion of self-sufficiency and simple living. All of these visions imagined a broader national unity either in connection or in confrontation with the world beyond Germany's boundaries, including the newly discovered territories.

On the political level, the "Germany" of the "Holy Roman Empire of the German Nation" was a flexible enough political union to allow its constituent members to take part in the expansion, but its loose federal structure precluded the possibility of imperial support for participation in the discoveries. The most substantial break between linguistic and political boundaries came at the end of the fifteenth century, when the Swiss Confederacy became the latest region to withdraw from the political institutions of the empire. What remained was an often uneasy conglomeration of sprawling territories governed by powerful princes, smaller principalities intent on protecting their prestige and liberties, and free imperial cities, all of which were subordinate only to the emperor. The governing bodies of the empire, such as the Imperial Cameral Court and the Imperial Diet, usually functioned as a means of maintaining the balance of power among these various estates and between the estates and the emperor, rather than as decision makers and policy implementers. As a result, the lower-level political units usually enjoyed an extraordinary amount of autonomy and acted as separate agents in international affairs. At the level of empire, however, the stasis and weakness resulting from the pronounced devolution of power meant that Germany was barely able to turn back the various threats from the Ottoman Empire, much less participate as a colonizing power in the voyages of discovery. The same political system that placed few restraints on those seeking connections with the expeditions of other states at the same time eliminated the option of a serious German colonial presence.

Political boundaries distinguished the Holy Roman Empire from its neighbors, as linguistic ones distinguished the German-speaking territories. In contrast, economic and cultural activities connected specific portions of Germany with the surrounding territories, while at the same time marking Germans abroad as members of a foreign community. For example, when trade took merchants to the shores of the Adriatic, the highlands of Aragon, or the Carpathian Mountains, they were bound to trade agreements and corporate structures established specifically for Germans. Within Germany, of course, these wealthy long-distance merchants would have been distinguished from each other by their place of origin and from most other Germans by their residence in substantial cities: in the fourteenth and fifteenth centuries, those of the Hanseatic League, and in the sixteenth century, the newly invigorated cities of Swabia and Franconia in the south, which swept past the declining Hansa. The Germany of international commerce was thus a clearly defined element, both outside and inside the German-speaking territories.

Cultural connections functioned in much the same way as economic ones. Italy was important as both a source and a contrast, as Germans ventured across the Alps to study law and medicine at universities such as Padua and Bologna, and Italians came north to conduct the business of princes and prelates.[14] Yet German students and travelers in Italy were still foreigners, and German humanism was not (and never could be) Italian humanism. The classical civilization whose heritage flowed with little difficulty into the Italian present had been destroyed by invaders from the north, and German humanists combined their love of classical texts and rigorous methodology with resentment at still being considered barbarians in humanism's homeland.[15] The differences between the northern and the Italian scholarly Renaissance extended beyond a simple emotional reaction to rejection, in that Germany's contentious relationship with the prized classical past prevented its scholars from simply answering Italian questions with the Italian answers.[16] Built into the scholarly endeavor that united elites from across Europe was a consciousness of national divisions that was particularly acute in the case of Germans looking south.

"Germany" in the sixteenth century was thus defined only partly by characteristics shared by all of its members: linguistic membership at its most expansive, political membership at its more circumscribed. What "Germany" meant was also defined by the knowledge, experiences, and associates of those who observed and commented on the European expansion. The Germany described in this work is limited to those German speakers with the time and connections to learn about the Spanish and Portuguese discoveries; its focus is thus on the centers of the circulation of information and goods: the populous cultural and commercial cities in the southern regions and the Rhineland. Within these limits, however, Germany was defined by a contrast with foreigners, whether encountered in texts or in person, which sharpened the sense of national belonging among the elites for whom travel and extensive reading were possible.[17] The newly discovered territories were perceived as part of a world already divided into Germans and foreigners, and it is part of the task of the present work to show how these mental constructs affected German understandings of the Iberian discoveries.

GERMANY AND THE OVERSEAS EXPANSION OF EUROPE

Situating the texts and images analyzed in this book within their German contexts is not meant to exclude the possibility of broader European commonalities; the claims made are not presumed to be (and in some cases are demonstrably not) unique to Germany. German observers and participants applied broader European categories in order to understand the European expansion, but did so within their own scholarly, economic, and cultural configurations. The flourishing of humanist scholarship in Germany, for example, called for the extension of ancient categories to new situations, while the robust entrepreneurial drive of the southern German merchant bankers produced an ongoing assessment of the commercial potential of the East and West Indies. These interests filtered the information arriving from the ports of Antwerp and Seville, the papal and imperial courts, and the publishing houses of Italy and France into "engaged representations" (to use Stephen Greenblatt's term) characteristic of Germany but derived from European frameworks.[18]

Understanding how Germans successfully integrated the European expansion into existing categories and why they wanted to do so, therefore, suggests the need to reassess the intellectual significance of the discoveries for Europe as a whole. The overseas expansion was important not because of the intractable challenge it posed to prevailing structures of thought, but because Renaissance Europeans believed that they could understand and cope with the discoveries. Convinced that India, Africa, and the New World were intelligible and accessible, merchants invested significant resources in the overseas trade, supplying goods and buying imports that fueled the economic exploitation of the East and West Indies. Audiences within Europe, meanwhile, were reassured that European structures of thought were capable of producing useful knowledge throughout the world, as long as experts such as cosmographers and botanists helped them make sense of new empirical data. Attaching the discoveries to familiar concepts even made it possible to understand certain aspects as new and strange, making possible the (eventually dominant) perception of the discoveries as novel experiences with transformative power. Germany thus provides a case study for broader European patterns of interaction, the German emphasis on the similarity of the newly discovered territories making German responses a particularly good indicator of how well the discoveries fit into Renaissance structures of thought. Explaining the German responses both resolves some issues that have long puzzled scholars and opens up new questions. For example, if German cosmographers in the 1520s were routinely and placidly using America to confirm the belief, found in ancient texts, that the torrid zone and the southern temperate zone were habitable and even inhabited (see chapter 2), why did the Spanish Jesuit José de Acosta still insist, at the end of the sixteenth century, that the ancients had asserted the impossibility of human habitation in these regions?[19] These differing interpretations demonstrate that portrayals of inherited knowledge, as well as portrayals of the East and West Indies, were influenced by agendas that must be recognized and analyzed.

THE CHAPTERS THAT FOLLOW explore how Germans adapted and stretched Renaissance frameworks to make the discoveries work for them. Chapter 1 examines the travel narratives that provided proof of the ability of Europeans to collect and use information about the newly discovered territories and that provided many details incorporated into other types of texts. In these travel narratives, the sheer wealth of information took the place, at least initially, of systematic discussions about the meaning of the discoveries and the nature of the newly discovered lands and peoples. Even in these cases, however, certain structuring principles and framing devices were used to connect "there" with "here." Subsequent chapters examine the selective deployment of information about the East and West Indies within the contexts and networks in which the news found "resonance." I use the criterion of "resonance" to avoid an exhaustive catalog of each place and way in which the voyages of exploration were mentioned, identifying instead the patterns of response in German understanding and the particular meanings thereby imparted to the discoveries. These patterns provide the themes of the subsequent chapters: chapter 2 covers the cosmographical literature; chapter 3 the initial enthusiastic commercial reporting on the economic expansion; chapter 4 the rejection of the spice trade on economic, moral, and medical grounds; and chapter 5 the German merchants' withdrawal from the overseas trade.

The original details may not have been systematic, but Renaissance learning was. The training, goals, and frameworks of Renaissance cultural arbiters determined why they worked so hard to interpret the discoveries in certain ways. Thus, the extensive discussion of these issues in the chapters that follow is not background information, but one half of the story. The presentation of the Spanish and Portuguese discoveries within existing parameters produced a view of the world as open to European investigation, control, and use.

A Note about Chronology

I have chosen to study the period between 1492 (when the Behaim globe, the first text to make reference to the circumnavigation of Africa, was produced) and roughly 1580, because these dates mark the initial phase of German assessment of the newly discovered lands and peoples. The chapters treat the resonant interpretations, all of which had their start in the first half of the sixteenth century, as static because they showed relatively little change over time. A cosmography from 1564 looked remarkably like one from 1507. The one exception comes in the commercial world, subject first to exuberance (chapter 3) and then to disillusionment (chapter 5), the two reactions marking, respectively, the earlier and later parts of the period under discussion. Even in this case, however, the frustrations of the German merchants came about as a result of structures that had been in place from the beginnings of colonial commerce. Around 1580, however, several developments introduced new themes and new frameworks into the depictions of the recently ("newly" being a stretch by this late date) discovered territories. Thus, although several important and substantial portrayals of the overseas landscape and the developing relations between the conquerors and

16

the conquered were published at the end of the sixteenth century, these accounts often gained their immediacy from the growing confessional split initiated by the Peace of Augsburg (1555), which had given both Lutheranism and Catholicism official status within the borders of the Holy Roman Empire.[20] As the divide between Protestantism and Catholicism spread to all forms of cultural representation, the (Catholic) Spanish and Portuguese expansion into the East and West Indies could hardly escape being used as ammunition by both sides.[21] When confessionalization penetrated every aspect of active and contemplative life, it lent a new significance to the discoveries for new sets of European audiences. At the same time that the religious landscape of Europe was being transformed, the imperial systems of Portugal and Spain (linked in 1580 by the union of the two crowns under Philip II of Spain) were being challenged by the upstart colonial powers of England and the Dutch Republic. The new religious and political circumstances promoted new interpretations that were not merely elaborations on earlier themes. While the conclusion suggests some connections with later developments, the years around 1580 were the end of the beginning.

A Note about Nomenclature

I have tried to make clear when I am referring to the historical America, which in the Renaissance referred to the southern mainland in the Western Atlantic, and the historiographical America, which refers more broadly to the New World as an entire region first brought to the attention of Europeans with the voyages of Columbus and the label of Vespucci. When a broader geographical region is meant in a historical context, I have used labels such as "New World" or "Spanish Indies" (which is meant to exclude Brazil). The designations "East Indies" and "West Indies" should not be taken to mean only the island groups currently so labeled, but the entire Indian/Pacific Ocean system on the one hand and the entire Western Atlantic system on the other. Where further geographical specificity is required, I have tried to provide it.

CHAPTER ONE

There and Back Again

THE TRAVELERS' TALES

IN 1508 A BOOK entitled *Newe vnbekanthe landte* (New Unknown Lands), filled with vivid accounts of journeys to distant places, was published in Nuremberg. A translation of a travel compilation published in Italy the previous year entitled *Paesi novamente ritrovati, Newe vnbekanthe landte* consisted of numerous letters from sailors, merchants, and kings about the recent Portuguese and Spanish expeditions.[1] In its form and content this volume typified the accounts of the Iberian expansion that circulated in Germany in the first decades of the sixteenth century. Like *Newe vnbekanthe landte,* most German publications on the discoveries came originally from abroad and found their way into Central Europe along the diplomatic, scholarly, and commercial channels that tied cities such as Augsburg, Nuremberg, Strassburg, and Basel to Italy, France, and the Iberian peninsula.[2] Germans interested in the European expansion thus read many of the same travel narratives as their counterparts in the rest of Europe. Now out of the hands of their original authors, the stories of discovery were further shaped by the decisions of compilers, translators, and editors about what to publish, how to combine and illustrate individual narratives, and how to explain the narratives' significance to their (hopefully numerous) readers.[3] *Newe vnbekanthe landte*'s compiler, who brought disparate narratives together into one volume, and its German translator, who wrote an extensive preface to the compiler's collection, shared the belief that the original traveler should not have the last (or the first) word. The expanded versions of *Newe vnbekanthe landte* published in German (1534) and Latin (1532, 1537, 1555) likewise reflected the growing amount of information about the discoveries available in Germany and the continuing interest in interpreting it for German audiences. The briefest outlines of the story told by *Newe vnbekanthe landte* and its successors will therefore be sketched here as a guide to what Germans knew, when they knew it, and what they were told about it.

The first "new unknown land" encountered by readers of *Newe vnbekanthe landte* was West Africa, as described in the Venetian Alvise da Cadamosto's narrative of his service in two Portuguese expeditions along the coast of Guinea in the mid-fifteenth century. Readers of *Newe vnbekanthe landte* were thus introduced to the themes of exploration, cultural clash, and economic exchange (including the purchase of slaves) in an African context. The significance of the South Atlantic explorations was made clear in the next set of texts, letters penned by a Florentine merchant residing in Lisbon, detailing Vasco da Gama's establishment of Portuguese trading and military bases in the Indian Ocean, including at the all-important spice centers of India. About the greatest of these emporia, the city of Calicut, the merchant wrote: "[It is] bigger than Lisbon and the inhabitants of the same are Indian Christians. [They] are neither white nor black." He noted as well the city's commercial importance: "In this city are merchants without number, Moors, [they] are very rich and all trade is in their hands. They have on their marketplace a very beautiful mosque, i.e., a pagan temple."[4] The account of Pedro Alvarez Cabral's subsequent journey to India featured the first appearance of western lands in *Newe vnbekanthe landte*. En route to the Cape of Good Hope, this captain of a Portuguese expedition made landfall at a spit of land he called Santa Crucis, in what is now Brazil, describing the territory as "overflowing with many trees, many rivers, many deer, yams, and cotton," and its inhabitants as "gray-colored, and [they] go naked without shame, have long hair and also long beards, [and they decorate their bodies]. And their houses are made of wood and are covered with the branches and leaves of trees. And they have many wooden columns in the middle of the same houses."[5] This sequence of texts cobbled together a report on the new Portuguese sea route to India around the Cape of Good Hope, the first to be published in Germany.

While Christopher Columbus's *Letter to Santangel*, describing his

1492 voyage, had appeared in both Latin and German editions at the end of the fifteenth century,[6] *Newe vnbekanthe landte* bypassed this text to provide a more comprehensive account of the western expeditions. Its main narrative, the *Libretto de tutta la navigatione de re de Spagna de le isole et terreni novamente trovati,* originally published in Venice in 1504, was an abbreviated version of Peter Martyr d'Anghiera's first *Decade of the New World,* written by the Italian humanist from his position at the Spanish court. D'Anghiera's text covered the early years of Spanish exploration in the Caribbean, encapsulating Columbus's initial Caribbean discoveries and his landfall on the South American mainland, as well as Alonso Niño's voyage to the latter region and Vincente Yañez Pinzon's expedition farther south, to the mouth of the Amazon. *Newe vnbekanthe landte* then provided accounts of Portuguese voyages to this same region, beginning with *Mundus Novus* (New World), a letter describing discoveries in the southern hemisphere that had already been published over a dozen times in nine German cities.[7] *Mundus Novus,* attributed (most likely incorrectly) to the Florentine navigator Amerigo Vespucci, was yet another description of a long voyage to a strange land, in this case one filled with man-eating savages who "have no goods of their own, but everything is held in common. They have neither king nor government and each is his own master. They take as many wives as they please, and son copulates with mother and brother with sister."[8] To the immensely popular and well-known *Mundus Novus* were added two more accounts of Portuguese discoveries to the west: a second report on Cabral's voyage to Brazil and beyond, and a report from the Venetian ambassador about Gaspar Corte-Real's discovery of land well to the north of the area where Columbus and Vespucci had concentrated their efforts. From these scattered narratives, a reader could gain a sense of the intensity of the Iberian effort and the immensity of the lands the western expeditions had stumbled upon.

Having established the main outlines of the Atlantic voyages, *Newe vnbekanthe landte* then returned to the situation on the Indian subcontinent, recounting the Portuguese success in establishing the Cape voyage as a viable trade route and da Gama's success, during his second voyage, in negotiating a (tentative) peace with the king of Calicut, allowing the Portuguese access to the most renowned trading center in India. The report of "Joseph," a native informant brought back to Portugal, provided details on Indian social stratification, religious practices, political organization, and foodstuffs; it was the final text included from the original *Paesi novamente ritrovati. Newe vnbekanthe landte* continued with a new addition, a letter from the king of Portugal to the pope, celebrating the Portuguese victories over local Muslim rulers in the Indian Ocean, framing this new conflict as part of the ongoing struggle against the traditional enemies of Christendom.[9] *Newe vnbekanthe landte*'s survey of the initial stages of the Portuguese and Spanish expansion thus encompassed an eclectic range of material from a variety of sources, united through the common feature of deep-sea navigation and loosely grouped by geographical destination.

The next version of *Newe vnbekanthe landte,* the 1532 Latin edition entitled *Novus Orbis regionum ac insularum veteribus incognitarum* (New World of Lands and Islands Unknown to the Ancients), was substantially longer, but much of its new material simply amplified existing themes.[10] The Portuguese material was augmented by yet another letter from the Portuguese king to the pope, relating victories in India and Malacca. A partial counterpoint to the Portuguese king's portrayal of triumphant Christian militarism was provided by the *Itinerario* of Ludovico di Varthema, which had earlier been published in German in 1515. In the *Itinerario,* the Bolognese nobleman recounted his travels in disguise through much of the Middle East and India, recording his own lively and not entirely believable adventures as well as the customs and natural resources of lands from the Levant to the Spice Islands. Even Varthema adopted the crusading spirit, however, in his final adventure: his participation in a victory over a Muslim fleet (for which he was knighted) and his successful return voyage by Portuguese ship around the Cape of Good Hope. The New World section of *Novus Orbis regionum* added later publications by authors already included in the original compilation. *Quatuor Navigationes* (Four Voyages), attributed (most likely incorrectly) to Amerigo Vespucci, elaborated on the themes of the *Mundus Novus* letter in its description of the course of four voyages, two for Spain and two for Portugal.[11] The more sober *Libretto* remained in the new edition, its narrative of Spanish expansion updated through an additional publication by d'Anghiera entitled *De nuper . . . Repertis Insulis* (On Islands Recently Discovered),[12] which focused on the early exploration of the Yucatan peninsula.

Novus Orbis regionum also expanded *Newe vnbekanthe landte*'s geographical and chronological scope by including accounts from earlier centuries and narratives about regions closer to home. The *Book of Marco Polo,* which described the Venetian merchant's thirteenth-century journey to and from the court of the Great Khan in Cathay, led readers along the trade routes of Central Asia to the magnificent cities of China—filled with beautiful buildings, great wealth, and idolaters—returning via an ocean route to India that allowed Polo to regale readers with some of the wilder tales about the inhabitants of various tropical islands.[13] Interspersed in the material about voyages to the East and West Indies, meanwhile, were accounts of peoples whom the German translator later labeled "the most noteworthy and powerful peoples of the Old World": the inhabitants of Sarmatia (the European and Asian lands to the northeast of Germany), Tartaria, Muscovy, Prussia, and the Holy Land.[14] The accounts of the Iberian expeditions now appeared as merely the latest and most far-reaching of European attempts to describe the world.

Additions to subsequent editions of *Novus Orbis regionum* returned to incorporating published materials on the Spanish and Portuguese expeditions. The 1537 edition included Maximilianus Transylvanus's *De Moluccis,* first published in Germany in 1523, which recounted the voyage of Ferdinand Magellan along the coast of South America, through the straits that bear his name, and across the vast Pacific to the East Indies. *De Moluccis* continued to follow Magellan's ship, *Victoria,* after its captain's death in the Philippines, as it limped its way around the Cape of Good Hope back to Spain.[15] By the time of its appearance in the 1555 edition of *Novus Orbis regionum,* Hernan Cortes's conquest of Mexico had been announced through news pamphlets[16] and through *De nova maris Oceani Hyspania narratio* (Nuremberg, 1524), a Latin edition of his letters to the king of Spain regarding the capture of the Aztec capital Tenochtitlan. *Novus Orbis regionum* included the latter text, along with an addendum of three reports proclaiming the early success of Christianizing missions, which had already accompanied a second edition of Cortes's letters from Mexico.[17] The steadily increasing literature on the European expansion thus contributed to *Novus Orbis regionum*'s widening chronological and geographical horizons.

Vernacular audiences were also expected to have a healthy appetite for travel narratives of all types, as indicated by the new accounts included in Michael Herr's 1534 translation of *Novus Orbis regionum,* entitled *Die New Welt.*[18] Herr continued *Novus Orbis regionum*'s practice of including reports about regions long familiar to Europeans, as well as newly discovered territories. *Die New Welt* featured new translations of two texts by Peter Martyr d'Anghiera that had previously been available only in Latin: *De legatione Babylonica libri tres,* an account of d'Anghiera's trip to Egypt, and his first three *Decades of the New World,* which covered the early years of Spanish settlement in the Caribbean basin in great detail—thus covering the gap between the *Libretto* and *On Islands Recently Discovered,* already part of *Novus Orbis regionum.*[19] Of the texts subsequently included in *Novus Orbis regionum,* Transylvanus's account of Magellan's voyage was not included in *Die New Welt* or ever translated into German, but a separate German edition of Cortes's letters from Mexico was published in 1550 in Augsburg.[20] German publishers, editors, and translators made available a steady supply of stories about the initial Portuguese and Spanish voyages and the establishment of empire.

Travel narratives by German authors did little more than supplement the basic catalog offered by *Newe vnbekanthe landte:* they did not deviate in style or theme from their Iberian and Italian counterparts. While most of the stories composed by Germans who had ventured overseas would have circulated in oral or manuscript form, accessible only to friends and associates,[21] five accounts did find their way into print. Balthasar Sprenger's account of a Portuguese voyage to India was published in 1509, and Ulrich Schmidel's account of his service in a Spanish expedition to the Rio de la Plata region, in present-day Argentina, in 1567. Two short accounts by Nicolas Federmann (1557) and Philipp von Hutten (1550) narrated the campaigns of conquest and attrition in the Venezuela colony of the Welser merchant firm.[22] The only account to be republished in the period under review, the narrative of Hans Staden, began uneventfully enough with Staden's service in a Portuguese garrison in Brazil, but the plot picked up when his capture by the Tupinamba Indians gave him ample opportunity not only to pray to God for deliverance (He eventually obliged) but to observe Tupinamba rituals, including one of direct relevance to Staden: their practice of eating prisoners. Staden's *Warhafftig Historia . . . der Wilden, Nacketen, Grimmigen Menschfresser* (True History . . . of the Wild, Naked, Savage Man-eaters) was the most successful of the German travel narratives, with four editions published in 1557.[23] These German compositions, aimed from the beginning at audiences in the heart of Europe, confirm the ongoing interest in tales of the European expansion.[24]

To sum up this exercise in analytical bibliography: Germans could read narratives about many of the significant events in the European expansion, most often authored by travelers from elsewhere in Europe but translated and packaged within Germany. It was deemed appropriate not only to combine accounts of the Portuguese voyage to India with those of the Spanish and Portuguese voyages to the New World, but also to add other material that placed the recent expeditions within a panorama of expanding European knowledge of all parts of the world. To explain how Germans made sense of the discoveries, therefore, it is necessary to examine both the travelers' texts and the German contexts.

As is clear even from the cursory survey just provided, the travel narratives published in Germany are intricate texts offering a rich variety of information about the experiences and observations of numerous travelers. Because they are so culturally and psychologically revealing, these sources have attracted much careful and insightful analysis from historians and literary scholars alike.[25] The usefulness of these studies for understanding German responses to the European expansion, however, is limited, as scholars have saved their most scrupulous attention for a single aspect of these texts: the narratives' role in recording and creating ethnographic distance. Boiling down a complex scholarly literature necessarily results in some distortion and oversimplification, and I hope I make clear in the following pages my debt to others' interpretive insights for certain parts of my analysis. With this caveat, however, it should be noted that the dominant view of how travel narratives should be read relies implicitly or explicitly on the concern with novelty and alterity laid out in the introduction to this book. In this interpretation, ethnographic difference is central to these texts because Renaissance Europeans, driven by both the incomprehensible novelty of the native cultures and the need to justify the colonizing powers' superiority and right to rule, resorted to dichotomous classifications: European or "Other," civilized or barbarian, Christian or pagan, colonizer or colonized.[26] These intellectual sledgehammers crushed the true complexity of native cultures, while the blanket of colonial pretensions smothered the very real challenge posed by ethnographic variety to existing ideas of humanity. The dichotomous categorizations could not always be maintained; as many studies have stressed, these initial delineations of radical difference as the basis of superiority were marked by hesitancy, instability, and performativity, because the boundaries between Europeans and natives proved notoriously subject to transgression and dissolution.[27] European categories were thus, according to current scholarship, unsuccessful in making sense of the true and substantial differences between cultures because established ideas were crude tools used to make false claims. Difference was both a fundamental reality and an imposed schema, and the scholarly value of these narratives lies in exploring how their authors responded to this tension.

But the reasons that modern scholars study these texts are not the reasons, according to the available evidence, that these texts were published and read in Germany. Travel narratives were published for all types of German audiences; the educated elite could ponder sober Latin tomes such as *Novus Orbis regionum,* while even the barely literate (along with the educated elite) could understand cheap pamphlets, such as the numerous German versions of Vespucci's *Mundus Novus,* with their short texts and large woodcut illustrations.[28] The German cultural arbiters who brought this wide variety of material to the attention of the wide variety of German readers consistently stressed the meaningful connections between "there" and "here" made possible by these texts and images. German audiences were encouraged to read these accounts to understand the broad patterns of natural variation, human behavior, and divine intervention that governed their own worlds as well. The descriptions of difference that dominate current scholarly discussion were crucial to this approach, but so were the ways in which both difference and similarity were made intelligible, believable, and meaningful. Seen from the perspective of German commentators, such staple accounts of the European encounter as those by Columbus, Varthema, and Vespucci are revealed to be about much more than ethnographic distance, suggesting that the role these travel narratives played in shaping the interpretation of the discoveries is larger than previously understood.[29]

The next section of this chapter shows how the travel narratives themselves fostered readers' sense of connection with the overseas world by portraying the voyages as comprehensible traversals of space and time to peoples and landscapes familiar in their foreignness. The subsequent section examines how these messages of continuity and intelligibility were further strengthened in the "paratexts"—the surrounding material furnished by editors, publishers, and illustrators.[30] This material provides two different kinds of evidence about the reception of the travel narratives by German readers, revealing not only how the paratexts' authors interpreted the original texts, but also which interpretations and explanations they thought would best appeal to a broader German readership.[31] To link the new accounts of exploration to the hopes, fears, and expectations of their audiences, German paratexts portrayed the newly discovered territories as objects of curiosity and as sites of historical action, incorporating them into a timeless, world-encompassing display of natural variety and human experience. The appeal to curiosity required an emphasis on the unfamiliarity of the newly discovered territories, but the equally important lens of history brought into focus the similarities between here and there. When German paratexts stressed the novel and different aspects of the newly discovered lands and peoples, therefore, they did so because it was culturally useful, not because it was politically or intellectually indispensable. In my analysis, the idea of difference is not restricted to colonial agendas and straightforward "Self/Other" comparisons: inherited ideas about the diversity of the world made difference a more open category that was more receptive to the seemingly insignificant details with which Renaissance travel narratives teem. Colonial claims, as the final section of this chapter demonstrates, found little resonance in the German context. Even though German commentators did not claim a specific political or moral authority over non-European cultures, however, they did claim an ability to understand them, assess them, and use them to advance ongoing debates.

THE AUTHOR'S TALE

Renaissance travel narratives were mediated texts constructed after the fact to serve particular purposes and to communicate certain ideas to European audiences.[32] In one form or another, all travel accounts were designed to enhance the status of the traveler. To accomplish this task, as Michael Harbsmeier has pointed out, the traveler-author needed on the one hand to "participate in the stay-at-home's world and prove that he belongs there" and on the other to "refer with his narrative to other worlds, in which only he as the traveler has participated."[33] Fulfilling these requirements was only possible if readers were able to recognize the distinctive aspects of the travelers' experiences and the links to their everyday world. As a consequence, travel narratives, whether emphasizing difference or similarity, made the overseas world legible.

Narratives of voyages to the newly discovered lands took readers along on the journey by using the elements of actual travel to organize their descriptions of events and places.[34] Each of these journeys had a starting point, then a sojourn in a foreign territory, followed by a return to the familiar origin—all reference points that helped orient the reader. After explaining the reasons for the voyage of Magellan to the Spice

Islands, Maximilianus Transylvanus started him out on his journey: "Therefore Magellan departed with five ships from Seville on the tenth day of August, in the year 1519." Equally precise was his information on the return of the eighteen survivors: "Safe and unharmed they arrived at the port near Seville on the sixth of September."[35] The journey proceeded through the enumeration of recognizable distances: days, weeks, miles, or leagues. Even if the distances were astounding, they were neither unimaginable nor immeasurable: "To travel from Lisbon to this city, Calicut, is 3,800 leagues. To travel there and return home again, they have 34,200 Italian miles. Imagine, what time is required! 15 or 16 months, and that is only if they do not stop or lose time, according to what they say."[36] Not only were the terms of travel familiar to audiences, but the days and miles had been traveled by the explorers as proxies of the armchair traveler.[37] Only when a place had been reached (or when the traveler had come close enough to hear about it through local accounts) was information about the place provided, as in this passage from Marco Polo describing the region between Cathay and India: "On leaving Chamba and sailing south-south-west for 700 miles the traveller reaches two islands, one big and the other smaller, called Sondur and Condur. As these are uninhabited, let us leave them. Another 500 miles towards the south-east brings us to a large and wealthy province of the mainland whose name is Lokak."[38] Marco Polo then described the customs of the inhabitants, their political situation, and their natural resources. In portraying their discoveries as the results of a journey, the authors of travel narratives did not just privilege their own experience, but included their readers by demonstrating that what they had experienced was part and parcel of a shared physical world.

The importance of this mundane recounting of less-than-extraordinary travel can best be shown by other texts available to Renaissance readers that failed to provide such guidance and reassurance. In the popular medieval tale *St. Brendan's Voyage,* the Irish monk and his companions simply leave the island of lost souls, or the hermit sitting on a rock somewhere in the Western Sea, and sail an unspecified distance for an unspecified amount of time in an unspecified direction.[39] A similar sort of indeterminacy plagues the latter part of the *Book of John Mandeville,* which recounts the travels of "Mandeville" to the Holy Land, the eastern isles, and even the Earthly Paradise. The first part of Mandeville's *Book* includes effusive descriptions of the many land and sea routes to Jerusalem, but farther east both traveler and reader lose their way amid remarks such as "The land of Lamori is about fifty-two days away from the land in which St. Thomas lies and one goes from St. Thomas's land to Lamori through many wild wastes, sometimes over sea, sometimes over land." [40] Even more discouraging than the text's failure to orient the reader is the traveler's failure to travel. Mandeville reaches the outskirts of the Earthly Paradise, but he admits that "no person can get in through natural means due to the great fire and water and wild animals and also darknesses," [41] a point he brings home by recounting the sad fates of those who have attempted it. Even the great Alexander was unable to conquer this terrain. This section, like the section describing the enclosed tribes of Gog and Magog, is oddly impersonal, because Mandeville simply asserts the impassability as fact, rather than as knowledge gained through his own unsuccessful efforts. [42] In the one instance in which he does dwell on his own struggles as a traveler, it serves as a warning to others. After traveling through the "Devil's Valley" (Teufelstal), with its inevitable winds, beasts, darkness, and tempting treasure, Mandeville concludes, "And I would tell no one to go therein since no one knows how it will turn out for him." [43] Even more vivid images of inaccessibility were featured in the chivalric literature popular with audiences in Germany as in the rest of Europe, in which lands were reachable solely through magic means. [44] In *Die Mörin,* magical oil and a letter written in blood transport the hero, a dwarf, and a tent over the ocean and "through the clouds and firmament" to the East. [45] In contrast, the travel narratives, in representing the overseas territories as accessible within the realm of human endeavor, rooted these lands in a world of possibilities for the reader as well as the explorer. [46]

For the reader to understand the second important point of a travel narrative—that what the traveler had seen and experienced was truly extraordinary—the representation of distance, danger, and difference also had to take recognizable forms. Authors of Renaissance travel accounts therefore used clear guidelines derived from ancient and medieval accounts to portray their encounters as exotic. [47] The travel authors assumed that readers would expect, for example, that the distant parts of the world would be inhabited by peoples with customs, and even bodies, different from their own; that Islam would be a fearsome and well-armed foe of Christianity; and that travel would be arduous and dangerous. The appearance of the startlingly new, the outlandishly strange, and the extremely perilous in travel narratives therefore served

29

to emphasize the links between the author's experiences and categories familiar and comprehensible to readers.

Individual elements of danger and difference enhanced the image of the traveler still further when woven into familiar dramas of chivalric adventure and Christian suffering. Chivalric tales, which could not provide a model for travel, could provide a model for adventure, as flesh-and-blood conquistadors joined literary knights-errant in triumphing over great odds in exotic settings, creating indispensable moments of suspense and high drama.[48] Heroes emerged in all parts of the globe, as both Spanish and Portuguese commanders achieved stunning victories over far more numerous enemies. For example, according to his narration of a sea battle between the Christian fleet of Portugal and the Muslim Indian fleet of Calicut, Varthema participated in a true test of faith and courage, placing the familiar opposition of besieged Christians and powerful infidels in a new setting. The opposing navy's ships, he wrote, resembled a forest upon the waters, so great was their number. In response, Almeida, the leader of the Portuguese, like an "honest manly captain" (redlicher Mannlicher hauptmann), gathered the troops together and gave them a rousing speech, charging them to remember the sacrifice of Christ. When the battle began in earnest the next day, numerous "noble" and "honest" captains (ritterlichen hauptmann) distinguished themselves by their feats of bravery, ultimately resulting in such a decisive victory for the Portuguese that a royal Indian ally commented, "These Christians are a courageous and manly people."[49] The presence of the Muslim Indian fleet is essential, adding an exotic threat to this display of masculine honor and right religion.

In other accounts, the enemies are less substantial but equally powerful, as storms, shipwreck, hunger, and fear become the constant companions of the voyagers. Far from being a deterrent, the voyage's difficulty became a source of pride and privilege. The Venezuelan conquistador Nicolas Federmann was at pains to point out that, although the Portuguese voyages into India and Malacca were longer and required a great deal of effort and endurance, "they go no more than eight days without seeing land."[50] Varthema explained in his preface that no one who read his *Itinerario* could doubt "the great care, daring, and almost unbearable effort" required of him "for the pleasure of seeing such strange things."[51] Although Federmann and Varthema did not go quite so far, the idea that enduring fears and hardships could lend a voyager unique wisdom and insight often slid into the familiar language of Christian suffering.[52] As Anthony Pagden has shown, travelers to America "saw the sea journey as an ordeal, almost as a rite of passage which could convey either purity or a special kind of vision to those who suffered it and survived."[53] Vespucci described the intense feelings he and his companions experienced on sighting the land he would come to call the "New World" after a difficult and stormy ocean crossing: "Still in such fears and such ragings of the sea and sky, it pleased God on High to show us inhabited land and new countries and an unknown world. That we were overcome with great joy upon this sight one can well imagine. . . . The great grace and mercy of God surrounded us as we came to this land, for we had run out of wood and water and could have only survived on the sea a few more days. To Him be given honor and glory and thanks."[54] The grace of God was likewise manifested during the course of Hans Staden's captivity and eventual deliverance. Privileged access to new and strange lands and customs was the reward obtained through God's power and grace and through human endurance. The sights seen had to mark the extraordinariness of the journey by being unmistakably worth the trip. Therefore, Vespucci's tropical paradise filled with leaderless men engaged in unlimited sex, and Staden's wild, fierce, and cruel man-eaters had to be as intellectually accessible to readers as they were physically remote.

The basic elements of the European travel accounts circulating in Germany were thus designed to make the travelers' experiences, both extraordinary and ordinary, intelligible. The feats of the explorer are measured against real human endeavors and frailties. In portraying travel as both adventurous and commonplace, these texts promoted the assimilation of the new territories by subjecting them to European structures of thought. The conventions of travel deployed in the narratives of discovery provided a space both for the depiction of the sensational, the exotic, and the hazardous—elements that stressed the foreignness of the foreign lands—and for the equally necessary reminders that explorers were participating in experiences, such as traveling, fighting, or enduring hardship to gain knowledge, that could happen anywhere.

THE EDITOR'S TALE

When German editors and publishers added illustrations, prefaces, and other paratextual material to entice and educate German consumers, they likewise connected accounts of the Spanish and Portuguese expeditions with an existing repertoire of images and ideas about travel to distant lands. Illustrations, such as those that graced early editions of Columbus's *Letter to Santangel* and Vespucci's *Mundus Novus,* drew crude connections between these new accounts and familiar themes through the display of stock images of ships under sail, naked people, and kings in command.[55] More substantial links between the old and the new parts of the world were drawn through the practices of compilation so evident in *Newe vnbekanthe landte* and its heirs, which brought accounts of the Portuguese and Spanish voyages, and even of travel to regions such as Muscovy and Egypt, together as a single set of stories. Broad surveys of the nature and variety of humanity were standard fare in the Renaissance, and texts such as Aeneas Sylvius Piccolomini's descriptions of Asia and Europe, Polydore Vergil's *De rerum inventoribus* (*On Discovery*) and Joannes Boemus's *Omnium Gentium Mores Leges et Ritus* (Customs, Laws, and Rites of All Peoples) were joined in the 1530s and 1540s by a series of world descriptions published in Germany that incorporated reports about the East and West Indies into their expositions of human geography.[56] These world descriptions included the *Chronica* of the Frankfurt publisher Christian Egenolff and the *Weltbuch* of the freethinking Sebastian Franck and were epitomized by the massive and popular *Cosmographia* of Sebastian Münster, which included hundreds of pages on the history and geography of European and Mediterranean regions and dozens of pages on the newly discovered territories of Africa, Asia, and America.[57] Even these world descriptions could be bundled together with other accounts; in 1567 the Frankfurt publisher Sigmund Feyerabend combined Sebastian Franck's *Weltbuch* and Fernão Lopes de Castanheda's *Von erfindung Calecut* (On the Discovery of Calicut) (a history of the Portuguese in India) with a reprint of Hans Staden's New World travel account and the first publication of Ulrich Schmidel's.[58] By surrounding individual travel accounts with stories and images of other times and other places, German publishers coaxed the newly discovered lands and peoples into established perspectives for understanding travel to distant lands. The paratexts, like the travel narratives themselves, both showcased the exotic and exciting aspects of the travelers' tales and embedded them within a familiar series of referents that connected these stories of adventure to the readers' world. On the one hand, the paratexts tried to draw the attention of curious readers to accounts of the marvelous, while on the other they claimed that readers could learn valuable moral lessons through understanding these accounts as history.

The travelers' tales entered a Renaissance Germany filled with descriptions and depictions of objects and peoples that satisfied curiosity and provided historical perspective. Classical writings on the things to be seen and the lessons to be learned by travelers to distant lands circulated in new editions and translations. For example, the *History* of Herodotus contained both extensive ethnographical discussions of barbarians such as the Scythians and a dramatic history of the wars between the Persians and the Greeks,[59] while Pliny the Elder drew on a long tradition of marvel writing within Greek and Roman culture to catalog the monstrous and marvelous races of Africa and India (the so-called Plinian races) in his *Natural History.*[60] Solinus, Pliny's redactor, went so far as to focus solely on the world's oddities—animal, mineral, and vegetable.[61] The Renaissance preference for ancient texts gave new weight to Greek and Roman accounts,[62] but medieval texts also contained invaluable knowledge about the variety of the world. Medieval creations, such as the great Eastern Christian potentate Prester John, whose fabulously wealthy and pious court was located by legend in India and by history (in somewhat diminished form) in the Kingdom of Abyssinia,[63] and the Great Khan of Cathay, described in all his opulence and wisdom in Marco Polo's *Book,* presented further visions of exotic, but wise and just, kings. Medieval elaborations on ancient accounts such as the stories of Alexander the Great's travels through Asia preserved and enhanced the ancient tales of the marvelous and the moral.[64] The world described in the books of Marco Polo and John Mandeville was different from that of the ancients: it was more extensive, its political and religious configurations had been transformed by the rise of Islam and the irruption of the Tartars, and it was now the stage for sacred Christian history.[65] Yet these changes simply provided more material to ponder, as indicated by the layered approach of Münster's *Cosmographia.* For his section on India, for example, Münster began with descriptions derived from Pliny, then added tales derived from Alexander's travels and information lifted from Marco Polo, before finishing (in a section entitled "New India") with details culled from Varthema's *Itinerario.*[66] The new material derived from the overseas expansion thus added to the overall weight of knowledge, perhaps confining inherited accounts to a smaller space, but leaving them in place as a firm foundation. All the layers could then be mined using the same interpretative tools. These tools enabled German commentators to fit the newly discovered lands and peoples within a recognizable and meaningful moral universe, but did not automatically encourage visions of European superiority or colonial domination.

CURIOUS TALES

Many authors and editors appealed to readers' curiosity, a recognized selling point and a culturally nurtured attribute to be sated by viewing or reading about marvels and wonders—that is, people, places and things that represented nature at its most fanciful and extreme.[67] The elements of difference that were already an essential part of the travel narratives' structure stood for this purpose on their own as objects of delight. When Varthema's great effort and endurance gained him the pleasure of seeing "strange things," he promptly promised to share this pleasure with readers of his *Itinerario* who had stayed comfortably at home. The Nuremberg merchant Michael Behaim, just the type of reader Varthema envisioned, responded to a letter, from his brother in Lisbon, replete with descriptions of Portugal and "parrots and other strange things which they bring from India," by reminding his relative "how much I enjoy strange things."[68] The enjoyment of the exotic was meant to be shared. The increasing (and increasingly displayed) collections of curiosities turned the possession of objects from abroad into social capital. The full development of the "cabinet of curiosities" culture, complete with instructional literature on the items' assembly and display, was a later development, but even in this earlier period, tangible representations of the exotic were a socially distinguishing mark.[69] Thus, in 1514, the king of Portugal, with much fanfare, sent numerous animals, including an elephant and a rhinoceros, to Rome, where the surviving animals (which did not, unfortunately, include the rhinoceros) were paraded in front of the Supreme Pontiff.[70] In Germany, smaller, more manageable animals, above all parrots, were preferred.[71] The Augsburg lawyer Konrad Peutinger was especially proud of his bird, writing to fellow humanist Sebastian Brant, "I want you at some point to see my parrots (papageios) speaking like humans (I don't call them 'psitacos' [as Pliny did], since they have a different color than Pliny describes), and the many other things that have been sent to me from India by our factors: woods, bows, skins, shells, and so on."[72] Michael Behaim was so eager to obtain a parrot that he proclaimed in his request, "I don't care whether it can talk or not."[73] Letters and manuscripts received from abroad also provided privileged access to desired information. The Nuremberg factor Jörg Pock, setting out from Lisbon to India, recognized the importance of such communication, promising Michael Behaim, "Truly I want to write to you often for a while, and to do the same from India." The privilege bestowed by transoceanic ties went both ways, however, as Pock recognized: "So you should too write me a very good letter every year, about the strange things that have transpired in Germany, so I will tell you what is strange in India."[74] For those without their own personal Pock, printed travel accounts or Albrecht Dürer's print of the pope's rhinoceros could meet the desire to acquire knowledge of strange things.[75]

As Pock's plea for reciprocity indicates, the strange was not confined to the newly discovered lands and peoples, even though it was particularly likely to be encountered there. Ancient texts, for example, described the peculiarities of Northern Europe, a region at the edge of the inhabited world from the perspective of Mediterranean civilization. According to Solinus, Germany held not only innumerable savages but birds whose feathers glowed at night and a mysterious substance called "amber."[76] When Northern European authors later came to write about their home region, they retained elements of this wonder, even if they also satisfied local tastes by providing orthodox histories and boilerplate descriptions of European territories and cities. The Alpine regions of Switzerland, for example, rated a chapter in Münster's *Cosmographia* on the "wild and strange animals and kinds of game" that could be found there, complete with illustrations.[77] The heightened sense of wonder with which German readers were expected to approach the newly discovered territories was at most a quantitative, not a qualitative, change from the way they could perceive the world as a whole.

Difference was thus a constant theme in texts new and old. While it encompassed the idea of "Otherness" so useful and fateful in setting strict boundaries between colonizers and colonized, this focus on difference was not confined to a harsh oppositional model.[78] If foreign peoples did not follow standard European practices, whether dietary, sexual, or sartorial, this assertion opened the door for extensive descriptions of the customs they did practice. There were, it turned out, many ways of violating the European taboo against eating human flesh, many substances that could be consumed in place of bread and wine, and many types of sexual relationships outside exogamous monogamy.

Even physical difference created numerous possibilities, as can be seen through the example of the Plinian races, considered monstrous because of the disarray in their physical form: some had dog's heads, some had no heads, some had one giant foot, some had two giant ears, some had no nose, and some subsisted solely on the smell of apples. These catalogs of human and natural diversity familiarized readers with the category of difference and established benchmarks for the inclusion of new phenomena in this category.[79]

German paratexts enthusiastically fit the inhabitants of the East and West Indies, with their various penchants for widow-burning, man-eating, wife-swapping, and betel-chewing, within this long and vigorous tradition of the marvelous. Jobst Ruchamer, in his preface to *Newe vnbekanthe landte,* stressed the rich variety of the Iberian discoveries: "For they have discovered in those same places wonderfully beautiful and pleasing islands with naked black peoples who have strange and unheard-of customs and ways. [They have discovered] also strange and marvelous animals and birds, exquisite trees, spices, various precious stones, pearls and gold, highly prized by us, but these same items are common to them." [80] More tersely, the translator of the Portuguese chronicler Castanheda referred to the "various unheard-of types of people, strange customs, and wonderful plants and animals" that the explorers, both Spanish and Portuguese, had seen.[81] Pamphlets, the established genre for transmitting news of the latest strange event, ominous portent, or monstrous birth in Europe or elsewhere, were used to frame the discoveries as a series of fabulous encounters and spine-tingling events.[82] The flourishing curiosity industry harvested the travelers' tales for all that could be labeled "strange" and "new."

Striking visuals also helped drive home the theme of recognizable difference. The marvelous dominated a pamphlet showing a group of "the people . . . who were discovered by the Christian king of Portugal," wearing elaborate feather-work creations, but otherwise naked. The promiscuity that Vespucci reported among them was indicated by a couple fondling each other in the background, while the everyday nature of their anthropophagism was indicated by a family preparing and consuming human limbs. The caption stripped the *Mundus Novus* letter down to the "familiarly strange" [83]:

The people are therefore naked, handsome, brown, well-built in body.
The heads, necks, arms, private parts, and feet of the women and men are

covered a little bit with feathers. The men also have many precious stones in their faces and chest. No one possesses anything, but instead all things are common. And the men take the women that please them, whether mother, sister or friend, they make no distinction. They also fight with one another. They also eat one another that are killed and hang the meat of those who are killed in the smoke. They live to 150, and have no government.[84]

Images such as this one, and the woodcuts that accompanied the German translation of Vespucci's *Four Voyages,* heightened the sense of difference through juxtaposition and the selective use of available information. However, the representational repertoire also included less oppositional modes for portraying difference, as seen in Hans Burgkmair's panorama based on Balthasar Sprenger's India voyage,[85] and in Christoph Weiditz's drawings of the Nahua he observed in Spain.[86] Burgkmair's panorama documented the variety within humanity, carefully showing the distinctive footwear reported for the inhabitants of "Allago" and the elaborate costumes of "Arabia," while depicting the natives of these regions in family groupings that connected them to each other and to viewers in Europe.[87] Similarly, Weiditz's drawings portrayed not only the new arrivals from the Spanish Indies, but also Moriscas and both black and white slaves. The category of difference, which already encompassed a wide variety of human customs and circumstances, always had room for one more.

In Renaissance Germany the discussion stopped at difference; the unusual was generally not further cataloged or assessed as part of a moral hierarchy or scientific schema.[88] While certain cultural and physical attributes were often mentioned, they were not accompanied by an explanation of their importance, and it was rare for descriptions to begin or end with an encapsulating judgment. Marco Polo might say of the people living in Dagroian that they were "out-and-out savages," or Balthasar Sprenger might state that near Bezeguiche (Byssegicks) there were many "wild people" (wilder menschen),[89] but it was far more typical for authors to include a mixture of traits, some praiseworthy, some earning condemnation, and some simply reported. A description of "Great Venice" (gross Venedig), as the city of Tenochtitlan was named in an early pamphlet on Cortes's expedition, reveals this pattern: "It is immeasurably rich in gold and cotton handiwork and honey. Every day there is a market where copper coins are used, as well as weights and measures. They have good justice. Their bread is made from millet. There are no animals in this country except for dogs, which they butcher and eat. They have much honey and also eat human flesh. They are obedient to their king."[90] The apparent delight in details reflected the interest of curious readers in variety rather than interpretation.

The moral guidance given to their readers by German commentators was directed at assuring them that the new and the strange had a place within a proper Christian life, not at encouraging them to impose a proper Christian life on the inhabitants of the overseas territories. The threat posed by difference was that the allure of the unfamiliar could distract Christians from more suitable objects of contemplation. Not all violations of the expected order were troubling, of course, as miracles served as evidence of God's power. However, unlike pilgrims, whose travel to holy sites and holy relics was part of a sacred vision that bound this world and the next through visible signs, those who sought out (in book or in person) the marvels at the edges of the earth could easily lose their way amid sensual delights and transient pleasures that brought the soul no closer to God.[91] Sebastian Brant's 1494 *Narrenschiff* (*Ship of Fools*), the first German-language text to mention the discoveries, referred to this danger directly. A moralizing poem on the various perils (or foolishnesses) that can entrap the body and with it the soul, the *Narrenschiff* contains a passing reference to the "gold islands and naked people" discovered by the Portuguese and Spanish as part of a longer diatribe against the investigation of the world, particularly its description and measurement. As Brant says, "He whose mind is set on wandering, is not able to serve God completely."[92] Placing an audience in the position of curious readers could put their souls in danger.

If German commentators took the trouble to explain how these stories of the strange in fact aided Christian contemplation, they further integrated the newly discovered lands and peoples into a unified vision of God's creation. As the world, like the human soul, was a work of God, its correct contemplation led one closer to God.[93] Thus, although travel accounts stressed the difference between the perils of the traveler and the comforts of the reader, this sanctioning of curiosity put the two in analogous positions: just as the traveler could gain knowledge only after perilous passage, so the reader could gain insight into the divine only after perilous reading. The paratexts helped by reclassifying marvels as early and permanent miracles, as in this remark that accompanied the numerous small woodcuts depicting the Plinian races in the 1493 *Nuremberg Chronicle:* "Since the Almighty God knew with what similarities and variety he composed the beauty of the world, he wanted also to bring wondrously formed men into the world." [94] Joining in the chorus, Ruchamer argued that translating *Paesi novamente ritrovati* into German was necessary "so that everyone could recognize and learn about the great marvelous wonders of God the Almighty, who made and ornamented the world with such a variety of peoples, lands, islands, and strange creatures." [95] For, asked a scholar who translated Cadamosto's account for the Duke of Bavaria, "what could be more pleasing or entertaining to an honorable and noble mind than that it sees before it as it were the situations of lands and peoples, their manners and strange customs, as well as many wonderful stars, sea creatures, lordly deeds, and God's omnipotence?" [96] The idea that the monstrous races and wonders of this world were also part of God's creation stretched back at least as far as Saint Augustine's *City of God,* but it was reinvoked in these instances to justify the consumption of seemingly frivolous texts.

Sanctioning the objects of curiosity with reference to the divine order had consequences beyond validating curiosity. It necessitated acceptance of the unorthodox as God's will. [97] Sebastian Franck, in his own unorthodoxy, represents an extreme position: "For the marvelous customs and thousand religions described herein will give you much understanding and take you far, because you must acknowledge that these strange people, laws, and ordinations are still human and must be accepted as human. . . . Also remember that the world is wide and almost unending and filled with the works of God, that he cannot hate." [98] Sebastian Münster was less enthusiastic, although equally inclusive: "[God] distributed humankind across the face of the whole world and adapted each according to the character of the land in which he lives. So that the Moor in his country is able to bear the heat of his heaven . . . and so that each one [can] live from the food of his land, which to another would be not only tasteless but physically harmful. Who in this country would want to drink horses' blood like the Tartars or eat dog's meat like some people in Africa, or live on human flesh like the Canibales [an example omitted from later editions] and other even crueler peoples? . . . And because they therefore are accustomed to live according to the character of their land, they live as well as we do according to the character of ours. But every thing comes from God, who manages and supplies all things according to his pleasure, to Him be praise and honor forever. Amen."[99] Whether, as Lorraine Daston and Katharine Park describe the dilemma, "wonders appeal because they contradict and destabilize . . . [or] because they round out the order of the world,"[100] including marvels in these texts was always "an act of containment: that these wonders cannot be explained is a result of human limitations, but whatever they are, they have a place in the divine plan."[101] Taking advantage of the concept's familiar and expansive nature, German paratexts stuffed the category of difference with overseas objects, customs, and landscapes, and then directed the contemplation of these elements, now classified as exotica and novelties, into channels instructive for the Christian observer and profitable for the German publisher.

HISTORICAL TALES

As the translator of the Portuguese chronicler Castanheda moved from praising the wonders of the discoveries to lauding their value as history lessons, a new set of concerns entered the picture: "If histories are to be fruitfully and usefully read, it is not the least important that they are well-ordered and narrated, and that the reader is properly instructed in not only the story, but also in the reasons and causes, why this or that was considered or examined. For although by most of those who eagerly read such new histories, more emphasis and attention is given to whether something marvelous, previously unheard-of, and strange is reported and described in it, nevertheless, sensible and experienced people know to tell themselves that many a more important, higher, and greater use, than simple pleasure of reading about strange things, may be taken from history."[102] Christian Egenolff likewise reminded the readers of his *Chronica* that it was best "if one not only sees and marvels at the stories, but also pays attention to the doings of the Lord in them."[103] The concept of "history" to which these writers referred was a history composed of exempla: paradigmatic situations and actions from which the reader could derive an understanding of proper and improper behavior. The explorers' experiences were thus ripped from their original setting and generalized to situations that people at home could expect to encounter. Readers could see "in Cortes a hero and also the character of a faithful and loyal servant, who would let neither danger nor opposition nor anything else turn him from his master's orders." [104] Princes and nobles could learn how to lead, punish insubordination, and reward loyalty. Common people could learn how to obey. Soldiers could see by example how disciplined and loyal the Spanish troops were, but could also learn that great and useful deeds were not always rewarded, as the examples of Columbus and Balboa showed.[105] Rather than taking place on incommensurate moral terrain, the actions of Christians in the East and West Indies could be scrutinized according to the same standards that applied at home.

The practices of foreign peoples could also be used to comment on specific circumstances in Germany. The image of unscrupulous priests (*Pfaffen*) loomed large in the Lutheran Michael Herr's dedication letter (to the Count of Hanau) in *Die New Welt*. First, priests instructed the inhabitants of both Calicut and the Caribbean to worship the devil. Furthermore, in Calicut they forced the king to lead "a miserable and pitiful life," forbidding him to eat almost all foods "fit for humans," by which Herr meant that they restricted him to a vegetarian diet. What the king of Calicut endured, however, was not unique: "For some people have also forbidden us many types of food and drink, which rules they themselves do not observe"—just as the priests in Calicut, unlike the king, "eat what they like." [106] The other side pointed out parallels as well; when Peter Martyr d'Anghiera reported in *On Islands Recently Discovered* that the priests in Palmaria, a region of Central America, abstained from sexual intercourse, the 1524 edition added this comment: "Note against the heretics of our times who want priests to be able to marry and teach that they not observe Lent." [107] The readers' attention was drawn to specific practices not because they were different from German customs but because of their (seeming) identity with local practices, whether desirable or undesirable.

Beyond very specific comments such as the ones above, and general exhortations to read the texts for exempla, German commentaries with a historical bent did not lay out how their readers should perceive the newly discovered lands and peoples. To serve as historical exempla, however, not only did European activities overseas have to be considered comparable to those on home soil, but the natives had to exhibit parallels in their practices and nature with readers at home. If the inhabitants of Hispaniola, for example, were possessed of a different nature than the Spaniards—or, more to this point, the Germans— then their simple lifestyle could not serve as a spur to greater piety in Europe.[108] In the numerous descriptions of battles, both the native populations and the various European factions appeared as "just another" noble opponent, cowardly enemy, loyal friend, or untrustworthy ally. Peter Martyr d'Anghiera's *Decades of the New World,* for all their interest in cataloging the novelties of nature and human society discovered in the New World, are at the core masterpieces of humanist exempla. The negotiations with the local caciques, the traps set on both sides, and Columbus's attempts to deal with rebellions among the Spaniards and the natives are stories about universal human characteristics. All of the human actors could be judged by the same (European) standards, which meant that accounts of European failure and native heroism could also provide moral enlightenment. Universal standards for judging human behavior were thus used here not to categorize the natives as savage but to assert the usefulness of these travel narratives to German readers.

IMPERIAL TALES?

The imperial visions of Portugal and Spain were explicitly based on moral judgments, derived from Christian and classical concepts, about the false religion, deviant customs, and primitive technology of the natives they sought to conquer.[109] When German commentators extended European understandings overseas, however, they arrived only rarely at assertions of European, or even Christian, superiority. The direct assertions of moral authority and the civilizing mission so prominent in the rhetoric of imperial powers were not the inevitable result of European perceptions, but were produced in response to colonial imperatives. The markers of barbarity would have been familiar to most Renaissance German readers, of course, because the term had been so clearly and frequently applied to the Germans who had confronted the Roman Empire from the far side of the Rhine and the Danube. These ancient barbarians appeared in Münster's *Cosmographia* as fierce warriors in rude surroundings who paid little attention to agriculture (but a lot to beer), were not familiar with gold and silver coinage, and "on certain days offered to the god Mercury human sacrifices." [110] As Stephanie Leitch has shown, these ur-Germans initially provided the visual repertoire for portrayals of New World inhabitants, but such "wild-men" references were quickly dropped as alternate representations became possible.[111] Meanwhile, unlike English writers on the New World who saw equivalents between their stalwart archers and the bow-wielding native inhabitants, and between the freedoms of the ancient Saxons and the native polities,[112] German authors and commentators studiously eschewed connecting the German past with the East and West Indian present, to the point of avoiding the word "barbarian" when describing the newly discovered peoples.[113] The parallels might still have occurred to readers, but it was apparently considered neither helpful nor desirable to point out the resemblance between these newest examples of simple-living forest dwellers and the uncivilized Germans of antiquity.

When it was deemed appropriate, the language of the European civilizing mission was used, but this vocabulary was always applied to the colonizing powers. On the death of Charles V, Holy Roman Emperor and King of Spain, the eulogy published in Augsburg contained, amid reflections on his military actions against the Turks and the split within the Church, praise for Charles's activities overseas: "As with Alexander the Great, the situation of the conquered peoples is better, barbarians are being turned into civilized men, and, what is most important, followers of Christ." [114] Neither Charles nor Alexander was held up as a model for Germans to follow, however.[115] The original German-language translator of Castanheda's first book on Portuguese India condemned in his preface the customs of most the peoples described in the book, "because in that place there is no discipline, no shame, no law, no justice, no crafts, no art." He then expressed his disbelief, tempered only by the assurances of many eyewitness accounts, "that real live human beings should sink to such cruelty, unreason and furthermore bestial way of life." What this display of unworthiness required of his readers, however, was only the recognition "that we thereby have even more reasons to thank God for the great gifts that he has mercifully granted and bestowed upon us and other countries. Which would not be appreciated as much if they were not set against and compared to those who do not have them." [116] The translator then described the changes that had taken place as a result of Spanish or Portuguese rule. The fate of the inhabitants did not worry him nearly so much as inspiring gratefulness in his readers for the superiority of the life that Christians enjoyed in Europe.

German commentators interpreted the lessons learned from the exploration and conquest solely for the benefit of audiences at home;

the judgments they issued were only locally applicable and imposed no requirement (and urged no responsibility) to change the lives of the people used as exempla. Even when commentators thought Europe really did have something to bring to the rest of the world (the Christian faith), they applauded the actions of others rather than urging new colonial undertakings. Indeed, while defending travel as a useful activity sanctioned by God, Sigmund Feyerabend did not envision proselytizing or civilizing missions. Just as those who required spices had to travel to the tropics, so those in need of "good governance" (gute policey) should learn by visiting well-regulated countries, as the Romans had with Greece.[117] The civilized should wait for the uncivilized to come to them for help.

The characteristics that called forth such condemnation from Iberian observers, particularly anthropophagism and the unencumbered lifestyles of the populations initially encountered by Columbus and Vespucci, provoked merely fascination in Germans. As Daston and Park have shown, monsters were interpreted in different ways—as objects of contemplation, wonder, investigation, horror, or fear—depending on the circumstances and intellectual stakes.[118] Categorical assertions of Otherness that put ethnographical descriptions at the mercy of predetermined schematic divisions served Iberian colonial imperatives,[119] just as the broader categories of the marvelous and the historical met the needs of German commentators trying to make these stories meaningful for readers outside the imperial context.

BECAUSE TRAVEL NARRATIVES were brought to the attention of German publics to inspire contemplation of human and natural diversity, and divine and human will, readers did not require an accurate and complete account of the discoveries.[120] As explorers and colonizers for Spain and Portugal reached farther regions, added new plots and characters to the history of expansion, and provided more detailed examinations of lands and peoples, German publishers eagerly recycled the narratives of Cadamosto, d'Anghiera, Vespucci, Cortes, and Varthema. When it came time for Sebastian Münster to describe the newly discovered lands and peoples in the *Cosmographia,* he reached for *Novus Orbis regionum,* the 1532 Latin edition of *Newe vnbekanthe landte.* When the Duke of Bavaria had narratives of discovery translated for his family's personal use around 1580, *Novus Orbis regionum* once again served as the source.[121] Some new information did arrive in Germany in the middle of the sixteenth century, but it tended to be announced only in an ephemeral pamphlet or to remain as an isolated manuscript.[122] Other histories of exploration and conquest, which have been regarded by modern scholars as central to understanding the European assessment of the newly discovered lands and peoples, seem to have remained entirely outside of Germany's intellectual orbit in the period under study, including the works of Oviedo[123] and Gómara and the chronicles of the Peruvian conquest by Zárate and Cieza de Leon.[124] The absence of the major works about the Incan empire is perhaps most telling, given not only the climatic denouement with the native ruler Atahualpa, but also the use of *quippu* for recording information, the rituals of human sacrifice, and the spectacular engineering accomplishments of the Incan Empire—all apparently fascinating to other European readers.[125] This satiability of German interest in the expanding world was the result of how the information about the discoveries was used: by fitting the discoveries into the more general frames of reference that made them meaningful for German audiences, the commentators stripped them of their uniqueness. Once the appetite for sensationalism had been stilled by the reports on the "wild, naked, and fierce man-eaters," and the appetite for ennobling and inspiring stories had been sated by the histories of Varthema, Cortes, and Castanheda, there was no room or need left for the large amounts of similar material available in Italy and Antwerp. The limited amount of new material (as opposed to the significant quantity of recycled material) published in Germany in the century after the voyage of Columbus thus reflected not so much a lack of interest on the part of Germans as the way their interest had been created and satisfied.

German commentators on the Iberian expansion were variously horrified, titillated, edified, and amazed. They were not surprised. The new, the strange, and the marvelous were not new in the Renaissance, as both the medieval and the classical traditions had preserved, clarified, and manipulated a rich legacy of wonders, oddities, and novelties. The Renaissance texts of discovery added to this material but did not completely supersede it, as evidenced by the inclusion of Marco Polo's text in *Novus Orbis regionum.* In addition to finding an anchor within such prior descriptions, the readers of travel narratives were guided from distant shores back to familiar harbors through the conventions of travel and the efforts of commentators and publishers to explain the relevance of this material. Therefore, although the effect of a specific encounter or anecdote, or even an entire section of the narrative, might be destabilizing, raising questions about European abilities to navigate the murky shoals of cultural contact, religious conversion, and scientific observation, the structure of the texts and the content of the paratexts helped readers see the Indies as extensions of their own realities. In the German case, interests of audiences limited not only the scope of material consulted but also the political and colonial ambitions thereby engaged. If the colonial dynamic was largely absent from German representations of the discoveries, European mastery of the world was still present in a different guise, as outside cultures were made susceptible to observation and judgment through their incorporation in the marvelous and the historical.

To what extent these attitudes were successfully transferred to readers must, for the most part, remain a matter of speculation, although I have pointed to some of the structural and rhetorical features designed to control interpretation. However, when various German observers combed through the travel narratives for specific types of information that they could then incorporate into an already established field of knowledge, such as cosmography or commercial calculation, they did leave traces of their reading. As the following chapters show, these distinct forms of reading rendered the discoveries intelligible and significant on their own terms, yet they all confirmed the ability of European forms of knowledge to make sense of the expanding world.

CHAPTER TWO

Plotting the Discoveries

THE COSMOGRAPHIES

THE *FOUR VOYAGES* OF Amerigo Vespucci opened with a set of observations decidedly different from the sensational descriptions of sexually voracious women and gluttonous cannibals for which its author has become famous: "In the year of Our Lord 1497, on the 20th day of May, we set sail from the harbor of Cadiz in four ships. To the islands once called the Fortunate, now the Grand Canaria, situated at the edge of the inhabited west in the third climate, we set our first course; above this place the North Pole rises 27 ⅔ degrees and it is 280 leagues from the city of Lisbon . . . the wind blowing between the south and southwest." [1] This passage hardly seems gripping, but it would have seized the attention of the many sixteenth-century readers familiar with the discipline of mathematical geography, or cosmography. [2] Even readers new to the field of cosmography could have grasped the significance of this passage, because *Four Voyages* first appeared in Germany as an appendix to *Cosmographiae introductio,* a short cosmographical treatise by the Alsatian humanists Martin Waldseemüller and Matthias Ringmann. [3]

If texts borrowed the language and concepts of cartography, maps replicated in visual form features of the narratives described in the previous chapter. On the *Mercarthen* (sea chart of the world) drawn by the Strassburg physician Lorenz Fries, for example, some geographical forms are universal; mountains appear on the Asian peninsulas just as they appear between Italy and Germany, and shorelines throughout the world are neatly punctuated with rivers. Other iconographic elements highlight the distinction between the European and Mediterranean core and the edges of the earth. The forest of names (of cities, kingdoms, and rivers) that covers the region from the Baltic to the Mediterranean coast gives way at the periphery to isolated geographical features, as well as scattered small drawings that mirror the narratives' interest in displaying difference in all its variety. In the East, a king (identified as the Great Khan) sits magnificently enthroned in a luxurious encampment, while in the South Sea two Javanese islanders carve up a human body. Anthropophagites appear again to the west, in the New World, along with a large rat-like creature, and in Norway a slightly more fearsome beast stalks the polar landscape. Africa contains a mixture of enthroned kings and strange animals, as befits a land home to both Prester John and the rhinoceros. Signs of the extension of European power, meanwhile, are present in the Neptune-like figure of the Portuguese king placed by the Cape of Good Hope and in the Spanish flags scattered throughout the lands of the Western Atlantic. The new sea route to India is shown in its entirety, while the potential of the western lands seems to rest more in their unexplored (and apparently undefended) hinterlands, shown as vast white spaces covered only with decorative elements. Even more direct links to the tales told in the travel accounts, whether historical, curious, or imperial, can be found in the framed texts staggered throughout the *Mercarthen,* which were derived (via an intermediate source) from that trusty travel compilation *Newe vnbekanthe landte.*[4] A caption in the Indian Ocean, for example, provides the following summary: "The land of India is very large and there are wondrous peoples there with strange countenances very unlike our own. [There are] several varieties of precious stones and spices. They go naked there, except that they cover their private parts. Christians live there as well. This was discovered by the King of Portugal in 1495."[5] These remarks encapsulate the themes (of attainability, variety, and intelligibility) that the map shares with the travel narratives.

Maps such as the *Mercarthen,* however, operated first and foremost within cosmographical principles that subordinated individual landforms to an abstract, mathematically based system applicable everywhere on the globe. On the *Mercarthen,* the Tropics of Cancer and Capricorn, the Arctic and Antarctic Circles, and the equator are prominently displayed, while latitude, longitude, and the winds are indicated around the border. The same hierarchy prevails in the explanatory text that was published with the *Mercarthen,* the *Uslegung der Mercarthen* (Explanation of the Sea Chart): the opening chapters explain cosmographical concepts such as "what the lines that are drawn in many directions through this map mean," while additional geographical and ethnographical information about various regions, including the newly discovered territories, is provided only after the general cosmographical introduction.[6] The descriptions of those who had traveled overseas play second fiddle to the firsthand expertise of Germans learned in cosmographical theories and procedures.

The wielders of cosmographical theory, such as Fries and Waldseemüller, had a stake in the extension of their knowledge to the newly discovered territories: confirmation of the universal nature of the mathematical truths that they purveyed. The new discoveries could not stand apart from this system; they either had to be omitted from the discussion or, as they usually were, incorporated into established cosmographical concepts. The result was the demonstration of a kind of mastery, in that the language, images, and calculations of cosmography affirmed the ability of European knowledge to work in new environments, lending a sense of stability and assurance to even the most disorienting aspects of travelers' experiences.

Cosmography's "utility" as a "tool for interpretation" of new empirical information has been underestimated or ignored in most accounts of the discoveries' impact on European learning.[7] Scholars have generally characterized the then dominant Ptolemaic system, derived from classical sources, as a closed and bounded world, which had to be broken apart, shattered even, to incorporate the unexpected and disruptive discoveries. Above all, the "fourth continent," America, has been imbued with an obvious and irreducible novelty. Thus, Columbus's discovery has been called a "cosmographic shock for Europe" because of its incompatibility with "the traditional cosmographic dogma."[8] Edmundo O'Gorman argues that seeing America as an entity separate from the Old World caused "the crisis which . . . had threatened the ancient concept of the world [to reach] its final climax."[9] Efforts to correlate ancient writings with more recent discoveries or to minimize the distinctiveness of the newly discovered territories (both of which were required by cosmography's drive toward universal applicability) are portrayed as retrogressive clinging to a "traditional framework" that prevented the correct perception of the discoveries.[10] Within this historiographical context, the reliance of humanists, including cosmographers, on classical texts has been viewed as an obstacle, rather than an aid, to the accurate assessment of reports arriving from overseas.[11] German cosmographical texts—which devoted endless pages to discussions of ancient terms, theories, and questions that the discoveries should have rendered obsolete, while relegating the new lands to cursory treatments in their final pages—are seen as textbook examples of the humanist handicap.

In contrast, I trace the ways in which the compatibility between the old and the new was demonstrated through the successful extension of cosmographical categories to the new lands. The viability and importance of the classical tradition have already been ably defended by Anthony Grafton: "Authoritative texts provided the Europeans of the Renaissance with the only tools they had for understanding the thoughts and values of alien societies. Like other tools, these often broke in the hands of those who used them. . . . But many of them also showed astonishing flexibility and resilience, changing as they were used and often changing those who used them." [12] Cosmographers, taking advantage of the flexibility of ancient theories and the universal nature of the cosmographical system, unhesitatingly swept the East and West Indies into their worldview. In so doing, these writers and mapmakers endowed the overseas territories with a significance that these lands had a priori lacked, but that they now derived from their place in the cosmographical framework. As a consequence, the accumulation of new empirical data posed few problems. Instead, difficulties arose because the new information was tentative and incomplete; the challenge then became to present this information in a manner that emphasized the eventual perfectibility and certainty of the mathematical claims of cosmography.

Although cosmography has not been granted a central role in the European incorporation of the discoveries, cartography has been granted such a role, as scholars have dramatized the ways in which maps were used to create and display European political and commercial mastery.[13] Through creating the illusion of an omniscient and omnipotent viewer, scholars have argued, maps and mapping mentalities first allowed glory-craving monarchs and spice-seeking merchants to visualize access and control.[14] After acquiring the territory (to a greater or lesser extent), powerful interests created symbolic devices that promoted ideologies of European superiority and dominance, while hiding behind the maps' facade of impartial authority.[15] This analysis, however, begs the question: how did the maps' depiction of land acquire the status of an impartial and authoritative representation? In examining maps alone as "the basic filter both for discovering and interpreting" the overseas territories,[16] scholars have ignored how the framework of textual cosmographical knowledge, such as that provided in the German cosmographies studied here, made maps intelligible and believable.[17] Cartographical claims of control seemed viable only because cosmographical claims did.

This chapter begins with an explanation of what cosmography was and of how this ancient science was updated to meet the needs and interests of its practitioners in Renaissance Germany. Most of these concerns would have been familiar to scholars in other parts of Europe, although they were given particular inflection by the intellectual dynamics of German humanism. After establishing why Germans wrote cosmographies, I then show how their handling of the newly discovered territories reflected the homogenizing nature of their cosmographical mathematics and their adeptness, acquired through describing regions closer to home, at handling historical change and expanded knowledge. The cosmographical literature also featured discussions of a number of technical questions that demonstrate how cosmographers combined the flexibility of the ancient inheritance with the appearance of new lands to proclaim their expertise. Their determination to display their mastery did not waver in the face of the limits of cosmographical knowledge and the difficulty of meeting its technical requirements. Instead, cosmographers and cartographers relied on a number of techniques and tricks to cover these (temporary) deficiencies. The different treatments accorded to Africa and America resulted from the interplay of these cosmographical interests, practices, and limitations. In both cases, however, by explaining the new discoveries within the Ptolemaic framework, cosmographers transformed them into objects of European knowledge and understanding.

LOCATING COSMOGRAPHY IN RENAISSANCE GERMANY

Although on the surface a highly abstruse and abstract discipline, cosmography was an integral part of German Renaissance learning, claiming the attention of a broad range of scholars and readers prior to and independent of the discovery of the East and West Indies. Its characteristic delight in ancient questions and in the technical mastery of calculation and terminology (qualities that enabled a precise and expert discussion of the new lands) originated in the interests of humanists and mathematicians, who pursued cosmography because this ancient science gave them a seemingly secure method to fix the place of Germany in the world and the place of the world in the universe. The Indies were just along for the ride.

Usually the responsibility of the mathematics professor at a university, cosmography was considered a subtopic of astronomy in the *quadrivium*, the mathematically based second tier of disciplines.[18] As Peter Apian proclaimed at the start of his *Cosmographicus liber* (1524): "Cosmography . . . is of the world: which consists of the four elements . . . as well as the Sun, Moon, and all the stars, and the description of all that is covered by the vault of the sky. . . . It proves according to mathematical demonstrations. And it differs from geography because it divides the land through the circles of the sky, not through mountains, seas, and rivers, etc."[19] In cosmography terrestrial position was related to astronomical phenomena through the "circles of the sky," such as the equator, the tropics, and the ecliptic, which could be described and dissected according to mathematical degrees and angles.[20] More precise astronomical observation and calculation would allow an observer to determine the latitude and longitude coordinates of his position.[21] The abstract terms of cosmography were given visual form in armillary spheres (see fig. 1), which used the circles of the sky to trace the spherical shape of the earth.[22] Through concentrating on the predictable skies rather than on the malleable surface of the earth, Renaissance cosmographers imparted order and harmony to the world.

Drawing on a number of reservoirs of cosmographical expertise, particularly regarding the technical aspects of calculation and instrument making, cosmographical publication began rapidly expanding in Germany in the last decades of the fifteenth century.[23] The University of Vienna was especially noted for cosmographical study, producing such graduates as Johann Regiomontanus, the premier mathematician, astronomer, and cosmographer of the late fifteenth century, and Peter Apian, author of the aforementioned *Cosmographicus liber* and professor of mathematics and astronomy at the Bavarian University of Ingolstadt in the first half of the sixteenth century.[24] Regiomontanus eventually

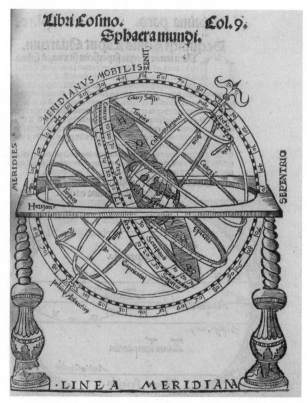

FIG. I. *Armillary Sphere, from Peter Apian,*
Cosmographicus liber (Landshut: J. Weissenburger, 1524),
col. 9. Courtesy of the John Carter Brown Library
at Brown University.

settled in Nuremberg, taking advantage of its superior metalworkers, experienced printers, and willing patrons to establish first himself, and then astronomy, as an important center of the city's intellectual life.[25] Strassburg publishers such as Johannes Grüninger and Johannes Schott also contributed to the outpouring of cosmographical publishing, re-using their prized cartographical woodcuts for numerous atlases and individual wall maps, while the city of Basel and its university provided another critical mass of scholars, publishers, and readers. This level of expertise and output put Germany at the forefront of the European-wide interest in cosmography and cartography.[26]

Ancient authority was crucial in giving cosmography a legitimate place in Renaissance scholarly investigations, but the discipline's classical credentials encouraged, rather than hampered, further cosmographical investigations.[27] The *Geography* of Ptolemy of Alexandria was the seminal classical text, setting the mathematical basis and technical methods for the discipline. Reintroduced into the Latin West during the Renaissance by Italian scholars,[28] the *Geography* was enthusiastically received in Germany as well, with the first of many German editions appearing in Ulm in 1482.[29] Essentially a manual for mapmakers, the *Geography* featured a highly technical (and occasionally obscure) discussion of how best to determine the geographical position of specific places (book 1); a list of latitude and longitude coordinates for significant cities, rivers, and other points of geographical interest (books 2 through 7); and instructions for drawing map projections (book 8). Copies of the world and regional maps that had customarily accompanied medieval manuscripts of the text rounded out the presentation of ancient geography.[30] The world map was constructed according to the first of the map projections described by Ptolemy, and the maps as a whole displayed the geographical features listed with such care in the body of the *Geography,* with reference to the mathematical model of the universe that undergirded the text. The maps therefore represented the culminating achievement of mathematical cosmography, providing a comprehensive summary of ancient knowledge about the world.

Ancient works, including not only the *Geography* but also such treatises as the *Cosmographia* of Pomponius Mela and the *Sphaera* of Proclus Diadochus,[31] along with the cosmographical sections of such noted works as Pliny the Elder's *Natural History* and Strabo's *Geography,*[32] were only the beginning of cosmographical investigation in Renaissance Germany, as scholars found it essential to explicate and update the material presented. Through this renovation humanists became adept at manipulating and refining texts to smooth over obscurities and inconsistencies in the literature. Johann Vernerus's 1514 translation of the *Geography*'s first book, for example, consisted of the original text, then a paraphrase of the original text to ensure that its meaning was clear, then a supplemental section to provide additional information.[33] While most editors did not go to quite the extremes of this three-tiered approach, they did add explanations of the more difficult sections, indexes to the maps, lists correlating modern place names with ancient ones, and information gathered from more recent sources about natural (and some not-so-natural) phenomena and customs in the various regions of the world.[34] The new cosmographical treatises of the Renaissance, such as Apian's *Cosmographicus liber,* while marking their debt to the ancient sources through extensive citations and encomiums, were even bolder in their approach, solving the structural problems of the classical texts by rearranging the material from various sources into a clearer expository form. The renewal of cosmography thus invited innovation as much as renovation.

Cosmographical study in Germany was also prompted by a need to register historical change, further emphasizing this discipline's potential to encompass and describe new developments. On a basic level, cosmography was pitched to readers as essential to understanding historical texts, because a knowledge of geography would help them decipher poetical, scriptural, and literary references.[35] The author of a short cosmographical treatise for a popular audience claimed that cosmography was important to the learned and unlearned man alike, so that he could understand not only his own position on the globe but also "what is preached and otherwise told to him about the various lands in which God and His saints have everywhere performed miracles and revealed right Christian truth to the whole world."[36] Placing events in geographical space also placed readers in historical time, because cosmographers often had to note that the names, political affiliations, and even physical appearance of the regions and cities had changed over the centuries.[37] The marking of change was particularly important for Germany itself, because classical texts made it abundantly clear that earlier Germany had been a land of uncultivated forests inhabited by barbarians. In response, German scholars authored numerous descriptions of local and national geography to depict the Germany they knew and to assert its cultural distance from the ancient descriptions. The "urge to portray country and people so that Germany's place among the nations might be re-established" prompted Germans to apply the principles of cosmographical measurement to their own territory, producing new maps that measured the changing landscape of German achievement.[38] The gap between the ancient world and the modern, which editors of the classical texts acknowledged with their annotations and paraphrases, was emphasized by geographers, who used cosmography to establish historical as well as geographical distance.

Cosmography could work as a secure anchor across time and space because of its mathematical foundation.[39] As Ptolemy himself had stated, "Only mathematics can provide sure and unshakeable knowledge to its devotees, provided one approaches it rigorously."[40] This sentiment was echoed in the preface to the 1543 edition of Regiomontanus's *Epitome* of Ptolemy's *Almagest:* "[Mathematics] has as great certainty as any other discipline, as indeed it solves its questions not by credible arguments, as the rest of the arts, but entirely by indubitable demonstrations."[41] Cosmography's practical applications were dependent on the clear answers provided by mathematics. Learned medicine, for example, placed considerable weight on astrological influences, so physicians needed accurate information about planetary position to determine astral influences, "critical days" of an illness, and so on.[42] Rudimentary astrological tables requiring basic cosmographical knowledge were also available to popular audiences in the form of almanacs and self-help manuals.[43] Cosmographical calculation was valuable because it provided specific information about the relationship (past, present, and future) between terrestrial and celestial positions. Although cosmography's importance as a branch of learning was predicated on its assistance in matters close to home, cosmographers, in establishing their ability to provide knowledge across time and space, fostered their ability to deal with the newly discovered territories in precise and expert ways.

Because the cosmographical system was universal, the numerous texts issued to explain it to German audiences concentrated first and foremost on explicating its basic principles, based on its classical foundations. A steady stream of new editions of Ptolemy's *Geography,* by such luminaries as Willibald Pirckheimer and Sebastian Münster, replete with commentary and double-page maps, issued from presses in Strassburg and Basel. Manuals for university students were another important genre, and to augment the reprints of standard textbooks such as Sacrobosco's *Sphere,*[44] professors such as Peter Apian, Henricus Glareanus at Basel, Kaspar Peucer at Wittenberg, and Samuel Eisenmenger (Siderocrates) at Tübingen authored cosmographical treatises.[45] Cosmographers also sought to educate lay audiences. Just after the first Latin editions of Ptolemy were issued, a German-language cosmographical text appeared in Nuremberg, covering concepts such as the Tropics, the zodiac, parallels, and meridians.[46] In his *Cosmographia,* Sebastian Münster drew on the expertise he had gained in editing Ptolemy to provide a brief outline of mathematical geography in Book I. The difference between this short German exposition and the kind of learning on display in something like Joachim Vadianus's massive Latin commentary on Pomponius Mela's *Cosmographia* is in one sense profound, as Vadianus's text invited scholarly readers to scrutinize, compare, and judge the knowledge of cosmographers ancient and modern, while Münster's introduction contented itself with a straightforward, authoritative presentation, minimizing controversies and complexities.[47] Yet both texts were ultimately designed to cement the faith of readers in the universal applicability and usefulness of the discipline of mathematical geography.

As it had in Ptolemy's *Geography,* cartography provided the ultimate display of cosmographical knowledge, and publishers obliged by producing numerous maps and globes. Martin Waldseemüller's 1507 world map was not only the first map to label the New World "America," but also the first in a long series of printed world maps, including Peter Apian's 1520 *Tipus Orbis Terrarum,* Waldseemüller's 1516 *Carta Marina,* and Fries's *Mercarthen.* Behaim's 1492 globe, created for the Nuremberg city council, was a handmade affair, but Waldseemüller and the Nuremberg cartographer Johann Schöner produced printed globe gores that could be assembled into paper spheres. As noted earlier, these maps and globes were typically accompanied by explanatory texts such as *Uslegung der Mercarthen.* The *Cosmographiae introductio* of Waldseemüller and Ringmann, which guided readers through the *Four Voyages,* also guided them through Waldseemüller's 1507 world map, with chapters on basic geometrical principles, the astronomical circles, the · system of parallels (lines of latitude a set distance apart), and the names and directions of the winds.[48] In this division of labor, cosmographical texts provided the concepts, and the maps then connected the concepts to specific landforms, proclaiming the cosmographical system's ability to serve as a reference structure for the entire world, known, unknown, and newly discovered.

THE COSMOGRAPHICAL TEXTS AND THE EXPANDING WORLD

German cosmographers happily ventured into the new terrain of the Portuguese and Spanish discoveries, but only to apply established techniques and concepts. There was no point in including information that cast doubt on the carefully constructed system they had spent so much effort in learning and explaining. Fortunately for cosmographers, the newly discovered lands proved susceptible to incorporation: as new empirical information, they did not disrupt and could even strengthen the system's theoretical underpinnings.[49] By placing the information derived from the Portuguese and Spanish expansion on the side of experience rather than theory, cosmographers could celebrate the advances in empirical knowledge that this information did represent, while preserving the integrity of Ptolemaic theory. Difficulties arose less from the theories than from the paucity of information, and the cosmographical display of the East and West Indies was therefore carefully crafted to create the appearance of authoritative knowledge.

The revival of Ptolemaic cosmography, which freed conceptions of terrestrial space from the theological/eschatological concerns of medieval geographic traditions, laid the world open to uniform investigation. The key to understanding the Ptolemaic system was, as Samuel Edgerton has pointed out, "imagining the globe . . . as a homogenous surface ruled by a uniform geometric grid." As a result, "terra incognita would be susceptible to the same rational, quantitative measurement as the inhabited world." [50] The Ptolemaic system implied a full 360 degrees of longitude, even if only 180 degrees were depicted on the maps. The same held true for latitude. Ptolemy's widely used first projection put the equator approximately two-thirds of the way down the map, which reached over 60°N in latitude, but only around 24°S.[51] The unequal distribution of land did not, however, mean that the earth was not symmetrical; each hemisphere would, in the natural course of things, reach 90 degrees by the pole. Geometry was universally applicable, rendering ancient cosmography, in the words of Frank Lestringant, "anticipatory in mathematical terms." [52]

Ptolemy himself had prepared his *Geography* with the eventuality of further discoveries in mind,[53] so that techniques for assessing and incorporating new empirical information were readily available to his Renaissance heirs. Not only had Ptolemy stressed the changing nature of lands and their inhabitants, but he had noted that constant vigilance was required to make the necessary adjustments as new or updated information became available. In his text and maps Ptolemy stated clearly when the limits of his information had been reached. For example, describing the boundaries of "Scythia beyond Mt. Imaus," he placed "Interior Scythia" to the west, "Seris" to the east, "India beyond the Ganges" to the south, and "unknown land" (terra incognita) to the north.[54] This pattern was repeated for numerous other regions. It was possible to claim Ptolemaic authority for updating Ptolemy, and Renaissance cosmographers freely referred to him as a model in just such circumstances.[55]

The mastery of cosmographical science thus created an ability to recognize and celebrate the new. The extension of Ptolemaic calculation over the whole of the globe did not obliterate the distinction between ancient and modern empirical knowledge; it made possible the precise demarcation of the boundaries between the two. Correlating ancient place names with currently identifiable locations through philological investigation was a prominent part of cosmographies and other geographical texts. Despite the seeming reliance on the ancients to provide meaning, the process of translation necessarily illustrated the limits of the classical texts. Not only had names and languages changed, but many important sixteenth-century sites were not listed at all in the classical sources. In determining what the ancients knew, Renaissance cosmographers also established what the ancients did not know.

The discussion of the Iberian discoveries in Willibald Pirckheimer's *Germania per brevis explicatio,* which listed equivalents for hundreds of places in Germany and a few farther afield, illustrates how correlation could be used to emphasize new knowledge.[56] Pirckheimer, a Nuremberg humanist and translator of Ptolemy, provided the corresponding names for some dozen locations that the Portuguese had reached in the East, including the "Aurea Chersonesus" ("Malaqua") and "Symila" ("Calecut or Chossin"). He then questioned whether the islands "recently discovered by the Iberians" (Hispanis) really were unknown in all ages past. Relying on two passages in Aristotle's *De admirandis in natura auditis,* Pirckheimer first identified the outcroppings in tuna-rich waters discovered by the Phoenicians with the islands of "Medera" and "Faial or Noua Flandria" (in the Azores). More daringly, he then discussed Aristotle's description of a fertile paradisiacal island discovered by certain Carthaginian merchants who had sailed beyond the Pillars of Hercules. Fearing that its liberty would be threatened if the fame of this island spread, Carthage had kept its location a secret.[57] Immediately after this citation from Aristotle, Pirckheimer provided the following information: "Accordingly, it was ascertained by the observation of an eclipse, which was in September 1494: the island of Hispana [Hispaniola] is 4 hours distant from Seville; that is, 60°, as the extent of a circle is 360°, the middle of this island is about 20° in polar elevation."[58] He then gave the locations of several other islands. What might be read as an attempt to preserve the validity of ancient knowledge in the face of the challenge brought by the explorations is better seen, I think, as a celebration of the success of the voyages in clearing up an ancient mystery and exposing secrets the Carthaginians had tried to keep hidden for all time. The passage in Aristotle that referred vaguely to these unnamed islands could now be properly annotated, and the achievements of the explorers placed in their proper light, through the wonders of correlating old and new information.

Pirckheimer's identification was not universally accepted, but the process of correlation was central to locating the lands (re)discovered by Spain and Portugal in the cosmographical tradition. For example, the Fortunate Isles, located in the *Geography* off the west coast of Africa, marked the edge of Ptolemy's known world and a common point from which to measure longitude (the original prime meridian, if you will). The venturings of the Spanish and Portuguese into the Atlantic in the fourteenth and fifteenth centuries had uncovered several island groups, of which "the Canaries" seemed to match the Fortunate Isles most closely in number and position, although the fit was by no means perfect.[59] Authors thus invariably referred to this group of islands using some version of the formula "the Fortunate Isles, which are now called the Canaries," as Vespucci did in the quote that begins this chapter. The concern with locating islands whose existence was attested to in the ancient sources, even if this meant acknowledging possible errors in the original information, indicates the importance attached to comparing ancient and present knowledge. The Fortunate Isles/Canaries served as recognizable landmarks, indicating that the end of the ancient world had been reached, both in actual voyages—they were a standard port of call for all journeys west and south—and in the cosmographies. The renaming indicated the rediscovery of these islands: it made clear both the passage of time and the equaling, and eventual surpassing, of the ancients.

In the context of this innovating spirit, the revelation that the ancients were not omniscient was neither startling nor the direct result of the maritime European expansion.[60] Fifteenth-century editions of Ptolemy's *Geography*, both manuscript and printed, contained *tabulae modernae:* updated maps of the regions most familiar and central to European scholars.[61] The 1482 Ulm *Geography*, for example, included four modern maps (of Scandinavia, Italy, Spain, and the Holy Land).

These maps not only reflected new political boundaries, religious land-marks, and nomenclature, but also, where necessary, corrected inaccurate geographical information. For example, the modern maps routinely adjusted the angle of the Italian peninsula to the European mainland and completed the outline of the Scandinavian peninsulas. Redrawing maps of familiar areas catered to readers' patriotic and religious concerns and demonstrated the expertise of modern cosmographers, thus meeting the needs of both consumers and producers of cosmographical knowledge. Meanwhile, only five of the twenty new maps in the 1513 Strassburg *Geography* (including the world map) depicted any portion of the newly discovered territories. In addition to two maps of Africa, one of India and places farther east, and one of the Western Ocean or New Land, there were nine maps of Europe; new maps of Asia Minor, the Holy Land, and Crete; and four local maps showing three regions of particular importance to Strassburg.[62] This pattern was repeated in the written material, the texts spending many more pages commenting on and correcting what the ancients had said about Europe than expounding on the deficiencies of their knowledge of the regions at the limits of the known world.[63] These home-based challenges placed a more severe strain on ancient knowledge than the expanding world did, because they demonstrated that the ancient authors were incorrect, not just incomplete. Yet the basic cosmographical structure remained firmly in place.

Based on their analysis of ancient knowledge, cosmographers were fully prepared to declare the East and West Indies an expansion of the known world beyond the limits established by Ptolemy, joining a long list of territories added since the classical period. When Sebastian Brant, in his 1494 *Narrenschiff,* proclaimed, "They've also since discovered in Portugal/and everywhere in Hispania/Gold islands and naked people/about which previously they had no knowledge," he meant this remark as the conclusion to a longer list of new discoveries: "Since then [the age of Ptolemy and Strabo] they've found many lands beyond Norway and Thyle/Such as Iceland and Lapland/where before they thought there was nothing."[64] The Iberian discoveries thus fit smoothly into a systematic comparison between Ptolemy's delimitation of the known world and current knowledge about its extent, which became a standard component of the cosmographies. Henricus Glareanus's *De geographia* included a section following his discussion of the three traditional parts of the world (Europe, Africa, and Asia) on "regions beyond Ptolemy," which encompassed not only the region "beyond Spain and the Fortunate Isles . . . totally unknown to Ptolemy," but also the regions of the extreme north; the islands of Zipangri, Java, and others to the east of the Asian mainland; and southern Africa.[65] Waldseemüller and Ringmann explained that a description of the whole world had first been developed by Ptolemy and was "then increased by others, recently by Amerigo Vespucci truly more broadly illuminated."[66] The discoveries were most consistently mentioned as part of the ongoing expansion of the known world, a process that was in no way inimical to the Ptolemaic tradition.

The world beyond the limits of Ptolemy's knowledge, German cosmographers insisted, was still susceptible to the principles of Ptolemaic calculation. The Ptolemaic system, for example, delineated the habitable world through seven climates (zones of latitude one half-hour in breadth), each named for a prominent city or other geographical feature that it contained.[67] Although initially tailored to the central portion of the northern hemisphere, the list of climates was easily expanded north and south by late fifteenth- and early sixteenthcentury cosmographers.[68] In his *Cosmographicus liber,* Apian added names to two further climates in the northern hemisphere: Rhipheon and Danias. He then divided the southern hemisphere into climates by reversing the northern ones: the first climate south of the equator was called "Anti Dia Meroes," the second "Anti Dia Syenes," and so on.[69] The discoveries fit easily into this elastic schema, as shown in this quote from Waldseemüller and Ringmann's *Cosmographiae introductio:* "And in the sixth climate towards the Antarctic lie the further part of Africa, recently discovered, and Zamzibar and Java minor and the island of Seula and the fourth part of the world."[70] The assignation of latitude and longitude coordinates, another essential element of the Ptolemaic system, was also crucial to the display of cosmographical integration. In Johann Schöner's 1515 *Luculentissima quaedam terrae totius descriptio* (A Very Proper Description of the Whole Earth), the route between Lisbon and Calicut/Malacca was laid out through a listing of geographical landmarks, complete with latitude coordinates. A small sampling will suffice: "Rio San Lorenzo 10.15 S., Angradas Aldas 16.20 S., CABO BONA SPERANZA 34.0 S., at that point there is a turn of the shore and the land to the east and a little to the north Abaia de la Goa 33.0 S.," and so on.[71] Apian's *Cosmographicus liber* contained a listing of latitude and longitude coordinates similar to those in

Ptolemy's *Geography,* but expanded to include new discoveries in Asia, Africa, and America, such as "Madagastar Insula 105.0|23.30 . . . Zipangri Insul 250.0|15.0 . . . Caput S. Crucis 345.0|14.0."[72] Through placing these newly discovered locations within the established disciplinary framework, cosmographers confirmed that framework's universal truth.

The apparently smooth transition between the old and the new was further demonstrated by subjecting them to the same principles of calculation. As Johann Dryander proudly proclaimed, his astronomical *annulus,* an instrument used for stellar (as well as other) measurements and for the derivation of the associated numerical values, was portable in function as well as in form, since a user could adapt the *annulus* to any location in the world simply by calibrating it to the correct latitude. Dryander even helpfully provided a latitude catalog at the end of the instruction manual, either anticipating far-flung users or simply driving his point home through listing, over several pages, all the places where his instrument would still work. Of course, German and European cities dominated the list, and the Africa section was limited to northern African cities, but among the "Asian Cities" Dryander threw in Calicut (7 degrees latitude), Hispaniola (20 degrees latitude), and the Moluccas, which "have no latitude, because they are under [at] the equator."[73] Cosmographers did not hesitate to expand other types of calculation to include new locations. Siderocrates, in explaining how to figure the distance between places whose longitudinal difference was greater than 180 degrees, set up the problem in this manner: "The island of St. Jacob in America has in longitude 356° 0'. Land's end in Spain 4° 23'." At first glance, he explained, the difference would appear to be 351° 37', but if one figured the distance of each location from the longitude of the Fortunate Isles (i.e., the prime meridian), the true difference would be calculated as 8° 23'. He then repeated the lesson using Saint Jacob again, this time with Lisbon, and then "Spagnolla" (Hispaniola) and Grand Canaria (the largest of the Fortunate Isles).[74] Kaspar Peucer's mathematically more adept treatise, *De dimensione terrae,* likewise explained the translation of differences in latitude and longitude into terrestrial measurements such as miles through examples involving "Lysibona" and "Calecuthum," and "Taprobana" and "Vmbria."[75] The suitability of these places for such calculations emphasized their compatibility and commensurability with familiar European places. The capacity to assign an island a number and to use that number to measure the distance between the island and Spain, in both degrees of longitude and miles, removed it from the realm of the marvelous and placed it within a regularized system of European origin. Thus situated in the system, the territories were ready to be interpreted.

THE INTERPRETATION OF THE DISCOVERIES

Through their matter-of-fact manipulation of the new empirical data, cosmographers proved that it was possible to extend calculation. Through their manipulation of theoretical possibilities to match the new empirical findings, moreover, cosmographers not only insisted on the continued viability of ancient categories, but gave their interpretation of the discoveries pride of place in resolving ancient controversies over, for example, the habitability of the torrid zone or the existence of the Antipodes. Neatly preserving for themselves the arbiter role, they triumphantly used their expertise to assert the superiority of the information derived from the Iberian expeditions over ancient suppositions.

The successful modification of the theory of the "five zones" reveals the German cosmographers' seemingly inexhaustible ability to use ancient explanations and the latest discoveries to arrive at foregone conclusions. The zone theory divided the earth into one torrid, two temperate, and two frigid zones on the principle that the closer the sun's rays were to perpendicular, the more heat they imparted to the region they struck.[76] The torrid zone was bound by the Tropics of Cancer and Capricorn, because the sun climbed directly overhead only in this region during the course of the year. The frigid zones lay between the Arctic and Antarctic Circles and the poles, that is, in those areas so far removed from the sun's rays that at least one day a year was spent in total darkness. Between the torrid zone and the frigid zones were the two temperate zones. In the zone theory's original form, "frigid," "temperate," and "torrid" went beyond temperature measurements, also assessing the possibility of human habitation. The frigid and torrid zones were described as "uninhabitable" on account of, respectively, excessive cold and excessive heat, while the two temperate zones were regarded as "habitable." This distinction served two purposes: it marked out measurable differences between the zones, and it elegantly illustrated the effects of astronomical phenomena on the earth's surface. As a description of where people actually lived, however, it was less helpful. Practiced in exegetical emendations to classical texts, Renaissance cosmographers stepped in to clarify the situation. Thus, Waldseemüller and Ringmann, after declaring that the polar zones were "uninhabited, frozen by the constant cold," and that the heat of the sun made the middle zone "torrid and uninhabited," continued: "Rather when we say inhabited or inhabitable, we understand well and easily inhabitable and for uninhabited or uninhabitable, inhabited only with struggle and difficulty."[77] Cochlaeus expanded on this definition by labeling the "uninhabitable" regions "unfit for human life."[78] This approach allowed the preservation of the distinctions between "too hot," "too cold," and "just right" that the basic zone theory propounded, while taking into account empirical evidence of human habitation in these regions.

The flexibility apparent in the redefinition of "uninhabitable" and "habitable" was even more evident in the erudite Latin texts that devoted space to expounding on previous disputations about the zones' size and character. In the mixture of ancient texts and medieval commentaries, one could find support for almost any position, all undergirded by the same understanding of the universe. Renaissance cosmographers used the technique of the "philosophical present" to bring these various viewpoints into conversation, while preserving for themselves the ultimate task of proclaiming a winner based on the accumulated knowledge of previous centuries.[79] In making use of ancient ideas to explain new empirical evidence, Renaissance cosmographers preserved classical knowledge while elevating their own status.

In the case of the frigid zones, there was general agreement among ancients and moderns that they were cruelly cold and that any inhabitants must be living wretched lives indeed.[80] Observations of peoples living in the northern frigid zone, made possible as European interests spread further and further north and northeast, pointed out the necessity of a migratory lifestyle in these regions, giving no cause to examine further the assumption that the absence of sustained sunlight throughout the year rendered the frigid zone unfit for human habitation. There was, however, to quote the medieval philosopher Albertus Magnus, "great doubt about the torrid zone."[81] The basic position held that, due to the perpendicular rays of the sun, which struck every part of the torrid zone, the whole region from the Tropic of Cancer to the Tropic of Capricorn must be hot to the point of being unfit for human habitation. However, an impressive array of scholars lined up in opposition to this opinion. The most significant was Ptolemy, whose first two climates, which marked off portions of the inhabited earth, lay at and to the south of the Tropic of Cancer, and thus in the torrid zone. Ptolemy also placed "Ethiopians" well within the torrid zone, and discussed the effect the heat of the sun would have on their physiognomy. Other classical authors, such as Pliny and Strabo, also located population centers in the torrid zone, belying claims that the heat made the region completely uninhabitable.[82]

A further problem—or rather, a further opportunity for Renaissance scholars to display their ability to explain empirical observations with ancient theories—arose from reports, even in ancient texts, indicating not only that people lived in the torrid zone, but that some lived very well indeed. The first issue could be (and was) dealt with through the simple method described above: even if the area was inhabited, no proper society could develop there. However, advanced civilizations apparently did exist in such places as the island of Taprobana, located at the equator, in the heart of the torrid zone. There was even a rumor that Paradise was to be found someplace nearby. How to explain this idyllic setting located where the sun should make the weather intolerably hot? The medieval philosopher Albertus Magnus provided a set of explanations in his writings (republished in the Renaissance) which were recapitulated in full in Vadianus's commentary on Pomponius Mela's *Cosmographia*.[83] A temperate climate was said to result from the blending of hot and cold; thus, the temperate zones lie between the frigid and the torrid zones. An argument could therefore be made that at the equator, hot and cold were also equally balanced. For as the sun's approach created heat, and the sun's retreat created cold, then the movement of the sun between the Tropics perfectly balanced the approach and retreat of the sun at the equator. This balance between hot and cold was also reflected in the length of day and night. As each is always twelve hours at the equator, what the day heats, the night cools down, to use the common phrase. The proponents of a temperate band at the equator also emphasized the calefactory nature of the direct rays of the sun. The closer the angle of the rays to perpendicular, they argued, the greater their impact on the surface of the earth. For several reasons, it was possible to argue that the sun tarried longer overhead at the regions at and adjacent to the Tropics of Cancer and Capricorn than it did at the equator. Therefore, these regions were uninhabitable, or close to it, while the equator remained blissfully balmy. These arguments provided the solution for those who perceived a conflict between reports of abundant life at the equator and the torrid zone's supposedly desolate nature. This virtuosic performance served no apparent practical purpose, because the Portuguese and Spanish never consulted German cosmographers about the advisability of establishing outposts in tropical regions. But to dismiss these elegant explanations on such grounds is to miss the point: their ultimate beneficiaries were, as intended, the theories about the effect of the sun's movement on the earth's surface and the scholars who propounded them.

Satisfied with having reconciled theory and experience in this matter, cosmographers turned to two related questions stemming from the writings of the ancients: whether human life was possible south of the equator and, if so, whether it was extant. The Iberian expeditions, of course, had already established that the answer to both questions was a resounding yes. German cosmographers, however, again surrounded straightforward answers with elaborate discussions of previous opinions, characteristically giving themselves a chance to display both their own learning and their ability to trump ancient questions with modern certainty. In answer to the first question, their sources agreed: the symmetry of the earth created a temperate southern zone to go with the northern one. The classical tradition, however, was less clear on whether "habitable" meant "inhabited." The strongest argument against the existence of populated areas south of the Tropic of Capricorn was the lack of empirical evidence. Why had no contact ever been made across the middle zone? While this argument could be countered by noting the difficulties of travel through the extreme heat of the torrid zone, for those operating within the structures of Christian thought, the impassability of the torrid zone was an argument against, rather than for, the existence of human life in the southern temperate zone. Saint Augustine, in *The City of God,* provided the classic exposition of the difficulty. If the distance was (in his formulation) too great to be traveled, then how could any descendent of Adam ever have crossed it to populate the southern temperate zone? Even if there were land in the southern temperate zone, and a pleasant climate, Augustine insisted, there could be no human beings.[84] The purported impassability of the torrid zone was thus at the heart of arguments both for and against the presence of humans in the southern temperate zone. However, as was the case with "uninhabitability," in the face of new evidence, Renaissance German cosmographers simply transformed "impassability" into a relative rather than an absolute term and continued the discussion about the people whose existence on the far side of the world had now been confirmed.

The ancient cosmographers, in tandem with speculating about the existence of people on other parts of the globe, had developed names and definitions for them that provided a crucial link between the abstractions of cosmographical science and concrete terrestrial locations. In these terms, imaginative descriptions were marginalized in favor of precise definitions dependent on cosmographical relations, as can be clearly seen in the case of the "Antipodes." The name "Antipodes" carried with it a wonder-laden response, cultivated by centuries of regarding such potential beings as belonging to the "monstrous races" and, hence, as being on the fringes of humanity as well as on the edge of the known world.[85] A little of this wonder carried over into the cosmographies, particularly around the interesting fact that there could be people whose feet would touch ours if the intervening mass of the earth were removed—which is what "Antipodes" literally means. In keeping with the focus of the cosmographies, though, the discussion remained firmly rooted in consideration of place rather than appearance or nature.

The Antipodes did not exist "out there" in inconceivable space, but in relation to the coordinate system and other cosmographical terms, particularly the Antipodes' two cognates: the Perioecis and the Antoecis.[86] As the cosmographers explained to their readers, their Perioecis were those people who lived on the same line of latitude and the same meridian as they, but 180 degrees apart from them in longitude. The Perioecis shared with the readers all yearly rhythms: the seasons came at the same time, the days grew longer and shorter at the same rate, and the length of the longest day was the same. The difference could be seen on a daily basis: when the readers had day, their Perioecis had night. The opposite was true of the Antoecis, who lived on the same line of longitude as the readers and whose latitude was the same number of degrees away from the equator as the readers' position, but on the equator's other side. As a result, daily rhythms matched: noon and midnight occurred at the same instant. The variations were instead seasonal: when the readers had summer, their Antoecis had winter, and the readers' longest day was their Antoecis' shortest. The final term combined the first two: the readers' Antipodes lived on the same line of longitude as their Perioecis and on the same line of latitude as their

Antoecis. Almost everything about the Antipodes, according to cosmographers, was in opposition to what their readers experienced: the Antipodes had night when they had day and winter instead of summer. These terms were thus relative to a specific point on the earth; there could be no "Antipodes" without the establishment of an original point, so readers were thus told that they were antipodal to those the text labeled Antipodes.[87] Furthermore, no specific characteristics were attached to the people at the readers' antipodal point, apart from their experiences of the sun's movement. This attitude was starkly illustrated in a comment by Vadianus, who remarked that even if an antipodal point fell in the midst of the ocean, preventing regular habitation, a passing ship (which might very well contain Europeans, given their globetrotting proclivities) could provide instant (albeit temporary) Antipodes.[88] Whatever its previous connotations, the term was now reliant for its meaning on cosmographical knowledge about the movement of the sun.

Through this precise terminology, which allowed them to seize control of the debates about the distribution of human habitation around the globe, Renaissance German cosmographers made the discoveries serve their purposes. In answering the question "Is the torrid zone habitable?" in the affirmative, Johannes Stoeffler first called on Ptolemy, pointing out by book, chapter, and even map the peoples and cities he had located between the Tropics. Stoeffler's next argument was less specific but apparently final: "And in our age the Kings of Portugal and Castile have discovered very many regions and islands under [at] the equator and in nearby areas. Enough said [Satis est]."[89] In like manner, when Albertus Magnus stated that the southern temperate zone was habitable, the editor of the 1515 edition of *De natura locorum* placed the following annotation beside this declaration: "Behold he concludes that it is habitable at 50° beyond the equator, as Vespucci has discovered and described by his voyages in previous years."[90] For his discussion of the historical meaning of "Antipodes," leading to his assertion of their existence, Vadianus relied on a whole panoply of arguments, drawing equally from ancient authors and modern reports. Thus, the tradition of an uncrossable equatorial ocean was wrong, as the navigations of the Portuguese had shown. Furthermore, any concerns that affirming the existence of the Antipodes went against scriptural tradition were dismissed by citing the example of the Apostles, who, in their wanderings, had conformed to the current cosmographical definition of the term:

"I doubt not that the word of Christ spread to India and the ends of Spain and Libya. But in these parts, separated by 180°, the location of the Antipodes very plainly must be discerned." [91] As cosmographers set the terms of the debate, they were able to flourish the evidence of the discoveries at suitable moments, endowing the new lands with significance of the scholars' own making. Through such remarks the new was introduced as the final proof of ancient contentions, not as a stunning reversal of them. [92]

Cosmographical confidence was in the end displayed through the blithe application of these supposedly controversial terms to the newly discovered territories. [93] Kaspar Peucer pointed out, for example, that the inhabitants of the two Atlantic islands then appearing on maps, Parias and America, were Antoecis. [94] Johannes Stoeffler used America, "discovered in our time on the order of the King of Castile," to make a slightly trickier point: that those living at the equator likewise had Antipodes, even though they would experience identical days and corresponding seasons, unlike Antipodes anywhere else on the globe. Nevertheless, their position relative to each other—according to latitude, longitude, and a line passing through the center of the earth—in every way conformed to the cosmographical definition of the term. Therefore, the inhabitants of "Nacaduma a city on the island of Taprobane (according to Ptolemy book 7, chapter 4 & Asia Map no. 12)" (at 0 degrees latitude and 128 degrees longitude) were directly opposite the inhabitants of the western province of America, likewise at 0 degrees latitude, but at 308 degrees longitude; and the Americans "therefore are the Antipodes of the Nacadumensians." Just in case anyone had not been following, Stoeffler explained how to determine that, in fact, the difference between 128 degrees and 308 degrees was 180 degrees. [95] This passage took both the existence of the newly discovered territories and their position within the Ptolemaic grid for granted, concentrating instead on a technical question about cosmographical definitions. Taking the concern with definitions one step further, Peter Apian used the just-explained term "Antipodes or Antichthones" to clarify his next set of terms, which divided people according to where the noon shadow falls during the course of the year. The "Heteroscii," for whom the noon shadow always falls in the same direction (north in the northern hemisphere, south in the southern hemisphere) were, for example, "we and our Antichthones." [96] The matter-of-fact use of these terms demystified them, displacing their connection to the marvelous with a place on a regular globe, subject to predictable solar movements.

The only real difficulty cosmographers faced in these discussions was the paucity of accurate observations. Conflicting empirical reports, for example, supported a variety of statements about the torrid zone. In 1509 Waldseemüller explained that the frigid zone was cold enough to make the region uninhabitable and the sea frozen, "as the merchants know who travel from England, Norway, and Scotland." Likewise, the barrenness and heat of the torrid zone could be attested to by pilgrims, "who have been to Jerusalem and to St. Catherine's mountain [in the Sinai]," as well as by merchants, "who have traveled to India, Alexandria, Calicut and overseas, where pepper and all spices grow." [97] Some years later Michael Neander asserted that the equator was most temperate, although the rest of the zone was truly torrid: "thus it is testified by the experience of the navigations." He drew on specific voyages, including that of Varthema, to illustrate his point.[98] Ancient theories proved flexible and malleable enough to bear the weight of the new discoveries, and cosmographers took full advantage of this fact, even while waiting for conclusive evidence. Because the newly discovered lands occupied a known and plotted position within cosmographical calculations and cosmographical terms, they could be used to further cosmographical investigation.

DISPLAYING COSMOGRAPHICAL CERTITUDE

This apparently seamless integration of the newly discovered territories into the cosmographical system, with precise placement on the latitude/longitude grid making possible knowledgeable consideration of questions about habitable zones and the Antipodes, was based on an illusion of accuracy, for there was much that was imprecise and jerry-built in the application of cosmographical methodology. Measuring instruments, including clocks, were not precise, and the movement of the sun and stars did not match precisely the theories that described their behavior, leading to inaccurate and variant readings.[99] Furthermore, because the gathering of cosmographical data was not a high priority in many regions or for many travelers, most places lacked even the meager certitude that contemporary instruments could provide. Instead, longitude and latitude were guesses, based on a place's distance (usually measured in travel time) from a location whose coordinates were a bit firmer. The ability to fix locations in the East and West Indies was particularly inadequate, as shown by the tendency of the recently discovered lands to float around on maps. On Peter Apian's 1520 world map, for example, the western edge of Marco Polo's island of "Zipangri" was shown at approximately longitude 262 degrees from the Fortunate Isles, while on Sebastian Münster's map from his 1540 *Geography*, a differently shaped "Zipangri" has a western edge at approximately longitude 233 degrees.[100] In extending their knowledge to the entire globe, cosmographers ran the risk of exposing the limits of that knowledge.

Through their emphasis on the reliability of the cosmographical method, no matter where on the globe it was applied, cosmographers stressed the eventual perfection of cosmographical knowledge, rather than its current incomplete state. Many texts invited readers to put cosmographical principles into practice through concrete examples. Johann Schöner, for example, led readers of his *Luculentissima quaedam terrae totius descriptio* through the determination of the latitude and longitude of his hometown of Bamberg,[101] while Peter Apian included instruments and instructions for figuring the altitude of the sun and locating the meridian, along with tables to aid in the basic calculations he introduced.[102] The results were only approximations, but in incorporating readers into the process of observing and measuring, they confirmed that cosmographical calculations produced tangible and verifiable results. A substantial number of texts aimed at nonspecialist audiences eschewed technical discussions and examples of calculations altogether. However, in omitting such technical aspects, cosmographers made the principles and results of cosmographical investigation all the more accessible.[103] Apian included numerous *volvelles* (paper instruments with moving parts) in his *Astronomicum Caesareum,* allowing readers to determine planetary position without any mathematical computations, so that "the universal theory of the heavens could be reduced to instruments, without numerals and without calculation."[104] Turning the *volvelles* produced quick and apparently precise results, reinforcing the credibility of cosmographical calculation by sidestepping its complexity.

Readers' engagement with maps was also used to reinforce the impression that cartography could produce true and verifiable knowledge. Even elementary tasks were painstakingly explained in the accompanying texts. If one knew the latitude and longitude of a particular place, readers were told, it could be located by tightening a string connecting the two latitude markings, then doing the same for the longitudinal coordinate; where the strings crossed would be the desired location. The numerous cross-references, textual and cartographical, within the new editions of Ptolemy's *Geography* likewise provided readers with a hands-on activity that required them to participate in the verification of cosmographical knowledge. One could look up the name of a town under its current name, find its ancient name, look under that name to find which of the regional maps it appeared on, look under the listing for that map to find its exact coordinates, and finally look on the map with these coordinates to see displayed the place one had set out to find. The exact experience was reproducible by every user of the text: the latitude and longitude coordinates were consistent within the book, however far off the mark they were regarding the actual location.[105] This closed system could also be used to produce maps. Glareanus instructed the readers of his introductory text that, when making a globe, they should begin by marking the poles, the meridians, the parallels, and the degrees. Only then would geographical features be added, "which are easily to be obtained from maps or tables."[106] This self-referential process emphasized, for those not directly involved in astronomical observations and measurement, the certainty and predictability of cosmographical concepts and calculations.

Maps vividly portrayed cosmography's ability to put the world at readers' fingertips, but they also posed the challenge of convincingly displaying a world still only partially known. Printed maps in particular had to present an authoritative front. Unlike manuscript maps, which often merely adopted the style of portolan charts, carefully delineating known coastlines and ignoring unknown coastal regions and all the hinterland, printed maps favored clear black lines outlining an entire piece of land, even if this meant relying on speculation to complete the outline. The outlines of Asia were difficult enough to determine, with the constantly shifting shapes of the three peninsulas that represented India, Malacca, and Cathay, but at least they could be approximated on the basis of either classical information or that provided more recently by Marco Polo and the Portuguese expeditions to the East. The landmasses in the Atlantic, on the other hand, had been only recently discovered, and that in a piecemeal manner. This inconvenient fact did not deter cartographers from showing the unknown west coasts of these lands, as well as the partially explored east coasts. Occasionally,

FIG. 2. *1520 World Map of Peter Apian.*
Courtesy of the John Carter Brown Library at Brown University.

the line denoting the shore would be accompanied by a qualifier, such
as the remark "The land further is unknown" (vlteri[us] terra incognita)
on the 1520 Apian world map (see fig. 2). Relying on words in the absence of geographical features also worked where the coastline was well
established but the interior had not yet been penetrated by Europeans.
The map of southern Africa in the 1513 Strassburg *Geography* contained,
instead of information about the interior, the large legend, "This area
remained unknown to the ancients," thus masking modern inadequacies with more glaring ancient ones.[107] In lieu of such window dressing,
many mapmakers favored placing unknown territories at their maps'
edges, where they could discreetly tail off, leaving the precise forms of
far distant countries to the imaginations of their readers.[108] The New
World, as its Atlantic and Caribbean coasts were the only parts of it

securely mapped, was often tucked into the lower left-hand corner of world maps, leaving out its western and southern coasts. Through these techniques, mapmakers emphasized the certainty of their information and drew attention away from their uncertainties and speculations.

Maps also transmitted the certainty of cosmographical knowledge through their portrayal of navigational competence. As they did in all other aspects, the maps here took their cue from the cosmographical texts, which discussed how cosmographical calculations facilitated deep-sea navigation (the essential component of the Spanish and Portuguese expeditions), linking the technical advances in astronomical observation to the discovery of new lands. For Peucer, the knowledge of the ancients was limited by their inability to travel great distances, an obstacle the moderns had clearly overcome.[109] As Glareanus told his readers, with the aid of the astrolabe, the quadrant, and the sky, they could determine their location anyplace on earth.[110] As a result, Behaim could assure the readers of his globe that "no one should doubt since the world is round [simpel] that one can sail or travel everywhere as it appears here."[111] Unlike travelers, therefore, cosmographers stressed the ease of ocean voyages and remarked on feats of science rather than personal valor.

Maps solidified the impression that technical mastery led to mastery of the seas by eliding the differences between the haphazard nature of the portolan charts (the traditional tools of the navigator) and the maps produced through cosmographical science. Portolan charts, with their emphasis on practical information of use to the mariner and their arbitrary placement of the guiding rhumb lines, seem completely incompatible with the easily transferable, carefully controlled, Ptolemaic grid system.[112] The traditions of portolan charts, however, were explained to landlocked Germans by Lorenz Fries in a way that emphasized their scientific certainty. The rhumb lines that ran through the seas on his *Mercarthen,* he declared, were used by sailors to determine which winds they should sail by and to reorient themselves should they be thrown off course by a storm, "all of which (with the help of astronomical instruments) takes place through these lines."[113] The *Mercarthen* itself shows both rhumb lines and a latitude/longitude grid. Likewise, Gemma Frisius, in his additions to the text of Apian's *Cosmographicus liber,* explained how to relate the two traditions. If one knew the variations in longitude and latitude of two places, it was easy to know "in which direction of the sky to point the prow" and, from that, which

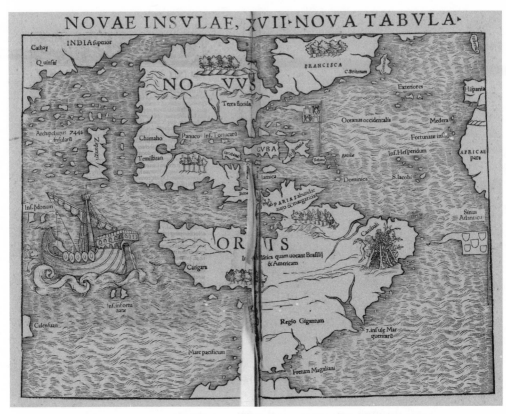

FIG. 3. *1540 New World* (Novus Orbis) *Map of Sebastian Münster, from Claudius Ptolemaeus,* Geographia universalis, *ed. Sebastian Münster (Basel: H. Petri, 1540). Courtesy of the John Carter Brown Library at Brown University.*

wind to use.[114] With the aid of the techniques and instruments outlined in the texts, readers were assured, cosmography would not lead mariners or anyone else astray.

The ultimate confirmation of the achievements and certainty of astronomical navigation lay in the map illustrations. In contrast to the travel narratives, which regaled their readers with tales of tragedy and woe on the high seas—sickness, mutiny, and shipwreck—the maps revealed no such details. In seas featuring artfully scattered whales, mermaids, and other marvels of the deep, ships under full sail were carefully positioned, not in the areas that the creatures inhabited,[115] but along the major routes connecting the new territories with the old.[116] Behaim's 1492 globe showed a ship sailing off the coast of Madagascar and one near the Azores. The only ship on Waldseemüller's 1507 map sailed toward the coast of "America." In a final example, Münster's maps for his 1540 edition of Ptolemy's *Geography* showed two carefully placed ships: one sailing around the Cape of Good Hope and the other sailing in the Pacific along the equator (see fig. 3). With their black lines and confident ships, maps provided visual reassurance of Europe's navigational competence.

When cosmographical terms and measurements appeared in travel narratives, as in the passage from Vespucci's *Four Voyages* cited at the beginning of this chapter, this cosmographical talk lent the text an air of certainty and gave readers a sense of belonging to an understandable universe.[117] Vespucci followed this opening of *Four Voyages* with the locations of various key landing sites, including the first mainland the expedition encountered: "It was distant from the islands of the Grand Canary 1000 leagues, more or less; it was inhabited, and was situated in the Torrid Zone. This we ascertained from the following observations."[118] In *Mundus Novus,* Vespucci again showed off his cosmographical prowess, this time determining his ship's position—to the amazement of the captain and the relief of his comrades—after a huge storm had blown it off course. As he somewhat condescendingly explained, sailors knew only the lands to which they had sailed before, knowledge that was of no use when "only the altitude of the heavenly signs was our guide and showed us the truth of hidden things and the same was made known to us by the quadrant and the astrolabe, as they all recognized."[119] It is not surprising that in the cosmographies Vespucci was praised as an "excellent mathematician" as opposed to an "accurate eyewitness."[120] In the narrative itself, Vespucci's professed abilities as the former enhanced his credibility as the latter. Johann Dryander's preface to Hans Staden's account of his voyage to Brazil demonstrated most clearly the potential of cosmographical knowledge for opening the way for the assertion of eyewitness authority. Although, he said, people might not believe that there were places on the earth where the sun did not rise for half the year and the longest day lasted six months, or that in other places there were two summers and two winters, those who understood these sciences "do not doubt these things." This succession of astronomical truths, however, should convince those about to read this tale of wild man-eaters that some things that were strange and unusual to the common man were nevertheless true.[121] Rather than experience being used to judge theory, theory in these cases was being used to create authority for experience.

Information from the travel narratives also found its way into the cosmographical literature, as in Fries's *Uslegung der Mercarthen*.[122] It was standard procedure to include short summaries of the political entities, inhabitants, natural resources, and curiosities of the "parts of the world" at the end of the presentation of cosmographical theory. While these in-text accounts lacked the complete integration of mathematics and description that the maps were able to achieve, they worked on the same principle. The closest textual equivalent of the maps' integration could be found in Peter Apian's *Cosmographicus liber* and Johann Schöner's *Luculentissima quaedam terrae totius descriptio,* where much of the texts' geographical information was contained in the coordinate listings. In many entries the precise numbers for latitude and longitude of a particular site would be followed by tidbits about its famous citizens, historical events, or economic role. For Marco Polo's city of Quinsay (longitude 226.00°, latitude 37.40°), Schöner noted that it was "the biggest city in the whole word, having in circumference 100 Italian miles, in the middle of which is a large lake, having 1200 bridges." [123] Regarding the city of Lac (longitude 166.30°, latitude 21.40°), Apian commented, "The inhabitants go naked, worship the cow and are idolaters; they are very just and hold liars in contempt." [124] This technique substituted the impersonal authority of the compass, astrolabe, and precisely placed summary for the personal authority of a specific traveler's experience. A veneer of seemingly exact details demonstrated the earth-encompassing nature of the cosmographical system. Readers who investigated closely would see that much of this exactitude was a facade, but they would also have become more fully initiated into cosmographical theories and procedures that promised eventual perfectibility.

AFRICA AND AMERICA IN THE COSMOGRAPHIES

The discovery of a new sea route to India around the Cape of Good Hope and the discovery of land in the Western Atlantic were always discussed in the cosmographies within the context of the cosmographical system and were thus never viewed apart from these assertions of expertise and control. The different treatments accorded to Africa and

America reveal how the cosmographical framework shaped the assessments of these distinctive and important advances over ancient empirical knowledge. Because the shape of Africa had both a firmer foundation as a source of ancient controversy and a clear and complete outline as a result of the Portuguese navigations, the discovery of the Cape of Good Hope held a more prominent place in the cosmographies' text and graphics. In contrast, America was subsumed under the (not mutually exclusive) categories of "part of the world" and "island." The application of these terms to the newfound western territories, rather than representing, as some historians have argued, a revolution in cosmography and a shattering of the familiar, finite image of the world, instead resulted from the use of familiar cosmographical concepts to explain (and, in so doing, limit) the implications of the expanding world.

It should be stressed, in keeping with their conflation of the Spanish and Portuguese discoveries, that the cosmographers placed far greater emphasis on the discovery of a series of unknown lands through deep-sea navigation than on one or another particular discovery. However, if the cosmographers chose to highlight one discovery above all others, they considered the Portuguese exploration of Africa the most important. It had confirmed that both the torrid zone and the southern temperate zone were traversable and inhabited.[125] In addition, it had extended Africa well beyond the point of Ptolemy's knowledge and, by revealing its circumnavigability, provided a direct point of contact with the ancients. Antiquity offered conflicting information as to whether Africa was circumnavigable. The maps in Ptolemy's *Geography* usually showed the Indian Ocean as enclosed, although this was not indicated in the text itself. Pliny and others, however, without supplying the specifics needed to set all suspicions to rest, did mention sailing voyages from one side of Africa to the other.[126] Some authors simply proclaimed that Ptolemy had been wrong and that new information was better than old.[127] Those who wished to stress the continuing validity of ancient disputes could also do so, with the added benefit (as was the case with the question of the habitation of the southern temperate zone) of being able to resolve the dispute in the end. Thus, Münster cited the Portuguese voyages to prove that Pliny and Pomponius Mela were right in stating that Africa was circumnavigable.[128] Marking out a measurable increase in knowledge from the time of the ancients, the Cape of Good Hope became a sign of intellectual progress for those who knew enough of the ancient heritage to appreciate its discovery as "progress."

Since the revised shape of Africa could be represented in its entirety, it was brought visually to the attention of cosmographical audiences as well. The title page of Apian's *Isagoge in typum cosmographicum seu mappam mundi* (Introduction to a Cosmographic Image or World Map) contained a depiction of the eastern hemisphere, showing Africa as circumnavigable and omitting America entirely. The importance of the sea route around the Cape of Good Hope determined the labels on the map as well: only Venice, Portugal, and Calicut were labeled, and two ships sailed across the Indian Ocean.[129] Waldseemüller's 1507 map placed enough significance on the circumnavigation of Africa to break the borders of the map to show the route in its entirety.[130] In contrast, the southern part of the island labeled "America" simply faded into the border (see fig. 4). The significance of the voyage around the Cape of Good Hope was also noted on the 1516 Waldseemüller *Carta Marina* and on its progeny, Fries's *Mercarthen*. In the strait separating Madagascar from Africa was a drawing of a triumphant king of Portugal, with the legend "The victory of the most Christian King Emanuel of Portugal."[131] Because the African voyages had revised Ptolemy, note could also be taken of them on Ptolemaic maps, as on the map accompanying Gregor Reisch's basic textbook, *Margarita philosophica*. On the land bridge enclosing the Indian Ocean by connecting southern Africa with Asia, the editor inserted a comment: "Here there is not land but sea, in which are islands of wondrous size, but which were unknown to Ptolemy."[132] As easily demonstrable and verifiable knowledge, the circumnavigation of Africa fit smoothly into demands for cosmographical expertise.

The New World was a different matter. Because it was an addition— not a correction—to the established worldview, and because knowledge of its shape and position was incomplete, this discovery lacked the panache of the circumnavigability of Africa. Although perfectly willing to recognize America as new, Renaissance cosmographers did not seek out further opportunities to exploit this designation. Instead, they concentrated on more precise classifications that established America's place within their system: was this a mainland, an island, a part of the world? For many modern historians, this process of categorization has loomed large, as the acknowledgment that this landmass was not part of Asia, and that it should be listed as a new part of the world, has been portrayed as presenting the gravest of challenges to received cosmographical wisdom.[133] From the standpoint of mathematical geography, however, the addition of another part of the world presented merely an empirical question. Likewise, the question of America's isolation from Asia was tentatively resolved (the final answer did not come until the discovery of the Bering Strait in the eighteenth century) according to the rules and traditions of cosmographical nomenclature.[134] Apparently revolutionary decisions were in fact the result of cosmographers trying to establish their authority over incomplete information.

"America" through most of the sixteenth century meant specifically and exclusively the southern mainland. The other islands all bore their own names and were described as "adjacent to America," in the same way that "Sicily" and "Sardinia" were adjacent to Europe. The northern landmass, often labeled "Parias,"[135] was usually shown as separate. If the region as a whole was meant, the term "Occidental India" or "Occidental Indies" was preferred. The extension of the name "America" from the southern landmass to the northern was not concurrent with the depiction of an isthmus connecting the two and is a process deserving more detailed study.[136] Because the northern landmass, as the century progressed, was often represented as simply a bulging part of Asia, with a narrow isthmus connecting it to the southern landmass, a separate name for the latter may have seemed preferable. Therefore, the "America" that first received the label "part of the world" was specifically the southern landmass.

"Part of the world" was the highest cosmographical category for dividing the earth's surface, bestowed on the basis of geographical, rather than political, theological, or cultural, considerations. As Siderocrates explained: "The surface of the earth was customarily divided by the ancients again in three, by more recent scholars in four. The threefold division is Europe, Africa and Asia, the fourfold Europe, Asia, Africa and America."[137] The original claim for America's significance was made in Vespucci's *Mundus Novus* letter, and Waldseemüller and Ringmann, in the *Cosmographiae introductio,* took Vespucci's assertion to mean that the new landmass should be placed on par with the others, as the fourth part of the world.[138] While some commentators continued to list only three parts of the world, many German cosmographers, led by Johann Schöner and Peter Apian, took up the new label, without disrupting the rest of their cosmographical thinking. As the quote from Siderocrates indicates, America was simply tacked on to an otherwise unrevised list.

FIG. 4. *1507 World Map of Martin Waldseemüller* (left)
and detail of Western Atlantic (above).
Courtesy of Libraray of Congress, Geography and Map Division.

Characteristically for the cosmographies, Siderocrates attributed no special significance, beyond custom, to the original tripartite world. The expansion of the list resulted solely from the extension of empirical knowledge in recent times. This expansion was significant, however, as it raised America's importance beyond that of those lands extending east, south, and north of the ancient world, which had also just come to the attention of Europe.

America's classification as the fourth part of the world often guaranteed it a conspicuous place in the descriptive portion of a cosmographical text, thereby stretching the ability of cosmographers to display certitude to the limit. As mentioned earlier, the exposition of cosmographical theory was usually followed by brief summaries of what the individual parts of the world contained. America would have such a section devoted to it, as would the other three parts of the world. There was one difference, however: the other parts of the world, being much better (or at least longer) known, could be more extensively described. As readers progressed through the descriptions of Europe, Africa, and Asia, a series of interlocking regions, described in convincing detail, spread out before them. The standard description of each region, like Ptolemy's remarks on "Scythia beyond Mt. Imaus," featured a listing of its boundaries and an enumeration of significant cities, rivers, mountains, and other geographical features. For a German cosmographer of the sixteenth century, fulfilling these requirements for America was absolutely impossible. The various landfalls onto the mainland and conquistadorial expeditions into the center produced no coherent image, and Germans were not sufficiently informed of the administrative development of the Spanish colonies to replace their lack of knowledge about the contours of native settlements with information about the developing colonies. Instead, cosmographers devoted the space allotted to America to a mention of its discovery and an account, often drawn verbatim from the travel narratives, of its inhabitants and natural resources.[139] Geographical detail was almost entirely absent, but the wealth of details about what was known about America apparently left no room on the page for any acknowledgment of all that the authors did not know.

America's status as a "part of the world" placed heavy informational requirements on cosmographers, while its simultaneous designation as an "island" made it possible to sidestep some of these requirements. America's insularity was particularly prominent in written cosmographical works, beginning with Waldseemüller and Ringmann's *Cosmographiae introductio,* and continuing as late as 1561, when Neander explained that "because however [America] is enclosed on all sides by the sea, it is an ISLAND."[140] America's separation from the other parts of the world made it an island, not a continent, according to the categorization laid out in Apian's *Cosmographicus liber:* "An island therefore is that part of the land which is separated from the larger parts of the land and is washed on all sides by water. A peninsula or chersonesus . . . is clearly not an island nor a continent, but instead is almost on all sides surrounded by water, however connected by some neck to the continent. . . . A continent is said to be all firm and fixed land which is neither an island nor a peninsula nor an isthmus. But the whole is stable and united to itself." [141] The assertion that a sea separated America from Asia, far from increasing the importance of the new land, minimized its significance. As Klaus Vogel has pointed out, new islands were constantly being discovered, so adding one more, even if it was labeled the fourth part of the world, was not a big step. [142] America simply joined a long list of islands to the west of Europe, including those discovered on Columbus's first voyage. In his recounting of the "islands of the ocean and the sea," Johann Honter stated that to the west were "Dorcades, Hesperides, Fortunatae, America, Parias, Isabella, Spagnolla & Gades." [143] As new areas were discovered and named, they were simply added to the list, the "island" of Peru being the most conspicuous example. The cosmographers' designation of lands reached by the voyages of discovery as islands was a survival strategy, a placeholder until more complete information could be obtained.

The marginal status of islands in the cosmographical texts stemmed from their existence on the borders and in the crevices of the world. Islands appeared in the texts under a separate listing, either at the end of the section on a particular part of the world or as a completely separate section. The information traditionally provided for islands was far less extensive than that provided for the parts of the world: major cities and the location of an island's center were the only attributes typically listed. In those texts that did not provide coordinate listings, only a vague indication of general direction or location was given. All of the Mediterranean islands, for example, would be listed together without any greater specificity about exact location. As islands were, by definition, surrounded on all sides by water, their relation to neighboring landmasses could be left an open question. [144] Conceiving America as an island, rather than as connected by some as yet undetermined means to Asia, had definite advantages, helping cosmographers assuage concerns about the limited information available on this newly discovered part of the world. America could then be successfully, if tentatively, integrated into a cosmographical system—the insufficiencies of knowledge glossed over and the conformity to recognized forms stressed.

For cosmographers, the deficiencies of experience, at least as it was transmitted to them in the form of half-drawn portolan charts and incomplete (from a geographical standpoint) travelers' accounts, posed the most formidable challenge. They were delighted when (as in the case of Africa) new discoveries allowed them to definitively solve ancient geographical puzzles, and they were coy when they knew enough to proclaim an advance in knowledge but not enough to precisely define this advance. In so doing, cosmographers not only displayed their expertise by containing the newly discovered territories within the confines of their discipline, but gave the discoveries a significance they would not otherwise have possessed. In this sense, Africa and America were treated equally.

IN 1512 JOHANN COCHLAEUS told readers of his edition of Pomponius Mela's *Cosmographia* not to worry about Vespucci's discoveries (even if the accounts were true), for they "contribute nothing or altogether little to cosmographical and historical knowledge." [145] Cochlaeus did, however, demand that his readers attend to two substantial additions to Mela's slim text. In the first new section, he presented a more orderly and complete version of the cosmographical system than Mela had introduced, developing such themes as the structure of the universe, polar elevation, and the five-zone schema (which, as discussed above, he qualified to take modern explorations into account). In the second addition, Cochlaeus provided a new description of Germany, including six pages on his home city of Nuremberg detailing its remarkable progress since the dark days of the ancients. These additions perfectly illustrate the issues driving cosmographical discussion within Germany: erecting and maintaining a usable cosmographical apparatus that enabled truth claims and then using that system to document the changing fate of human societies of particular interest to German audiences. The knowledge produced under these circumstances had already established that the ancient authorities were indispensable, but not infallible. In that sense, Cochlaeus was right: America did have little to offer.

In another sense, however, Cochlaeus's dismissal does not reflect the attitudes of many of Germany's most prominent cosmographers, who embraced the latest news they could obtain about the discoveries; eagerly passed along selected information to a broad array of audiences; and filled the edges of their maps with new mainlands, islands, and extensions of known land. With a little effort, the lands "outside Ptolemy" could reward investigation and incorporation. [146] The Spanish and Portuguese expeditions in particular could help refine and verify the system, while demonstrating (yet again) the limits of ancient knowledge. Moreover, they provided another opportunity for present-day cosmographers to situate themselves as either authorities (in the case of nonspecialist audiences) or arbiters (in the case of more devoted scholars), elevating themselves over both ancient authorities and modern explorers. In return, cosmographers certified the Spanish and Portuguese discoveries as providing new and significant information within an established system of knowledge.

CHAPTER THREE

Accounting for the Discoveries

THE COMMERCIAL CORRESPONDENCE

W HEN YOUNG MEN SIGNED UP as junior agents (factors) with
one of the flourishing south German commercial houses,
their contracts typically contained a standard set of stipulations, including prohibitions against gambling, consorting with women and
bad company, and using general funds for personal purposes, as well
as an agreement to be at the disposal of the firm's partners. A contract
signed in 1511 and another signed in 1523 by factors joining the Imhoff
firm of Nuremberg contained, in the usual phrasing, an agreement to
go "wherever needed and ordered, by water or by land," with, in one
case, the important condition that "no land or region [is] excluded,
except for India, but including Lisbon," and, in the other case, that
"no land or region [is excluded] except for India."[1] Jörg Pock, an agent
for the Hirschvogels of Nuremberg, agreed in 1520 to a different set
of conditions, which laid out his obligations during his stay in India.
Pock agreed not only to conduct the requested business transactions
promptly and honestly, but also to "give each year an honest, clear, upright, honorable accounting, and also to send said accounting with the
ships that sail from India to Portugal each year, and also to include a
list of the cargo loaded into these ships in India and what kind of spices
remain available in India, all of which to check and establish as clearly
as possible, and to write down and send by a certain associate."[2]

Why were such measures necessary? Why did newly hired agents guard so carefully against the possibility of being sent to India as representatives of a German commercial firm? What allowed the geographical horizons of commercial expertise to expand so far? Why was the keeping and sending of faithful accounts deemed the essential method for communicating a factor's overseas experiences? The answers to these questions relate not only to Europeans' ability to travel to new locations (covered in the previous chapter), but also to their ability to exploit these lands for commercial gain. Rather than standing paralyzed on the shores of Europe, unable to comprehend these new discoveries, German merchants jumped at the chance to participate in the globalizing trading system. They acted so quickly because from these new sources and along these new routes came familiar and highly prized products, including spices, precious metals, jewels, hardwoods, and expensive cloth. A long-term and ongoing reorganization of the commercial and financial systems of Europe had given south German merchants a prominent position. Even more important, through coping with the increasing commercial sophistication of Europe, these merchants had grown adept at tools and practices that proved adaptable to the extraction of overseas goods. The key to this extraction is revealed in the specific orders given to Jörg Pock: precise calculation—of risk and opportunity, profit and loss, supply and demand—remained the sine qua non of mercantile procedures. The merchants' rapid and enthusiastic response to the establishment of a direct link between Lisbon and the spice emporia of India and to the discovery of gold and silver in the Spanish Indies shows that German commercial agents viewed the overseas world as understandable and manipulable.

Yet, as Mary Poovey has demonstrated in her analysis of bookkeeping manuals, precision and accuracy are not the same thing, and merchant practices depended on numerous "constitutive fictions." As narrative entries were transferred into mathematical forms of record keeping, the emphasis on arithmetical precision "required anyone who wrote in the [account] books to act as if these fictions were true and, in so doing, to help make them so."[3] In creating the appearance of rule-governed order, the numbers of the double-entry system privileged certain kinds of information: "quantity over quality and equivalence over difference."[4] I would like to take this analysis a step further and examine how such formulations, in practice as well as in theory, systematized the varied cultures and landscapes into just so many producers and providers of accessible goods whose worth could be calculated. Through the success of their ventures, merchants not only increased their wealth, but also demonstrated their competence in assessing and controlling risk and reward in areas newly opened to European exchange and exploitation.

Commercial opportunity was always a recognized part of the European expansion, which was of course driven in part by the well-established belief that riches were to be found in the East. The fabulous wealth of the Orient had been described by the ancients and confirmed by medieval travelers. Maps from the period, such as the Behaim globe, consistently note the abundance of gold, spices, and other natural resources in far-distant regions. Behaim relied on Marco Polo for the following notes about the island of "Cipango": "In the island grows a vast amount of gold; precious stones and pearls also grow there." [5] From their inception the expeditions targeted the sources of these desired goods. According to the 1508 travel compilation *Newe vnbekanthe landte,* Columbus's goal was to "find islands to the west, adjacent to India, where there is an abundance of precious stones and spices, as well as of gold, which is easy to come by." [6] The association of the voyages' destination with tremendous wealth was a commonplace for contemporary observers of the European expansion.

This image of "gilded abundance" functioned in two ways: it prompted a careful evaluation of how best to tap into these sources with economic acumen and military might, and it acted as a fairy tale that elicited the same pleasure as the wonders of the East. [7] These two effects were not mutually exclusive, and combined they created a powerful force that pulled men overseas. [8] When discussing how the treasures of India, Africa, and America influenced European representations of the discoveries, however, scholars have almost exclusively stressed the marvelous aspects of this wealth. The use of travel narratives, with their tendency toward the fantastical, to analyze the perception of the discoveries has enhanced this trend. The wonder in this analysis is sustained above all by unspecificity: incalculable wealth and innumerable riches lie in the vast region known simply as "the East." According to Gita Dharampal-Frick, Sebastian Franck's depiction of India in the 1534 *Weltbuch,* which represents a "kind of synthesis of contemporary knowledge," centers around an image of India as the Earthly Paradise: "Blessed with all the riches of nature, India is a land of plenty, where neither want nor disease exists. . . . Jewels and mountains of gold increase the natural wealth to the point of immeasurability." [9] The response elicited through such portrayals, scholars have claimed, was an emotional one, based on dreams and desires. For example, Columbus's story about the willingness of Caribbean natives to trade goods of great value for trinkets prompted Peter Hulme to acknowledge, "Accountancy is lodged at the very beginning of the European colonial venture." But Hulme's overarching point remains, however, that "intimately entwined with that accountancy is the question of power," as Hulme is interested in the sweeping gaze of a political power with ever-expanding aspirations, rather than the precise gaze of a merchant concerned with the prospects of a particular voyage.[10] Louis Montrose's analysis of another text with overt political and imperial aims, Sir Walter Ralegh's *Discoverie of Guiana,* also subsumes the financial motives of the expedition under a more general rubric that stresses the irrational aspects of the conquest: "Greed is here the common denominator of 'Western desire.'" This point is further driven home by Montrose's inclusion of "the spectacular myth of [the golden king] El Dorado" as part of "the discourse of wonder."[11] If they do give prominence to the material promise of the newly discovered territories, scholars have disregarded the mediation and manipulation required to obtain and use this wealth, limiting themselves to describing a European desire that envisioned effortlessly acquired wealth that could be carelessly translated into physical well-being, social success, and emotional happiness. This perspective is based on and strengthens the idea that the source of such delights was a place so new and different that European rules did not apply. It certainly made sense for promoters of overseas expansion (such as Columbus and Ralegh) to create this impression, but the extraction of the riches of the Indies proceeded along lines more realistic in principle and more rewarding in practice.

In neglecting the intellectual implications of commercial correspondence, scholars have missed the way these documents demonstrate the successful extension of European categories and practices overseas. Dreams of splendor may have been excited from afar by images of incalculable and uncataloged riches, but their fulfillment required going beyond marveling at wealth to entering it into a system of exchange, where its worth would be established and its value equated with other desired goods. Seeing the golden mountains was beside the point if the gold could not be removed from its original context and circulated. Observers of the voyages of exploration, both those weighing the costs and benefits of risking the trip themselves and those content to await the results on European shores, judged success on the basis of the voyages' ability to extract, transport, and measure, as well as to discover, the wealth of the Indies.

Transforming the natural and human resources of the newly discovered lands into objects of exchange called for training in commerce and accounting—in other words, for merchants. Among those lining up to profit from the treasures of the Indies were Germans from the wealthy and populous cities of the south, who came to be involved at almost every stage in the process of extracting and distributing colonial goods. Their presence was neither as overwhelming as that of the thousands of Spanish and Portuguese who engaged in both large-scale and petty trade along overseas routes nor as crucial as that of the Italians, particularly the Genoese, whose financial backing of the expeditions was unrivaled. Nevertheless, an examination of German participation demonstrates that entering into commerce with the Oriental and Occidental Indies defined particular questions as essential to understanding the discoveries and their impact on Europe. Rather than containing images of inconceivable wealth, the commercial correspondence was driven by a desire to calculate commensurability: to discover and confirm the types of products, the amounts available, their value in Europe, and the potential for profit.

THE NEW COMMERCIAL LANDSCAPE

German merchants were able to extend their operations and commercial calculations into the new arenas opened by the Iberian expansion because this trade was conducted on terms recognizable from existing patterns of European commerce. In the decades before Columbus, da Gama, and Magellan, German merchants were already engaged in trade that took them from Eastern Europe to Italy to the Iberian Peninsula. The hallmark of economic exchange in Europe in the late medieval period was its system of negotiated trading privileges, which determined who could sell what to whom under what conditions. The Germans in Venice, for example, had to reside at the so-called German House (Fondaco dei Tedeschi), hire a Venetian agent for all transactions, and spend any money earned from the sale of imported merchandise immediately within the local economy. Within these networks German merchants exported the products of German soil (metal ores, grain, and wood), as well as the products of German artisanship (metalwares and cloth).[12] They imported, among other items, luxury wares from Italian ports. Some goods, such as fine cloth, were manufactured in Italy, but others, above all spices, arrived in the ports of Venice and Genoa via the well-established Mediterranean trade routes that brought products from India and the East Indies by way of the Islamic kingdoms of the eastern Mediterranean. Not only did German merchants provide spices to local markets through the Frankfurt fair and other distribution points, but they also acted as middlemen in the transport of spices to Eastern Europe. None of this would change much over the next century: German merchants would still go forth in search of spices, bringing cloth and metal to trade.

By the time of the establishment of the new oceanic trade routes in the sixteenth century, recent developments within European economic structures had not only demonstrated that German merchants could adapt to changing circumstances, but had also prepared the way for significant German commercial involvement in the overseas expansion. The most characteristic aspect of the economic reorganization of the Renaissance was the increasing dominance of large firms, which had the capital necessary to invest in the new types of highly profitable economic ventures. The introduction of new production methods in the weaving and mining trades gave an advantage to those with the capital to employ new forms of labor and technology.[13] Cloth, particularly fustian (a mixture of linen and cotton), came increasingly from the looms of weavers dependent on a merchant for the supply of their raw materials and the distribution of the finished product. In mining, a new smelting process using lead was introduced that separated silver ore from the surrounding copper ore, providing both extra silver and purified copper. The development of new pumping and deep-mining methods also required substantial investments of money and know-how. Such protoindustrial structures were well developed in Germany. The Fugger family of Augsburg, for example, established a manufacturing center for fustian on their property of Weissenhorn,[14] while their fellow Augsburgers, the Welsers, along with many other members of the urban elite, owned shares (*Kuxen*) of mining and smelting operations.[15] The staples of the long-distance trade thus fell increasingly into the hands of those with access to significant concentrations of capital.

Money itself, in the form of loans, bills of exchange (which were often loans in disguise), and long-term leases of extraction privileges (such as tax farming), became a prominent trading item for the most substantial German commercial firms. The ambitious royal houses of Europe needed large amounts of ready cash to raise armies, finance state projects (including the voyages of discovery), and display themselves with appropriate pomp. However, the limited sums due to them from taxes, grants from their loyal subjects, and other traditional sources of income no longer sufficed. As a result, they turned to the merchants of Italy and Germany for advances. The Holy Roman Emperor Maximilian I relied most heavily on the Augsburg firms of the Fuggers and Welsers, but often sought aid further afield, for example, in appealing to the Tuchers, Imhoffs, Hirschvogels, and Fütterers of Nuremberg for a loan in 1508.[16] Maximilian was only one of the many rulers who sought aid from German merchants.[17] As loans were always demanded in large amounts and on short notice, lenders had to have the financial stature and strength to scrape together the necessary sums quickly, either from their own supplies or through their good credit with business associates.

A final aspect of the new commercial landscape also hinged on the fiscal strength of the German firms. Often (and often under duress), rulers would guarantee repayment of private loans from a specific source of royal or ducal income. For the princes of sixteenth-century Central Europe, one of the most stable sources of income were their territorial mines. Therefore, through their loans to the powerful, German merchants were able to secure control of much of Europe's silver and copper supply.[18] The silver mines of Tirol, for example, first came under the control of the Paumgartners, who were in turn driven out by the Fuggers at the end of the fifteenth century.[19] In Spain, the most eagerly sought means of debt repayment was the lease of the Maestrazgos— the income of the three knightly orders that had become part of the Crown's revenue when Charles V was appointed their collective head. The Fuggers and Welsers, both holders of long-term leases on the Maestrazgos during the sixteenth century, devoted much money and attention to turning a profit from the grain, wine, and quicksilver that formed the principal parts of the orders' income. Thus, not only was long-distance trade necessary to build up the capital reserves required to participate in the money business, but the money business increasingly became a necessary prelude to acquiring access to the most lucrative trade goods.

The changing economic system produced changes in the commercial topography of Central Europe. Medieval trading powers like the

Hansa and the city of Regensburg lost some of their importance to south German firms.[20] These firms, concentrated in Swabia and Franconia, grew strong enough on the basis of their location at the crossroads of the trade in metal, cloth, and spices, and their early participation in the economy of money, to overtake their competition within Germany and even to rival the Italians.[21] These merchants included established patricians, such as the Gossembrots and Herwarts of Augsburg and the Behaims of Nuremberg, as well as more recent arrivals. The Fugger and Welser families of Augsburg both grew within the space of a century from relatively humble cloth merchants to phenomenally powerful entrepreneurs. Other less well-known but still internationally active families included the Höchstetters and Paumgartners of Augsburg and the Imhoffs, Hirschvogels, and Tuchers of Nuremberg. The commercial predominance of southern Germany was increased by the firms' habit of drawing employees (who sometimes could acquire enough experience and capital to establish their own firms) from among their relatives, friends, and neighbors, in that order. A dense network of expertise in the dominant transactions of the early modern economy developed in southern Germany, centered on the free imperial cities of Augsburg and Nuremberg. This expertise gave German merchants a firm footing in the organized chaos of European commerce and stepping stones into the new commercial opportunities.

THE OVERSEAS TRADE

The European expansion, rather than rendering such expertise obsolete, made possible its extension into new parts of the globe, thus laying the foundation for merchant claims that the newly discovered territories were comprehensible in economic terms. The trade in luxury goods was by no means disrupted; the whole point of finding a new route to the Indies, after all, was to tap into the profits that the Italians had for centuries derived from this trade. Spices such as pepper and ginger continued to be imported, only now they arrived more often in Portugal than in the Italian ports. Other products that had earlier been the exclusive province of the Mediterranean trade, such as brazilwood and precious stones, were now available for purchase through Portuguese agents in Lisbon and Antwerp in exchange for German goods. Although the exploitation of the Spanish colonies in the New

World took longer to develop, soon precious metals, pearls, sugar, cattle hides, and medicinal products started flowing into the port of Seville. Overseas commerce flourished because it was based on the staples of the long-distance trade.

The initial response of German merchants to these new trade routes was guided by their existing expertise. Their long-standing involvement in the lucrative, well-established spice trade made them respond with more energy and enthusiasm to the initial reports of the Portuguese discoveries. For Wilhelm Rem, a member of a prominent Augsburg merchant family,[22] Vasco da Gama's expedition was the first of the Iberian voyages worth mentioning in his city chronicle. For the year 1499, he noted: "The King of Portugal sent three ships out to sea in 1497, to seek India and strange lands. They brought the king good news, that they found Calicut in India, where spices grow." [23] A later chronicle also reports on the successful spice voyage of 1499, subsuming the discoveries of Columbus and Vespucci as an afterthought in the narration of da Gama's success.[24] The importance of spices was also indicated by the merchants' activities in Portugal and Spain. Although the establishment of Portuguese trading forts along the African coast in the course of the fifteenth century had brought supplies of gold, ivory, and slaves to the metropolis for several decades before da Gama's expedition, the activity of German firms increased notably with the discovery of the sea route to India.[25] In 1505–6 a consortium of German merchants, including the Fuggers, Welsers, and Höchstetters of Augsburg, and the Imhoffs and Hirschvogels of Nuremberg, outfitted three ships to sail with that year's India fleet.[26] When the king of Portugal decided to shift the main distribution point for his spices to Antwerp, the German firms followed suit, giving increased emphasis to the Antwerp offices and reducing or closing their offices in Portugal.[27]

Their eagerness to acquire spices even took the German merchants to Spain, specifically drawn by the possibilities of a new sea route to the Pacific Spice Islands, first mapped out by Magellan's crew, which would bypass the Portuguese-controlled eastward route. Their hopes for the new route caused the Fuggers and Welsers to contribute substantial sums to the voyage of García de Loiasa, sent out to cement Magellan's gains.[28] The prospects for circumventing the Portuguese dimmed, however, when the ragged remnants of Loiasa's crew were taken prisoner by the Portuguese, then died out completely when Charles V ceded his claims to the Spice Islands to the king of Portugal in 1529 for the sum of

350,000 ducats. Despite Spain's failure to secure access to the spice trade, its possessions in the New World soon eclipsed earlier and competing sources of other prized and familiar goods, particularly gold, silver, and pearls. In addition, the lands of the Western Atlantic became noted for two plants that before had required a journey to Arabia or India: brazil-wood and sugar. The increasingly obvious potential of Spain's overseas possessions and the increasing indebtedness of the ruling Habsburgs to German merchant houses prompted German merchants to incorporate Seville into their commercial activities. In 1518 the Hirschvogel factor Lazarus Nürnberger, previously the family's representative in Lisbon, traveled for the first time to Seville. He returned to the Spanish port in 1520 and soon settled there permanently, marrying the daughter of the prominent printer Jacob Cromberger and acting as an agent for various German firms, as well as investing and trading on his own.[29] Both the Fuggers and the Welsers set up networks of agents in Spain, and the Welsers extended their operations in 1526 to Santo Domingo and by 1530 to Venezuela.[30] By the middle of the sixteenth century, the new patterns of trade had become part of routine commerce, continuing to supply Europe with goods whose profitability had been firmly established prior to the voyages of discovery.

The involvement of German firms came as a result of their strong economic position within Europe, so that the opening of new trade routes enhanced the importance of already established practices. Because silver and copper were the preferred exchange for spices on the world market, the south German firms became even more indispensable through their increasing control of the mining industry.[31] Their access to staples such as shipbuilding materials, iron goods, and grain made them welcome in Seville as well as Lisbon. The trade in money was also a crucial component of their indispensability. Both the Portuguese and Spanish Crowns, chronically short of funds, were advanced large sums by commercial firms.[32] As major actors in the arenas of both long-distance trade and finance, the German merchants were intrinsic to the Iberian economic arena.

Any barriers German merchants faced to full participation in the overseas trade arose from the policies of the Iberian kings, rather than from any inability to cope with a global economic system. As they did throughout Europe, German merchants had to negotiate access to the trade around the Cape of Good Hope and across the Atlantic. In allocating permission to participate in this lucrative opportunity, the rulers of Spain and Portugal were governed by the typical concerns of political and financial expediency. The king of Portugal's need for copper and capital persuaded him to grant new trading privileges to the Welser firm in 1503, including tariff reductions on goods imported from overseas. He quickly extended these privileges to all German firms with 10,000 ducats of investment capital.[33] The brief relaxation of the Crown's strict control over the spice trade that made possible German participation in the 1505–6 voyage also came about as the result of the king's financial difficulties. The note the Welsers' agent made about his preparations for this voyage stressed the legal prerequisites: "On the first of August we signed the contract with the King of Portugal to equip three ships for the voyage to India."[34] The successful and profitable completion of this expedition only enhanced the German firms' desire to continue in the trade,[35] but the interests of the Crown again shifted. Intent on maintaining control over such a profitable venture, the king established a general royal monopoly over the spice trade, regulated by the official *Casa da India*. The German firms, prohibited from direct participation, had to be content to obtain their pepper in Lisbon and Antwerp, where the king satisfied his need for liquid capital and trade goods by signing exclusive pepper-distribution contracts with international firms in return for advances of cash and precious metals.

Similarly, the Germans' encroachment on the Spanish overseas trade did not so much reflect their capacity to handle new situations, colonial relations, and exotic locales, as their familiarity with the patterns of the European commodity and money markets. Gaining access to the Atlantic trade likewise depended on royal decree. Initially, trade with the Spanish colonies was limited to subjects of the Spanish king. In 1524, however, foreigners were allowed to participate in overseas commerce, which was regulated by the *Casa de Contratación* (a parallel institution to the Portuguese *Casa da India*), through the port of Seville. In 1525 the restrictions on foreigners traveling to the Spanish Indies were lifted for the Genoese and for subjects of the Holy Roman Empire, and the requirements originally placed on them were eliminated the following year.[36] The Spanish expeditions aimed at breaking the Portuguese monopoly on trade with the East Indies were also opened to foreign investment, due to the usual lack of available domestic capital. Although Magellan's voyage to the Spice Islands via the westward route was purely funded by the Spanish, the succeeding voyage of García de Loiasa tapped into broader sources of support.[37] The opportunities the weak structures of royal finance created for German participation were contrary to the ideals of royal power, but completely standard in practice.

The height of German involvement in the Spanish colonial empire came with the granting of conquest and settlement rights in Venezuela to the Welsers in 1528–30.[38] The details of the contract indicate that neither side was so blinded by hopes and dreams of incalculable wealth as to neglect the careful division of responsibilities and rewards. The contract stipulated that two outposts (each with three hundred colonists and, if deemed necessary, up to three forts) be built in the territory over the next two years. In addition, the Welsers were to supply fifty miners to the Spanish provinces in the New World. In exchange, the colonizers were to receive exclusive rights of exploration and conquest, with many export duties eliminated or reduced to ease this process. The financial rewards included a handsome salary promised to the governor from the province's income, a temporary reduction in the royal tax on precious metal exports, and the right to enslave "rebellious" Indians.[39] While the contract committed the Welsers to new and unaccustomed military and administrative roles (duties that they in any case passed along to their agents), the contract itself was not an innovation. First, it was consistent with the exploration and colonization grants that the Spanish Crown was handing out left and right. Second, the Venezuela contract formed part of a series of agreements signed between Charles V and the Welsers, in which the Welsers' expertise and financial capabilities were exchanged for royal permission to engage in lucrative trading opportunities.[40] Thus, immediately prior to the Venezuela contract, the Welsers were granted licenses for the import and sale of four thousand African slaves to the Spanish Indies. Merchants became colonizers because such contracts fit within recognized patterns of economic extraction.

Although Philip II renewed the restrictions on foreign participation in the economy of the Indies, following the same logic as the king of Portugal, the financial strength of the German firms nevertheless allowed them access to the territory's natural resources by the back door of loaning substantial sums. As noted earlier, the king of Portugal relied on the deals he struck in exchange for his pepper in Antwerp to finance upcoming voyages. Firms that bought pepper therefore had to be in a position to advance large sums, a condition that favored the capital-rich south German firms.[41] In the Spanish case, the loans to the Crown, which had earlier been repaid through the Maestrazgos or through other local sources of Crown revenue, were increasingly secured through the king's share of the shipments from the Spanish Indies. Thus, in 1530 Sebastian Neidhart was guaranteed repayment for a loan of 40,000 ducats with pearls from the Caribbean.[42] In the Fugger books the same phrase appears repeatedly in entries about repayment and promises of repayment: "To be delivered in the gold [or gold and silver] of the Indies."[43] The same qualities that made the German merchants prominent within the European economy guaranteed their access, through one means or another, to the products of the Oriental and Occidental Indies. They were astute in evaluating new opportunities, insistent on a recognizable potential for profit, and flexible about the exact form and conditions of the commercial venture.

MERCHANTS AND GEOGRAPHICAL EXPANSION

For German merchants sitting in their counting houses in Augsburg, Nuremberg, Antwerp, or Lisbon, the essence of the discoveries was that the world had now been opened to the practices of European exchange—an economic opening that accompanied the geographical one discussed earlier. The elements of travel literature and cosmography that appeared in German merchants' writings worked in tandem with specifically commercial elements to make dreams of wealth seem plausible. As Jerry Brotton has pointed out, the idea of the availability of the entire world, graphically represented by maps, also had economic implications: "One of the most effective aspects of the possession of a map recovered from the rigours of long-distance travel was its ability to instill in its owner a belief in his possession of the territory depicted, or, within the concerns of commercial entrepreneurs, access to the territories portrayed in their maps and across their globes."[44] Thus, the plentiful notations on maps such as Behaim's globe and Fries's *Mercarthen* regarding the abundance of gold, silver, and other natural resources were not taunts but invitations. The promise of cosmography found resonance in merchant networks, as illustrated by two route descriptions produced in this context. The first example comes at the beginning of a book of trading customs completed in 1506 by a member of a prominent Augsburg firm.[45] Starting with "Lissabon," the miles from one landmark to the next around the Cape of Good Hope are provided:

From Lisbon to Grand Canary Island   240 . . .
From Grand Canary Island to the Island of St. Ago   250 . . .
From the Island of St. Ago to the Cape of Good Hope
    by the direct route   1400 . . .

But the sailors must travel so that they almost touch the shores of Brazil
on account of the wind so that they must sail an additional 400 miles
or so

From the Island of St. Ago to first landfall in Brazil   450[46]

The signposts for the journey from Nuremberg to Peru were likewise
noted by the Nuremberg merchant Hieronymus Koeler in his history
of a thwarted journey as a member of a Welser expedition, an itin-
erary that included Seville (700 miles from Nuremberg), the Canary
Islands (300 miles from Seville), and Santo Domingo (700 miles from
the Canary Islands).[47] In such cases, the presentation of exact mileages
stressed the new territories' reachability to the enterprising merchant.

Conducting trade in, as well as with, the Indies provided tangible
proof that the globe was accessible to Europeans. A steady trickle of
German commercial representatives traveled overseas. The actual number of their voyages is less significant for present purposes than is the
possibility they represented to those involved in trade. Their journeys'
impact was increased by the fact that a number of them composed
news-filled letters or even more formal travel accounts, making their
experience available to a wider audience. One, Balthasar Sprenger, the
Fugger factor with the 1505–6 expedition to India, published an illustrated narrative of his journey.[48] In addition, two Hirschvogel factors
sailed to India; Lazarus Nürnberger stayed for less than a year, but Jörg
Pock spent the rest of his life there as a jewel merchant.[49] Both wrote
letters to friends at home in Nuremberg.[50] Gabriel Holzschuher, sent
abroad by the Augsburg merchant Konrad Rott in 1580, wrote a carefully preserved letter home and promised to write more.[51] Another set of
commercial travelers left their fate to be recorded by others. In a *Familienbuch* (a recounting of a family's origins, births, marriages, deaths,
and notable accomplishments) for the Holzschuher family of Nuremberg, a simple notation appears: "Peter Holtschüher . . . died unmar-
ried on the return voyage from Calicut, whence they bring pepper"—
bringing home the physical reality of the trip to this no-longer-fanciful

land.[52] The Tucher family, fellow citizens of the Holzschuher, noted in their *Familienbuch* the history of one family member, Endres, who "served the Herwarts and traveled to Portugal and the new-found islands" sometime after arriving in the Netherlands in 1512.[53] Even those sent overseas who lacked a family member with enough sensibility to inscribe their fate for posterity (and there are many whose identity is known only through non-German records) would have illustrated the expanding world to friends and associates at home.[54] Sometimes it must have seemed as if everyone belonging to the small, tightly knit community of south German merchant firms had a friend or relation overseas. When the Tucher firm went in search of a new employee, the one they found in Ulm had not only a sizable inheritance to invest, but also "two brothers who are in the service of Bartholomew Welser in Santo Domingo."[55] The Imhoff factors' insistence that they not be given a now-possible assignment to India reflects this kind of local knowledge about the extension of travel possibilities through navigation.

While Renaissance cosmography and cartography explained where a place was, and provided some assurance that getting there was possible, they did not make places meaningful in economic terms. Merchants shared the cosmographers' interest in precise location, but for commercial rather than scientific reasons, which meant that a place acquired significance because of the products available there. Merchants were attuned to differences in place because trading circumstances varied so much from city to city and country to country and because products varied widely in quality and price depending on where they were acquired. The Augsburg book of trading customs, in addition to marking the landmarks and mileages of the sea route to India, noted the following gradations of lacquer: "The best kind grows in a land called 'Irgon.' The second kind grows in the land of 'Kirnalli.' . . . The third and worst kind grows near Calicut."[56] Merchants sprinkled their texts liberally with place names not (or not merely) to show off their globetrotting prowess, but to locate as precisely as necessary the sources of desired commodities.

The correlation of place with product is also a feature of the published travel narratives, particularly those that began as letters written by merchants. In these accounts detailed descriptions of natural resources often provided exactly the plotting of commercial opportunities that turned Calicut into "the land where pepper grows." Scanning the lands of the Western Atlantic for their economic meaning, the author of *Copia der Newen Zeytung auß Presillg Landt,* most likely a German merchant,[57] described both the product and its source: "They also found cana fistula in the land . . . they also have beeswax; they also have in the land a kind of spice that burns on the tongue like pepper, which grows in a pod with many small kernels." The possibilities for future success were also carefully noted: "You should also know that they bring sufficient indications that they are reportedly around 200 miles from the Cape towards us, in that Cape they were in a harbor and river, where they had indications that inland there was much silver and gold, also copper."[58] A remark that the author had purchased several fur pelts from the same fleet bolstered the image of economic potential with evidence of successful economic extraction. India's economy was similarly presented in elaborate detail. Thus, among the earliest news German audiences received about these fabled lands, reached after centuries of isolation and decades of searching, was the information that "around the abovementioned city of Calicut cinnamon and pepper grow well, but [they are] not of very good quality. But cloves come from lands farther away. There there is also enough rhubarb and other such spices. The ginger on the mainland is very good."[59] The commercial plotting of the European expansion, like the geographical plotting, explained the significance of the discoveries through asserting their compatibility with European systems of classification.

CALCULATION IN THEORY

The intersection of cartographic and commercial mapping only allowed the merchant to envision the "land where pepper grows" as accessible. Merchants, however, also needed to be convinced that the pepper itself was accessible. In this instance, accessibility meant availability through recognized trading procedures based not on a delight in the marvelous or the lure of the unknown, but on calculations of exchange, whether of money or of goods. The commensurability of the overseas trade with the principles of commercial assessment was thus indispensable for the interest and participation of German merchants. The essential tool for the extension of commercial practices was one that was already crucial in European trading contexts: quantification. Promoted as a method of bringing order to the otherwise chaotic world of commercial exchange, quantification integrated exotic goods from faraway lands into established practices through categorizing, counting, and measuring them. What little remains of the commercial correspondence of this time reveals the energy and technical capability expended on gathering precise economic information at the expense of gaining a broader understanding of the overseas world.

By the sixteenth century, the logistical and financial challenges of long-distance trade and the newly developing commercial structures had produced sophisticated tracking and accounting procedures.[60] The economic landscape of Europe and the Mediterranean around 1500 was a patchwork of different currencies, weights, measures, trading restrictions, and tariffs. These conditions, while burdensome and costly, produced merchants experienced in a bewildering variety of political and economic conditions. More than a bureaucratic chore, the complex process of calculating and recording accounts was essential to commercial training throughout Europe, as is indicated through its prominence in merchant manuals of the period.[61] One type of manual, the *Rechnungsbücher*, provided instruction in the mathematics necessary for commercial transactions,[62] while another provided guidance on figuring profit and loss, and still another provided information on the newest technique in bookkeeping: the double-entry system developed by the Italians.[63] The intricacies of the market thus produced a body of expertise in how to master the market.[64]

This body of expertise shares several characteristics with the knowledge produced by cosmographers. Historians have identified mathematics as an important meeting ground for elite culture and craft culture, and this convergence also applies to the high science of cosmography and the low science of merchant accounting.[65] The same cosmographers who made certain aspects of their knowledge available to the broader public also composed practical treatises on arithmetic, including its commercial applications. Both Peter Apian and Gemma Frisius, renowned cosmographers, composed *Rechnungsbücher*, Apian in German, Frisius in Latin.[66] These texts went beyond the standard arithmetical operations to explain the Rule of Three, alligation (proportionality in metal alloys), and calculations of interests—all distinctly mercantile concerns. The transferability of expertise suggests parallel lines of operation. Both of these forms of calculated knowledge were enclosed systems, whose accuracy was guaranteed with respect to other parts of the system and aligned with mathematical precision.[67] While the precise figures recorded in the account books, like the exact latitude and longitude coordinates listed in the cosmographies, elided the instability and imprecision of the original measurements,[68] the systems' validity was demonstrated through using the numbers to achieve concrete goals such as astrological predictions or price comparisons. The end results proved that these systems produced useful and accurate knowledge.

Good bookkeeping, according to its proponents, produced controlled, useful information: "Bookkeeping is a methodical record or description of a merchant's business, as well as other concerns, such as household expenses, rents, interest, and other administrative matters. So through subtle and methodical order and skill put together, and without mistake or harm put into good account, just as if it were laid on a balance or scale. . . . In addition, without such orders and skill, the final totals cannot easily be obtained from the business and accounts without mistake or harm.[69] In addition to these benefits, bookkeeping could also control people, because the methodical reentry of figures into different accounts and the regular tallying of balances made both innocent mistakes and sinister misuse of funds more difficult.[70] Such surveillance was particularly important in long-distance trade, because agents operated at a remove from the direct supervision of the partners, and communication could be infrequent. The Fugger employee Matthäus Schwarz took such problems seriously in his manuscript treatise on bookkeeping, devising specialized methods for recording transactions between various branches of the firm and for reporting to the head office in Augsburg, promising that "thereby no master can be deceived."[71] Proponents and practitioners of regularized accounting thus held out these systems as bulwarks against the acknowledged uncertainties and difficulties of economic transactions.

Bringing order from disorder was accomplished through precise recordkeeping and precise calculation. Therefore, merchant manuals of the era were filled with numbers: how to add, subtract, multiply, and divide them; how to calculate equivalencies between them; and how to manipulate them in a variety of word problems introduced to give the lessons a real-world flair: "Item a man buys 20 pounds of saffron at 4 fl. per pound, 30 pounds cloves at 15 ß per pound, and 60 pounds of ginger at 25 ß per pound. He wants to sell these at a profit of 10 fl. per 100 fl. How should he price a pound of each spice and what will be his total profit?"[72] The calculations were then carried out, showing how the exact prices and the total amount received could be figured. While it was unlikely that a merchant would ever be able to set his prices to come up with such a tidy profit as 10 percent, this problem and similar ones helped students see the universal applicability of such mathematical manipulations, regardless of the merchandise.

The homogenizing effects of mathematics were clearly demonstrated in other problems, such as those demonstrating the calculations required to translate currencies, weights, and measures into comparable forms (the same currency for all prices, the same yardstick for all length measurements, etc.). Following a listing of current exchange rates, the manuals would explain how to get from, say, Reichsthaler to Venetian ducats, or from a Regensburg cloth measure to one in Flanders. They would then provide practice problems so that the student would become comfortable comparing a purchase transaction conducted in Venice with a sale transaction conducted in Frankfurt. The successful solution of these problems depended on the student reducing every element to a common system of measurement, a feat accomplished using ratios, so that the numerical qualities of each item—amount, price, cost, and so on—had to be determined according to their relation to another set of numbers. Whatever their origin, the results would all be presented according to a single standard.

All could then be entered into the records according to the principles of bookkeeping. The information required for proper bookkeeping focused on the transaction, reducing it to its economic elements: items purchased, source, date, price; items sold, buyer, date, price. The clearest sign of the limited but precise data demanded by merchant correspondence and bookkeeping was its abbreviated style. These documents typically contained only shorthand references to place names, goods, and people—their position in the merchant network apparently needing no further comment. The purpose of these texts was to note and communicate the exact numbers (amount, prices, ratios) that could eventually be translated into the critical figures of profit and loss. Profit, furthermore, was not merely a figure; it was tangible proof that commercial calculations worked, despite all the approximations, manipulations, and constitutive fictions inherent in trading and accounting practices.

CALCULATION IN PRACTICE

Merchants found that their basic modus operandi worked perfectly well when dealing in the trade in exotic goods, whether overseas or on European shores. The coastal cities of India serve as an obvious case in point, as "the organizational structure of procurement and trade that . . . traders encountered . . . was both efficient and sophisticated." [73] The practical result was that the principles of the merchant manuals could be applied to trade in Calicut as they could to trade in Venice. As the 1506 Augsburg book of trading customs proceeded from trading center to trading center, it outlined expected expenses, prices, and exchange rates and offered advice on local customs and procedures. The text began with Italy, including such information as how spices should be "garbeliert" (i.e., sifted to rid them of impurities) in Genoa and measured in Venice.[74] The next part of the text went beyond the standard European entrepôts to cover India by way of the Portuguese strongholds along the coast of Africa. Occasionally, information useful to the traveler was given, such as the fact that "Quiloa" was tributary to the king of Portugal, while "Melinde" was allied with him, and that the water in "Motzabick" was unhealthy to drink.[75] The point of this section, however, is revealed in its extensive descriptions of the markets of India, complete with instructions on what to buy and how to buy it: "In Cochin: Pepper is bought by the 'bachar' and not by the 'farasoll.' And each bachar, when it is cheap, costs 180 'fanomen.' One bachar contains 20 farasoll. With this condition, that the payment is made half (or at least one-third) in copper. The price of copper is around 11 to 12 crusados for a 'quintal' or 'zentner.'" [76] The text continues with advice about the purchase of nutmeg, red sandalwood, brazilwood, tamarinds, rhubarb, incense, cinnamon, rubies, and pearls (to name just some of its entries). The distant origin, exotic nature, and high cost of these commodities did not prevent them from being bought and sold according to measurable standards.

It was essential that goods in India be available at calculable rates for the elements of trade to be integrated into an overall business strategy. Overseas traders thus exported the procedures for gaining commercial knowledge, allowing them to import desired products. When the Herwart factor Jörg Imhoff set sail for India, he began an account book to keep track of his transactions overseas. The document begins:

Praise be to God 1526   28 April
On April 28, debt owed to the account, from Jörg Herwart and Co. that
I received from Hans Sayler, which I took with me in cash to India.

f. 40000

The document continues in this vein, listing receipts of goods, debts, and purchases. Included among the purchases are a substantial number of jewels, all carefully entered in the approved manner:

> On December 25 Jörg Herwart and Co. must have from the account that bought and did thus in the abovementioned "maca" letter N°1: 2 small diamonds costing 3 gold pardaos (R[eichstaler] 1080). Further, 1 fairly large ruby costing 14 pardaos in gold (R[eichstaler] 5040). Further 1 ruby costing 2100 R[eichstaler]. Further 1 ruby, which some say is a spinel, costing R[eichstaler] 750. Further a small garnet cut to a pattern.
> Total of 6 pieces for   R[eichstaler] 8970.[77]

These transactions were proof positive of the accessibility of the "priceless" jewels of the East.

The ports along the Indian Ocean, with their recognizable commercial systems, lent themselves particularly well to the type of confidence expressed in these texts: a European merchant, with the proper experience and know-how, could trade and even prosper in this environment. German merchants were less informed about trading customs in the lands along the Atlantic and Caribbean shores that had been opened to European investigation for the first time by the Portuguese and Spanish voyages. In part, India's accessibility was made more apparent by its role as the established source for the all-important spices and by the India fleets' initial openness to foreign participation. In contrast, trade with the Guinea coast, Brazil, and the Spanish Indies was more strictly controlled and produced fewer essential staples of the German long-distance trade. However, these regions were not left outside the scrutiny of the commercial gaze. First, the travel accounts about these territories provided ample evidence that trade with the native populations was possible and profitable. Alvise da Cadamosto described an African ruler with whom he would soon develop a lucrative trading relationship as follows: "I also had had reports from some Portuguese, who had had dealings with the King [Budomel], that he was an honorable man, and a prince who could be trusted, and that he honorably paid for that which he bought."[78] The tentative Spanish explorations of the Caribbean basin were marked as much by trade as by skirmishes and (as Columbus's story of acquiring gold for trinkets indicates) could be well worth the trouble. Second, trade between these territories and Europe was regularized by the imposition of Spanish or Portuguese

trading outposts and/or colonial administration, which either inter-
acted with or replaced indigenous trading patterns. All four parts of
the world, therefore, were integrated into a single system of exchange
that could be coordinated with European practices.

The ultimate proof of the success of the Spanish and Portuguese
in extracting the wealth of these western territories was the arrival of
sugar, pearls, gold, and slaves in Lisbon and Seville. Upon their arrival,
all these were available through commercial transactions, and at this
point, the Germans tried once again to systematize their information
about gaining access to them. The third part of the Augsburg book
of trading practices, a "Triffasband" (book of tolls) written in 1514–15,
reflects the German merchants' increasing sophistication regarding the
structures of the worldwide trade. The book discussed the conditions
under which various products were sold at various emporia and the
costs of handling and shipping them. "Callachutt" warranted a price
listing for spices and metals, with the caveat that "these abovementioned rates were in effect at the beginning of the trip in 1503, without
a doubt they are now higher or lower."[79] The next city listed was (logically enough for a merchant) Lisbon, where, the manual explained,
the old weight of fourteen ounces per rotel was used to sell "all spices,
drugs, brazilwood and all things that they sell in the House of India."[80]
Later, in the section addressing tolls, the author described the "zisa de
merzaria," which applied to sugar and "all foreign items which come
from foreign lands such as wedin, painted cloth from India. Further, all
parrots, monkeys, long-tailed monkeys, and civets."[81] The procedures
for paying tolls and for ship inspection were explained, as was the best
method for smuggling goods (import part of the cargo openly and legally, before bringing the rest of it in as contraband). At the end of the
section on Portuguese tolls was a listing of the goods available for sale,
beginning with local products but continuing on with "the goods and
merchant wares that come from the Land of the Blacks and Guinea,
which land belongs to the king and no one is allowed to travel to or
do business in without his permission." This listing was extensive and
precise:

> Item elephant tusks, which are very beautiful and large.
> Item malagueta pepper, or grains of paradise, in large amounts.
> Item red wood, from which they make knife handles in Germany and
> which is called wild sandalwood.

Item gold, from which they make the cruzados which no one, except on
account of the king, is allowed to export, under penalty of life and
goods.
Item leopard skins also come from Barbaria [a North African region].[82]

Lists were also provided for "the New Land or Brazilland" and for
"India, where the king has captured several cities, and to which no
one can ship without his permission."[83] As these listings indicate, the
prohibitions cited in the text did not make the products of these areas
off-limits to German acquisition or prevent German merchants from
locating and pricing them exactly.

Conditions overseas fluctuated, just as they did in Europe, but the
same general principles for imposing order on the world of economic
exchange always applied. When the owner of a private commercial
school in Nuremberg published his handbook of trading practices in
1558, the same types of information were still valued, and precision was
still important. The removal of German merchants from direct participation in the Indian spice market was reflected in the terse notation for Calicut, whose brevity contrasted sharply with the flood of
information available in the 1506 Augsburg manuscript: "In Calicut
or India they buy everything by the 'fomoss,' 20 of which equal one
ducat."[84] Two new developments overshadowed this inability to detail
the circumstances of the on-site Indian trade. First, Portuguese trade
with the East had been routinized: the few indications of it in the text
reveal its loss of novelty status—as, for example, the estimated prices
of spices "that come first from Malucca to Antwerp."[85] Second, the energy of the handbook's readers (as was the case in general with German
merchants at that point) was focused on understanding the complexities of the spice trade within Europe. In the section "concerning the
Lisbon trade," the first topic was "How trade was conducted a few years
ago with the King of Portugal." The purchase of spices, "namely pepper, ginger, cloves, cinnamon, nutmeg, [and] mastic," was extensively
discussed, including shipping insurance, payment procedures, and
the garbulier necessary to remove unwanted substances from the bulk
spices.[86] Another section was devoted exclusively to the customs of the
House of India in Lisbon, obviously a key destination for the aspiring merchant. Shipping and handling costs to Antwerp were then discussed, and the proper accounting methods demonstrated, including
the tricky question of the loss of value resulting from the garbulier, as

a certain amount of impurities was usually taken into account with the initial sale price. This discussion took for granted the regular arrival of spices in Portugal, thereby nonchalantly asserting the successful extension of European practices.

The same concentration on the intra-European trade was evident in the discussion of Spain, for, as the author stated, "to travel to Anthiglia [the Antilles] or to engage in trade there, no one can do but those who are citizens of Seville, and [those who] have lived there for twelve years and were married—then they can trade, no matter what nationality they are." Therefore, the author explained how to acquire the goods that the ships brought from "Anthiglia," which he carefully enumerated: "There arrive normally every year twelve or more ships from Anthiglia in Seville, bringing around 600,000 ducats in gold, also around 3,000 marks of pearls and up to 3,000 boxes of sugar. Further, up to 500 quintals of cassia fistula, further up to 14,000 ox hides yearly. These ships also bring brazilwood, but not as good as that which arrives in Lisbon from Brazil. And these ships arrive more or less richly laden, than is described above, according to the time." The sorting, piercing, and purchasing of pearls in Seville were then discussed.[87] While the author freely admitted that the figures and procedures he was presenting were subject to change without notice, this fluctuation did not prevent an extensive presentation. For however much the details might change, the contours of the trade, the negotiations with the king, the relative prices, and the handling procedures were unlikely to be substantially altered. Furthermore, the text gave the student confidence that, however byzantine the vocabulary and procedures, and wherever they took place, they ultimately presented no hindrance to the effective pursuit of trading opportunities. The book stopped at the shores of the Atlantic because of legal, not conceptual, barriers.

German merchants preferred to specialize in the exchange of goods and money, their areas of expertise, but they were prepared to extend their European know-how more broadly in certain circumstances. Thus, the German commercial houses also brought their knowledge of new production methods into play in the mining industry of the Spanish Indies. The Welser factors made sure to negotiate mining rights with the neighboring province of Santa Marta in conjunction with their move into Venezuela.[88] The fifty miners the Welsers imported from the Joachimsthal region in Saxony certainly were expected to use their knowledge readily in the new environment, as did Hans Tetzel, the most successful of the German mining entrepreneurs in the Indies.[89] Beginning in 1546, Tetzel obtained the rights to establish ten copper mines in Cuba and to smelt and export all the copper ore mined on the island.[90] Upon the failure of his initial smelting attempts, Tetzel went where he could consult with experts: to his home city of Nuremberg. His subsequent return to Cuba to implement the revised methods was financed, in typical fashion, by a consortium in which other family members also invested heavily.[91] His enterprise is less important for its contribution to the economic development of the Caribbean than as an example of how the New World functioned as a territory for the application of German expertise, not as a place of alterity.

When new extraction methods appeared overseas, German merchants were quick to tie them into their existing interests. While the standard lead-based smelting method was initially used successfully in the Spanish Indies, it could not be used on the poorest ores. A new technique for the mass exploitation of these ores, using mercury, was then developed by Bartolomé de Medina, working on site in New Spain.[92] The method quickly spread throughout the region, leading to a spike in demand for mercury. German merchants had a long history in the mercury business: rights to the Almaden mine were included in the Maestrazgos, and rights to the Idrian mine (now in Slovenia) had been held by firms such as the Höchstetters and the Herwarts. The Fugger factor Sebastian Kunz now saw a bright new future for mercury, particularly if the Fuggers could gain the rights to the Idrian mine as well. According to the business plan Kunz laid out in 1558 for the mine's patron, Ferdinand I (Holy Roman Emperor and uncle to King Philip II of Spain), quicksilver was now selling for 150 ducats a quintal in "India," opening up a huge opportunity for Idrian mercury. Kunz even dismissed the possibility of Philip forbidding the importation of foreign mercury, because the local supply barely sufficed for the silver mines in Spain, much less for all the New World mines.[93] In the end, Philip made the export of mercury to the New World a Crown monopoly,[94] and the Herwarts renewed their Idrian contract with Emperor Ferdinand, but the Fuggers' rapid and specific response to the new developments indicates their full participation in this global and innovative industry.

Commercial expertise in the ongoing process of exploration and conquest was most importantly and most consistently displayed as a listing of numbers through which control and surveillance could be exerted. In the ports of Lisbon, Antwerp, and Seville—swarming with sailors, soldiers, commercial agents, and returned settlers who had been witness to all manner of people, customs, and events abroad—the factors of the south German commercial firms were trained to keep their eyes and fingers busy counting. Jörg Pock's India contract, despite the exotic destination, was typical in its insistence on honest and thorough recordkeeping. At the other end of the spice route, the Antwerp representative of the Imhoff firm was instructed to find out about "provisions for that year's India fleet, when the ships were going to arrive and what they were going to bring."[95] Factors were not being paid to provide either local color or scholarly descriptions.

The reports on overseas goods from the shipping and receiving ports show that the factors took these instructions to heart, translating plan into practice. From India, Gabriel Holzschuher reported: "At this time we will in my opinion prepare no more than 4 ships carrying 20,000 centners of pepper, although we ought to send 30,000 centners, but we couldn't obtain it. . . . Otherwise from other spices: cloves, nutmeg, ginger, mastic and cinnamon and from all other drugs, the necessary amount is going from here to Portugal, but very few jewels on account of war."[96] In the summer of 1504, the factors of the Ravensburg Gesellschaft in Italy reported to the central office: "In terms of spices, you understood, that a 'pasadi' came from Portugal, brought 1,400 lots of pepper, 60 of ginger, but of very poor quality, not appropriate for Germany, 20 lots of cloves, 40 of brazilwood and 50 centners of cinnamon."[97] A few years later, Endres Imhoff wrote from Antwerp: "News has arrived from Zeeland, that 7 ships from the fleet from Andalusia [in Spain] and 2 from the Canaries also arrived, but without any of the cash and money that should have been on board; no explanation so far has been given." He then went on to give news of the shipments from Lisbon, where "between 150 and 180 sacks of pepper, 20 to 24 sacks of ginger and a small amount of cinnamon were loaded on these 9 ships as contracted." Later he mentions that, according to reports from Lisbon, 3 ships from India should arrive at the latest in May, with 5 more arriving in August.[98] And in Seville, Cristoff Raiser reported to his superiors that "on June 5, 1558 a report arrived about 5 ships that arrived in [the Spanish port of] St. Lucar from New Spain. Here there was a letter from Terra Firma, given on 22 October, that the fleet that sailed from Spain last July also arrived safely, and a report of much gold and silver from Peru, that could be expected in the fleet sailing in October."[99]

These examples could easily be multiplied, because this type of information made up a substantial portion of all correspondence with the home office.[100]

The counting was important because it led to a more important number: price. The Tuchers' factor in Antwerp fully expected prices to rise after the meager shipments from "Calicut" in 1544, as only three ships had arrived, with two more probably lost at sea. He was concerned enough about the possibility of the last two ships surfacing unexpectedly that he devoted some energy to confirming the rumors of their loss, finally reporting to his superiors "that the 2 ships sank you have no cause to doubt."[101] Sixt Tucher wrote to his superior (and father), Lienhard Tucher, that the price for saffron in Aragon depended heavily on whether the Castilians were waiting to snap up the available supplies "on the journey to India" (p[er] die India). Because no ships were available to travel to "India" at the time he was writing, his worries about their demand driving up the price were eased.[102] Like the factors in Lisbon and Antwerp, merchants in India had to count ships, for normally "a bachar of cloves costs 400 fanomen, more or less, and 5 cruzados per centner, [but] when the ships do not arrive [in Calicut], cloves cost 500 fanomen per bachar and seven crusados per centner."[103] Monitoring the flow of goods to and from Europe not only absorbed a great deal of the merchants' time, but reinforced the impression that international commerce was governed by the same understanding of supply and demand that determined the price of staple goods in Augsburg.

German merchants were also quick to calculate the impact of the Iberian economic expansion on the commercial structure of Europe. Initially, their attention was riveted by the successful challenge the Portuguese mounted to the Venetian dominance in the spice trade. Wilhelm Rem's chronicle, after noting the success of da Gama's voyage, included among the noteworthy events of the year 1502 that "reports came from Venice to Augsburg, how 23 ships came from Calicut to Lisbon in Portugal, bringing spices . . . it sent shivers down the spines of the Venetians."[104] Christoph Scheurl, a prominent Nuremberg citizen, reported the same doom in 1506, when it appeared that the islands discovered by Columbus would prove a valuable source for spices: "You know that 14 years ago, under the auspices of the King of the Spanish and the leadership of Christopher Columbus there was discovered a new world, in a certain sense, and in it 600 islands . . . which of their own accord bring forth mastic, aloe, ginger and cinnamon, although not comparable to that of Ethiopia. This voyage brought upon Venice and [Nuremberg] a deadly blow, and a great benefit to Lower Germany and Leipzig, because the Sarmatians, that is, the Poles, Hungarians and Bohemians could buy their spices more easily and less expensively in Leipzig."[105] In extending his pessimism to Germany, Scheurl was unique, but in attributing significance to both what the colonial fleets brought back and where they brought it, he was part of a broader discussion about the eclipsing of the Levantine trade.

The narrative of the decline of Venice, while powerful enough to become a commonplace within the learned community, was not as accurate as it was compelling. Although the Portuguese did become the main importers for pepper and ginger, admittedly the spices most in demand, Venice continued to be an important center for spices such as cloves and nutmeg and was never completely shut out of the pepper trade.[106] Merchants, unlike more aloof observers, were quick to correct their initial impressions and adjust their strategies accordingly. The difference in the routes by which spices were brought to Europe was noted only through the notations "of Venice" and "of Calicut," used to distinguish spices available for sale in Venice from those available in Antwerp.[107] No mystique was attached to one source over another: availability, quality, and price were discussed and compared, the Portuguese fortunes in the Indian Ocean becoming just another component of the market calculus. As Anton Fugger phrased it when transmitting the news from Venice to his Spanish factor, "The Portuguese had suffered a great defeat in India, and many spices should arrive from Alexandria."[108] In the end, the important differences between spices "di Venezia" and spices "di Calikut" were how much they would cost and how much they would sell for.[109] This emphasis on monitoring the supply of specific goods transformed all the fluctuations of the international situation—the imposition of European colonialism, native insurrections, bad harvests, storms at sea, and other natural and man-made interventions—into comprehensible, concrete impacts on the merchants' bottom line.

The German merchant correspondence reveals that those involved in commerce with the newly discovered lands made sense of the Iberian expansion in terms of its utility to their interests. The economic possibilities created by the discoveries would not have been possible without the claims of the worldwide compatibility of exchange relationships and exchange calculations. Far from requiring special handling or a distinctive set of calculations, the valuable goods obtained overseas were measured, priced, taxed, and bought just like the cloth, timber, and grain that traveled from one European country to another. Indeed, the firm foothold of the southern German commercial firms in the consolidating economic landscape of Europe made possible the acquisition of the spices of India and the gold of Peru. Seen through the lens of these firms' systematic economic accounting, the colonial encounter seemed relevant only in its effects on the flow of commodities to and from Europe.

CALCULATING FORTUNES

If the sober accounting system of the merchants made the newly discovered territories seem accessible and trade with them profitable, by no means did it make them ordinary. As was the case with cosmography, fitting the discoveries into preexisting systems of thought made their significance all the more apparent. The reputation of eastern and western "India" as sources of extraordinary wealth, while it might have initially drawn on medieval tales of golden mountains, was confirmed only through detailed reports about profits won and treasures captured. Specificity of place, of objects, and of numbers elicited the wonder.

The primacy of calculation over vague legends is best illustrated through the imaginative tale *Fortunatus*, considered the first German prose novel.[110] *Fortunatus* contains many features drawn from adventure stories and fairy tales, including narrow escapes, disguises, court intrigue, a magical money sack that is never empty, and a magical hat that immediately transports the wearer anywhere he wishes. It is also, and not paradoxically, suffused with awareness of the commercial value of things. Thus, the king of England's jewels (whose theft nearly prompts Fortunatus's execution) are said to be worth "sixty thousand crowns."[111] Even the money bag is practical enough to dispense money in the currency of the land in which its bearer finds himself.[112] The precision of the marvelous elements of the tale is even more clearly revealed when Fortunatus, on his second epic journey, travels to the Near and Far East. He first sails to the entrepôt of Alexandria, where his gift to the sultan, estimated to be worth five thousand ducats, incites the jealousy of the resident Italian merchants. With the sultan's assistance, Fortunatus then continues on to Persia, Cathay, India (or Prester John's land), and finally Lumbet, "the land where pepper grows." This mention of the land itself apparently did not suffice for the author, who continued: "[Pepper] grows in a wild jungle called Thobar, and no pepper grows in the entire world other than there." [113] The geographical specificity of the "land where pepper grows" lends a concreteness to Fortunatus's travels. In a subsequent edition Fortunatus's destination is changed to "Calicut in the country and place where pepper grows. There there is a powerful king and overabundant heat; women and men go naked. There grows the very best pepper in all of India in the form of small green grapelets." [114] The inclusion of detail gleaned from travel reports indicates the fusion of the fantastical and the historical, as the object of desire became obtainable. Pepper did not come from some place vaguely to the east of Europe and to the west of Paradise; it came from Lumbet, which was taken to mean Calicut.

Pepper was not only an identifiable commodity; it also had an identifiable price. To match the five thousand ducats' worth of gifts that Fortunatus presents to him on his arrival in Alexandria, the sultan orders that "one hundred carg pepper" be given to Fortunatus, because the pepper "was worth as much as the jewels that he had given him." [115] The precise exchange value of spices is also important in the final negotiations between Fortunatus and the sultan over the magical hat, which Fortunatus had stolen from the sultan's treasury. The ambassador of the sultan, having run Fortunatus to earth in his native Cyprus, sets a specific price on this magical item. In return for the hat, he promises "that the King Sultan will load your galley with fine spices: pepper, ginger, cloves, nutmeg, and cinnamon and still others, so that the total is worth one hundred thousand ducats." Furthermore, he warns Fortunatus that this is the best deal he will be offered, because no one else in the world would give one-third as much for the magical hat as the amount the sultan is willing to give. [116] Spices had a universal and extraordinary value, but this did not prevent their value (or, for that matter, that of the magical hat) from being established and compared to their value in other markets.

The concreteness introduced into the fairy tale by the enumeration of the costs of things is the concreteness of the materially extraordinary. The gifts worth five thousand ducats that Fortunatus gives the sultan display his extraordinary wealth in the same way that the offer of one hundred thousand ducats' worth of spices reveals the extraordinary worth of the magical hat. The imagination of the German merchants was captured by the spectacular wealth of the newly discovered territories because tales were told, not of countless sacks of pepper or shipments of innumerable ducats of gold, but of measurably higher profits and measurable amounts of treasure. An early and significant example is the 1505–6 India voyage financed by the consortium of Augsburg and Nuremberg merchants. According to the chronicle of Wilhelm Rem, the profit from the voyage was 175 percent, which, he carefully explained to the uninitiated, "means that for each 100 ducats they gained 175 ducats, above and beyond all expenses." While not expecting his readers to doubt the truth of his assertion that Vasco da Gama had reached India, or that a strange new disease (which would later come to be called the French disease) had appeared in Germany in 1495, Rem did anticipate that this profit figure would be met with skepticism, introducing it with the comment, "I heard from a reliable source, who also was a participant."[117] If this number strained the limits of the believable, it was because it was measurably far above the usual returns.[118] The expectations for expeditions to the Indies remained high. When the Fuggers tried to recoup their losses from the failed Loiasa expedition to the Spice Islands by suing the Spanish Crown for their share of the 350,000 ducats that Charles V had received for ceding his claim to the king of Portugal, they claimed that they would have realized a profit of 400 percent had they been allowed to participate in the planned voyages to the East Indies.[119] While legal maneuvering was clearly behind the high figure, that it could even be mentioned was the result of the careful records kept of the enormous rewards achieved in the past.

The image of the Spanish colonies as lands of enormous wealth also had its basis in the evidence of calculation. While the shipments of sugar and pearls indicated the economic viability of the region as an area of exploitation, the discovery of the Incan Empire in Peru finally gave the pursuit of American treasure the same legitimacy in Germany as the search for the spices of India. Although, as discussed in chapter 1, the discovery of Peru received little notice in the world of printed travel reports, Peru's reputation among those tracking the flow of money and goods was far greater.[120] The discovery and, more important, the conquest of Peru by Pizarro not only established the wealth of the region, but represented the possibility that other civilizations like those of the Aztec and Inca were nestled somewhere in the vast interior of the landmass, waiting to be plundered. The image of astounding wealth was ultimately made convincing through the numbers.[121] Writing from Milan in 1538, an official of the Duke of Bavaria wrote to his employer: "In Seville there reportedly arrived a great sum of gold from the new-found Islands, a part of which is the Emperor's and a part belongs to other individuals, some speak of 8, others of 3 million of gold." [122] The lack of exact information did not keep this official from trying to pin a number on the shipment.[123] A manuscript report entitled "Report from India on the Gold Shipments of 1538" is far more specific, detailing the amounts of gold and silver coming from specific parts of the Spanish Empire and concluding that "the total gold and silver brought by the fleet for the Emperor alone amounts to 1 million and 65,000 pesos and each peso is calculated at 450 maravedis [and 375 maravedis equals one ducat]. And His Majesty still has in the city of Cuzco in Peru 800,000 pesos in gold and silver waiting, for which a fleet should be sent out." [124] Even merchants and other passengers, according to the author, still had riches waiting for transport from the New World. The method of extraction was different—plunder rather than trade—but the result was the same: a sizable profit for the expedition's sponsor.

Although in both cases claims to extraordinariness were predicated on precise calculation, the looting of the magnificent cities of the Incan Empire would seem to call on a different set of skills and produce a different set of emotions from those of a merchant trading copper for pepper in the stable exchange system of Calicut. At least in the case of the German accounts of conquistadorial expeditions, however, the appearance of Pizarro's treasure produced a fusion of merchant and military enterprise that meant that economic appraisal, as outlined above, remained a point of orientation.[125] In 1535, for example, a contract was signed by a company of French and German merchants then resident in Antwerp, setting out the conditions for their trade with Spain and, if it appeared profitable, Peru. The details of the contract stressed the usual merchant obligations, such as selling for the highest possible price and avoiding gambling and women, but stipulated different terms regarding the beckoning possibilities of the New World. If a member of the company found gold, silver, or gems in Peru, he had to report his discovery to his partners and split the profits with them evenly, regardless of their level of investment in the firm. After their arrival in Peru, or elsewhere in the newly discovered territories, any member wishing to join a conquistadorial expedition could leave the firm, under the condition that two-thirds of his loot would belong to the members of the company who had not joined the expedition.[126] That they were using Peru as their model is clear from the formulation of the contract, which explicitly allowed for a member to leave the company to undertake a military campaign.

A similar mixture is found in the undertaking of Lazarus Spengler the Younger, who in 1535 wrote home from Antwerp to Nuremberg, asking for part of his inheritance to finance an expedition "to the new island Baru."[127] He had consulted with the experts available in Antwerp about how best to proceed and estimated that 400 gulden would be required to pay for passage and purchase sufficient trade goods. With this money he formed a partnership with a relative in Antwerp, Hans Tucher, who had valuable connections in Spain. When another Tucher, Hieronymus, tried to reassure Lazarus's aunt about the prospects for success, he referred not to past myths but to recent examples: "A few days ago we received a letter out of Spain from Seville, that there were 2 ships that returned from the lands where they wish to travel, with many thousands of pesos in gold. Among the returnees is one of my former journeymen, who came with and brought over 8 thousand Rheinish ducats with him."[128] Together, Spengler and Tucher traveled to Spain, where new information caused them to set their sights on the Rio de la Plata region.[129] The first reports on this region were newly arrived in Spain, and Spengler described it as "a land in which wild naked people live and in which there is no wind, from this land just recently have returned those who discovered the land and arrived there poor, bringing back with them up to 40 to 50 and 60 thousand ducats as well as a large sum of pearls and gems."[130] Trade goods would serve little purpose now, for this expedition required a different kind of investment: a two-year supply of provisions. The first modern interpreter of the Spengler story claims that at this point the character of the enterprise changed, from "a more or less realistic business enterprise" to a "booty journey, basically a plundering campaign."[131] I would argue that the two, seen from the vantage point of prospective investors, were not really that different.

The Welser enterprise in Venezuela also reveals the close connection between commercial and conquistadorial expeditions.[132] Initially attracted to the province by the possibility of precious metals, tropical trade goods, and even a convenient strait to the South Sea and the East Indies, the firm quickly developed a new strategy and began searching for gold to conquer rather than mine. This enthusiasm was stoked on the ground by continuing hints, as campaigns pushed farther away from the coast, of a rich province available for conquest, but it was also fueled by the contemporaneous discovery of the Incan Empire.[133] The excitement generated by the conquest of Peru caused one of the leaders of the Venezuela expeditions, Philipp von Hutten, to complain in a letter to his brother: "People perhaps believe back home the rumors that all who travel to India must return rich," and that those who do not have only themselves to blame, "but where it is understood with what effort and danger riches are acquired here, and how many thousands of Christians these Indians cost and how some fleets can go astray, before one finds a Peru," there was a more sober accounting of the risks as well as the rewards.[134] Yet, although they might have differed in their estimation of the difficulty of finding the next Peru, both the conquistador in Venezuela and the observer at home agreed on the viability and profitability of the venture. Hutten's letters home are filled with details about the next big plan for striking it rich and new reports of others' success, such as the discovery of "a great wealth of pearls" in Cabo da la Vela.[135] If Hutten and others like him were frantically searching the south American mainland for "El Dorado" and other hidden treasures, they were acting not in the hopes of discovering a long-lost paradise, but in the conviction of tangible, measurable rewards.[136]

GERMAN MERCHANTS CAME to the new systems of overseas trade well prepared to make use of commercial principles to engage successfully in economic extraction. Accustomed to navigating the complex world of European trade, with its extensive Mediterranean contacts and its elaborate trading privileges that fused money and power in an uneasy relationship, German merchants were not intimidated by the new commercial reach of Portugal and Spain, but instead set about methodically gaining access to these new opportunities, taking advantage of their newly strengthened position within European commodity and financial markets. The south German merchant houses were convinced that they could make their investments in the overseas trade pay off because these enterprises were in most respects simply extensions of their activities in Europe. As a result, commercial calculation could also be extended into overseas transactions, creating the appearance of control through the required homogenization and quantification. At the same time that their self-referentiality reinforced the sense of stability, accounting practices also limited the commercial gaze to tangible assets and concrete exchanges. Within these restricted criteria for success, Europeans succeeded. They bought spices and precious stones and sold copper. They used technology, human labor, and violence to extract natural resources. They profited. The viability and the importance of the colonial enterprise were visible in the neat rows of figures and the measurably immense shipments of silver.

CHAPTER FOUR

Too Rich for German Blood?

THE SPICE TRADE AS
AN ECONOMIC, MORAL, AND MEDICAL THREAT

I N AN INFLUENTIAL PAMPHLET printed in 1519, the Reformation polemicist Ulrich von Hutten expressed a heartfelt if peculiar desire: "It is therefore my fondest wish, that no one ever be free of gout or the French disease, who cannot do without pepper."[1] In an extraordinary move, pepper, the highly regarded condiment and medicine that launched annual Portuguese fleets to India, was here disparaged as a sinful luxury and accused of producing rather than curing disease. To make his moral point about this exotic import, Hutten mentioned the "French disease," a new and virulent epidemic first recognized in Europe at the end of the fifteenth century, in the same breath as gout, a chronic condition that had haunted Europeans for centuries.[2] Whether new or old, both diseases were linked to overindulgent lifestyles, making them in this context appropriate punishments for pepper eaters. Yet Hutten had written this pamphlet to promote the use of guaiacum wood, a new arrival from the Spanish Indies, as a cure for the French disease. The wholesale condemnation of an Old World drug was thus used to encourage acceptance of a New World import. Hutten's precise configuration was unique, but the individual components of his argument were widespread in Renaissance Germany. The mixture of economic, moral, and medical considerations that animated Hutten's prose demonstrates the richness of the negative language available to German commentators when it came to discussing the harmful impact of the Iberian expeditions. This rejection of the overseas expansion was prompted not by new and disturbing extra-European developments, such as the discovery of new natural substances, or by the cruelties and exploitation of nascent European colonialism, but by domestic manifestations of greed and luxury that the centuries-old spice trade epitomized. Doubts about the benefits of the European expansion consistently arose in response to foreignness rather than newness.

The perceived economic, moral, and medical threats posed by the spice trade were all predicated on a more-or-less sharp distinction between the domestic and the foreign. Merchants, therefore, as the mediators and material beneficiaries of much of Germany's contact with the foreign, figured prominently as promoters of contagion. The issue of commerce's corrosive effects was made more urgent in the Renaissance by internal factors as well: the growing concentration of large-scale trading and production operations and the infusion of classical ideas about the dangers of dependence and luxury. Those who believed Germany was threatened by merchant greed encompassed the foreign in their complaints, and those who believed Germany was threatened by the foreign encompassed the merchants in their complaints. Overseas trade in general thus attracted broad anxieties about the contaminating effects of imported commodities, avarice, and materialism.

The prominent place of spices from India and the East Indies in this rhetoric of rejection demonstrates their visible and established position as a foreign commodity in the domestic environment. Used in both culinary and medicinal preparations,[3] spices created a direct, physical link between the native (body) and the foreign (ingested substance), ideally suited to represent the possibilities and dangers of bringing the foreign home. Their expense and their use as status symbols allowed spices to stand in for any number of other foreign luxury goods that provoked the wrath of moralists. In addition, those commentators disturbed by merchant behavior in general and the newly prominent and dominant south German merchant firms in particular found in the structures of the spice trade an unsurpassed opportunity to demonstrate the willful transgression of ethical boundaries by these powerful economic forces. Their very familiarity within European commerce made tropical spices tempting targets for critics.

In the end, most Germans did not heed Hutten's advice, continuing to indulge their pepper cravings and (as a result?) continuing to suffer from gout and the French disease. The Renaissance indeed witnessed a profusion of "worldly goods,"[4] many of them the products of the new global trading networks that were rapidly becoming arteries of desired consumer goods and mercantile riches. Perhaps because of its ultimate failure, the kind of resistance to the foreign that is analyzed in this chapter has received little scholarly examination.[5] Nevertheless, not only was this phenomenon a substantial component of the German response to the European expansion, with remarks about the dangers of trade and consumption appearing even in general commentaries on the discoveries, but this polemic also promoted a "negative incorporation" of the expanding world. While publishers, cosmographers, and merchants seized upon the identifiably useful information brought back by the expeditions and claimed, with greater or lesser degrees of enthusiasm, that they could manage the discoveries to their intellectual or material benefit, critics of Germany's overseas involvement were equally firmly convinced that they could appropriately categorize these goods as luxuries and predicted the dire consequences of their improper use within the changing German economic system. This gloomy assessment depended first and foremost on moral and juridical concepts developed to cope with the dynamics of European commerce, but it was also based on assertions of mercantile competence, such as those in the commercial correspondence described in the previous chapter. *Unsuccessful* forays into global markets did not produce these threats to Germany's moral, physical, and economic health. Rejection thus gave German commentators another set of tools with which to control the meaning and significance of the newly discovered territories.

The anxieties over the spice trade, furthermore, present a new perspective on the incorporation of botanical information and substances into European intellectual and commodity currents. While scholars have taken for granted the continued acceptance of the well-established East Indian spices,[6] the intrusion of hitherto unknown plants from the Spanish Indies (guaiacum wood, chili peppers, and maize, to name just a few) into the pharmacopoeia of Europe has received considerable attention. The main focus of such scholarly investigations has been the slow and painful process through which Renaissance botanical investigators, whose stubborn allegiance to authoritative texts had only been rendered stronger by humanism's sway over the discipline, recognized new plant species.[7] When this barrier to acceptance finally fell, the story continues, the new arrivals quickly became subject to enthusiastic and culturally transformative uses.[8] This interpretation mirrors the common interpretation of the cosmographical literature: an initial failure to attribute the correct significance to scientific discoveries unaccounted for in inherited texts was followed by a shattering of previous structures when the true meaning of the new objects was properly appreciated. The appearance of botanical knowledge based on novel experiences (above all in America), rather than on classical information, has thus been made the revolutionary moment, and the most significant one, for the discoveries' reception within Europe.

I argue, however, that the status of the familiar tropical spices as quintessential foreign commodities made them far more vulnerable to attack and subjected their importation and consumption to greater scrutiny than was the case with new plants. In the following pages I examine first the political deployment of criticism aimed at the spice trade during the *Monopolstreit* (conflict over monopolies) as part of a general assault on powerful merchants and their economic domination. While this particular legislative and judicial battle was largely played out during the intermittent meetings of the Imperial Diet, its rhetoric drew on a far more widespread discussion of the distinction between moral and immoral commerce and the dangers of unregulated economic exchange. The discussion's salience even to those who opposed other aspects of the Diet's agenda is illustrated in the next section, which examines the extension of the rhetoric of the *Monopolstreit* in the hands of the leaders of the Reformation. While envisioning both a greater threat from economic intercourse across national boundaries and a more radical system of restraints in response, Martin Luther and Ulrich von Hutten relied on the same analytical base for their attacks as did the Diet's representatives, placing the spice trade with India at the center of their polemics. The Portuguese accomplishments, intertwined as they were with the spice trade that provided so many points of contact with received wisdom, once again took precedence over the Spanish discoveries in the interpretation of Europe's overseas expansion.

The importance of attitudes toward the familiar tropical spices in shaping the reception of new American products is demonstrated in the final section of the chapter, which examines the herbals (handbooks on the medicinal uses of plants) produced in Germany shortly after the *Monopolstreit* peaked. The herbals' authors decried the German dependence on foreign medicinal substances, particularly tropical spices, and vilified the merchants who fostered this unhealthy reliance. Their disdain for these products was made most evident in the exclusion or marginalization of these substances from the scientific consideration accorded to the favored domestic plants. This discriminatory treatment complicates the notion that Renaissance scholars were bound by the material available to them from classical sources. The other side of this argument—that the same scholars ignored or rejected plants that did not have a secure place in their authoritative sources—is challenged by the appearance of New World flora in the same herbals that excluded some of the most widely used and lucrative Eastern spices. The chapter ends with a consideration of how and why the category of the native, which was guaranteed acceptance within the rhetoric of foreign danger, expanded to include recently discovered botanical specimens. As part of this narrative of the varying fates of spices old and new, I present the authors of the herbals as struggling to balance the stringent technical demands of humanist botany with contemporary concerns about corrupt commerce and with the need to purvey useful information to their readers. I therefore do not treat the appearance of new flora in European texts as the inevitable result of natural curiosity about these new substances. Instead, I follow the approach taken by Marcy Norton in her analysis of tobacco and chocolate in early modern Spain, examining the combination of factors that determined not only whether people paid attention to these new arrivals, but also how they categorized and assimilated them.[9]

THE QUESTIONABLE VALUES OF COMMERCE

One of the reasons the spice trade became an object of attack was that it epitomized transformations in the economic landscape that had sharpened anxieties about the potential threat of commerce to the moral and economic order of the community. The king of Portugal's pepper contracts with the prominent merchant families of Europe, as discussed in chapter 3, were characteristic of the consolidation of economic resources in the hands of a few large-scale entrepreneurs, such as the Fuggers and Welsers of Augsburg and their associates/competitors in Nuremberg. The spice trade could therefore be seen as embodying commerce in general and the new large-scale, capitalistic commerce in particular. If merchants incorporated new economic developments into established commercial practices, opponents of "big business" likewise had a tradition on which to draw: in this case medieval Christianity's (and particularly scholasticism's) ambivalent but detailed position on the purpose and procedures of commerce. These terms of analysis formed the basis for the negative incorporation of the European economic expansion.

Scholastic commentators[10] did not deny the necessity of commerce and even acknowledged that it could be part of a proper Christian life, under certain conditions. Moral merchant activity meant not only avoiding fraudulent practices, but also engaging in beneficial trade for the right purposes. The merchant profession in itself was morally neutral and was sanctioned for those who sought gain for the purpose of supporting their families or raising money for the poor. In contrast, those who practiced this profession solely for the accumulation of wealth sinned.[11] Furthermore, commerce fulfilled its role as part of a properly ordered Christian society only when it served the community by ensuring a supply of needed commodities and providing goods unavailable in the local economy. Any trade, however, that sought to overstep these boundaries placed its practitioners in moral danger and made itself vulnerable to regulation.

Although the elaboration of the dividing line between moral and immoral practices varied from author to author, the issues remained the same. The discussion revolved around what was understood to be the driving force behind commerce: material gain. While barter might have developed for the mutual satisfaction of needs, the buying and selling of goods in a system of exchange produced the troublesome result of profit. How profit could fairly and justly be determined and obtained was a key question in scholastic thought on commerce, linked to the question of "just price." A commodity's "just price" was established not through some abstract standards of fairness or inherent worth, but through market conditions;[12] it should incorporate such factors as production costs, availability, and consumer demand. Scholastic commentators also made specific provision for the expenses incurred by the merchant, from concrete costs, such as transportation and storage expenses, to less tangible ones, such as the merchant's effort and risk. A certain amount of profit was therefore built into a just price: "Businessmen may properly charge more than their actual costs because of the expenses, exertions, cares, qualities of industry, risks, and other reasonable engagements or burdens which they undergo in bringing together things useful to men or in preserving or setting out necessary things in the common market place, and because they remain [there] in order that anyone in need may promptly have such goods."[13] Allowance was also made for the greater effort required to gather information and transport goods and the greater risk involved in long-distance trade; merchants bringing goods from distant locations could thus fairly claim a higher profit margin. It was believed that the "common estimation"—that is, the customary market price for a good—already included a calculation of these factors. Barring fraudulent or unfair influences, the market price should coincide approximately with the just price. If the common estimation was flawed, or if there was no clear "going rate" for a particular good, then "the businessman ought to have recourse to elementary reason by weighing his expenses, the costs of labor, [and possible improvements to the good] and finally sell his goods by such criteria."[14] Merchant profit therefore held a legitimate and protected place. However, as the above quotation detailing the criteria for calculating profit indicates, because legitimate profit was based on defined inputs, merchants could not claim unlimited profits: merchant behavior was moral only within carefully defined parameters.

Explicitly forbidden were market manipulations that attempted to alter artificially one of the components of the just price. The accusation of engaging in such practices was a common and damaging one, and some of the more egregious transgressions helped forge a link between theological (and judicial) proscriptions and popular vilifications of merchants. The same derogatory terms would later appear in the debate over the spice trade, signaling the deployment of established negative stereotypes in the face of new economic mechanisms. Hoarding (*Fürkauff*), which interfered with the supply of a good, was a particularly charged example,[15] since it usually implied cornering the regional market on a staple good, such as wine or grain, in order to force the populace to buy the good at inflated prices set by the merchant.[16] It therefore clearly fell under those forbidden market manipulations that raised the price above the "just price." Hoarding also crossed the line between engaging in trade for the benefit of the community and engaging in trade for the sake of gain alone.

The practice of usury (*Wucher*) was another profitable business activity that posed a threat to both the soul of the merchant and the welfare of the larger community. Usury (the charging of interest on a loan) had been officially condemned by the Church for centuries, although return on an investment could be allowable under certain circumstances.[17] In outlawing usury, scholars relied on biblical exegesis and proclamations of usury's unnatural nature. Paradoxes typically cited to support the latter contention included the impossibility of transferring the use of money (conceived of as a consumable good) without transferring ownership and the impossibility of the sterile substance of money increasing (breeding, so to speak) on its own. In addition, interest received on a loan violated the requirement that the merchant labor for his profit; like the speculator, the usurer spent only time, which did not belong to him.[18] Usury was therefore comparable to market manipulations because gain was derived against the natural workings of the economy.

The measured considerations of scholastics fed into popular images of the merchant that emphasized the harmful impact of his financial power on a vulnerable populace.[19] Usury and hoarding both caricatured and defined this threat, as they went beyond a specific instance of fraudulent or unfair exchange to practices that systematically enriched merchants and impoverished the hardworking "common man." Usury in particular carried overtones of moral pollution through its association with Jews. In the 1509 edition of Sebastian Brant's *Narrenschiff,* a chapter was dedicated to "usury and hoarding" (Wucher vnd furkouff), condemning both transgressions in the final couplet: "He who wants to be rich, at the expense of the community, is a fool, / but he is not alone."[20] The perception of merchants as parasites went hand in hand with a belief in the closed economy, in which a finite amount of wealth had to be divided fairly rather than increased. Economic accumulation was therefore seen as a zero-sum game in which every gain was offset by a loss somewhere else,[21] connecting unjust profits with harm to the entire community. These practices were effective symbols of merchant misbehavior, even without an understanding of the scholastic argumentation.

The strength of the distrust of commerce was not due simply to the continuing influence of Christian thought and closed-economy logic; it also stemmed from the limited reach of commercial enterprise. Only in significant cities was commerce a defined profession and merchant a defined social estate. Even within those walls, their expansive commercial view was by no means universally shared, since the guilds (the backbone of the urban production system) operated, at least traditionally, as self-sustaining units.[22] The new entrepreneurial opportunities had an even more isolated impact,[23] as the chance to benefit from investments in such areas as mining or finance was limited by the concentration of firms engaged in these transactions in a small number of south German cities and by the wealth and connections required to become even a silent investor.[24] Even the politically powerful princes, who relied on the great merchant houses as bankers and financiers, dealt with merchants out of necessity rather than entrepreneurial zeal. The uneven economic development of Renaissance Germany thus failed to connect the interests of most of the populace with the success of merchants.

In the early sixteenth century, all of the apparatus of scholastic and popular disapproval was readily available to the reading public. The scholastic treatise of Johannes Nider, *De Contractibus Mercatorum* (On the Contracts of Merchants) (the source of the quotes above used to define moral commerce) was published in Cologne about 1468 and reprinted seven times before 1500.[25] For those unable to read Latin, the lawyer Cristofer Cuppener provided a handy introduction: "A pretty little book in German from which each person, no matter what rank, can learn what usury and usurious practices are . . . and what right and wrong business and trade is."[26] Martin Luther played the same tune, although a bit louder than others, in his *Von Kauffshandlung vnd Wucher* (On Business and Usury), published in 1524. All the elements were there: the assertion that commerce should benefit the community; the belief that the merchant should not use his position to obtain unseemly profit, but that profit should instead simply "pay [the merchant's] costs, and reward his effort, work and risk"; and the equation of just price with customary price.[27] Just how contentious the topic remained is illustrated by the disputation held by Johannes Eck and Johann Cochlaeus, one a professor of theology at the University of Ingolstadt and the other a humanist scholar from Nuremberg, on the subject of the "five per cent contract," a business arrangement that managed to accomplish through partnership what was forbidden by the usury prohibition.[28] Originally scheduled to take place in Ingolstadt, this disputation was forced to relocate by the opposition of local authorities. With the support of the Fuggers, that powerful Augsburg merchant family, the disputation was finally held in Bologna.[29] The criticism of the spice trade thus took place against the backdrop of a broad and ongoing discussion of the proper conduct of merchants, which made any questionable practices in the spice trade just another element of a long history of complaints aimed at merchants. The figure of the deceitful and parasitical merchant was the common threat that allowed all the varying networks calling for controls on the importation and consumption of spices to make their demands intelligible and urgent. The spice trade of the king of Portugal, and the pepper, ginger, and other spices obtained by German merchants, were placed at the well-traveled intersection of economic and moral thought.

THE SPICE TRADE AS MONOPOLISTIC

The *Monopolstreit,* or conflict over monopolies, questioned the value of the European expansion, particularly the Portuguese accomplishments in the Indian Ocean, by placing the conduct of merchants engaged in the spice trade in the glare of moral and judicial examination. This clash between entrenched standards and new events did not come about because the voyages to India represented a challenge that the older categories could not incorporate and thus had to resist, but because established categories could articulate a discomfiture with the intra-European economic developments of which the spice trade was a part.[30] "Monopoly" was a useful concept in the attack on merchants, because it bridged the gap between vilification (both scholarly and popular) and current practice. Monopolies violated the proper order in several ways. They clearly represented an intervention in the operation of the market, skirting dangerously close to *Fürkauff* and preventing the fair establishment of a just price. They enabled the merchant to charge whatever he wished and thus receive a profit well beyond that to which he was entitled. After reviewing allowable and unallowable trade, Nider concluded, "From these premises it becomes evident that it is unlawful for some men to buy up all the stock of grain or pepper in order that afterward they may be able at their pleasure to sell dearer."[31] From the perspective of a closed economy, the higher prices charged by merchants, and hence the higher profits attained, meant that the purchasers of monopolized goods were the losers; the merchants were sucking out wealth that should be deployed elsewhere. Charges of monopolistic practices were also helpful in demarcating a line between permissible and impermissible commerce, because they were aimed only at the large, capital-rich firms whose rise is described in chapter 3. The *Monopolstreit* thus raised the issue of shady practices in the spice trade as part of a calculated move against German firms that were seen as altering the balance of the domestic economy. The following history of the *Monopolstreit* reveals how the treatment of the spice trade was shaped by domestic political agendas and made possible by the creative application of the legal and moral categories just discussed to commercial developments.

The *Monopolstreit,* which reached its high point between 1521 and 1530, began as an attempt by the Holy Roman Empire's Imperial Diet to outlaw "monopolistic" practices and then escalated into legislation designed to eliminate the large-scale firms that were believed responsible for the monopolies. Although these measures enjoyed widespread support in the Diet,[32] they were halted by the emperor's intervention. While the impetus and the targets of the *Monopolstreit* were the powerful new corporations (*Gesellschaften*), with their penchant for gaining exclusive access to profitable goods, the structure of the debate and the legal system of the empire made reliance on traditional values and legal precedents inevitable. Roman law and scholastic theory formed the basis for the attack on the corporations and, through them, the spice trade from India around the Cape of Good Hope.

The extension of German commercial calculations overseas was interpreted in the *Monopolstreit* as a domestic matter that required control of local practices, rather than as a colonial matter demanding international intervention, because of the background and agenda of the Imperial Diet's members. As stated in the introduction, the Imperial Diet was the representative organ for the three estates of the empire: the electors, the lords (prelates and temporal lords), and the free imperial cities. In practice, the Diet functioned as a counterweight to the emperor, providing the estates a way to preserve relative autonomy in their own territories without precluding joint action in times of crisis. The Diet thus had the ongoing task of forestalling any initiatives on the part of its members or the emperor that might upset the balance of power, while simultaneously preserving the appearance of an active and engaged consultative and legislative body essential to the well-being of the empire.

The Diet met irregularly but frequently. For important occasions of state, the members of the estates would attend in person, but much of the day-to-day grind—hammering out proposed legislation; hearing complaints from various imperial constituencies; and responding to the emperor's requests, demands, and threats—was left to the delegated representatives of the electors, lords, and cities. The delegates, whose principal qualification was usually some form of legal training, would settle in for the duration (at least several months), keeping their employers informed through extensive correspondence. The staying power of these career legislative staffers was particularly in demand once the Reichsregiment (a smaller version of the Diet charged with representing its interests and implementing its legislation between meetings of the full Diet) was established in 1521.[33] The reports and recommendations that featured the polemic against the spice trade were the products of astute politicians trying to promote the interests of the Diet's members while protecting the image of the Diet as the caretaker of all inhabitants of the empire.

Appeals to values like justice and the common good of course served an important legitimating function for imperial elites, who wanted to maintain their position within the political and social structure of the empire. Something more than simple tut-tutting was at stake in this case, however, because measures against commercial misdeeds, unlike the prohibitions the Diet recommended against blasphemy, excessive ceremonial expenses, and drunkenness, were vigorously pursued. That political decisions could be driven by self-interest was widely understood; critics of monopolies assumed, for example, that the close ties of friendship and obligation between the authorities responsible for enforcement and the monopolistic German firms would prevent these authorities from perceiving and upholding the good of the community as a whole.[34] Naturally, those acting against the monopolies portrayed themselves as wholly disinterested, and indeed, they did stand to gain relatively little personally from their attacks. However, the lords and prelates who participated in the new financial and commercial markets only as consumers would have their social status most trenchantly challenged by the lavish displays of the new merchant princes. Meanwhile, the merchants' accumulating wealth was a tempting source of revenue for new imperial projects, most notably the Reichsregiment, which was to be financed largely through export/import duties.[35] The indifference of most participants in the Imperial Diet to the welfare of the large trading firms can thus in part be ascribed to their need to salvage their pride and pocketbooks, while using expressed concern for the "common man" as a front for their own discomforts.

The first step in the *Monopolstreit* occurred at the 1512 Diet of Cologne, when the term "monopoly" made its initial appearance. The usefulness of older ideas in the face of new economic developments is indicated by the minor modifications necessary to make them fit the new situation. The law used as precedent in this instance was Emperor Zeno's edict from the year 483, contained in the Justinian Codex, which forbade monopolies (but left vague the definition of this term) and included a list of exemplary goods. In its concluding document, the *Reichstagsabschied,* the Imperial Diet explicitly defined monopoly power in broad terms and revised the list of goods to fit the perceived new problems. The Diet described as monopolistic all activities that gave a merchant or a small group of merchants substantial control over prices, such as price consortia, agreements about price floors, and exclusive contracts.[36] Using the term "monopoly" as an umbrella, the Diet obtained a basis for legislative action against all practices that could be used by capital-rich firms to skew the market in their favor. Furthermore, whereas the original law had focused on basic foodstuffs, the list now began with those goods that had recently become the target of consortia and exclusive agreements: spices and metals. The article therefore began: "And as many large commercial corporations [Gesellschaften] have arisen in recent years in the Empire, and there are also certain particular persons who attempt to bring into their possession and power all kinds of wares and merchant goods, such as spices, ore, woolen cloth, and the like."[37] From the beginning of the *Monopolstreit,* therefore, the Diet's economic analysis inserted recent developments into a political/legal framework that gave the Diet the greatest potential for control.

The expansion of the legal definition of "monopoly" produced a convergence between concern about the recent monopolies and the new corporations that had created them and the familiar litany of merchant evils, paving the way for the wholesale negative incorporation of these new economic developments. This move is evident in the *Polizeiordnung* (police ordinance) drafted in committee during the 1521 Diet of Worms,[38] which reiterated the principles of the 1512 *Abschied,* the only changes being expansions in the practices considered monopolistic and in the list of exemplary goods.[39] Yet the new version of the article on monopolies, in both its title, "On Unseemly Hoarding [furkauffen], also on the Monopolies Forbidden to Corporations and Other Particular Persons,"[40] and in its elaboration of the reasons behind the prohibitions on monopolies, tried to make clear that these newfangled practices ran up against long-standing prohibitions. The key phrase was "improper price increases" (unzimblich teuerung), which referred to the merchants' ability, through controlling supply, to raise the price at will. Through their unfairly inflated prices, the merchants obtained "sudden excessive wealth" (schnell überschwenglich Reichtum).[41] Thus, through unjust practices, merchants charged unjust prices and thereby gained unjust profits (i.e., profits beyond what they had earned through their labor and risk). While the language of *zimblich* indicates the ongoing influence of scholastic categories, the language of *überschwenglich* points to the disproportionality caused by monopolistic practices, which, in the logic of the closed economy, signaled an economic as well as a moral threat. Through their high prices and their high living, the corporations were the embodiment of the selfishness and greed to which merchants could so easily fall prey.[42]

The 1521 *Polizeiordnung* dwelt at length on the harms produced by monopolistic practices, ranging from the general ("thereby extreme and high burdens are placed on every estate, high and low, rich and poor, that buys and uses these goods, against justice and fairness") to the specific. Two complaints had implications for the spice trade that would be drawn out in more detail outside of the Diet's debates. One allegation held that, through monopolies, much of Germany's gold and silver supply was exported in exchange for unnecessary and even harmful goods. The other accusation was that merchants, for the sake of "malicious profit," deliberately sold copper, a necessary ingredient in the manufacture of armaments, to the "infidels." (German copper did reach Islamic powers, but only through Venetian intermediaries.)[43] A full articulation of the difficulties and dangers that the spice trade involved, though, would have to wait until the Diet looked beyond monopolistic practices to the corporations themselves.

As the Diet's attack homed in on the merchants, spices became more prominently mentioned. A suggestion that "the abovementioned outlawed monopolies cannot be prevented, unless the merchant corporations are completely done away with," was already present in the *Polizeiordnung* of 1521.[44] When the Diet took up this issue again (in 1522–23, at the second Diet of Nuremberg), the agenda was consequently broadened to include *all* the misdeeds of the corporations, whether classifiable as monopolistic or not. Following the usual procedure, a committee was first assigned the task of determining the extent of the problem and suggesting possible solutions. In its final recommendations the committee cited the situation with spices, "which are one of their [the merchants'] foremost goods which is brought into and traded in Germany," as proof of its assertion that "large corporations and their accumulation of capital are in many ways disadvantageous and obstructive."[45] Beyond embodying potentially unfair business practices, the spice trade was so deeply embedded in the economic structure that it could serve as an example of even larger problems.

As the committee's full exposition of the situation shows, spices were not chosen at random from among the "foremost goods." Several characteristics brought the spice trade to the forefront, none of which involved its products' exotic origin or its role in the exploitations of European colonialism. First, unlike the trade in metals, the spice trade would not implicate any prominent Central European princes,[46] leaving the committee free to imply all kinds of nefarious collusion between the king of Portugal and the corporations. The real impetus behind the choice, however, was that the spice trade, and particularly the pepper trade, had always been the implicit model for the Diet when it addressed monopolies. The exclusive contracts with the king of Portugal were flagrant violations of the principle of fair trade. The first paragraph of the committee's exposition explains how merchants engaged in such monopolistic practices: "[If they deal directly with the king], they have no complaint or objection to how dear the King offers or gives these goods, but even occasionally give him more for them, but with the condition, that he sells these goods even dearer in the future to others who wish to purchase them." The result of these monopolistic contracts followed logically: the merchants were able to obtain consistently large profits by charging consistently high prices: "And therefore, such merchants have risked nothing, nor have they any loss, but great and excessive [uberschwenklichen] profit, because they can sell [the spices] afterward for as much as they like, and no one in the Empire can otherwise have or obtain the same." The careful documentation of the recent increase in spice prices indicates that the committee's attention was drawn to the spice trade because the imbalances produced by the corporations were almost impossible to ignore. The committee cited the case of cloves, which "went for example in 1512 for 19 shillings per pound (1 shilling = 3 creuzer), and in 1513, 1 gulden 27 creuzer; they now (in 1522) cost 2 gulden. And there is more than one kind of clove, which have all increased in cost according to their quality, such as pure cloves, fine cloves, clove stalks, and mixed cloves." Other spices listed included nutmeg, saffron, ginger, sugar, and pepper (which received the most extensive account).[47] The report then remarked on the harm caused by higher prices, specifically noting that the merchants gouged consumers even though spices had medicinal uses. Only after this exposé of the spice trade did the committee move on to general accusations against the corporations, such as the formation of consortia and the elimination of competitors, which it did not dramatize through elaborate case studies. The spice trade thus provided the most convincing proof that corporations inevitably harmed the general community.

The committee made its general targeting of the German corporations even more explicit in its suggestions for reform, which focused first on crippling the corporations through limiting their capital, their number of branch offices, and their ability to accept funds from outside investors. Only after addressing the broad economic issues that the spice trade typified did the committee turn to specific measures for the spice trade itself. Unsure that even its proposed measures would be enough to correct the market distortion and ensure that the king of Portugal did not continue to give free rein to the merchants' greed, the committee recommended that price controls be set, as scholastic thought demanded, according to the average going rate of a spice before the machinations of the merchants sent it skyward.[48] The importation of spices in and of itself, despite the few doubts raised in the 1521 *Polizeiordnung*, was considered a tolerable part of the German economy, as long as greedy Europeans were kept from exploiting it.

The recommendations of this committee marked the high point of the drive to tame the corporations and explain the reasons for doing so. After the second Diet of Nuremberg, the positions of both sides—of the Diet on the one hand and the corporations and their political allies on the other[49]—hardened into repetitions and elaborations on the same themes, before the urgency of the issue faded and the Diet turned its attention to other matters by 1540.[50] While the *Monopolstreit* did have some political consequences, to be discussed in the following chapter, the Diet was not successful in ending monopolies, breaking apart the corporations, or reducing the high price of spices. The various documents produced by the Diet and its committees did, however, begin to reveal the morally fraught role of spices in the German economy.

The Diet's proposals were not the result of some inner panic in the face of an external, inherently incomprehensible threat. Indeed, the fabulous profits harped on in the accusations had a measurable extent, not only in the 175 percent profit noted earlier for the 1505–6 voyage, but even more spectacularly in the case of Bartholomew Rem, an investor with the Höchstetter firm. Having contributed 900 gulden to the enterprise, after six years Rem sued the Höchstetters, saying that they owed him the staggering sum of 33,000 gulden. The Höchstetters demurred, saying that they owed him "only" 26,000 gulden.[51] Like reports of Peruvian wealth, reports of merchant riches were believable because of specific instances with precise numbers.

The image of the spice trade the Diet used to make its political point would even in certain aspects be recognized by the merchant networks discussed in chapter 3. For example, the committee illustrated the merchants' collusion with the king of Portugal with an example that resembled the word problems standard in merchant manuals: "For an example of this may be put forth: if the King of Portugal has offered a centner of pepper for sale for 18 ducats, they have given him 20 ducats or even more for it, but with the condition, that [he] should sell the same pepper or good to no one for less than 24 ducats in the next year or two."[52] Precise measurements similarly projected a sense of control over the situation: the chart showing recent price increases used numbers obtained from actual merchant records.[53] Furthermore, the committee devoted a paragraph to preliminary estimates of the flow of spices into Germany (over 36,000 centners of pepper and 2,400 centners of ginger) before concluding: "For a thorough inquiry of what normally is brought into Germany from Lisbon by way of Antwerp in terms of spices of all kinds, the best place to go is the customs in Antwerp."[54] In the Diet's considerations, just as in the commercial correspondence, spices were treated as goods that could be cataloged, measured, and valued.

The Diet's arguments consistently stressed the ease with which German merchants had become part of the now-expanded trade with India and the control they were able to exert over the situation. At the second Diet of Nuremberg, the committee in charge of monopoly legislation was so convinced that the indispensability of Central European metals to the king of Portugal made the German merchants more-or-less equal partners in the exchange that it suggested that the Diet exert pressure in the same way. In order to reduce German shipping losses on the sea route to Portugal (which unfairly raised the price of goods for German consumers), the committee wanted to require the king to ship all goods himself, thus relieving German merchants of the associated risks. If the king, as some on the committee feared, retaliated by shipping spices to ports far out of range, the committee proposed that he be denied access to German metals and so forced to reconsider, because "[he] cannot do without access to the metal from the German lands and he can accomplish nothing with regard to India without the same."[55] Above all, however, the profitability of the spice trade, and especially the supposed lack of risk involved, was proof that the German merchants understood the spice trade all too well. Their culpability depended on their willing and knowledgeable participation in the process of globalization.

The image of the spice trade presented in the documents of the Imperial Diet, while bearing some essential resemblance to the trade's actual practices and procedures, was a caricature. The switch to the new centers of Lisbon and Antwerp was depicted as complete, to the exclusion of the still-substantial Venetian spice trade.[56] Many of the spices cited as subject to the same manipulations as pepper in fact did not even pass through the hands of the king of Portugal; the most notable example is saffron, which was grown principally in Aragon and Italy. Neither did the king have the access to figs or almonds required to impose the contract system. The Diet's use of the extreme case of pepper indicates that it was attempting to assert control of the situation through a mechanism other than an accurate gauge of the international trading system. Pepper provided the ideal model for applying the laws against monopolies and the scholastic and popular strictures against merchants to the powerful southern German merchant firms. Because the firms—the truly troubling new development—could be conceptualized as dangerous, they could be handled. It was in fact a sign of the Diet's confidence in its understanding of the situation and its strong moral and political position that it placed the spice trade at the forefront of its attack on the corporations.[57]

SPICES AS LUXURIES

The *Monopolstreit* concerned the proper conduct of trade, with goods both domestic (metals) and foreign (spices) implicated in the Diet's criticism of corporate practices. When the question moved to the consumption of goods within Germany, however, the boundaries between the domestic and the foreign were more sharply drawn, with spices on the outside. The documents drawn up by the Imperial Diet hinted at concerns over the consumption of foreign commodities, but in the end they proposed no radical lifestyle alterations designed to separate once and for all the native from the nonnative. On the other hand, the leading polemicists of the Reformation advocated autarky as a way to preserve Germany's material and spiritual wealth. Unlike the Diet, therefore, which sought to regulate trade independently from consumption, the Reformers linked supply and demand in a wide-ranging condemnation of merchants and their imported goods.

As the criticism expanded from how the merchants acquired their goods and made their profits to the kinds of goods they imported and exported, the scholastic distinction between moral and immoral trade again provided guidance. The merchants were now assessed on whether their trade, even properly conducted, benefited the community, defined as the nation of Germany by all the participants in this discussion. For critics of foreign trade, the exchange between Germany and the rest of the world was inherently unequal. Germany had been blessed with all that it needed but not all that it wanted; therefore, to obtain desired foreign goods, Germany had to hand over its essential products. The exemplary transgressive commodities were luxury goods, particularly those that derived their value not (or not only) from skilled craftsmanship but from their distant and exotic origin. This economic division had physical and moral parallels as well, with Germany as the home of simplicity and hardiness, set in opposition to the softness and corruption induced by luxurious lifestyles. Luxurious consumption was a constant source of worry and a target of nagging throughout Europe; in Renaissance Germany attitudes toward foreign (particularly Italian) influences allowed temptation to be viewed as external, rather than endemic. As a result, concern could be focused on policing the borders of the nation, rather than on the actions of the individual.[58] The merchant now stood accused of making his profit through corrupting the German way of life. Because they came from outside the borders of Germany, spices joined a whole list of foreign commodities that were by definition unnecessary and undesirable. While their exotic and distant origin made their alien nature unmistakable, it did not make spices any more threatening than other luxuries from abroad.

The Imperial Diet questioned the necessity of foreign commodities twice in its proposals during the *Monopolstreit*. In the first instance, which did not implicate spices, but did set the framework for future attacks, the Diet inveighed against the dangers of the wrong kind of economic (and cultural) exchanges in the 1521 *Polizeiordnung*. To obtain the "golden cloth, velvet, satin, damask, goldwork, pearls and ostrich feathers" used for the "lavish magnificence of clothing and jewelry," an excessive (*uberschwenglich*) amount of gold and money had to be sent abroad, "since it all must be brought and bought from foreign lands."

Nor did the committee forget to point out the benefit to the corporations and merchants, who became rich and powerful as a result.[59] The opposition between foreign luxury and German simplicity was made even more evident in the argument that extravagant tastes, as well as expensive goods, had been acquired abroad and then brought back with disastrous results: "So this lavish magnificence does not come from our ancestors in the German nation, but the custom has only been introduced in recent years . . . that [here] one uses all the magnificence that in other kingdoms and countries is differentiated and divided up. For we know, that if in some foreign kingdoms and countries the nobility and others wear expensive clothing, nevertheless they cut costs in other ways; furthermore the same foreigners wear their expensive clothing for much longer than the High Germans."[60] The unthinking and unsophisticated adoption of foreign customs demonstrated the need to monitor the influx and use of the nonnative.

To supplement the calls for moderation that were a constant refrain when it examined the issue of conspicuous consumption, the Diet proposed regulatory and (its favorite) fiscal measures to sort out the essential from the dispensable. In addition to its call in the *Polizeiordnung* for sumptuary legislation to control excessive display, the Diet also developed a plan for an import/export tariff that distinguished between staple goods, such as grain, wine, livestock, cheese, salt, leather, hops, and fish, which would not be taxed, and specialty goods, whose use should not be universal and which would be taxed. Spices here made their appearance along with other foreign luxuries: gold, silver, silk cloth, brocade, and all other foreign cloth, as well as sugar and all other kinds of seasonings.[61] The inclusion of these commodities on the tariff list indicates that the Diet neither expected nor wanted their use to be completely curtailed. The borders of Germany remained permeable, and, like costly clothes, spices had their place within the German nation.

The line between necessities and luxuries, and between Germany and the rest of the world, became starker under the influence of the Reformation.[62] As was the case with anticlericalism, the Reformation both drew strength from and strengthened the rhetoric of virtuous Germanic simplicity, without ever making the issue exclusively its own. Martin Luther and Ulrich von Hutten both made spices an intrinsic part of their attack on the presence of foreign luxuries in the German nation. Their polemics against German dependence on spices and other imported goods were heightened by their desire for a total reform of the

mind, body, and spirit. Against this envisioned purity they positioned
the greed, cunning collusion, and flamboyance of the merchants.

Both Luther and Hutten used the general critique of merchants
as a basis to make specific and timely charges that echoed those of
the Diet, indicating the broad resonances of this brand of economic
analysis. Their discussion of commerce was replete with references to
"monopolies" and spewed much venom at "corporations."[63] Like the
Diet, they distinguished between basic goods and luxury commodities. Luther, for example, conceded the usefulness of trade in those
items that "serve necessity and honor," such as "livestock, wool, grain,
butter, [and] milk." The radicalness of the Reformers' position was revealed by their insistence that foreign commerce was entirely unnecessary: the exchange was inevitably to Germany's detriment. Thus,
Luther declared, "Foreign commerce, which brings goods from Calicut
and India and like places, such as expensive silk and articles of gold
and spices, which serve magnificence rather than a useful purpose, and
which sucks out money from the land and the people, should not be allowed." The threat to Germany was both extreme and unique, for "we
have to hand over our gold and silver into foreign countries, making
the whole world rich, while we ourselves remain beggars." The solution, however, was simple: "The King of Portugal would have less gold,
if we would leave him his spices."[64] The division between good and
bad trade was given additional dimension by Ulrich von Hutten, who
linked self-sufficiency to the point of autarky with the hallowed German past. In what he described as the golden age of the Germans, "no
merchants came to them, bringing foreign goods. They also did not
desire such goods, but used only those things which grew locally. . . .
Their food was raised in the soil and air of the Fatherland."[65] Now
merchants were bringing in "the most trifling things," including "that
damned pepper, ginger, cinnamon, saffron, cloves," and other spices for
which Germans paid out their precious metals.[66] The reconfiguration
of global trade was casually acknowledged in these texts; the real threat
was the principle of foreign commerce.

Hutten extended his attack on the corrupting influence of merchants by examining the deleterious effects of "magnificent display,"
in which spices had a well-defined place. These passages rang with the
conviction—made both visible and fashionable by the humanist revival
of texts such as Tacitus's *Germania*—that the vigor induced by living
in circumstances that sustained life, rather than making it pleasurable,
was to be preferred over refined tastes and pampered bodies.[67] The

merchants were to be blamed for the current addiction to "luxury, banquets, lavish dishes, and gourmet foods," which destroyed the physical strength of Germans. For, Hutten insisted, as Germans in the past had only consumed food that grew in their native land, this food was therefore suited to their bodies. However, "now you do not use these [foods], but seek out delicacies, not to preserve the body, but to delight it. And the corruption and the steep fall into all kinds of diseases is extraordinary." [68] Unhealthy and luxurious living, finally, became a sign of moral turpitude when linked to the vices of the clergy. In his dialogue *Feber* (Fever), published in 1519, Hutten was visited by Fever in search of a victim. Understandably unwilling to take Fever in himself, Hutten cast about for a substitute. The guildsmen and other common folk were unsuitable, as their meager lifestyles would have quickly driven Fever out. Eventually, Hutten hit on the perfect target (and not just for his unwanted visitor): a high-living, well-connected local prelate. This "courtesan" had recently returned from Rome, "after he had learned from a Cardinal there how to live a soft life." The clergyman's lifestyle made him susceptible; as Hutten earnestly assured Fever, the recent returnee not only drank wine and ate pheasants, but "season[ed] [his food] with pepper, cinnamon, ginger and cloves." [69] Hutten's sarcasm then came full circle: the gluttonous minions of Rome might consume the spices, but the merchants were the ones who made these useless goods available in the first place. As Hutten's Fever reminded the clergyman he was hoping to infect, "Don't spare any herb or spice / it doesn't matter how expensive. Or if it's brought from India / grown in Arabia / came from the New Island / Pile it on! The Fuggers will bring more." [70] Through their influence over consumption habits, merchants had now moved beyond disrupting the sanctioned operation of the economy to threatening the essence of Germanness. Tropical spices were portrayed as illegitimate commodities because they fit so neatly into the category of corrupting foreign luxuries, making vivid the connections between the moral and the physical debilitation that the foreign produced.

SPICES AS MEDICINE

Categorizing spices as luxuries made them easy targets for moral outrage but did not confront the issue of their place in medicine, where a substantial apparatus of knowledge supported and explained their usefulness. As with much university-taught science in the late medieval period, the therapeutic use of tropical spices rested on the classical corpus and on medieval elaborations of classical texts. Greek and Roman medical practitioners had used tropical spices in their remedies (many are included, for example, in Dioscorides's *De Materia Medica,* a handbook of medical ingredients), and the use of elaborate and expensive preparations involving dozens of imported ingredients became widespread in Europe under the influence of the Arabic commentators on the Greek authors, causing classical theories about drug administration and efficacy to be expanded to encompass these preparations.[71] The works of Arabic authors such as Avicenna, Serapion, Mesue, and Rhazes became part of the standard curriculum in the medical faculties of medieval universities, enhancing the scientific foundation for the use of these "wondrous" ingredients.[72]

The opposition between foreign countries, which provided expensive luxuries, and the Fatherland (*patria*), which provided wholesome necessities, surfaced in the medical field through herbals published in Germany in the 1530s and 1540s.[73] Part of the humanist reform of medicine, these botanical handbooks for the preparation of plant-based remedies helped revitalize the ancient study of botanical simples (i.e., single medical substances). Proclaiming that only humanist expertise could create useful knowledge out of supposed ignorance and chaos, the new breed of botanical investigators tried to establish their authority over a difficult, contested, and rapidly changing field. The return to ancient texts reconfigured the production of pharmacological knowledge in a number of ways, including providing a structure, complete with a vocabulary, for the presentation of new plants as viable materia medica and providing a basis from which to challenge the dominance of the compound medicines derived from Arabic texts. In neither case, however, did humanism determine the inclusion or exclusion of different plants in these herbals, which instead was determined according to an agenda that bore a striking resemblance to the polemic outlined above. The result was that the arbiters of botanical information transformed selected New World plants into usable substances, while transforming tropical medicinal spices into luxuries whose use enriched only merchants and signaled danger to the German population.

The botanical Renaissance in Germany was marked by the appearance of the herbals of Otto Brunfels, Hieronymus Bock, and Leonhart

Fuchs in the middle decades of the sixteenth century.[74] The study of plants was clearly a lifetime devotion for each of these men, but its connection to medicine also provided avenues for the enhancement of their professional standing and their means of support.[75] Brunfels, a former monk, established himself as a schoolteacher and author of theological tracts in Strassburg before receiving a medical degree in Basel and, shortly before his death, obtaining the post of city physician in Bern. His *Herbarum vivae eiconeb* [sic] (Living Images of Plants) was published in 1530, in handsome folio, illustrated with large woodcuts. Two years later Brunfels came out with a German version entitled *Contrafayt Kreüterbuch,* which eliminated some of the detailed philological discussion but presented the same herbs with the same medical content. Hieronymus Bock likewise combined medical with theological interests, working at various times as a doctor, court gardener, and Lutheran pastor. His *New Kreütter Buch von underscheydt, würckung und namen der kreütter, so in teutschen landen wachsen* (The New Herbal on the Distinction, Effects, and Names of Herbs Which Grow in German Lands) was originally printed without illustrations, but his publisher saw to it that the two succeeding editions contained a complete set of woodcuts.[76] David Kyber's translation appeared in 1552 under the title *De stirpium, maxime earum, quae in Germani nostra nascuntur.* Leonhart Fuchs's herbal, *De historia stirpium* (On the Description of Herbs), bore the marks of its author's position as a professor of medicine at the University of Tübingen; while setting the standard for scholarship and quality of illustrations,[77] this text was too erudite and expensive to supplant Bock's more accessible version, despite the appearance of a German translation the following year.[78] Each of these botanists acknowledged the contribution of the other members of the botanical community in his work, and their combined efforts made the appearance of their rejuvenated form of botany something of an event.[79] In addition to enabling these men to parlay their botanical expertise into professional credentials and opportunities, these lavish volumes, published in numerous editions that continued to appear even after the authors' deaths, indicate that Brunfels, Bock, and Fuchs were successful in establishing their work's credibility and necessity before German audiences, both learned and vernacular. Because their authority was based on the standards and practices of medical humanism, their treatment of both Old and New World plants was regulated by humanism's scholarly expectations. Understanding how medical humanism operated, therefore, can both clarify why the depictions of newly discovered tropical flora in these texts confound current scholarly expectations and suggest more useful interpretations of them.

The goal of Renaissance botanical investigation was the correct identification and use of plants to produce successful remedies, linking the reputation of botanists to their ability to recognize medically useful plants rather than to their intrepidity in seeking out new plant species. The search for effective knowledge was retarded not by humanist intransigence but by practical obstacles that made acquiring and communicating authoritative information enormously difficult. The most educated and elite group of medical practitioners, physicians, were responsible for the tricky domain of internal medicine, where diagnosis and treatment were hampered (even prevented) by the almost complete lack of invasive procedures, the absence of reliable and precise diagnostic tools, and the ignorance of causative agents such as germs and viruses. Due to the lack of straightforward explanatory mechanisms, physicians, like other medical practitioners, were forced to fall back on experience to guide their assessments, but were simultaneously confronted with a relatively rudimentary system for sharing case studies based on the slow diffusion of written commentaries or personal contacts.[80] The claims of learned medicine were thus fragile, open to charges of ineffectiveness or rival claims of expertise from empirics and other nonelite practitioners. In the face of this uncertainty, physicians and apothecaries based their claims to authority on the classificatory and explanatory mechanisms they derived from texts.[81]

Medical humanism, like its relatives in other fields of inquiry, sought elusive truth through a return to the original texts of the classical period, with new and corrected translations facilitating a proper understanding and appreciation of the wealth of ancient knowledge.[82] Helped along by the appearance of previously unexamined texts and new editions of old favorites in Greek and Latin, some medical writers started to make distinctions between the original texts by Hippocrates and Galen and the commentaries and compilations produced in succeeding centuries by Arabic authors, whose writings, they claimed, were marred by mistranslations, inaccuracies, and unnecessary additions.[83] The most important botanical component of this medical Renaissance was the *De Materia Medica* of the Greek author Dioscorides, which described the appearance and medicinal uses of a wide variety of substances, including plants.[84] Renaissance German botanists saw in

Dioscorides not only a source but also a model for the kind of information that would free medicine from the tentacles of medieval commentary and the grasping paws of unlearned empirics alike. All plants, old and new, would therefore need to be fitted within this system of proper knowledge.

Medical humanism shared important attributes with the cosmographical humanism discussed in chapter 2. While humanism did not necessitate the search for new lands or new herbs, it did encourage the validation of national possessions (in this case plants rather than places) through their inclusion in the knowledge of the ancients. However, attempts to correlate ancient knowledge with present surroundings forced humanists to confront the limits and difficulties of the classical canon.[85] Dioscorides, like Ptolemy, had described a world centered on the Mediterranean, something of which Renaissance authors were well aware: "Dioscorides also did not write about all countries, but about Greece. Galen also measured his herbs for Greece and in part Italy, and not for Germany." [86] This displacement meant that German botanists accepted the ancients as the starting point in classifying plants, not the final word.[87] In addition to problems caused by the shift in geography, there were problems caused by the passage of time: changes in language and the process of cultural transmission had resulted in confusion about the correct identification of some plants, in addition to several different plants being called by the same name and the same plant being called by several different names.[88] Making use of ancient knowledge thus required considerable adaptation and innovation. On the one hand, the historical gap could be bridged (but not closed) through intensive philological efforts requiring even closer scrutiny of the texts. On the other hand, as numerous historians of botany have noted, these discrepancies promoted a new reliance on ancient models for empirical observation.[89] Like maps, the drawings of plants visually connected ancient terminology with the latest information collected on the ground.[90] The authority of both the cosmographer and the botanist was established not only through their familiarity with ancient texts but also through their role as arbiters of authenticated knowledge, new as well as old.[91] In both cases, finally, scholars had to rest their claims of expertise on incomplete knowledge, with the promise of future improvement and ultimate success.[92]

THE DOMESTIC STANDS ALONE

In their herbals, the German botanists cataloged domestic plants (almost) exclusively, justifying this selection criterion in surprisingly similar terms.[93] Certain plants of New World or Mediterranean origin were included, but with specific reference to their nativized state or the nativization process in Germany. Meanwhile, despite their presence in the original classical texts and in the classical revival, tropical spices were deliberately and ostentatiously excluded from the catalog of simples.[94] The domestic, in botanical terms, was therefore not an unchanging category, but one that contained the possibility of incorporation. This possibility was further demonstrated by the consistency with which new plants were given the trappings of classical simples. The herbals' focus on transportation rather than origin as the boundary between the domestic and the foreign made merchants once again transgressors.

The efforts of German botanists to glorify German plants and include New World ones were validated by medical humanism's acknowledgment of the importance of empirical research for correctly identifying and describing materia medica.[95] To improve medicine, the plants in the field needed to be accurately correlated with the entries in the handbooks of medicinal preparations, or, where such entries were lacking, the plants needed to be properly cataloged. These modern problems could be solved through the application of an ancient technique, for according to Fuchs, ancient authors "traveled through a great part of the world, so that they could not only observe with their own eyes herbs of all kinds, but also handle them with their own hands and taste them, so that plainly they could gain additional information by this method; learning not merely their image, but all about their properties."[96] Medical humanism's empirical focus was likewise demonstrated through the herbals' increasingly standard inclusion of detailed illustrations drawn from life.[97] The demand for physical, not just textual, familiarity accounts in part for the slow diffusion of New World plants into the herbals. Botanists were prepared to recognize and catalog new plants, but they could not simply be discussed sight unseen. The Dioscoridean model of personal observation thus helped promote the authority of learned medicine and naturalized the turn toward the domestic.

The idea of empiricism also provided a schema for expanding knowledge. The acceptance of New World flora into the category of the domestic (by the time of Fuchs's 1542 herbal, the plants discussed and depicted include maize, chili peppers, pumpkins, and beans) was indicated first by their treatment in these texts. They were never introduced without a systematic presentation according to the standardized categories[98] derived from Dioscorides: name; habitat; botanical description; drug properties or types of action; medicinal usages; harmful side effects; quantities and dosages; and harvesting, preparation, and storage.[99] References to the classical sources, a technical vocabulary, and observed data were all used to generate the appearance of sufficient knowledge.

In this process, the botanists acted as arbiters, deciding when and how the classical authorities should be invoked and when experience was of paramount relevance. The first (and far from simple) task when confronted with an unidentified plant, whether of local or foreign origin, was the matter of its name. A classical identification was the gold standard, because the rediscovery of authentic ancient prescriptions seemed like a faster and more reliable means of expanding the drug repertoire.[100] The thinking behind botanical identification parallels the medical establishment's initial determination to give the new "French disease" a name derived from Greek or Arabic sources. As noted in one modern study of the disease: "A *real* [i.e., classical] name . . . would have meant that the disease had *identity* and could be found among the authors. That would have been the key to understanding it; that is, knowing its causes, nature and treatment; in other words its place in the whole network of rational medicine."[101] In the absence of such certainty, the disease "could not be handled by the theoretical apparatus of learned and rational medicine, on which the reputation and advantages of the university-trained physician rested. He was in no better position than the empirical practitioner who claimed to have a specific, that is, a remedy proven by experience rather than reason."[102] Hence, the botanists devoted considerable attention to connecting their specimens to those described in the ancient texts, asking for help from their friends and readers when they were unable to establish a link.[103] The difficulties of lining up the bewildering variety of names and plants did not relieve botanists of their primary duty of fitting botanical specimens into established medical knowledge.

When labeling plants from the overseas territories, botanists conducted the standard search for classical equivalents or, failing that, provided names that still indicated affinities with known qualities. Hieronymus Bock commented at length on the relationship between chili peppers and the East Indian variety of pepper, concluding finally that the descriptions of the two did not match, but that he would let the name of the chili pepper stand because its fiery heat matched that of the Indian pepper.[104] Fuchs, in his discussion of the same plant, referred in contrast to Pliny's description of *Siliqvastro:* "this plant is called by the most appropriate name from Pliny, Book xx, Chapter xvii, 'Siliquastrus,' from the very large and long pods which it brings forth." In a heroic effort at correlation, Fuchs listed other names as well: "There are those who call it Spanish pepper, others Indian pepper, some even pepper of Calicut. Avicenna seems to name it Ginger 'caninum.' In German one can say Calicut or Indian pepper."[105] Likewise, Bock labeled "Foreign beans" (Welsch Bonen), recently arrived in Germany, with the Dioscoridean name "Smilax hortensis" and also related them to plants mentioned by Galen and Avicenna.[106] Establishing all the variations in nomenclature and connecting them to one plant, represented by one picture, was an approach developed to bring order to the chaotic botany inherited by the humanists, but it worked just as well with new plants, giving them the legitimacy granted by a scientific name.[107]

Once a plant's name had been established, at least provisionally, its properties had to be detailed. Each chapter thus reviewed the plant's various forms (*Genera*), a standard plant (*Forma*), where it grew (*Locus*), its growing cycle (*Tempus*), its "temperament" (*Temperamentum*), and its effects (*Vires*). The links to the classical system and nomenclature were indispensable for this process, especially the idea of "temperament," which connected botanical substances to the Galenic system of humors.[108] The basis of the schema was the correlation of the four qualities (hot/cold, wet/dry) with the four humors in the body. Blood was hot and wet, yellow bile was hot and dry, phlegm was cold and wet, and black bile was cold and dry. According to Galen, disease was caused by an imbalance in the humors of the body: too much blood, bile, or phlegm. Plants therefore had to be categorized according to their ability to contribute to the amount of one or more of the four qualities in the patient's body, with the understanding that an imbalance would be corrected through infusing the body with the opposite quality or qualities. Thus, a fevered patient should be given cooling foods, and so on. Some substances possessed a quality to a greater degree than others, and a four-tiered system developed to rank a substance's cooling, heating, moistening, and drying effects. Renaissance botanists also provided this information as best they could for the new arrivals. For Fuchs, experience would confirm that in chili peppers the Galenic qualities of heating and drying dominated (*valenter excalfacit atque desiccat*).[109] Bock, thanks to his identification of *Welsch Bonen* with *Smilax hortensis,* could quote Galen about its effects,[110] while Brunfels took a broader approach: "[They are] like other beans, but somewhat more tender and milder to eat."[111] Fuchs, having described maize's temperament as apparently identical to that of wheat, then declared that its *vires* were likewise the same.[112] Through this contextualization, the new plants from the Occidental Indies were incorporated into expert knowledge, making them safe from ignorant amateurs, while demonstrating their usefulness to humanistic medicine.

In cases where there was insufficient information, botanists looked to fill in the gaps any way they could. Bock went so far as to make inquiries of a humble peddler when he saw him selling large kernels similar to those described by the Greek author Theophrastus and to other kernels of the *Welschen Korn* and was informed that these (maize) kernels "came from India."[113] In the case of chili peppers, Bock's search for information about Asian pepper took him not only to Theophrastus and Dioscorides, but also to the "Meerfart" of "Aloysius," presumably a reference to *Newe vnbekanthe landte,* the travel compilation that began with the narrative of Alvise da Cadamosto.[114] Ultimately, however, the truth would be established through the determination of scholars themselves, as in Brunfels's extensive and illuminating consideration of "Rittersporn" (a local plant): "I have also made inquiries for a long time among scholars and herbalists about this flower named 'Rittersporn,' what kind of a Latin or Greek name it could have in Dioscorides or Pliny, but I haven't yet been able to find out. Therefore I will then save its description until another time when I have been better informed about the same. For those plants which cannot be determined from Dioscorides, Pliny, Galen, and the ancients, these I hold all for uncertain. In the meantime, we would want to stick with its old name and call it 'Consolidam regalem,' for so the moderns and the barbarians call it, until someone else comes who christens it better." It should be noted that Brunfels's uncertainty about the name did not prevent him from giving as complete an account as possible of its form, location, and drug properties.[115] That the investigation would be ongoing was simply assumed, as in Bock's remark about maize (a New World plant): "I have at this point learned no specific information about what this plant medicinally is suited for, except that one can bake a fine bread from this grain; its temperament is very similar to wheat's."[116] The result was that an impressive amount of ink was spilled about these new arrivals, even though much of the page was filled with explanations about how much more remained to be learned.

Despite these plants' being incorporated into the classical schema, there were still signs within the text that marked them as domesticated rather than domestic. In some cases a name would point to a plant's foreign origin. Fuchs gave maize the name "Turkish wheat" because it "came to Germany from Greece and Asia,"[117] while Bock labeled it "Foreign [Welsch] wheat or Turkish wheat" since "that is how all foreign plants that come to us are called, by the name Welsch."[118] In another case Fuchs remarked in his description of various kinds of cucumbers that the second type (the "Turkish Cucumber") was foreign (*peregrinus*).[119] Another sign of nonnative origin was a plant's inability to tolerate the colder extremes of the German climate. Bock commented that the sensitivity of *Welsch Bonen* to early spring and late fall temperatures indicated "that such a fruit has come to us from a warm nation."[120] The presence of these plants in Germany was thus marked as an innovation.

The herbals interpreted the arrival of new plants not as an invasion, but as an enrichment. Unlike customs, these plants, when they crossed borders to take root in a new country, became less rather than more threatening. The welcoming German soil nativized the plants, even if they still bore some traces of their original status, as the opening comments in Bock's section on maize indicated: "Our Germany will soon be called 'Felix Arabia,' since we have acclimated to our soil so many foreign plants from foreign lands day by day, among which the great foreign wheat is not the least. It was without a doubt first brought to us by the merchants from warm and fertile lands, because it likes good soil and cannot tolerate in particular any cold or frost, just like the foreign beans."[121] The limits of this approach are seen in the extraordinary handling needed to raise aloe, which originally came from Greece (according to Bock) but had since been transplanted to Italy, the Netherlands, and (most important) Nuremberg. The method for preserving it through the cold of the Nuremberg winter had been developed by an apothecary: "Herr Jörg Oellinger plants this foreign aloe every year in the summer in his garden, where it grows a little bigger. With the approach of winter, he digs it out and hangs it in his study . . . it cannot tolerate the winter cold in the garden, and, although it grows the best and most profusely in autumn, winter arrives too soon, and that is a reason why in our lands it cannot be brought to bloom." [122] Aloe's ability to grow in German soil, no matter how tenuous its hold, was the key factor in its inclusion in Bock's herbal.

In the same way that the inclusion of chapters devoted to maize, chili peppers, and beans signaled the domestication of these plants, the lack of chapters covering pepper, ginger, and cinnamon signaled their marginal status in the sixteenth-century German botanical revival. [123] Brunfels turned his attention to simples such as cardamom, myrrh, and papyrus (topics that he admitted were included in other humanist texts) only in the appendix attached to the second volume of his herbal. Indian pepper received Bock's full consideration only in a supplemental work, his *Teütsche Speiszkammer* (German Pantry), published in 1550. [124] As its title indicates, this text examined foods in use in Germany for culinary, rather than medicinal, purposes. While Bock never ceased to comment on the physical effects of ingested substances, pepper was consigned to the role of condiment rather than drug.

In another sense, however, tropical spices were central to the agenda of the German botanists, as shown by the frequent references to them throughout the herbals. Their reputation as desirable exotic medicines was sometimes invoked and sometimes dismissed, always with the goal of raising the status of domestic plants, so that foreign ones could once again be proclaimed unessential luxuries. One tactic was to proclaim some domestic plants to be just as good as a tropical variety. For example, Brunfels noted that lovage was used by the ancient Ligurians in place of pepper, and Bock remarked that hazelwort was similar to the "exquisite nard from India." [125] The praise of the native also encompassed the praise of the nativized. The "German Austrian" (teutsch Osterreichisch) saffron grown around Vienna, Bock proclaimed, was now praised above saffron from its original growing regions in the East. [126] Brunfels acknowledged the force of distance in enhancing reputation with the comment that valerian would perhaps be more highly valued "if it were brought here from overseas." [127] The exalted status of tropical spices was thus called upon to heighten appreciation for simple German herbs.

Both Bock and Brunfels went one step further, proclaiming in their herbals that Eastern products were not appropriate medicines for German bodies. Fuchs's strident commitment to pure Galenic medicine prevented him from tossing out ingredients with a documented use during the classical period (although even his allegiance did not extend so far as to recommend tropical spices unequivocally),[128] but Bock and Brunfels tried to use the humanist framing of their texts to give their pharmacological revisionism the full sanction of this broader movement.[129] By simply disregarding the ancient development of compound medicines, they linked the distinction between simples and compounds to the distinction humanists made between (good) Greek medicine and (corrupt) Arabic medicine: "I call however the simple drugs both the simple herbs, roots, seeds, flowers, and bark, and their boiled and steeped compounds from wine, oil, water, honey, vinegar, and sugar, in which are not mingled together the one with the other, or three or five into one; truly, sometimes 40 are mixed together without discrimination or judgment. I believe this kind of drug was unknown to the ancients, or certainly they combined the simples with some kind of discrimination."[130] In contrast to *simplicia,* which were the proper accompaniment to classical medicine, compound medicines, or *composita* (a term that now designated elaborate preparations requiring numerous varieties of tropical spices), were an Arabic intrusion. The neglect of basic botanical studies that he was trying to correct, Bock explained in his preface to the Count of Nassau, had arisen in part because academic medicine concentrated solely on "the unknown Mesue and the Arabian author Avicenna." Despite their difficulties with these texts, university doctors insisted on prescribing "their long prescriptions or compound mixtures of many Arabian spices." As a result, the German *simplicia* "that previously one had to know from the Greeks, such as Dioscorides and Galen, have been thrown to the wind and disregarded."[131] The harmful foreign *composita* thus served as the foil for the beneficial native *simplicia,* in a scientific as well as a moral sense.

Ancient medicine did provide, as all three botanists agreed, a rationale for preferring local medicines as remedies, and this discrimination between the native and the foreign was also injected into the herbals. The idea that a certain drug would not be equally efficacious in all instances had its basis in the Galenic approach, which called for medicinal preparations to be adjusted according to the age, habits, and underlying temperament of the patient.[132] As geographical location was also thought to affect temperament, Brunfels argued that the use of *composita* was unwise. It was natural for the Arabs to turn to substances such as pepper, because these were native to the tropical climates that they called home. What was unnatural was for Germans, living far removed from the fiery heat of Arabia, to impose these same plants on their bodies: "Foreign herbs may have stronger natures, but they are therefore not acclimated to our climate. As Almighty God has given our lands their own wine, fruit and bodily nourishment, why wouldn't he also give us temperate herbs so that we can use them?" [133] Bock also maintained the importance of like consuming like. People's "eagerness for anything new," especially for exotic goods transported from far away at great expense, led them to "cast into neglect and contempt" that which is "everywhere available at home, and without a doubt more suited to our bodies, and indeed that which grows under the same sky with us." [134] While tension remained between this argument and the concurrent one that some German herbs were adequate substitutes for tropical spices, such programmatic statements worked to delegitimate tropical spices as European medicines. This negative incorporation of East Indian products, like the selective positive assimilation of New World plants, occurred through careful recalibration of ancient frameworks to meet new demands and new circumstances.

SPICES AS LUXURIES (AGAIN)

The goal of both of these moves (i.e., comparing local flora with foreign rivals and dismissing the importance given to the distant origins of these rivals) was to convince readers that spices were not necessary for their health. Instead, they could rely on good German herbs: "We Germans may celebrate our own herbs as much as other nations. If other lands such as Ceylon and Malacca have cinnamon, cloves, nutmeg, and mastic, etc., we have gentian, juniper, and choice saffron, not to mention many other valuable herbs, roots, seeds and fruits, which have received their properties and strength, like the other, foreign, spices, which grow on the far side of Calicut, from God. The greatest folly is that we are not thankful to the one God, who created all such things for the well-being of humanity, nor are we satisfied with them." [135] Fuchs was also far from insisting that medicine required imported drugs: "And why should we despise so greatly the familiar and common, when usually more strength is contained in them, than in those which are imported from the most remote and furthest parts of the world, and gathered with very great expense?" [136] By rating the domestic as equal to, if not better than, the foreign, the herbals depicted the spices used in the *composita* as luxuries, mocking those who valued them more highly because of their distant origins.

When rejecting spices as superfluous, the botanists drew upon the same rhetoric of luxury as laid out earlier in the chapter. The use of costly spices became, for example, yet another form of conspicuous consumption, dependent on commerce: "If the rich want to pay any price, they can be guided by India and Arabia. Who wants to object to that?" The sensible solution, in contrast, was German simplicity. Bock, although stating explicitly that he did not wish to disparage the tried and true compound medicines, implicitly categorized them as trifles, recommending that "pious and simple household heads [haussüatter]" not be ashamed to rely on the simples described in his book, remarking that they would thereby "avoid in part the notable expense spent on the compounded foreign unknown substances, and will allow us to be satisfied with the common gifts of God, which he gives to each in abundance." [137] Avoiding the lure of luxury was, of course, an ancient virtue. According to Brunfels, the ancient Ligurians used lovage in place of pepper, not because they lacked pepper but because "they preferred to use their own plants, rather than go to great expense for riches from foreign lands, for that which they could get at home for free." [138] The expense of spices had become a sign of folly rather than value.

The unnecessary expense of foreign commodities was made all the more evident in Hieronymus Bock's *Teütsche Speiszkammer*, where Germany was again portrayed as a land rich in the basic necessities of its inhabitants. Because of Bock's focus on physical health, many of Germany's benefits were tied to a specific geographical location and hence could not be bought, sold, or traded: "Perhaps other nations, such as Arabia, Egypt, Libya, and India, can rightfully boast, because they have the best gold, the most magnificent jewels, and many splendid and delightful spices. While in these areas they have the advantage over other lands and are more richly blessed by God, on the other hand they frequently lack the humbler things, such as sweet spring water, bread, wine, wood, meat, vegetables, healthy air, and many other everyday things, which we have and are able to get in our German land in sufficient and abundant quantities." [139] Bock then renarrated Ulrich von Hutten's story of the decline from ancient German virtue, brought about by dependence on foreign goods. In contrast to current nobles, who sent large amounts of money hither and thither in search of spices, their forefathers (though also powerful and prestigious lords) had been content with their daily bread. Now imports fueled a culture of excess, which brought nothing but poverty and premature death.[140] Given this unfair exchange, commerce became once again not only superfluous, but dangerous.

Like the Imperial Diet, the botanists who blamed Arabic influence for the triumph of *Composita* located the problem not in the original usage, but in its transfer to a new environment, where it must be sustained with imports. Both Brunfels and Bock compared Germans to monkeys who enthusiastically imitated others, without considering the rationale behind the imitated behavior. Using tropical spices might have been natural in Arabia, where they were as familiar as leaves and grass were to Germans, but just because Arabs prescribed them did not mean that Germans had to do the same.[141] Indeed, Bock placed the blame, as well as the harm, at home: "The fault lies with us, for we Germans first, and then afterward other nations as well, fetched all technique and medicine from Arabia and since in that land many exquisite and delightful spices grow, we have them brought over and mimicked those unknown things, just like apes. Everything, whether spice or drug, must be brought to us from foreign lands with great expense, even at the present time." [142] This quote again shows concern with the exotic as the foreign-out-of-place. The calls for change and reform were directed inward, at the point where international exchange had a domestic manifestation.

The driving force behind the overindulgence and abject dependence of the German population was easy for these medical reformers to spot: merchants. Warnings about fraud, adulteration, and other scams involving tropical spices linked spices with the folly of commerce and the machinations of merchants. The real possibility of such deception had prompted the city of Nuremberg to hire official spice inspectors,[143] and the emperor to forbid ginger tampering,[144] but when Bock dwelt at length on the various tricks of "spice peddlers" (wurtzkremer), including selling false saffron, passing dried white bread off as ginger, and labeling oak bark as cinnamon, the real target was not the ineffective enforcement of such legislation, but the "peddlers and idlers" (kremer vnnd müssiggenger) and their spice-craving, gullible customers, whose increasing numbers made it "no wonder that the German nation alone should by these means become poor and a laughingstock." [145] Adulteration was thus the extreme end of the problem of profit-seeking merchants confronting a luxury-seeking public.

Ultimately, botanists placed most of the blame on the merchants as professional and powerful border crossers: "Indeed there grow in Germany many good and healthy spices, that can equal the imported foreign spices, but we are not satisfied with them. Instead, we must go continually to India, and to Calicut in search of spices. This is all the merchants' doing, for they know how to sell us the spices."[146] The benefits of German *simplicia* for the common man and for national morality are summed up in a poem written by a scholar who also edited Bock's herbal. Here the image of the scheming merchant, burdened with care, is contrasted with that of the simple German farmer, content with his small world: "He doesn't sit in the counting house / He isn't weighed down with usury / He doesn't have to pay interest to anyone on his own sweat and labor / He doesn't cause inflation by debasing coinage / He doesn't have distant trade offices / Or need to fear the impact of Venice / Or need to know what's available in India / and all their varieties of spices / Which is the sugar from Candia / which is the sugar from the Canary Islands / He doesn't need to wait for the ship from Portugal / But is content with his own herb garden." The poem then goes into raptures about the gustatory delights awaiting the farmer in his herb garden.[147] This poem combines the Imperial Diet's fear of the predatory merchant with promotion of the pharmaceutical value of *simplicia,* fusing economic with medical analysis. German humanist botany gave the critique of commerce a scientific basis and made it one of the selling points of a new study of local plants. The immediate surroundings thus supplanted distant lands as the source for medicinal products, and German gardeners and botanists supplanted merchants as experts in these needed goods. As a consequence, the commercial results of the Portuguese and Spanish expeditions were categorized as expendable, explicitly mentioned only to be dismissed.

THE DEBATE OVER GUAIACUM

So powerful were these contrasting images of simple living versus merchant greed that they were used to promote and disparage the most prominent new drug from the New World: guaiacum wood.[148] Guaiacum's efficacy as a cure for the French disease was disputed, and certain participants in the debate who wished to influence the broader lay public borrowed significant components of their arguments from the attacks on the East Indian spice trade.[149] Guaiacum's most prominent supporter, Ulrich von Hutten, described it using language that echoed that used to promote German *simplicia* and argued that the abstinence required for the guaiacum cure strengthened much more than physical fiber. Its most prominent detractor, Paracelsus, decried its foreign origin and touted the benefits of an alternative mercury cure.[150] Despite guaiacum's obvious status as a recently discovered substance from the recently discovered Spanish Indies, both of these men, for the sake of polemic, positioned it with reference to familiar tropical spices.

Ulrich von Hutten, an outspoken opponent of merchants, let his enthusiasm for a medicine from which he had personally benefited override his concerns about who profited from its use.[151] Instead of treating guaiacum as an unwanted foreign import, he contrasted it with the much-loved and much-hated *composita* in his 1519 pamphlet *De Guaiaci Medicina et Morbo Gallico* (On the Medicine of Guaiacum and the French Disease), introduced at the beginning of this chapter. What *De Guaiaci Medicina* lacked in medical and botanical sophistication, compared with the subsequent herbals, it made up for in scorn. High on the list of Hutten's targets was the great regard accorded to compound medicines with exotic ingredients. To explain their unwarranted high status, Hutten focused on the motives and morals of doctors, at times bringing them perilously close to merchants. He consistently complained about ignorant doctors who "want us to regard nothing unless collected in the potion are the three parts of the world compounded. . . . Of what do they approve, where there is not expense?"[152] While Hutten did not rely on the authority of academic medicine, but rather on the wisdom granted by his experience as an educated consumer of medicine, in questioning the value of foreign drugs, he was in perfect accord with the German Renaissance brand of pharmacology.[153]

Hutten did not hide guaiacum's foreign origin; he described the island of Hispaniola and even the initial anxiety that the wood, due to its long journey across the Atlantic, would not work in Germany as well as it did in the New World.[154] However, he drew a more important distinction between simple and compound medicines, through which guaiacum, in being contrasted with expensive, elaborate concoctions, took on an almost German stolidity. Hutten was so adamant that guaiacum should only be used as a simple that he devoted a chapter to the subject: "That This Medicine Does Not Tolerate Admixture" (Qvod Admixtionem non ferat Medicina haec). Even the purgative that should be taken at various points in the cure should be "some simple, but not at all a medicine compounded from many." As proof that no *composita* were required, Hutten pointed to their absence from guaiacum's homeland, whose "barbarian" inhabitants lacked the medical experts who now prescribed and proscribed for the sake of their own profit rather than for the health of their patients: "There are no doctors, no exotics, no canons [of Avicenna], no aphorisms [of Hippocrates]." [155] By consigning exoticism and expense solely to *composita*, Hutten collapsed the distance between guaiacum and native German plants, and between guaiacum's West Indian users and its German consumers. [156]

Hutten also drew an analogy between the medical regimen required for the guaiacum cure and the moral regimen required for Germany's cure. The recommended medical treatment involved internal and external application of a guaiacum decoction, accompanied by sweating baths and an abstemious diet: a little poultry, a little bread, and little or no alcohol. Sexual intercourse should also be avoided during and immediately after treatment. These requirements provided Hutten with an opening, and in a chapter entitled "Against Luxury, in Praise of Frugality" (Contra Lvxvm, Parsimoniae laus), he introduced themes that would reappear throughout his satirical career. Hutten's grandfather is used as an example of correct living, because, despite his high rank and important positions, this nobleman had "never allowed in his house pepper, saffron, ginger and that kind of foreign seasoning, neither did he lay aside his clothing made from our wool, although at some point on account of a deed well done, he was given expensive clothing." [157] The joys of the native also came through when Hutten described the strengthening drink he took during his cure: "But I leave the cinnamon, nutmeg, storax, citrus fruit, saffron, cloves, musk, camphor and these very expensive things to those addicted to pleasure and luxury." In contrast, he was satisfied with a drink containing herbs "all our own," such as cumin, anise, coriander, roses, violets, and sage, which were "very powerful and approved by any doctors with judgment." [158] But his compatriots, rather than heeding Hutten's sage advice, were busily buying up overseas products using proceeds gained from selling products native to Germany, thereby enriching only the Fuggers. The punishment for this overindulgent lifestyle was disease. Going beyond his sarcastic comments about pepper eaters, Hutten argued that the French disease was more virulent among Germans because of their intemperance in eating and drinking. [159] (Foreign) luxuries, merchants, and disease again appeared as a triad, but guaiacum wood's connection with the first two was concealed in order to elaborate on the lessons to be learned from its (supposed) success in fighting the third.

Paracelsus, interested in dethroning the guaiacum cure in favor of a mercury treatment, wrote in terms of a foreign substance imposed for the profit of merchants. He made his recommendations about appropriate treatment of the French disease in a series of tracts, the initial 1529–30 publishing flurry continuing as his catalog of works was expanded and reprinted. Paracelsus's iconoclasm is deservedly a subject of much historical investigation, and his defense of the mercury cure reveals a great deal about his idiosyncratic approach to medicine, but certain elements of his attack on guaiacum reveal instead his connection with broader concerns about commerce.[160] Guaiacum's success was due, Paracelsus argued, not to its efficacy, but to a sinister collusion of powerful clerics and merchants. He asked the doctors who supported the cure, "Have you learned nothing at school, except that you must learn your craft from the Fuggers, and the Cardinal [a reference to Matthäus Cardinal Lang, a member of the emperor's commission on guaiacum wood] must be your tutor?"[161] Their promotional efforts were necessary because common sense dictated that a cure would be found where the disease existed; there was no need to go gallivanting around the world: "This disease is German, and not Greek, French and not Arabic."[162] Guaiacum wood had been brought to Germany, Paracelsus insisted, not to benefit those suffering from the French disease, but to benefit the most prominent merchant family of Augsburg, which had seized control of the guaiacum trade. The Fuggers, he claimed, "brought it for no other reason, than for their own profit," and unscrupulous doctors used it even though "[they] know that in [their] own land the houses and streets are full of the sick people that the wood has ruined."[163] This accusation was made not on the strength of established fact (no evidence exists that the Fuggers ever had or aspired to have a monopoly on the import of guaiacum), but on the continuing association among corporations, monopolies, and imported medicines.[164]

THE SPICE TRADE AND THE OVERSEAS EXPANSION OF EUROPE

The use of images from the spice-trade debate to advance or hinder the guaiacum treatment demonstrates that the spice trade provided a structure for discussing the impact of the European expansion as a whole. The idea that spices were foreign commodities that disrupted domestic harmony (economic, moral, and physical) also found its way into more general histories of the discoveries, where the problems with commerce were brought forward to attack both the motivations and the accomplishments of the discoverers. As the rhetoric of rejection intruded into the narrative of the European expansion, it continued to reflect anxieties about commercial success, rather than commercial disappointment or disillusionment.

The ample evidence of the importance of commercial motivations in reaching places such as Calicut, the land "where pepper grows," could cast a shadow of doubt on the legitimacy of the whole enterprise. Sebastian Franck, for example, attributed the expansionist urge to three factors: "the Venetian nobility, the merchants' curiosity and hunger for gold, and the sea voyages of the King of Portugal and Spain." [165] This passage covers who, why, and how, but the merchants' role was the only aspect that brought out a moral judgment. Vadianus, in his cosmography, took a drier approach, but still presented the discovery of the new sea route to India as the result of the less attractive side of humanity: "Perhaps to this part we admit some certain thanks to be owed to greed and luxury, in general great banes of human affairs, because they have opened this part of the world, for so many ages untouched by us, and they have freed the tottering faith of the ancient stories, by such oft-repeated proof, of all suspicion of error." [166] The Strassburg preacher Johann Geiler von Kaisersberg, in his Latin version of the *Narrenschiff,* even subsumed the discoveries completely under the category of greed, shifting the Iberian expeditions away from the rubric of geographical curiosity where Brant had originally placed them. Under the heading "To travel out of greed" (ex cupiditate), Kaisersberg first remarked that "everyone knows" that merchants travel to farthest India seeking riches at great risk, before reminding his readers that, "in our time, west of the Hesperides King Ferdinand has discovered in the high sea innumerable people." Showing where his true concerns lay, Kaisersberg then immediately launched into a brief tirade against the introduction of "new and perverse customs, foul and foreign appetites and clothing into our lands" by (who else?) "greedy merchants." [167] The ubiquity of such critiques impelled Sigmund Feyerabend, in his introduction to Castanheda's history of the Portuguese discoveries, to explicitly defend the spice trade as part of his wide-ranging positive appraisal of travel and exploration: "And since some regions have a very cold climate, God invented a way, by voyages and travels, that the hot spices such as ginger, cloves, pepper, and cinnamon could also be brought to these places, so that with these aids the cold stomachs could be warmed, and the people thereby live longer." [168] The characterization of merchants as agents of God was infrequent in Renaissance Germany, but whether they served God or Mammon, their commerce structured moral judgments about the voyages that they made possible.

The particular importance of the spice trade in connecting questionable commerce with unquestionable navigational accomplishment is evident in the 1556 edition of Sebastian Münster's *Cosmographia*.[169] In the chapter on Portugal, following a recitation of the accomplishments of Prince Henry the Navigator, the following passage appears: "But it turned out, that these voyages caused great harm to the Germans, French, English, Danes, etc. The Portuguese navigation not only made more difficult for other nations the passage to India, but also made it so that spices come to us with a large profit for the Portuguese and our noticeable harm. For they keep that which is good, and what is not they sell to us at very high prices. . . . But Damianus [a Goes], a Portuguese, attempts to apologize for his compatriots and blames the *fürkauffer*, who buy all the spices for themselves, and squeeze the middlemen so much, that they must make the common man throughout Europe pay. These harmful *fürkauffer* should be driven from the land and not tolerated in all of Europe." [170] The switch in this passage from the Portuguese activities overseas to the harmful impact of commerce was characteristic of German commentators. The concern about the damage caused by the Iberian expansion and the desire to regulate it appeared at exactly the moment when the foreign became the domestic. These brief comments tapped into the much larger reservoir of learned skepticism, popular distrust, and polemical venom about the destruction wrought by successful merchants.

THE CONTINUAL REFERENCES to spices and the spice trade, even (or rather, especially) after the Portuguese discoveries reconfigured trade routes and commercial procedures, demonstrate that these foreign culinary and medicinal plants were regarded as a discernable threat whose impact could be analyzed and contained. The quiet insertion of nativized New World plants into the botanical repertoire was also designed to display learned mastery, this time of the natural world, through tying new plants into classical nomenclature and Dioscoridean categories. The moral, economic, and scholarly concerns that drove these differing treatments of New World plants and tropical spices were prompted by domestic developments. Unlike Spanish legal and theological experts, who judged the worth of the overseas expansion and the legitimacy of Spanish claims with reference to the characteristics of the native populations and the justness of the emerging colonial order, German commentators' assessments stopped at national boundaries. This inward focus reflected not only Germany's absence from the colonial system but also the significant changes then taking place within the German economic and religious landscape. The spice trade was attacked in the *Monopolstreit* and the Reformation in the service of much broader, but nationally focused, agendas. Doubts about the benefits of the overseas expansion thus focused not on the figure of the colonial oppressor (as they would in the Black Legend literature of the end of the century), but on the figure of the merchant. As the next chapter will show, while German merchants were successful in preventing the Diet from limiting their overseas activities, they also began to have, for very different reasons, significant doubts about their participation in the Iberian colonial sphere.

CHAPTER FIVE

The Sorrows of Young Welser

THE COMMERCIAL MISFORTUNES

I N A 1547 LETTER to Bartholomew Welser, the Welser agent Christoph Peutinger complained about a difficult encounter with the
emperor's officials in the royal camp at Ulm. Peutinger had gone to
collect payment on an outstanding debt, but instead found himself being importuned for an additional loan. Sensing that the emperor, who
in the next year would capture the rebellious city of Augsburg, had the
upper hand, Peutinger struggled to gain as much imperial goodwill
with the limited Welser resources as possible, while the emperor's staff
worked every angle to double the offered loan amount. Temporarily
put off by Peutinger's declaration, "I can't do any more, even if you have
me flayed alive," the emperor's financial officer returned as Peutinger
was finishing his letter to report on Charles's dissatisfaction with the
initial loan offer. The officer's incessant demands finally prompted a
testy Peutinger, as he reported to Welser, to reply, "If I had that mountain in India [New Granada] that was just discovered, I could easily
continue to hand out money without getting any in return."[1] This telling exchange on the one hand exposes the increasing rifts between the
south German merchant firms and the princes of Europe, which made
the (barely) controlled chaos of Renaissance commerce still more un-
predictable. On the other hand, the New World in this passage appears
as a source of wealth capable of rendering its possessors generous, even
flighty, with their money. Someone was reaping the benefits of the dis-

covery, but it was not the Welsers. The narrative of victimhood here had changed from that detailed in the previous chapter, in which a vulnerable German populace was being swindled and morally and physically debilitated by greedy merchants. Now hardworking merchants were being threatened and thwarted, while their potential wealth slipped away into other hands. What new realities did this attitude express, and did it alter the earlier perceptions of the overseas territories as sites of predictable (and favorable) exploitation?

In two ways, one rhetorical and one tangible, German merchants expressed dissatisfaction with the conditions of trade with the newly discovered lands. First, during the height of the *Monopolstreit* and their activity in the overseas spice trade, German merchants bewailed the various (almost) catastrophes that had either befallen or threatened the Portuguese spice trade from India, dwelling at length on the frailty of the commercial connection between Europe and its overseas territories. Second, German merchants subsequently curtailed their investments in the overseas trade. The trajectory of cries of misfortune was chronologically distinct from the trajectory of disengagement. Only after midcentury, well past the *Monopolstreit,* did German merchant firms reduce their involvement in the global economic enterprise created and managed by the Spanish and Portuguese. They now sought to limit their exposure as creditors to the Iberian kings, one of the most important guarantors of their access to overseas opportunities. They ended their ventures in the Spanish Indies. They hesitated to enter into contractual arrangements for the purchase and distribution of pepper.[2] By 1580 the configuration of the spice trade no longer fit the pattern described during the *Monopolstreit,* as the shipping routes of Portugal (now united with Spain) came under increasing attack from the Dutch and the English, and as the Fuggers and Welsers (and the Imhoffs and Hirschvogels) ceased to be prominent players in international trade. Both the claims of commercial hardship and the eventual deflection of investment away from overseas trade opportunities were responses to domestic or intra-European developments. In neither case did German merchants alter their private view that the newly discovered territories would richly reward entrepreneurship if only the conditions were right.

This transformation in German commercial attitudes, therefore, did not result from the dissolution of merchants' bright hopes in the thick air of the incommensurably alien world that the New World was finally revealed to be. Merchants did not express the deep disillusionment of the mid-sixteenth-century literary figure Barchilon, the creation of the Spanish priest Pedro de Quiroga, who declared, "The dream of the wealth of this land [Peru], and of this century . . . is [all] a dream and a mockery."[3] Benjamin Schmidt has also analyzed the struggles and disappointments confronting the Dutch western colonies by the middle of the seventeenth century, when incompetent administrators, insignificant or nonexistent profits, recalcitrant native populations, and intense intra-European competition had combined to make the Dutch identify "the New World, and especially Brazil, with dissipation and decline."[4] Such expressions reveal that for many settlers the overseas territories— with their internal dissension, violence, unequal distribution of the limited available wealth, and unending labor requirements—were becoming not depressingly new and strange, but depressingly similar to Europe.[5] For Germans at the end of the sixteenth century, however, the fabled riches were still tangible.

As Germans described the situation, the rewards of overseas trade remained accessible to Europeans, but German merchants were experiencing increasing difficulties in elbowing their way through the mass of competitors for the available wealth. The chief source of the merchants' anxieties was their vital, yet tenuous, connections with the monarchies of Renaissance Europe, through which they obtained access to colonial ventures. They had always felt encumbered by the terms the Iberian kings set for the extraction and acquisition of colonial goods, terms that were part of a more comprehensive approach ("plan" would imply too much coherence) to all the economic opportunities controlled by the Crown. The risks and costs of doing business in this way would eventually prove almost entirely prohibitive. The miscalculation therefore revolved around the relationship between south German merchants and their principal debtors, the monarchs of Europe, not around conditions overseas. German commercial failure thus occurred in spite of the riches of the Indies, whose "inaccessibility" was determined (first in rhetoric, then in actuality) by factors closer to home.

THE USEFULNESS OF RISK

From the first flush of success in their overseas ventures, the long-distance trading companies and their allies in legal and political circles were at pains to point out the factors that increased their effort and risk and diminished their rewards. Such arguments appear in a string of thought papers (*Denkschriften*), legal briefs, and pleas for intervention addressed to the emperor and the Imperial Diet. These texts were composed in response to the attempts (discussed in chapter 4) to regulate the size, shape, and "monopolistic" activities of the corporations. All of the documents examined for this analysis came from inside the walls of the free imperial city of Augsburg, yet another indication of the limited public support available to the corporations. Konrad Peutinger, the Augsburg city secretary, trained lawyer, and Welser in-law (as well as father of the harassed Christoph), was responsible for outlining the position of the merchant firms during the *Monopolstreit,* sometimes in his own name, sometimes as the representative of the city of Augsburg. That his views indicated a broader consensus among merchants about how to approach political harangues is demonstrated by their early appearance in a response drafted in 1507 by Jakob Fugger to a forced loan attempt by Emperor Maximilian.[6] The purely reactive nature of these texts is responsible for their somewhat jumbled style, but the complaints about the hazards of overseas trade consistently appear to justify the profit of merchants and the price of spices. While for the most part this rhetorical use of the dangers of India fell on deaf ears, its presentation here serves as a reminder that even expressions of the global economy's unmanageability can be read as a political stance, rather than as a representation of reality.

Citing the difficulties of obtaining spices was part of a larger strategy by the merchants' defenders to gain political allies and justify the corporations' actions and presence in the economic landscape. The merchants' defense strategies always relied on challenging the specifics of the Diet's proposals, without challenging the traditional theories that underlay the Diet's attack. By not arguing that all commerce was beneficial, that monopolies should be allowed, or that the unrestrained self-interest of the individual was the best regulatory mechanism, the merchants' advocates tied their response to the same understanding of the moral ethos of commerce as that held by their critics. Since they did not argue that the discovery of the sea route to India required the fundamental revision of economic ethics, it was necessary to show that, first, corporations in and of themselves did not violate the principle that commerce should exist to benefit the community and, second, that the practices of the corporations cited by the Diet, including but not limited to those in the spice trade, did not cross the line from permissible to impermissible trade. The merchant as portrayed in the Augsburg documents was the valued leader of an essential enterprise, whose upright attempts to provide for himself, his family, and the members of the community dependent on his unrelenting labor for their daily bread were constantly being threatened by the risks and obstacles of the long-distance trade. The spice trade provided an excellent example of such hardships: shipping losses, uncertainties of supply and demand, the shifting and disadvantageous policies of the Portuguese Crown, and now even the "envy and hate" of men with at best a superficial and biased understanding of the efforts and benefits of commerce. The continual references to the frustrations of the India enterprise were part of an overall strategy to portray the merchant as a victim, at the mercy of the forces of nature, trade, and irrational emotions.

The argument that merchants and their firms contributed to the well-being of the community relied on the Diet's position that a certain demand for foreign commodities was inevitable and morally neutral. Therefore, the commercial firms that were large and financially powerful enough to engage in international trade (i.e., the corporations) were providing a necessary service. As Jakob Fugger put it to Maximilian, the corporations "take out of the Empire that which is surplus to other places where there is a need, and bring from foreign lands into the Empire that which is needed."[7] That the merchants did not justify the existence of demand for their goods is perhaps the clearest sign that the consumption of foreign commodities, while in constant danger of attack as morally lax and un-German, was never in danger of dying out in practice. However powerful Ulrich von Hutten's autarkic vision was as rhetoric, it was politically impractical.

Given that borders were permeable and trade legitimate, German merchants could even pose as heroic preservers of the nation's economic health, ensuring that wealth was kept away from foreigners, not sent out to them: "If the German merchants and corporations did not bring spices from Portugal into this country, the Italians would bring them, and therefore receive the benefit themselves; in the same way the Venetians would set spices much higher at their pleasure, that the German merchant, because he is more hard-pressed, would not do and would not be able to hold firm in selling. If then the Italians receive this benefit before the Germans, the damage to the German nation that would result is easy for anyone with sense to see."[8] This statement reoriented the issue of national aspirations and welfare, setting German corporations against those of their rivals, the Italians, the French, and the Flemish, rather than setting the simple German lifestyle against foreign luxuries.[9] The merchants also pointed out that crossing boundaries could even bring wealth into Germany without requiring domestic consumption, arguing that much of the corporations' business was conducted outside of Germany: "For the well-known corporations conduct very little of their business proper in the German lands, but instead mostly between Italy, Spain, France, Portugal, Hungary, Poland, the Netherlands, etc. and so from one place to another."[10] The corporations thus did to other nations what at all costs should be prevented from being done to Germany.

Corporations not only accumulated wealth that would otherwise dissipate to foreign lands, but spread it around. While ostensibly the various segments of society who benefited were mentioned to show how corporations contributed to community welfare, this argument also astutely reminded those in power of what they gained from the current arrangement. Therefore, Peutinger's argument that the proposed prohibition on outside investments at fixed rates of interest would deprive those of all ranks, "nobles, urban citizens, widows, orphans," among others, of a secure source of income[11] was in part merely a prelude to a specific consideration of the impact of diminished trade on the revenues of German princes: "Not to mention in addition the disadvantage, harm, and decrease to His Imperial Majesty and Royal Highness in Hungary and Bohemia, also the Electors, lords, and authorities of the German nation in their tolls."[12] The redistributive effects of corporate trade were presented as reminders that people other than the great merchants profited from commerce and that the mechanisms of distribution would be disrupted if the regulatory measures the Diet proposed were implemented. The corporations did not enjoy an unfairly large share of the closed economy's resources, but instead accumulated resources abroad and disseminated them (albeit selectively) at home. The merchant's commercial activities thus in principle never clashed with his civic obligations, and foreign spices worked harmoniously with domestic interests.

The corollary to the contention that the corporations' practices were beneficial was that they were moral—a separate, if related, argument. When this second argument was made, the discussion switched from the usefulness of commerce to questions of monopoly and "just price."

The corporations were quick to agree that improper commerce should be prohibited and violators severely punished.[13] Konrad Peutinger's tactic was twofold: first narrowing the definition of improper trade, and then delineating the conditions of international trade in a manner designed to show how easily it fit within his definition of moral commerce. At this point, the spice trade took center stage, as it had when the corporations were vilified as market manipulators. The merchants now claimed a superior knowledge of the spice trade that gave them a correct understanding of its inherent unmanageability and risk.

The corporations' defenders used the example of the spice trade to dwell on the minor incidents of misinformation and faulty reasoning in the Diet's outline of commercial collusion and legislative remedies. The committee report issued at the 1522–23 meeting of the Diet presented many details about the spice trade to show how clearly its configuration violated the proscriptions on monopolies in particular and the ethical standards for merchants in general. Undermining the factual basis of these assertions would weaken the Diet's overall case, and therefore Peutinger expended much ink on correcting individual points. For example, when pointing out that saffron does not come from Lisbon, as the committee's report had incorrectly stated, Peutinger cited this confusion between the Diet's strongest case (pepper) and other expensive spices as proof that the Diet had acted "partly from error and partly, among other things, from mistaken logic."[14] He countered the complaint that the corporations were profiting from the sale of copper to the infidels by patiently pointing out that, since the Portuguese were not in the habit of letting foreigners travel to India, nor the Venetians of allowing free trade with the Turks, any copper trade with the enemies of Christendom had to be carried out by these middlemen and could not be the fault of German merchants.[15] Although they were merely a supplement to the basic acceptance of the Diet's procedure and the basic counterattack of portraying the merchant as victim, these details were nevertheless useful in highlighting merchants' superior knowledge of the spice trade.

Just as the Diet had expanded the scope of practices encompassed by the term "monopoly" to reflect current business procedures, so Peutinger tried to limit the term to a definition so rigorous that the spice trade was obviously excluded. He therefore insisted that "monopoly" applied only in a situation "where a single or several individuals bring solely into their hands a type of commodity or some such thing that is commonly sold in the cities or in the country." [16] This narrow definition rendered legal the other methods tagged by the Diet as unfair market meddling (such as price consortia, or the control of most, but not all, of a market). Peutinger then could argue about the spice trade, with technical accuracy, that no one of "sound mind" (sanae mentis) could say that any one corporation could monopolize the market, in the face of the king of Portugal's control over the supply. Furthermore, many corporations in Germany looked to places outside of Portugal, such as Venice and Genoa, for their supply. "On this account," Peutinger declared, "[the corporations] do not exercise a monopoly, nor even, if any wished to, would they be able to, because they are not powerful enough." [17] In presenting a more complex picture of the spice market in Europe than that sketched by the Diet, Peutinger nevertheless over-stressed the amount of competition and choice available to traders. Just because the spice market was unstructured enough that no one entre-preneur (not even the king of Portugal) could pull all the strings, it still included structures that created opportunities for the manipulation of prices and the amplification of profits. Peutinger's argument here con-cerns legal definitions, not observable effects, and his discussion of the spice trade was composed to counter the Diet's portrayal of an easily manipulable environment.

In another argument entirely aimed at exempting spices from the prohibition on monopolies, Peutinger insisted on defining spices as luxuries. The exemplary goods listed by Emperor Zeno's law, Peutinger argued, were all basic necessities. Spices, however, did not fall into the category of essentials, for they "are used more for delight and pleasure than for everyday bodily nourishment. And in my opinion neither pep-per, ginger, cloves, mastic nor others of this kind fall under the purview of this article." [18] Because calling spices a luxury good was a common tactic used by those commentators who opposed their presence in Ger-man culinary and medicinal preparations (see chapter 4), this argu-ment was unlikely to promote the merchants as providers of a necessary service. The argument's limited utility is indicated by its restricted use; it appeared in its full-fledged form only in one text at the beginning of the *Monopolstreit*. Only within the legal framework created by the Ro-man law as applied by the Diet did it make sense to declare that spices were luxuries.

Unlike "monopoly," which, as defined by the Diet, clipped too close to actual practices for comfort, the "just price" of scholastic analysis proved quite helpful to the merchant cause. While the corporations' advocates, like their opponents, never explicitly identified the legal and theological background of their logic, their explanations were aimed at justifying their practices in these very terms. In chapter 4, I argued that the two signs of an unbalanced economy were the merchants' sudden wealth and the spices' steadily rising prices. The committees of the Imperial Diet charged with investigating these phenomena presented the marketplace for spices as the playground of German merchant firms. The merchants countered with a depiction of the spice trade in which a multitude of factors outside their control not only made their profits less than commonly imagined, but also relieved them of blame for high prices. The result was the argument that current rates for spices barely compensated those involved for their worry, risk, effort, and achievement. Through portraying themselves as victims of circumstance, merchants could use "just-price" analysis in their defense.

Substantial profits and visible wealth were, in the world of the *Monopolstreit*, moral liabilities, representing surpluses made possible only by taking advantage of consumers. Apparent surplus wealth was also an economic liability, presenting an inviting target for others with big ideas and empty wallets. In this context, setbacks like the one Jakob Fugger carefully outlined to Emperor Maximilian were, paradoxically, *good* news. In the aftermath of the hugely successful 1505–6 voyage, Fugger reported, the king of Portugal decided to end the open financing of the India fleets and institute a royal monopoly. He therefore confiscated the spices from the recently arrived fleet, including those on the three German-financed ships, and would only agree to release a certain amount of the pepper each year, with the promise of payments of sugar and money in exchange.[19] Any profits, Fugger reported mournfully, were now up to the king's good faith.[20] The dynamic between the king and the merchants will be discussed in more detail below; the important point here is that this difficulty was made much of, not to discourage investment in the next venture (as stated in chapter 3, the 1505–6 venture, if anything, fueled German interest in a direct route to Indian spices), but to portray the merchants as less effective in gathering wealth.

If money was not pouring into merchant coffers, then why were prices so high? The Augsburg documents in defense of corporations claimed that high prices were due to market conditions beyond merchants' control (but not their understanding), above all fluctuations in supply. Difficult conditions in India and along the sea route were trotted out to justify higher prices at the point of purchase and the point of sale. One of Renaissance Germany's most extensive documentations of the commercial upheavals caused by the Portuguese presence in the Indian Ocean (with a few additional complaints thrown in for good measure) appeared in Fugger's letter to Emperor Maximilian:

> In the matter of spices, the majority [of the price increase] comes from the fact that the Portuguese King with his armada is continually engaged against the King of Calicut. Calicut was the principal city of India to which spices from all over come, and are there bought by the Moorish merchants who ship it to Mecca and on to Alexandria. The Portuguese king, however, for the past several years has captured so many ships loaded with spices from the Moors with his armada, and damaged them so much, that they have left the trade via Calicut and have searched for other ways to bring the spices to Alexandria, mostly overland, so their expense is increased and the amount decreased compared to what was transported by water in more peaceful times, since Calicut is now not a center of trade, but of war, which has driven people away. Spices do not arrive in the same amounts as previously from Malacca and other places. As is due to the inflation and short supply, the Portuguese king keeps the pepper and does not sell to anyone for less than 22 cruzados the centner. When it is sifted, ten to twelve pounds of sand, filth, stones, etc. are in each centner [and other costs], in addition to effort and the risk of life and goods, so that they cannot be sold cheaply.[21]

By 1530, Peutinger was placing less stress on the calamitous effects of the Portuguese arrival, focusing instead on the structures of trade around the Cape route as a particular problem of the India trade: "Every year not more than once, approximately in autumn, several fleets from India come, with all kinds of spices, one year less or more than another." He also linked supply problems to conditions that might affect crops at home as well as abroad: "Of each spice and in each individual location for the same, not only does God bring forth more in one year than in another, as also happens here with wine and grain as well as other crops, but also that sometimes these spices come from India to Portugal more undamaged or damaged, or unequally because of the course of the war." [22] In comparing spices to familiar staples that did not stand under suspicion of monopolistic manipulations, the corporations' defenders tried to show that prices could rise for legitimate reasons. The trade with India appeared beset with problems that were not unique to exotic locales, but recognizable versions of the hardships of European trade, rendering even the difficulties similar.

Furthermore, whether or not the flow of spices had indeed been hampered or cut off by conditions in India or on the way to European ports, the high chance of mishap meant that merchants who participated in the spice trade could justifiably attain higher profits to account for their greater risk and effort. Although acknowledging legal limitations on business activities in a petition to the emperor on behalf of the city of Augsburg, Peutinger carefully enumerated all of the contributions that should be compensated by higher rewards: "For self-interest [aigner nutz], when a person may rightfully have and seek it, is by no one easily refused or excluded, not only in business, but in all things, and much less to be forbidden by law to those trading corporations and other merchants who put forth their body, life, property and possessions, effort and work, and who do not conduct business illegally, and are therefore much more justly to be permitted self-interest than those who in contrast do nothing." [23] Peutinger explained a great deal through applying this general rule to the spice situation. Each merchant, within the proper limits, was allowed to serve his self-interest by charging what the market would bear. Attaining the greatest profits possible at a given time, Peutinger claimed, was particularly sanctioned in cyclical trades like the spice trade, where one or more years of low prices had to be made good when prices rebounded. [24] Just-price analysis could even rescue the king of Portugal from the charge of exploitative business practices. While Peutinger was more than happy to throw part of the blame for high prices on the king, who did in fact sell his pepper for a set price, the Augsburg lawyer refused to allow even this practice to go without justification: "For it is known that His Majesty in the Indies for the past 30 years has deployed his best troops of nobles and commoners, as well as all of the income that His Majesty receives not only from pepper and all other spices, but also from all his other kingdoms and dominions, against the infidel in India, whence His Majesty has the spices brought, from which it is easy to see that His Majesty lays much more out than he makes through sales." [25] The king is here transformed into a merchant, and the costs of exploration and conquest (here emphasized rather than minimized) are transformed into so many factors of production.

In the documents produced in favor of the corporations' existence and actions, their Augsburg defenders discussed the spice trade extensively to nullify its use as an exemplary case of the corporations' threat to the economic and social well-being of Germany. They argued that the corporations' opponents not only were ignorant of the minutiae of trading patterns but had also failed to comprehend the hard realities of doing business across hazardous waters in distant countries with goods that were hard to cultivate and easy to spoil. Recitations of the dangers of the Cape route and the encounter with India thus appeared in Germany in an attempt to remove the taint of immoral trade from spices. For the difficulties of colonial commerce to justify merchants' practices, however, they had to be factors that recognizably influenced price. As a consequence, the documents did not describe an exotic locale filled with unimaginable threats, but an overseas world that tried to produce, sell, and transport spices the way Europe did wine and grain. Foreign trade was still fraught with dangerous implications for Germans, but in these texts it was the German merchants who were threatened by the standard risks and obstacles of long-distance trade, allowing the potential for failure to justify their success.

THE USEFULNESS OF POLITICAL POWER

The story of the *Monopolstreit* is only partially that of a disputation over the morality of commerce and the validity of citing the spice trade as an example of merchant wrongdoing. It is also the story of the increasing political dependence of the German merchants and bankers on the crowns of Renaissance Europe. During the *Monopolstreit,* the opposing sides raised the issue of the power dynamics between the Spanish and Portuguese monarchs and the German merchants to strengthen their cases for the merchant as manipulator or the merchant as victim. Both images avoided the complexities of the situation. The Iberian kings and the German merchants all entered their agreements with an agenda and with leverage: the monarchs' political power and military might, and the merchants' liquid capital and access to needed supplies and trade goods. As long as their interests both ran to establishing a viable, well-financed, and open system of colonial exchange (a blissful situation that existed for a relatively short time), royal and commercial interests colluded rather than collided. However, the same political control and will that enabled the Spanish and Portuguese crowns to establish and maintain a foothold overseas, and that opened up possibilities for the foreign merchants soon swarming in Lisbon, Seville, and Antwerp, would be used as the century progressed to aid the monarchs' accumulation of power and prestige, not to reward or strengthen the commercial houses of Germany.

The final disposition of the *Monopolstreit* reveals how much the merchants had come to depend on the substantially greater political strength of Charles V, Holy Roman Emperor and King of Spain. With the Diet vigorously denouncing the corporations and issuing proscriptions against them, the merchants' advocates did not rely on the persuasive power of their counterarguments to turn back the attack.[26] The severe sanctions the Diet proposed against the corporations were turned aside by the direct intervention of the emperor.[27] When the Diet turned its attention from outlawing monopolies to crippling the corporations, the city of Augsburg sent an embassy to the Imperial Court in Spain. In response, Charles issued two important decrees. In the Madrid Law of 1525, he in essence went back to the *Reichstagsabschied* of the 1512 Cologne Diet, which, while forbidding certain monopolistic practices, lacked both the stringent punishments and the stringent supervision of the corporations that were the central features of later proposals. In the Toledo Edict, Charles explicitly excluded mines and metals from any monopoly legislation, a move designed to protect the most important source of his creditors' wealth, and hence his cash flow.[28] While the Diet did not quietly accept this (to its mind) interference from the emperor, neither was it in a position to nullify it. Consequently, the decrees guaranteed the corporations a degree of legal protection and a great deal more room to maneuver, until interest in the issue petered out.[29] The *Monopolstreit* produced little political vitality within the Holy Roman Empire, but it showed conclusively that the fates of the German merchant houses were inextricably tied with those of the monarchic states.

In the *Monopolstreit,* the emperor weighed in on the side of the merchants, but in a growing number of cases, the interests of the king of Portugal or Spain diverged from those of the merchants. The confiscation of the cargo from the 1505–6 voyage was one such instance. On the Spanish side, the hopes of those who financed García de Loiasa's voyage, designed to cement the claim to the Spice Islands established by Magellan's expedition, were dashed when, as mentioned in chapter 3,

Charles V decided unilaterally to cede his rights to these discoveries for a cash payment of 350,000 ducats. It was a typical royal move—settling for the immediate gratification of ready cash instead of banking on the potential of much greater gains. While it was made with calculation, it was not made according to merchant logic.

The balancing act between royal power and commercial power continued to set the terms of overseas trade, but developments within Europe did not favor the global trade aspirations of German merchants and bankers. The problem for individual bankers was that, as the financial systems of Europe continued to shift and develop, the initially requisite relationship of trust was superseded by the far more arbitrary relationship of unbridled greed.[30] Wilhelm Rem summed up the relationship between his colleagues and the Portuguese king upon noting the latter's death in his chronicle for the year 1522: "He was a great merchant, who did business with the German merchants himself, but often he didn't conduct the sale the way he had promised them."[31] The kings discovered that they could unilaterally, if not break, then at least alter the terms of the accord more or less with impunity: delaying payment, reducing interest rates, or substituting one method of payment for another. Merchants had no way of enforcing contracts except with the threat of withholding future loans, a threat that lacked teeth due to the numerous merchant-bankers waiting in the wings, eager to take the place of those who refused to extend additional credit. Furthermore, many merchants, including several significant south German firms, were still tied by outstanding debts and unwilling to sever the link entirely. Merchants, who had earlier been in a position to demand extraordinary surety for their extension of credit, were now unable to control the system of debt financing that they had helped create. The *Monopolstreit* showed what the rulers could do that the merchants could not, thereby revealing the precariousness of the merchants' overseas position.

THE (LIMITED) USEFULNESS OF COURTS OF LAW

The merchants' connections with monarchs were their most important source of gain and loss, but similar dynamics of collaboration and competition also existed within the merchant community. The suits filed by one merchant against another reveal a pattern that would come to define the relations among German merchants, the Iberian kings, and overseas wealth. For a growing number of German merchants engaged in trade with the newly discovered territories, the experience they related to the courts, to each other, and to themselves featured the real riches of the Indies being diverted from their true owners illegally (or at least unfairly) on their way to or within Europe.

A small number of preserved court cases relate to the transaction of business among Germans overseas. The three cases examined here concern the jewel trade with India, in which foreign merchants were allowed to participate under the supervision of Portugal. The dangers of the India trade, which had been a prominent element in the corporations' defense against the Diet, make their appearance again in these documents, under two guises. Pleas of hardship were occasionally used as exculpatory tools explaining failures to report in, pay up, or deliver. However, many of the practical impediments firms faced are also evident in the suits. These impediments, like the risks outlined in response to the Diet's anticorporation proposals, were merely overseas variations on those encountered within Europe itself. Information and goods were lost en route, the distance from the home office dissipated control over the branch offices, supply and demand were difficult to gauge, and trade was subject to annoying and disruptive levels of state interference. The increased expanse of time and distance involved in trade with the newly discovered territories to the west, the south, and (above all) the east magnified these problems. Factors in branch offices from India to Lisbon to Antwerp disrupted the orderly conduct of business through their personal peccadilloes, unsavory business dealings, lax reporting to the home office, and refusal to follow orders.[32] Such difficulties only led to suits, however, because the parties involved believed that substantial wealth had nevertheless been acquired.

Certain that Jörg Pock's years in India could not have been spent in vain, the Hirschvogel factor's heirs sued his former employer, Endres Hirschvogel, for Pock's outstanding wages and payment of an outstanding debt in proceedings that began in 1530. Hirschvogel's response drew on a familiar tactic: dwelling on the difficulties of commerce. He was unable to determine the extent of his factor's estate because Pock, despite his faithful promise, had never sent back an account to his employer of money spent and jewels acquired (a copy of his will at least had made it back to Lisbon). If that were not enough, the king of Portugal had frozen all of Pock's assets pending payment of a

10,000-ducat debt (the circumstances of this debt are not clear). These objections, however, were not enough to set aside the relatives' claim that there must be *something* coming from India to which they were entitled. Eventually, the parties agreed to mediation, settling finally on a sum of 600 gulden to be paid to the plaintiffs, with an additional 20 gulden for their costs.[33] In this case, the claim that Pock had successfully acquired property in India was not disputed, although the amount and its availability were. Indeed, the expectation of wealth was realistic enough that, despite Hirschvogel's attempts to dismiss the claims of Pock's heirs, they in the end received a substantial sum.

Endres Hirschvogel also appeared as the plaintiff in a complaint filed with the city of Nuremberg in 1531, arguing that it was not the unprofitability of trade with India but the deviousness of those at home that kept his firm from reaping the profits of its investments. According to a letter he wrote to the Nuremberg City Council, the dispute centered around an agreement signed between the Hirschvogel firm and the Augsburg firm of Christoph Herwart. Hirschvogel's father had agreed to make available the services of his factor in India, the same Jörg Pock, in exchange for one-third of the profits of Pock's transactions for Herwart. This apparently straightforward agreement hit two snags: Pock's delay in sending home accounts of his transactions, and the Herwarts' refusal to pay the requisite portion after the first year. The suit was prompted in part by the hopelessness of ever resolving the first problem; as Endres Hirschvogel reported, "Now, however, Jörg Pock has never returned, but died in India in 1529, without ever sending me a final accounting." But Hirschvogel's request for redress was also prompted by the conviction that the Herwarts had continued to profit from their association with Pock. Hirschvogel therefore dismissed Herwart's reason for rejecting his initial plea for restitution—that there were no profits to be shared—by insisting "that we both several times split equally several stones that Jörg Pock sent from India, from which half I profited greatly." As was the case with Pock's heirs, the insistence on the reality of overseas profits was apparently effective enough to produce a settlement offer. Hirschvogel, however, rejected the proffered 1,000 gulden, claiming that his share "by itself amounts to over and above twenty thousand gulden."[34] Such claims would only reinforce the image of India as a land of calculable wealth.

The thorough entrenchment of such transactions in the calculations of merchants is illustrated by two other aspects of the case. At one point,

Hirschvogel tried to preempt any argument that the contract, signed as it was in Lisbon, was not binding on the Hirschvogel and Herwart firms by citing the business sense of his father, in whose name the contract had originally been signed. It was inconceivable that his father would have provided Pock's services gratis, since he "risked a good sum of money on him" through the capital he had given Pock to invest and the costs he had undertaken for Pock's expenses in India.[35] Here the investment required to participate in the India trade was used as a self-evident part of the logic of overseas commerce. Hirschvogel also proposed that the question of profits could best be settled by an examination of the ultimate authority: the Herwart account books. That source could be counted on to determine the truth of commercial encounter.

In the third case, filed by Georg Herwart against Hans Welser in 1548, and based on events in the 1530s, the same stock characters appear: the recalcitrant factor, the conniving and deceitful business associate/competitor, and the precious jewels that had fallen into the wrong hands. According to Herwart, Welser had conspired with his agent in Lisbon, Hans Schwetzer, to do business with the Herwart factor, Jörg Imhoff, then in the jewel trade in India, thus breaking the terms of Imhoff's contract with Herwart and illegally obtaining profits from the sale of jewels that should have gone to the Herwarts. The case documents are extensive, and much of the argument ran to legal technicalities, such as which court should have jurisdiction and whether the prima facie case had been made. However, neither the existence of the jewels nor the wealth they represented (estimated at around 12,000 ducats) was in dispute.[36] Hans Welser even admitted purchasing the jewels, but only as an independent transaction with Hans Schwetzer, without knowledge of the latter's conspiracy with Imhoff.[37]

The strains produced by the conditions of the India trade were always present in the transactions documented in this case, too. India appeared as a distant place, where the normal contractual context was stretched to the breaking point. Jörg Imhoff was the object of rage in a letter that Herwart wrote to Welser in 1543, before the matter was brought to court: "For I want to prove, that Jörg Imhoff has turned against me in Narsinga with a horrendous amount of money and goods, like an errant knave; [he] never wanted to give me an account and I could not set the law on him in that heathen land."[38] So desperate was Herwart to receive some kind of accounting from Jörg Imhoff that in 1539 he sent a notarized letter to Imhoff in India promising him one-half of all profits on the goods that he either shipped out or brought back himself (a substantial improvement over his original contract), with the condition that Imhoff send back by the first ship home a true and clear account.[39] Imhoff's guilt extended beyond his business obligations to familial ones, as Schwetzer thought it necessary to remind him: "It would be good if you consulted your conscience and did not allow your wife in Augsburg to starve to death."[40] Ultimately, though, the renegade was seen as neither freed from his responsibilities nor immune from the conventional inducements. It would be possible to bridge the gap of time and space, as Herwart confidently declared in the 1543 letter to Welser: "[I will show] that from my goods which Jörg Imhoff stole and carried away from me, around ten to twelve thousand ducats came into your possession."[41] The distances involved did not preclude the expectation of an eventual fair adjudication.

Exasperation with the policies of the king of Portugal also cropped up in the correspondence filed as evidence in the case of Herwart and Welser, but neither the expense nor the irritation was high enough to discourage continued participation in the India trade. Hans Schwetzer experienced considerable difficulty in trying to ship goods purchased with the profits of a jewel sale from Lisbon to India. In the midst of what should have been routine preparations, as he plaintively reported to Imhoff, the king decreed that only Portuguese citizens would be allowed to travel to India. Since the goods' departure could not be delayed, Schwetzer quickly married a Portuguese woman ("the daughter of a man of inferior station, without a dowry," according to Hans Welser's version of events in his letter to Imhoff in India).[42] However, even that was not enough, as officials required a year's residence before the citizenship requirement would be satisfied. Therefore, Schwetzer was forced to hire a Portuguese substitute and hand the goods over to him for safekeeping, without any official indication that the merchandise belonged to the Germans. With the substitute's death on the journey, Schwetzer's shipment became entangled in logistical (figuring out what he had sent and where it had gone) and legal (trying to claim it) predicaments.[43] The king of Portugal's regulations, however, were merely a sideshow to Herwart's attempts to obtain his share of the 12,000 ducats that Welser had gained from the successful transactions of Imhoff and Schwetzer in India.[44] The disruption in the proper flow of goods had been caused by people who could be brought to account in a local court of law.

THE DANGERS OF ROYAL FIATS

In this litigation among merchants, the king of Portugal loomed as a figure of arbitrary power, on which part of the blame for the merchants' frustrations could be placed. As Hans Welser explained to Jörg Imhoff about the shipping delays, "It is all however the King of Portugal's fault." [45] Beginning in the middle of the century, royal power was exercised with decisive and damaging results, as illustrated by the Fuggers' dealings with Charles V and Philip II of Spain. Once again tangible rewards for the efforts of German merchants appeared, only to be diverted. Because individual interactions between monarchs and merchants signaled broader changes in policies and in the balance of power, the examples described here had a direct impact on the participation of the entire German merchant network in overseas commerce. Even though the Spanish and Portuguese colonial strongholds became more entrenched and international trade more regularized during the course of the sixteenth century, German firms directed their energy elsewhere. Their policy toward the newly discovered territories tended less toward expansion and more toward retrenchment, firm after firm switching its operations from seeking out new wealth to securing a return on funds and effort already invested. The reason for the frequent failures to obtain such returns was not that the wealth of the Indies had proved a "dream and a mockery": pepper, nutmeg, and cloves still poured in from India and the East Indies; gold and silver from the mines of Mexico and Peru; brazilwood, sugar, pearls, and precious stones from throughout the tropics. But these imports were increasingly directed to fulfilling the immediate political agendas and expediencies of the crowns, rather than maintaining their relationships with their merchant-creditors.

A good example is the transfer to the Portuguese of all rights to the Spice Islands for 350,000 ducats. A Spanish merchant and Fugger associate, Christobal da Haro, was the first to seek restitution from the Spanish Crown for the losses thus incurred, not through the failure of the voyages (Magellan's crew had, after all, found the Spice Islands), but through the transfer of rights to the king of Portugal. Following da Haro's partial success, the Fuggers filed suit in Spain in 1539 for the loss of their original investment (with interest) and the presumed profits of all Spanish voyages to the Spice Islands that were part of this endeavor (which, as mentioned in chapter 3, they estimated at 400 percent, based on the returns on the Portuguese voyages). The suit itself revolved around the validity of Fugger claims to the whole enterprise, as the Fuggers had only contributed to the succeeding and less successful voyage of Loiasa, and both the initial and final decisions went against the Fuggers' claims.[46] The real sign of danger, however, was that with his transfer of territorial rights to the Portuguese, Charles V had turned a commercial investment into a function of sovereignty and the Fuggers' potentially successful enterprise into funds for his treasury over which they had no claim.

The Spanish sale of the Spice Islands was a one-time superseding of commercial hopes by royal imperative. This dynamic, however, would soon become a pattern with regard to the gold and silver from the Indies, initially so alluring as security for loans. The issue was not that the metals had failed to materialize, for the reports of the Fugger factors and other agents consistently mention the arrival of large amounts of gold and silver in the port of Seville. These riches usually found their way unerringly from the Spanish Indies to Spanish shores; they ran into many obstacles, however, on their way to the Fuggers' coffers.[47] The clearest representation of where the merchants' true difficulties lay came in 1557, when, having received a shipment of silver from the Spanish Indies as repayment for a debt, and having received permission to ship the precious metal out of the country, and having made it as far as the Low Countries, Fugger representatives had to stand helplessly by while Philip II confiscated their treasure in order to continue the war against France.[48] The endless uncertainties of Spanish finances were only to a slight extent caused by the uncertainties of the trans-Atlantic crossing, as the placement of the word "hoping" in the following statement by a Fugger factor in Antwerp, written in 1561, makes clear: "The King of Spain should pay off something to my masters, something they are all hoping will happen, since the fleet from Peru arrived fairly richly laden this month of October in Seville."[49] The ultimate sign of royal control over the precious metals of the Indies and their use as payments on the state debt came with suspensions of payments to all creditors, first in 1557, then in 1560, then in 1575.[50] These actions did not wipe the slate clean, but they did give royal officials an extraordinary amount of control over the terms of repayment. Interest rates would be reduced, or the debt would not be allowed to appreciate after a certain date. Most important for the German merchants' view of the newly discovered territories, the decreed method of repayment would not be shipments from the Spanish Indies, but *juros*—essentially treasury bonds that were already circulating for substantially less than their face value. The gold and silver of the Indies lingered as a forlorn hope. When the dukes of Bavaria were given the legal obligation of recovering the Spanish debts in the name of the sons of Hans Jacob Fugger at the end of the sixteenth century, their agents compiled lists detailing the arrival of precious metals from the Spanish Indies.[51] These continuing reports documented not only the steady production of wealth in the colonies, but also that its arrival in no way guaranteed the repayment of Fugger debts and the realization of Fugger investments. In the end, the reality of the gold and silver shipments from the Indies, which could be easily and immediately deployed to further their goals, was tempting enough to those in charge of organizing and leading the Renaissance monarchies to overcome concerns about damaging their future credit (or the solvency of their hapless creditors). While the shipments from the New World represented a form of financial security for Spain (albeit only partial and increasingly subject to the predations of Spain's European competitors), for German merchants they turned into a reminder that he who makes the rules gets the gold.

Recovering from these difficulties in obtaining repayment on loans was, for many firms, hindered by the overall economic stagnation in southern Germany and by the waning of the entrepreneurial spirit on which the leading firms had been founded. The Fugger heirs, for example, became more interested in cultivating an aristocratic lifestyle than in new economic opportunities, while the Hirschvogel firm disappeared entirely with the death of the last male descendant.[52] But the disillusionment's roots went deeper. The appearance of new companies and the continuing trade in staple goods such as grain, wine, and copper could not mask structural shifts that eroded the sources of the region's economic might and access to the overseas trade.[53] State bankruptcies (in France, as well as Spain)[54] and the gradual reorganization of oceanic trade routes around the developing Dutch and English ports were crippling long-term problems.[55] The retrenchment of the German firms in the overseas trade thus should be seen as part of an overall contraction in their role in the world economy, which, if anything, sharpened the frustration and disappointment at the diversion of the wealth of the Indies.

THE WELSER RETREAT IN VENEZUELA

Two dramatic events represent the failure of German merchants to maintain a presence in the overseas trade, highlighting both the rhetoric and the reality of commercial misfortune in the second half of the sixteenth century. The first case is the virtual abandonment of Venezuela by the Welsers, followed by the official retraction of the settlement rights originally parceled out to the firm. The second is the bankruptcy of the Augsburg merchant and speculator Konrad Rott, a downfall caused by his investment in the pepper trade under rules created by the Portuguese Crown. The explanations for the failure of these commercial ventures, with historical hindsight, rest ultimately with the imperatives of the Spanish and Portuguese crowns. Each of these cases also demonstrates a persistent belief in the presence of overseas riches, along with a persistent pessimism and frustration at the requirements for getting at them.

The Welser colony in Venezuela began, as discussed in chapter 3, around 1530 as a mining/trading venture extending from the Augsburg firm's European activities.[56] Within a few years, however, with visions of rich provinces dancing in their heads, a succession of Welser governors marched inland, following their instincts, the lay of the land, and the intimations of the Indian tribes with whom they came into contact—in the hopes of enormous financial gain. This diversion of resources from production and settlement to exploration affected not only Coro, the one town established by Europeans, which dwindled into a mere staging area and hospital for the sick and disabled, but also the future development of the colony, as little attempt was made to establish settlements in more suitable locations or to investigate less profitable but nevertheless sustaining production options, such as cattle raising. Small amounts of gold were obtained through trade and capture, but the Welser expeditions were unsuccessful in reaching their main goals.[57] The parent Welser firm eventually decided that further investment was not worthwhile and in effect abandoned the colony to its own devices. The situation in the colony deteriorated with infighting, the increasing hostility of the remaining local native populations, and the unhealthful coastal climate. The final Welser-appointed leaders, Philipp von Hutten and Bartholomew Welser (son of the head of the family), were executed by a mutinous Spanish captain, leaving sole authority in Venezuela in the hands of a governor appointed by the *audiencia* of Santo Domingo. In 1556 the Council of the Indies, after more than a decade of legal maneuvering, finally removed Venezuela from Welser control and integrated it into the regular administration of the Spanish Indies.

What seems, thus outlined, to be a story about the mirage of El Dorado and the failure of European expectations in the harsh reality of the colonial environment turns out on closer inspection to be a story about recalcitrant employees, real wealth that eluded the Welsers' grasp, and European political configurations in which German merchants played only a contingent role.[58] The legal challenge to the Welsers' proprietorship of the colony was precipitated by, of all things, the discovery of a rich kingdom—the expeditions' goal all along. New Granada, as the region came to be called, while by no means as magnificent as Peru, had enough of Peru's accoutrements to enable its conquerors to set themselves up independently and its Spanish settlers to prosper.[59] An expedition from the Venezuelan capital at Coro, led by the Welser employee Nicolas Federmann, even made its way in 1539 to New Granada, only to discover that it had been occupied for the past two years by Gonzalo Jimenez de Quesada, a Spanish soldier from the neighboring territory of Santa Marta. Quesada and Federmann jointly decided that control of the region and access to its wealth would best be secured by traveling to Spain to present the competing claims of Santa Marta and Venezuela. While Federmann took no explicit steps to weaken the Welser claim on the territory, he did agree that administrative control would remain with Quesada and put his men at Quesada's disposal. As part of the agreement, Federmann would receive land and part of the booty, an arrangement that expressly went against his contract with the Welsers, which, as was standard, required him to work for their benefit and not for his own.[60]

However, upon their arrival in Spain, Quesada and Federmann discovered that they had entered the far more difficult terrain of rumor and reputation and that Federmann, in particular, had not been favorably portrayed by reports and embassies from the Spanish Indies. Still intent on receiving recognition for his accomplishments, Federmann traveled to the Imperial Court, then seated in the Netherlands. Bartholomew Welser, the head of the firm that had hired Federmann, also happened to be at court on business, and their meeting had fateful consequences. Welser apparently accused Federmann of putting money belonging to the firm into his own pockets and had him arrested, whereupon

Federmann denounced the scandalous conduct of the Welser agents in Venezuela, alleging not only breach of the Welsers' original colonization agreement with Spain, but also smuggling and other illegal activities.[61] These accusations naturally caught the attention of the Council of the Indies, the branch of the Spanish state charged with conducting and monitoring affairs overseas. By now, the charges of misconduct were no longer merely a weapon in a private feud; they were a state concern. Thus, even though Federmann retracted his statements, his accusations against the Welsers continued to be investigated, becoming part of the continuing battle for control between the various local and central authorities: the governors on the ground in Venezuela, the *audiencia* in Santo Domingo, and the Council of the Indies in Seville.[62]

In both matters—the competing claims to New Granada and the defense of their conduct in Venezuela—the Welsers were now on the familiar, but increasingly unfriendly, terrain of court connections and bureaucratic proceedings. In the first instance, the neighboring province of Santa Marta, with both precedence (its captain, Quesada, had been the first to reach the rich province) and geography on its side, was awarded New Granada, at least until 1549, when it became a separate province with the establishment of the Audiencia de Santa Fe de Bogota.[63] The abrogation of the Welser claims to Venezuela was a somewhat trickier matter, since the official assigned to investigate Federmann's charges accused the Welsers of having violated not only the original contract (and thereby having forfeited the colony) but Spanish law as well, and made the firm's leaders personally liable for criminal charges and substantial fines.[64] Thus, long after the firm had lost interest in the continued administration and exploitation of the colony, its representatives in Spain fought for acknowledgment of its claim as proof that they had done nothing wrong. Legally, the Welsers were able to sustain this claim, and in 1555 the charges arising from the investigation were dismissed and the validity of the contract confirmed. What, if any, further use the Welser firm would have made of this opportunity is unknown, because, following an appeal by the Crown's attorney, the Council of the Indies partially reversed its decision. The original charges remained dismissed, but the original judgment stood, and the Welsers' rights were abrogated.[65] A political decision rather than a legal one, this verdict by the Council of the Indies was yet another sign that royal and bureaucratic prerogative now superseded obligations to merchants where the two clashed.[66]

The Welser disillusionment with the Venezuela enterprise was very much part of the pattern described in this chapter: the newly discovered territories still figured as lands of opportunity, but attention now turned to the all-too-familiar figures who had caused this opportunity to be missed. Writing in 1543 to Franz Davila, a business associate in Santo Domingo, Bartholomew Welser expressed his regret that Federmann owed Davila money and advised keeping a close watch to see if his crafty employee had any hidden sources of money. Welser then commented on his own firm's difficulties with this individual: "He remains greatly in debt to this firm and has caused us much unpleasantness." The only hope in the situation lay in the land, not in the employees: "If the land would start to bear fruit, then you would know by the proceeds in what high regard you are held by all of us." [67] The Welser factor Jacob Rembold echoed and expanded on these complaints. Federmann's deception had even extended to his possessions: "His estate has slipped through our fingers, since he disposed of it in secret and under other names." The search for Federmann's estate was driven by a desire for restitution, since "he stole easily 6000 gold piasters from the new dominion, about which we have sufficient proof, and took them with him in gold; what he did with them, we will probably never be able to find out." [68] But the clearest example of missed opportunities was the failure to lay hands on New Granada, which instead had rewarded the efforts of the neighboring province. The resentment toward the near-ingratitude of the Spanish Crown, which had demanded so much and whose rewards seemed always to go somewhere else, was palpable in Christoph Peutinger's remark that *had* the Welsers discovered "that mountain in India," they *would have* money to burn (or to lend to the emperor, which at this point amounted to pretty much the same thing).[69]

The 1545 execution of Philipp von Hutten and Bartholomew Welser in Venezuela, justified in an after-the-fact show trial by the rebellious colonists, crystallized for their relatives and associates in Germany the problem of overseas ventures.[70] In addition to seeking the punishment of all those responsible for the deaths (in the end only the leader of the renegade group, Juan de Carvajal, was executed), Philipp's brother, Moritz, and Bartholomew's father, the same Bartholomew who had squabbled with Federmann, pressured the Spanish authorities to return the possessions of the two. In arguing their case to Charles V, they painted a vivid picture of New World wealth and Carvajal's villainy:

"Out of insatiable greed he took and villainously alienated from them all that they had brought, and had combined the men that came with them with his, with the plan, to seek out the rich lands and provinces, that the oft-mentioned von Hutten had discovered with his great effort and work and with the Welser money, and to enjoy their fruits by himself, which von Hutten and Welser rightly should have enjoyed."[71] Such pleas (particularly those made personally at the 1548 Imperial Diet in Augsburg) did serve the purpose of moving Charles to direct the Council of the Indies to investigate Hutten's and Welser's estates and restore them if possible to their families. However, private correspondence between the Welsers and the Huttens reveals that this narrative was not just a politically expedient story, but a personally convincing account of both the success of this latest venture and the events that had robbed them of their family members and their treasure. As Philipp's brother, Moritz, wrote to Bartholomew's father, "We are completely in agreement, that they were by no means without money and possessions, by which we suppose the perpetrators were moved to their crime."[72] This passage summarizes many of the themes of the commercial experience: treasure had been found, admittedly after much effort, but it had been stolen en route through a show of legality arranged by political forces beyond the merchants' control.

THE BANKRUPTCY OF KONRAD ROTT

Beginning in 1577, Konrad Rott, an ambitious Augsburg merchant, headed a consortium of merchants with exclusive rights to import and distribute the spices of the East Indies around the Cape route. The withdrawal of the former powerhouses that had earlier dominated the spice trade facilitated Rott's entry into this high-stakes, potentially lucrative field. His overextension in the credit markets of Europe, his inability to cope with the logistics of distribution, and the straitjacket of requirements imposed by the king of Portugal precipitated Rott's spectacular bankruptcy. Although his agent reported some difficulties in obtaining the requisite amounts of spices in India,[73] the extraction of colonial goods was the least of Rott's problems. In the records of Rott's transactions and in his subsequent defense of his actions, the pepper itself appears as the one sure thing.

Konrad Rott had engaged in smaller transactions for the Portuguese

Crown before taking on the challenges that produced his downfall, including supplying copper, still an essential component of German trade with Portugal. In 1575 he took a major step upward by entering into the so-called Europe contract for the intra-European distribution of pepper for the next five years. This contract, as all the others had been, was more attuned to the financial needs of the Portuguese Crown than to the most suitable business arrangement. Rott agreed, in addition to contracting to buy a set amount of pepper for a set price, to pay a substantial sum up front and to aid in financing the purchase of grain and shipbuilding supplies for the India fleet. The commercial difficulties of the past decades were reflected in the fact that only Rott, a relative newcomer, was initially willing to sign on to this contract. The king had first sought takers from among his longtime creditors as a way of partial debt repayment, but firms like the Fuggers, the Neidharts, and the recently bankrupted Manlichs were in no position to extend the necessary financing. Nor, to be honest, was Rott, whose shaky credit situation prompted sniggers from Fugger factors, and whose financial viability was only restored by an Italian firm's entrance into the Europe contract.[74]

Buoyed by his successful foray into large-scale entrepreneurship, two years later Rott negotiated for the "Asia contract," a newly revamped plan for the financing of the India fleets. Rather than organizing the fleet and financing himself, the Portuguese king had decided to seek outside contractors who would be responsible for carrying out the whole venture, but with strict stipulations about amounts and prices. Again unable to fulfill the financial requirements of this contract by himself, Rott acquired two partners, a Portuguese firm and a Milanese firm. However, by this point Rott's financial straits had begun to resemble those of an Iberian king, and he sought a similar solution. He approached the elector of Saxony, who had already expressed interest in engaging in the copper trade with Portugal, with the proposal that the elector buy a fixed amount of Rott's pepper, with payment up front and in cash, for which the elector would be guaranteed exclusive distribution rights in Central and Eastern Europe.[75] This semibrilliant scheme started to unravel when Rott's partners refused to guarantee the elector's monopoly on distribution, a monopoly in any case doomed by the continuing arrival of spices through the Levantine route.[76] Europe was, in fact, awash in pepper, which meant delays in distribution and lower prices due to increased supply.[77] Unable to obtain more credit, and unable to keep his creditors at bay until the pepper market could bring its (uncertain) rewards, Rott fled the city of Augsburg at night, leaving his bankrupt status clear from the piles of debts and the limited assets. Rott's failure as a pepper merchant was due to the extreme demands for credit and the requirement of fixed prices imposed by the king of Portugal. The Europe and Asia contracts placed all the risk on the contractors, without lending them the needed flexibility to respond to fluctuations in supply or demand. Rott proved, even though he was able to pass along some of this risk to the elector of Saxony, unable to sustain the loss.

Although the hazards of the overseas trade with India that the merchants were so fond of citing had nothing to do with Rott's limited financial resources and clearly were not to blame for the oversupply of pepper, they do figure in Rott's subsequent attempts to restore his reputation, a task that he undertook in two extraordinary documents. The first, written shortly after his flight from Augsburg, purported to be a will composed on his deathbed, showing his debts and assets.[78] Subsequent investigation by the Augsburg City Council revealed not only that a traveler matching Rott's description had been seen alive and well in the days after Rott's reported death, but also that in his will Rott had greatly underestimated his debts and optimistically portrayed his assets.[79] The second document was a pamphlet that appeared in 1580, entitled "Conversation that Pasquinus had with Marphorio in Rome on 1 July 1580 about the affairs of Konrad Rott."[80] Far too favorable to Rott's case to have come from any source other than Rott himself or a close associate, the "Conversation . . . about the affairs of Konrad Rott" tried to present the case that entering into the contracts had been a reasonable decision and that the situation was still salvageable, although some complicating factors had arisen.

In both of these documents, pepper is held forth as the solution to all the problems, if only people would be patient with the logistics of cashing in on the supply. The first assets listed in the fake will included the pepper currently on hand in Lisbon, as well as the presumed returns on the money invested in fulfilling the Asian contract, unproblematically transformed into a liquid sum available to his European creditors:

> This past year I provided 100,000 Reichsthaler in cash to buy pepper and cloves in the Indies, namely 12,500 quintals that would be my share of

30,000 quintals, for which however I count no more as 25,000 to make the journey. Then ½ to the King, and of the other ½, my ⁵⁄₁₂ portion equals 5202, at 35 Reichsthaler [per centner]   R. 261,000.[81]

Leaving aside the question of whether that much pepper would actually reach Europe, the real problem was the difficulty of selling pepper for the presumed price; creditors had already expressed reluctance to accept pepper as payment because of the risk that the established rate would not translate into the actual market price.[82] Rott's belief in the pepper contrasted sharply with the cynicism he displayed toward debts owed by the nobility; here, at least, he seemed to be realistic: "In Lisbon I still have in terms of debts owed to me by the nobility there and then the King, around 100,000 Reichsthaler, which I do not count at all, if something is received, then it is found money."[83] The pepper payments, meanwhile, merely needed time for the commodity to reach Europe.[84] This point comes across even more strongly in Rott's pamphlet, which insists, against all plausibility, that Rott is not really bankrupt. In addition to blaming his problems on envious colleagues and the current political troubles in Portugal (in which the king of Spain would emerge as victor in the succession crisis), Rott portrayed India as his salvation: "Nothing would be lost, instead what is lacking in Europe you will find in India."[85] Europe was the source of difficulties and demands; India was the source of wealth.

Despite Rott's forced optimism, the attitude of most south German merchants who had been involved in the pepper trade in the sixteenth century was perhaps best expressed by the elector of Saxony, as he contemplated a lawsuit against Rott to try to obtain something in exchange for the false promises and the miscalculations of commercial power. Writing to his chamber secretary, he announced: "Since I see, that I was not born to the pepper sack . . . I have firmly decided on my part, to rid myself of this business and to state that for better or worse, it is of no concern to me; I do not want to spend the time I have left on such annoying business. . . . I have stuck my neck out, and want to be rid of this false business."[86] The image of the pepper sack is telling; it focuses on the merchandise already packaged and delivered to Europe. The "false business" to which the elector had fallen victim is merely a variant on the age-old tricks of the cunning merchant.

German merchants, despite, or perhaps because of, their cunning, eventually suffered significant financial reverses as a result of many of their overseas commitments. The complaints that had begun in an attempt to turn aside charges of immoral and illegal conduct in the spice trade signaled in the end real losses. German merchants were also right in placing the blame on their European system of associates, contracts, and competitors, rather than on the failure of the overseas territories to produce the required products. The sense of ill-usage reflected in the court records and in their remarks to each other, aimed at heightening their status as victims in an effort to make them even more viable plaintiffs, was perhaps unwarranted. The misfortunes of merchants, after all, stemmed from the same set of relations that had earlier rewarded them so richly.

THE RESPONSES OF merchant advocates in the *Monopolstreit* and the excuses of defendants in suits over Indian jewels show that tales of misery and woe, like those of new and strange things, were constructed in response to the expectations of domestic audiences. Likewise, the insistence that trading ventures to the East and West Indies were fundamentally profitable was designed to help those who needed to imagine the best possible outcomes—such as the Fuggers in the suit over the Spice Islands, the plaintiffs in the lawsuits, and Konrad Rott. When German merchants went beyond rhetoric to concrete measures, however, they staked their wealth on the economic commensurability of the newly discovered lands, seeking to overcome the difficulties of long-distance trade, now aggravated by greater distances and more infrequent communication, and continuing to invest in the new trade opportunities as they saw earlier ones rewarded. Their decision to reduce their presence in the transoceanic trade was prompted not by changing events overseas or by evidence that economic extraction overseas was becoming more difficult, but by developments within European commercial and political systems. The courts of Europe turned out to be more inhospitable than the jewel market of India or the high plains of New Granada.

Conclusion

Iɴ 1620, ꜰʀᴀɴᴄɪs ʙᴀᴄᴏɴ's *New Organon* used the example of Europe's geographical expansion to call for a wholesale reevaluation of inherited knowledge: "We should also take into account that many things in nature have come to light and been discovered as a result of long voyages and travels (which have been more frequent in our time), and they are capable of shedding new light in philosophy. Indeed it would be a disgrace to mankind if wide areas of the physical globe, of land, sea and stars, have been opened up and explored in our time while the boundaries of the intellectual globe were confined to the discoveries and narrow limits of the ancients."[1] Bacon's proclamation has usually been cast as the climax of the story about the discoveries' effect on European intellectual culture. In this interpretation of history, the expeditions of the Moderns cast such a blinding light on the deficiencies of the Ancients that the classical tomes that had earlier weighed down strivers after truth lost their importance and were replaced by the wings of experience and experiment. This view also secures Bacon's place in history as the first to propose a new and complete system of knowledge based on the observed realities of nature.

In the preceding chapters, however, I have told a different story about the discoveries' effects on European intellectual culture—a story in which Renaissance German commentators, responding to expectations, developments, and debates of immediate relevance to them, successfully used established concepts to explain the significance of events abroad to diverse audiences at home. Situated at the center of numerous trade and information routes, Germany's flourishing scholarly, commercial, and publishing communities were already well versed in handling the complexities of Europe's intellectual heritage and well aware of the importance of the successful incorporation of new information into prevailing ideas and expectations. Contact with the extra-European world in the preceding centuries had prepared Europeans to acknowledge and exploit information about the diversity of humanity and the natural world. Exploration of the European geographical and cultural landscape, which exhibited considerable variation in its own right, had also provided observers with much to examine and ponder. In addition, commercial connections across Europe and between Europe and the rest of the world had already introduced a range of goods, currencies, trading customs, and ways of distinguishing legitimate from illegitimate trade to European observers responsible for knowing such things. Germany had not been isolated from Europe, nor Europe from the rest of the world, and this interconnection required workable processes of cultural and economic exchange.

The political, economic, and intellectual developments that marked the Renaissance, which were new to Europe in ways that the newly discovered lands and peoples were not, enhanced Germans' need and ability to come to grips with the overseas expansion. The subsequent outpouring of representations and commentaries reflects the secure and vital place the overseas territories found in Renaissance German culture. The establishment of the printing press allowed accounts of new voyages to circulate widely within Europe, while at the same time making possible the editing and publication of numerous older texts and large compendia that placed the latest reports in broader contexts. The well-established trade connection between the metals of Central Europe and the spices of the East quickly prompted German merchants to set up shop, first in Lisbon, then in Antwerp, in response to the new Portuguese sea route to India around the Cape of Good Hope. At the same time, the growing commercial clout of the south German merchant firms gave them the necessary access to lucrative opportunities abroad, whether in the jewel trade of India or the plunder trade of the New World. The concerns of polemicists and politicians prompted by this seeming economic disequilibrium found not only a ready outlet in attacks on the spice trade, but common cause with the interests of medical humanists, who brought the division between the domestic and the foreign into their scientific investigations while establishing procedures for the incorporation of new flora. Humanism also changed cosmography, not by imprisoning cosmographical knowledge within ancient geographical limits, but by inspiring philological investigations that stressed the boundary between the new and the old, and, through the Ptolemaic system, furnishing scholars with the mathematical tools to assert eventual perfectibility across the globe. These efforts, intended to explain and control the meaning of the European expansion, also gave the discoveries status and significance within Renaissance culture.

The fit was not perfect. As much recent scholarship has shown, colonial environments, much less colonial populations, were never completely mastered by European imperial powers. Neither, however, were home environments, because physical realities and human behavior also proved difficult to measure and investigate in Europe. Much practice was gained in techniques to preserve the authority and usefulness of established structures of thought—when German publishers passed along news of northern marvels, when German botanists were faced with unknown local plants, when German merchants confronted fluctuating prices and recalcitrant factors in Antwerp and Italy, when German cosmographers included Scandinavia on their maps, and when German legal commentators explained why the new monopolies were illegal and harmful. German commentators extended these assertions of expertise, along with necessary elisions and sleights-of-hand, across the oceans to make analogous claims that bolstered their status and interests. The one instance in which confidence seems to have faltered—the commercial withdrawal from overseas opportunities—was the result of the merchants' inability to control events and circumstances on European soil. When it came to the overseas territories, confidence was maintained in the face of incomplete information and inadequate identifications through belief in the ability of established procedures to eventually produce valid results.

The German experience in the expanding world was not the universal European experience. Colonizing powers such as Spain, Portugal, and England engaged in the overseas world more intensively and in different ways than Germany (or Italy), which remained distant from direct colonial relations. Their representations of the newly discovered lands and peoples, however, can be read in the same way as the German responses: as attempts to make sense and use of the expansion through applying familiar categories. Categories like "new" and "strange," which stressed the distinctiveness of the overseas territories, gained increased importance when participants and observers wanted to magnify their, their countries', and their monarchs' imperial might and right through emphasizing the intrepidity of their travels, their privileged access to sights few Europeans had seen, and the primitive nature of the conquered peoples. Expressions of difference, as their appearance in German paratexts indicates, also found a place in explaining the expansion to audiences throughout Europe, particularly in appealing to a sense of curiosity and wonder. German commentators, however, usually found the label "just another" more useful and appropriate for extending to new territories expertise gained initially in, and primarily for, the handling of European scholarly investigation, polemical disputes, and commercial contexts.

Even imperialism was not just based on claims of difference. There were powerful incentives to fit the newly subject peoples into political categories and religious explanations, turning the natives into just another group of "subjects" or "Christians." While the imposition of these frames of reference obviously required a more profound (and profoundly resisted) transformation of the social and cultural order than did trading copper for pepper or ascribing Galenic qualities to maize, far more powerful repressive mechanisms were available. When these mechanisms failed, as they frequently did, European categories were once again mobilized to explain and minimize failure.[2] The more malleable nature of human societies (in comparison to geographical landscapes, commodities, and natural substances) produced, I would suggest, an even greater belief in their ultimate conformity to required categories.

It is essential to recognize such differences in the application of existing ideas because these variations demonstrate the importance of context for the form and the consequences of the extension of European categories. Many of the basic aspects analyzed in the preceding chapters were common throughout Europe: Germans were not unique in their travel narratives, maps, or accounting procedures, or in their scholarly, legal, and scientific thought. Travelers, texts, exotic merchandise, and merchants crossed borders. As a result, the German successes in incorporating the Iberian expansion have broader implications, particularly for explaining the intellectual changes in Europe that followed the discoveries. Bacon's assertion about the importance of Europe's expanding horizons and the numerous echoes of this idea in the seventeenth century cannot be viewed as spontaneous outbursts in the face of the inescapable novelty and alterity of the "new worlds," but instead must be seen as carefully constructed claims that placed the newly discovered lands and peoples at the disposal of a certain intellectual agenda. Two points about Bacon's biography highlight the problems of a straightforward connection between geographical expansion and intellectual revolution. First, Bacon himself never set foot on the other side of the ocean; the experiences he was writing about were not his own, and he was dependent for his understanding of events on the same type of textual and visual material on which Renaissance Germans had likewise based their conclusions. Second, for all Bacon's talk about "in our times," the voyages of Columbus and da Gama had taken place more than a century before the publication of these words in *New Organon*. Bacon's task was not to make sense of the initial, confusing, and frustratingly incomplete accounts of the expeditions—the task undertaken by German commentators during that first century—but to depict these earlier struggles in ways best suited to his purposes.[3] His account of the revolutionary impact of the discoveries must therefore also be taken as an "engaged representation" about events in which he did not participate. In this case, the geographical failings of the ancients form the backdrop for Bacon's claims about the independent and iconoclastic nature of his proposed knowledge system.

Such enthusiasm was not limited to Bacon, as a sustained interest in novelty characterized European elite culture of the late sixteenth century and the seventeenth century. It seems that, although the discovery of new worlds occurred during the Renaissance, the celebration of new worlds was a phenomenon of Baroque culture, which exalted both the new and the strange in their own right. A budding genre in the late sixteenth century, the *Wunderkammer* (cabinets of curiosities) came into their own in the seventeenth. Furthermore, as Paula Findlen has argued for the Italian case, "If sixteenth-century collections were noteworthy for their encyclopedism, resulting in the indiscriminate inclusion of every natural object, mid-seventeenth century collections were distinguished by their exoticism, which invested such categories as 'wonder' and 'marvel' with new meaning."[4] Likewise, Benjamin Schmidt has noted that prints from the Low Countries in the later sixteenth century and into the seventeenth "celebrate[d] that which is new in America: that which had been foreign, strange, and unknown before it could be counted among the *nova reperta*."⁵ What Stephen Greenblatt describes as the "frequency and intensity of the appeal to wonder in the wake of the great geographical discoveries"⁶ thus grew stronger as the initial stages of the discoveries grew chronologically more distant.

This delight in things outside previous knowledge and common experience was then rendered intellectually productive through conceptualization and systematization. The new became subject to a "theoretical curiosity" that concentrated more on categorizing the new than on experiencing it.⁷ The *Wunderkammer* epitomized this trend. These collections incorporated objects brought back from the East and West Indies into a world-encompassing schema of knowledge defined by the categories of *naturalia* (works of nature), *artificia* (works of art), and *scientifica* (works of technology).⁸ The things that the travel narratives had stuffed into the category of novelties and exotica were now unpacked and arranged alongside other examples of the workings of nature and human artifice, in a microcosm of the world's variety. Crocodiles, Native American weapons and featherwork, and tortoiseshell and lacquer objects from the East were displayed, as were extensive collections of European art, clocks, corals, ancient statuary, and fossils.⁹ Only through such variety could the new and the strange, whether of natural or human origin, be assigned its proper place in the world's order. The conviction that the world was in fact ordered, its elements joined together in harmony by systems of correspondences that the cabinet of curiosity could make manifest to its initiates, was signaled in the regular architecture and the symbolic decor of display rooms.¹⁰ The category of difference, which Renaissance participants and observers had extended to the new territories, found institutional expression in the *Wunderkammer*.¹¹

Not surprisingly for an institution meant to reflect the magnificence and power of its owner, the *Wunderkammer* made the diversity of the world visible and comprehensible in order to control it.¹² Moreover, the progression from the discovery of nature (*naturalia*) to the crafting of nature (*artificia*) to the control of nature (*scientifica*) revealed that the potential for human mastery of nature had not yet been exhausted. The manipulation of nature was integral to the program of the *Wunderkammer*, from the removal of objects from their original environment to display them within artificial settings, to the fascination with artistic attempts to imitate nature, to the interest in elaborate machines. The culture of curiosities was thus linked to the culture of the experiment, a link explicitly recognized in Bacon's program for the advancement of knowledge, which featured a "goodly huge cabinet, wherein whatsoever the hand of man by exquisite art of engine hath made rare in stuff, form, or motion; whatsoever singularity chance and the shuffle of things hath produced; whatsoever nature hath wrought in things that want life and may be kept; shall be sorted and included," and, equally significantly, a laboratory for the further investigation of nature.[13] Experience was now produced under carefully controlled conditions, in addition to being gathered through observation in natural settings. In either case, the advancement of knowledge, rather than its confirmation, had become a scholarly requirement. The "new models to explain a perplexing, increasingly expansive, and pluralistic universe" that began flying out of scholars' imaginations and onto the printed page reveal both delight in examining the world's potential and conviction that it could eventually be systematized.[14]

Renaissance German assessments of the Spanish and Portuguese expeditions help explain the development of this new approach to nature. First, they dispel the idea that Europeans were simply reacting to the inherent novelty and alterity of the New World. The new experimental philosophy did not discover the idea of novelty; it repurposed it for its own agenda. Moreover, no drastic change in empirical conditions forced the new more vigorously on the European consciousness as the sixteenth century drew to a close. Europeans confronted no unimaginable forms of market exchange, no tropical heat in the northern seas, and no un-Adamic extraterrestrials. In this respect, what Wolfgang Neuber postulated for the strange can be applied with equal force to the new: "The strange [new] cannot become reality any way other than in categories of the familiar. Strange [new] things are only permitted, in truth constituted, when a need for alterity [novelty] is present in one's own cultural context."[15] Just because European observers *could* classify aspects of the discoveries as new or strange did not mean that they necessarily *would*. Just because European observers could define the new and strange as essential elements in the investigation of nature does not mean they necessarily would.

The new philosophy could feature an intense and fruitful concern with the new and the strange in part, I would suggest, because the successful incorporation of the European expansion during the Renaissance made the new investigators of nature confident of their ability to master the world even (or especially) in the face of increasing variety.

The plausible application of the existing techniques of European travel, navigation, commerce, and moral investigation had made the discoveries real for audiences at home and opened the newly discovered lands and peoples to continued investigation and categorization within European structures of thought. The successful incorporation had even commodified the wonders of the Indies, which were cataloged, bought and sold, and valued in Baroque scientific culture as relics had been before them.[16] These philosophical and commercial transactions tied together the world in a system of manifest correspondences, an exoteric harmony to go with the more esoteric and occult order that underlay the *Wunderkammer*.[17] Therefore, even as existing intellectual frameworks were reworked and rebuilt in the centuries following the Iberian expansion, the presumption of their worldwide applicability remained. Subsequent interpretations of the territories reached by the Portuguese and Spanish expeditions (and French, English, and Dutch ones) began with the discoveries chewed, swallowed, and digested. All new explanations and classifications of natural phenomena were based on the assumption that Europeans could make sense of the entire world, even if their efforts were as yet incomplete. Europeans were eventually cognitively able to express doubts about the reliability of existing intellectual structures, and delight at objects and ideas that seemed to transgress them, because of their initial success at deploying these same structures.[18]

In addition to providing what perhaps can best be described as psychological comfort, the old systems in certain circumstances provided something far more tangible: hard data. The three early modern disciplines that Mary Poovey, in her *History of the Modern Fact*, identifies as producers of "facts," which where characterized by their ability to "simultaneously describe discrete particulars *and* contribute to systematic knowledge," were front and center in Germany's response to the discoveries: astronomy, botany, and merchant accounting.[19] All three disciplines produced usable bricks from which to build new edifices. An example from cosmography illustrates this process. At the end of the sixteenth century, when the cosmographical initiative had shifted from Germany to the Low Countries, the Netherlandish mapmaker Gerhard Mercator produced two major milestones in the history of cartographical publishing: the 1578 deluxe edition of the maps of Ptolemy's *Geography* (to be followed later by an edition of the entire text) and the famous *Atlas,* a *separate* set of *tabulae modernae,* the first volumes of which were issued in 1585. Modern scholars have seen in the separation of the Ptolemaic and the modern maps a declaration of independence from the classical tradition, but these publications in fact reveal Mercator's continuing debt to ancient knowledge.[20] The landmark characteristic of the *Atlas* was not its modern maps (which had accompanied editions of Ptolemy since the fifteenth century) nor their separation from a Ptolemaic setting (which Abraham Ortelius had already accomplished with his *Theatrum Orbis Terrarum*), but its provision of a substantial set of latitude and longitude listings along with systematically designed and calibrated maps.[21] Mercator was able to separate the *Atlas* from the *Geography* because he could now finally cobble together a *Geography* for his time.[22] Moreover, the updated information Mercator provided his readers was good, old-fashioned latitude and longitude measurements, achieved through good, old-fashioned techniques.[23] The complete data set that made possible Mercator's independence from Ptolemy was therefore based on the principles of Ptolemaic cosmography. The success of Mercator's *Atlas* demonstrates how the old made possible the new.

While my argument reconfigures the relationship between European intellectual changes and the extra-European world, the link remains essential. Europe had not developed in isolation—a point demonstrated by the importance of Mediterranean commercial and intellectual exchange in creating the flexibility and nuance of Renaissance knowledge practices. As the exchange of peoples, customs, and goods expanded, Europe's global connections were instrumental in changing political, scientific, economic, social, and even dietary practices, at home as well as abroad. To argue, as I have, that the newly discovered lands and peoples were made to fit within established conceptions is not to suggest that their long-term implications could be easily confined or minimized. The expansion of Europe ultimately proved transformative for all involved, but this transformation was itself influenced by the situations and demands facing those Europeans responsible for weighing, translating, disseminating, and acting on the European expansion. The study of cross-cultural exchange and conflict must be extended to include the intracultural.

When the Germans successfully explained the Iberian discoveries to themselves on their own (occasionally contradictory) terms, they were on the one hand minding their own scholarly, political, religious, and commercial concerns, and on the other hand contributing to a supra-regional discussion of the issues the discoveries raised. To what extent the German answers to the questions raised by the overseas expansion reflected or influenced European-wide patterns is a question best answered in definitive form by other historians. I have identified, however, some possible linkages to the historiography of other countries and of Europe as a whole. More than anything, the history of Germany's initial involvement with the Renaissance discoveries reveals the actors and processes that worked to turn the unwieldy mass of details about the haphazard, undisciplined, and hard-fought European expansion into a compelling story of European mastery and control.

Notes

ABBREVIATIONS

BHSA	Bayerisches Hauptstaatsarchiv, Munich
BSB	Bayerische Staatsbibliothek, Munich
FA	Fugger Archiv, Dillingen an der Donau
GNM	Germanisches Nationalmuseum, Nuremberg
HAB	Herzog-August-Bibliothek, Wolfenbüttel
IG	Borm, *Incunabula Guelferbytana*
RKG	Reichskammergerichtsakten
StadtAA	Stadtarchiv Augsburg
StadtAN	Stadtarchiv Nürnberg
STAN	Staatsarchiv Nürnberg
Statbibl. N.	Stadtbibliothek Nürnberg
SuStBA	Staats- und Stadtbibliothek Augsburg
VD 16	Bayerische Staatsbibliothek, *Verzeichnis der im deutschen Sprachbereich erscheinenen Drucke des XVI. Jahrhunderts.*

INTRODUCTION

1. The classic text is Elliott, *Old World and the New.*

2. The sense of Europe as an integrated cultural area was still developing in the fifteenth century, receiving additional impetus from the rise of Otto-man power, which encouraged the definition of a "Europe" in opposition to this new "Asian" power. See Bisaha, *Creating East and West*, 83–87. In my use

of the term "European," I do not mean to imply that the boundaries of this region, which included both Germany and the colonizing Iberian powers, were natural. I am simply acknowledging the existence of commonalities—including the suprastructure of the organization and beliefs of the Roman Catholic Church; the use of Latin by the educated classes; and more general political, intellectual, and economic ties fostered by geographical proximity, shared political concerns, and intellectual borrowings—that made representations of the discoveries mutually intelligible.

3. Pagden, *European Encounters with the New World,* 22, 36.

4. Major works exploring this theme include Greenblatt, *Marvelous Possessions;* Campbell, *Witness and the Other World;* Mignolo, *Darker Side of the Renaissance;* Certeau, *Writing of History.*

5. Phillips, "Outer World of the European Middle Ages," 62.

6. The comparison is drawn from Pagden, *Fall of Natural Man,* 11.

7. My understanding of knowledge acknowledges both its social construction and its claim to correspond to a verifiable external reality; see Shapin, *Social History of Truth,* chap. 1.

8. Said, *Orientalism,* 12.

9. For these shared characteristics, see Christine R. Johnson, "Bringing the World Home," 9–15.

10. See Jardine, *Worldly Goods.*

11. The phrase "imagined community" is drawn from Anderson, *Imagined Communities.* For this outline of the meaning of "Germany," I have most heavily relied on the connotations of "German" I have gleaned from the sources themselves. For useful overviews, see Silver, "Germanic Patriotism in the Age of Dürer"; Scales, "Late Medieval Germany"; Schnell, "Deutsche Literatur und deutsches Nationalbewußtsein."

12. Because the Imperial Court was highly mobile, multilingual, and only partially connected linguistically and culturally with Germany on the international scene, I have excluded it from consideration. I have included relevant material published in the Habsburg lands where appropriate.

13. In general, these more involved definitions of Germany narrowed the area being discussed to the confines of the German linguistic sphere. For minor exceptions, see Christine R. Johnson, "Bringing the World Home," 5 n.8.

14. Spitz, "Course of German Humanism," 392–97.

15. Stadtwald, *Roman Popes and German Patriots,* 61.

16. Even when the Italian model was followed, as was the case with German imitators of the *Italia illustrata,* the focus on local specifics automatically differentiated the result from the model. See Gerald Strauss, *Sixteenth Century Germany,* 19.

17. For the importance of communication and supra-regional connections, see Sieber-Lehmann, *Spätmittelalterlicher Nationalismus,* 347–62.

18. Greenblatt, *Marvelous Possessions,* 12. Recent analyses of the Dutch and Venetian responses to the discovery of the New World have also made clear the importance of the immediate context. See Schmidt, *Innocence Abroad;* Hodorowich, "Armchair Travelers."

19. Acosta, *Natural and Moral History of the Indies,* 39.

20. Neuber, *Fremde Welt im europäischen Horizont,* 55–57. See also Pieper's study of the reports on the destruction of the Huguenot colony in Florida, *Vermittlung einer neuen Welt,* chap. 3.1.

21. Protestant Europe developed the infamous "Black Legend" of the Spanish conquests, which drew on the polemics of Bartolomé de las Casas and further tales of Spanish cruelty toward the native inhabitants (not to mention the French colonists in Florida) to create an image of Catholic tyranny, realized abroad and possible within Europe. For the Dutch case, see Schmidt, *Innocence Abroad,* 91–99. Catholic Europe, meanwhile, developed its own narrative of struggle and triumph, epitomized by chroniclers such as Laurentius Surius and the Jesuit letters penned on missions abroad. For the dissemination of Jesuit letters on India in Germany, see Dharampal-Frick, *Indien im Spiegel deutscher Quellen,* 87–88.

I. THERE AND BACK AGAIN: THE TRAVELERS' TALES

1. For more on the original Italian text, see Böhme, *Grosse Reisesammlungen,* 12–23.

2. The importance of networks has been extensively documented (and perhaps a bit overstated) by Pieper, *Vermittlung einer neuen Welt.* For more on these networks, see Carina Lee Johnson, "Negotiating the Exotic," 6–7; Christine R. Johnson, "Bringing the World Home," 26–27.

3. Recent estimates place the literacy rate for the south German cities at around 30 percent, and evidence suggests that books reached a broad range of the population, including journeymen and other laborers. See Künast, *"Getruckt zu Augspurg,"* 11–13; Chrisman, *Lay Culture, Learned Culture,* 68–75.

4. *Newe vnbekanthe landte,* sig. dvi r–v.

5. Ibid., sig. eiiii r.

6. Columbus's letter was first published in Germany as *De insulis inventis Epistola.* For further editions, see the bibliography.

7. Vespucci, *Mundus Novus.* For complete information, see the bibliography.

8. Vespucci, *Mundus Novus* (Augsburg, 1504). Vespucci's authorship of this letter is in serious doubt; see Gerbi, *Nature in the New World,* 36. However, for the sake of brevity, and because Vespucci was regarded as the author of the letter in the sixteenth century, I will refer to the author of this letter and of *Four Voyages,* discussed below, as "Amerigo Vespucci."

9. This letter was one of several published in Germany. For complete information, see the bibliography.

10. *Novus Orbis regionum* reprinted the Latin translation of *Paesi novamente ritrovati,* by Arcangelo Madrignano, first published as *Itinerarium Portugallensium.* See Böhme, *Grosse Reisesammlungen,* 51.

11. The first five printings of the text, all in Latin, were in conjunction with the *Cosmographiae introductio* of Martin Waldseemüller and Matthias Ringman. For further information, see the bibliography. As is the case with the *Mundus Novus* letter, the text is no longer considered to be by Vespucci, but by an unknown forger. See Gerbi, *Nature in the New World,* 45.

12. This text was an abridged version of the fourth *Decade of the New World* (d'Anghiera, *De nuper sub D. Carolo repertis insulis . . . enchiridion;* also published in conjunction with the Nuremberg edition of Cortes as *De rebus et insulis noviter repertis,* and subsequently with the first three complete *Decades,* in 1533 and 1574).

13. For more information, see Larner, *Marco Polo.*

14. Specifically, the *De Tartaris liber* of Haithonius Armenius, the *De Sarmatia asiana atque europeae* of Michow, the *De legatione Moschovitarum* of Paulo Giovio, the *De Borusiae antiquitatibus* of Erasmus Stella, and the *Locorum terrae sanctae exactissima desscriptio* of Brocard.

15. Transylvanus, *De Moluccis insulis.*

16. The news pamphlets were entitled *Newe zeittung, von dem lande* and *Eine schöne newe zeytung.*

17. See the bibliography for a complete listing.

18. See also Böhme, *Grosse Reisesammlungen,* 62.

19. d'Anghiera, *De rebus Oceanicis & Orbe nouo decades tres,* contains the first three *Decades* and the abbreviated fourth one, along with *De Legationis Babylonica Libri Tres.*

20. Cortes, *Von dem Newen Hispanien.*

21. For the importance of oral communication within Augsburg, see Häberlein, "Monster und Missionare," 356–57. For other German travelers to Iberia, see Pieper, *Vermittlung einer neuen Welt,* 26–27. For specific examples of this type of transmission, see Christine R. Johnson, "Bringing the World Home," 45–47. For two letters from George Geuder promising to send Willibald Pirckheimer news "de nouis Hispano[rum] nauigationib[us]" from Spain, see Stadtbibl. N., Pirckheimer Papiere, 415, nos. 5, 8. A summary of German travel narratives from the earliest Indian voyages is available in Pohle, *Deutschland und die überseeische Expansion Portugals,* 189–218.

22. Sprenger, *Merfart,* transcribed in Hümmerich, "Quellen und Untersuchungen," 104–26; Schmidel, *Neuwe Welt;* Federmann, *Indianische historia.* Hutten's text, actually a compilation of some of his letters, appeared as an addendum attributed to Oviedo in Cortes, *Von dem Newen Hispanien.*

23. *Warhaftige Historia.* For editions, see the bibliography.

24. Because the financial viability of German publishers depended on sales rather than patronage, most printers "printed what they believed to be in demand" (Hirsch, *Printing, Selling and Reading,* 23).

25. For an example of such intensive analysis, see the following on the writings of Christopher Columbus: Pagden, *European Encounters with the New World,* chap. 1; Zamora, *Reading Columbus;* Flint, *Imaginative Landscape,* part 2; Greenblatt, *Marvelous Possessions,* chap. 3.

26. The use of these categories for exertions of imperial ambitions and control was established by Said, *Orientalism.* This model has also been applied to Renaissance texts: see, e.g., Islam, *Ethics of Travel;* Gerbi, *Nature in the New World,* 5. See also Greenblatt, *Marvelous Possessions.*

27. This analysis owes much to literary scholars, e.g., Barbara Fuchs, *Mimesis and Empire;* Fuller, *Voyages in Print;* Hadfield, *Literature, Travel, and Colonial Writing.* Historians have also noted the mixed messages about power and difference in these texts, e.g., Rubiés, *Travel and Ethnology in the Renaissance* and "Futility in the New World"; Grafton, *New Worlds, Ancient Texts.*

28. While lavish illustrated volumes could cost more than most Germans made in a year, pamphlets were sold for less than the average daily wage of a laborer. For general information about prices and wages, see Künast, *"Getruckt zu Augspurg,"* 185–96.

29. Later English accounts of exploration and encounter in North America, as Chaplin and Kupperman have argued, operated in multiple registers of similarity and difference, both of which were crucial for English negotiation and self-representation in this new landscape. See Chaplin, *Subject Matter;* Kupperman, *Indians and English.*

30. I take the term "paratexts" from Genette, *Paratexts* (I am indebted to Jonathan Rose for this reference). Genette's fundamental insight is that these supplementary materials are designed to control meaning (407). For competing themes in prefaces and texts, see also Schmidt, *Innocence Abroad,* 159. Paratexts, especially prefatory material, are also an important source base for Hart, *Representing the New World,* a study of English and French attitudes toward the Spanish Empire, and for Binotti, "Cultural Identity and the Ideologies of Translation."

31. Readers presumably did not always pay attention to such guidance, but two factors make paratexts especially valuable sources for understanding how German readers were likely to approach these texts. First, paratexts were immediately connected to the original texts, providing direct implicit and explicit commentary. Second, the commercial interests of German publishers meant that they tried to make the paratexts as persuasive to potential buyers as possible, thereby allowing a crude form of market research.

32. Travel narratives were often explicitly written as letters, as in the case of Columbus's *Letter to Santangel,* Cortes's letters from Mexico, and the merchants' letters in *Newe vnbekanthe landte,* or addressed to readers through

a prefatory letter, thus relying on epistolary conventions that stressed effective communication. Rhetorical training assigned particular value to making the unknown familiar to the intended audience. See Fitzmaurice, *Humanism and America*, 112–16. Of course, the travelers' experiences themselves were not naive sensory impressions, but likewise constructs. See Joan W. Scott, "Experience."

33. Harbsmeier, *Wilde Völkerkunde*, 19. Authors who recorded the experiences of others, such as d'Anghiera and Transylvanus, also shared in this prestige as privileged presenters of the story and shaped their accounts accordingly.

34. For analysis of the importance of movement to these accounts, see Zamora, *Reading Columbus*, 96–97; Kiening, "Ordnung der Fremde," 74–75.

35. Transylvanus, *De Moluccis*, sig. Aiiii r, Bvii r–v.

36. "Reise des Vasco de Gama," in Greiff, "Briefe und Berichte . . . aus Dr. Conrad Peutingers Nachlaß," 127–28.

37. See also Kiening, "Ordnung der Fremde," 88.

38. Polo, *Travels*, 251.

39. For example: "Darnach trug sy ein wind in das möre an ein statt" (*Sankt Brandans Seefahrt*, unpaginated). According to *VD 16*, *Sankt Brandans Seefahrt* was published eleven times between 1500 and 1521, principally in Augsburg, Strassburg, and Erfurt.

40. Mandeville, *Von der erfarüng des strengen Ritters*, sig. Giiii v. The Diemeringen translation cited here varies in certain respects from the Velser translation, but the basic elements discussed above remain the same, including the treatments of the Indies, the Teufelstal, and the Earthly Paradise. For a discussion of these translations and facsimiles of their first published editions, see Bremer and Ridder, *Jean de Mandeville. Reisen.* The Latin version, *Incipit Itinerarius Johannis de Montevilla,* contains significantly more cosmographical discussion. An excellent guide to these three (and other) versions can be found in Higgins, *Writing East.*

41. Mandeville, *Von der erfarüng des strengen Ritters*, sig. Mi r.

42. Ibid., sig. Kiv r. Cf. Sir Walter Ralegh's description of his journey into Guiana, an expedition that failed to find the fabled El Dorado. Skillfully analyzed by Mary Fuller as a text full of divergences, distances, and displacements, the *Discoverie of . . . Guiana* is also noteworthy for its insistence on successful, if arduous, travel, both achieved and planned. The defining feature of Ralegh's travel is therefore not its ease, but his ability to overcome seemingly limitless barriers to achieve the desired goal. See Fuller, *Voyages in Print,* chap. 2; Ralegh, *Discoverie of . . . Guiana.*

43. Mandeville, *Von der erfärung des strengen Ritters*, sig. Liii r.

44. For the widespread publication of certain chivalric texts, see Müller, "Augsburger Drucker von Prosaromanen," 342–43.

45. *Die Mörin,* fol. IIr.

46. This approach to space, as Padrón has demonstrated in *Spacious Word,* was different from the geometrical abstractions of Renaissance cartography that have long been credited with the extension of European control. Nevertheless, this linear travel was also a performance of mastery.

47. Thus, the many studies demonstrating that explorers arrived with a catalog of expectations that they used in deciphering landscapes and cultures tell only half the story. See, e.g., Grafton, *New Worlds, Ancient Texts,* chaps. 1–2; Flint, *Imaginative Landscape,* chap. 4.

48. See Jennifer Goodman, *Chivalry and Exploration;* Briesemeister, "Frühe Berichte," 248; Daston and Park, *Wonders and the Order of Nature,* 33.

49. The entire battle is narrated in "Capitel von der rüstung vnd des kriegs volck des künigs zu Calicut," in Varthema, *Ritterlich und lobwirdig Rayss* (facsimile), sig. riiii r–sii v.

50. Federmann, *Indianische Historia,* fol. Bii v.

51. Varthema, *Ritterlich und lobwirdig rayss,* sig. ai v.

52. This point is thoroughly and convincingly developed in Kiening, *Das wilde Subjekt,* chap. 3.

53. Pagden, *European Encounters with the New World,* 3.

54. Vespucci, *Von der new gefunnden Region,* sig. Aii r.

55. The generic nature of these images is made clear by their use in different texts. For example, the images on the title page of *De ora antarctica,* a Strassburg edition of the *Mundus Novus* letter, show a group of naked men walking in a hilly landscape and a sea filled with five ships loaded with people. These images bear a striking resemblance to those from an edition of *Navigatio Sancti Brandani* that was published in Augsburg in 1476. See Kohl, "Über einige der frühesten graphischen Darstellungen," 315. For another example, see Neuber, "'Garriebat philomena,'" 129.

56. Piccolomini's works are cataloged under his papal name: see Pius II, *Asiae Europaeque elegantiss. descriptio;* Boemus, *Omnium Gentium Mores.*

57. *Chronica* (ed. Egenolff); Franck, *Weltbuch;* Münster, *Cosmographia.* For information on Münster, see Geiger, "Münster, Sebastian M."

58. Feyerabend, *Erst* and *Ander theil dieses Weltbuchs.* Castanheda's text was first published as *Warhafftige vnd volkomen Historia.*

59. Lorenzo Valla's Latin translation of Herodotus was published in 1537 as *Herodoti Halicarnassei Historiographi Libri Novem.* An abridged German translation was also published: *[V]on dem Persier.* While removing much ethnographic material, this edition still contained descriptions of human variety, including some of the information about the Scythians. For more on this translation, see Gottlieb, *Europa in der Defensive,* 22 (for omissions).

60. A complete Latin edition of Pliny was published in 1523: *C. Plinii Secundi Naturalis Historiae opus* (Cologne: Eucharius Cerncornus). In 1543 a German translation of books 7–11, covering the "Menschen vnd Völcker wunderbarlichen gestalten," as well as animals, fish, and birds, was published as *Natürlicher History Fünff Bücher*, translated by Heinrich von Eppendorff. A later German edition of the same material, based in part on Eppendorff's translation, also included extensive interpolations from Gesner, Mattioli, and other investigators of nature, as well as addendums from the Scriptures and the Church Fathers, in addition to several brief passages derived from Varthema and d'Anghiera: see *Bücher vnd schrifften/von der Natur*. For the ancient tradition of marvels, see Romm, *Edges of the Earth in Ancient Thought*, chap. 3. For a catalog of the Plinian races, see Friedman, *Monstrous Races*, 9–21.

61. After numerous Italian Latin editions, Solinus's text was published in Germany as [*D*]*e Memorabilibus Mundi*; it then enjoyed several reissues bound with Pomponius Mela's *De Situ Orbis*. See, e.g., Solinus, *Rerum Toto Orbe Memorabilium*.

62. For the eclipsing of medieval sources by classical authorities, see Klaus A. Vogel, "Cultural Variety in a Renaissance Perspective," 19–20.

63. Following Portuguese contact with the Ethiopian ruler identified as Prester John, an Ethiopian embassy was sent to Pope Clement VII and described in *Bottschaft des groszmechtigen Konigs Dauid*.

64. For the medieval history of the Alexander legend, see Cary, *Medieval Alexander*. Renaissance German editions include *Historia Alexandri magni regis macedonie de preliis*, published in Strassburg in 1489, and Johann Hartlieb's German translation, *Das buch der geschicht des grossen allexanders* (Strassburg: M. Schott, 1487).

65. For a mid-fifteenth-century humanist text that recognizes and encompasses these changes, see Pius II, *Asiae Europaeque elegantiss. descriptio*.

66. Münster, *Cosmographia* (Basel: H. Petri, 1545), dcclv–dcclxi. (All references are to this edition, unless otherwise stated.)

67. For the broad cultural meaning of marvels, see Daston and Park, *Wonders and the Order of Nature*.

68. StadtAN, Familien-Archiv (FA) Behaim, E11/II, Nr. 585.

69. Pieper, *Vermittlung einer neuen Welt*, 276; Daston and Park, *Wonders and the Order of Nature*, 68–108.

70. Lach, *Asia in the Making of Europe*, 1: bk. 1, 167.

71. For New World parrots in Central Europe, see Pieper, *Vermittlung einer neuen Welt*, 251–53. Lucas Rem, the Welser factor in Portugal, also reported a brisk trade in "fremd niu papgey, [meer?]katzen, [und] ander seltzam lustig ding" (Greiff, "Tagebuch des Lucas Rem," 31).

72. Letter no. 48, "An Sebastian Brant. 1507 April 7. Augsburg," in Erich König, *Konrad Peutingers Briefwechsel*, 77–78.

73. Michael Behaim to Jörg Pock, Dec. 16, 1518, StadtAN, FA Behaim, E11/II, Nr. 582, Doc. 3.

74. StadtAN, FA Behaim, E11/II, Nr. 582, Doc. 12. In a letter from India (Cochin) dated Jan. 1, 1522, Pock in fact thanks Behaim for sending him news of the emperor's election, the latest on the wars in Eastern Europe, and a report about the "monk of Wittenberg" (transcribed in Georg Pock, "Der Nürnberger Kaufmann Georg Pock," 178–84, quote on p. 181).

75. For the importance of acquiring expertise, not just objects, see Findlen, *Possessing Nature*, 295. Dürer's 1515 woodcut was based on a sketch of the rhinoceros drawn by Valentin Fernandes. See Walter L. Strauss, *Complete Drawings of Albrecht Dürer*, 3: 1584.

76. Solinus, [D]e Memorabilibus Mundi, fol. XXv–XXIr.

77. Münster, *Cosmographia*, cclxx.

78. For analyses of the uses of "Othering" in travel reports (including the Othering of competing colonial powers), see Montrose, "Work of Gender"; Hartog, *Mirror of Herodotus*.

79. This comparison was enhanced by the world descriptions' practice of placing the ancient, medieval, and latest descriptions side by side. By the time the anthropophagites of the East Indies appeared in Münster's *Cosmographia*, the reader had already encountered Tartars who roasted their enemies and then tore at their flesh like wolves (dccxlvi) and Scythians who drank the blood of their foes and used their skulls for drinking goblets (dccxliii).

80. Ruchamer, *Newe vnbekanthe landte*, sig. ai v.

81. "Vorrede an den Leser" (translator's preface), in Castanheda, *Von erfindung Calecut*, sig.)(2 v.

82. For the importance of pamphlets to the culture of prodigies, see Daston and Park, *Wonders and the Order of Nature*, 181. Both *Mundus Novus* and the initial accounts of Cortes's expeditions appeared as pamphlets.

83. I take the term "familiarly strange" from Hulme, "Tales of Distinction," 170.

84. The text is derived from *Mundus Novus*. Vespucci, *Dise figur anzaigt vns das volck vnd insel*, reprinted in Colin, *Bild der Indianer*, 392. The woodcuts that accompanied the German translation of *Four Voyages* also stressed the nudity and anthropophagism of the natives.

85. Burgkmair's panorama was published once in 1508 and again in 1511, with altered illustrations and a shortened text. For further bibliographic details (including the 1541 edition), see Borowka-Clausberg, *Balthasar Sprenger,* esp. 33–44, 216–20. For a detailed discussion of the initial printings and their relationship to the text of Sprenger's *Merfahrt*, see McDonald, "Burgkmair's Woodcut Frieze."

86. Weiditz's book of drawings is preserved as GNM (Bibliothek) Hs 22474.

87. Leitch, "'Better than the Prodigies,'" chap. 3.

88. This failure to catalog has led many scholars to complain about the lack of discrimination and organization in the dissemination of information on other cultures by Renaissance German authors. See, e.g., Rubiés, "New Worlds and Renaissance Ethnology," 173; Hodgen, *Early Anthropology*, 146.

89. Polo, *Travels*, 255; Sprenger, qtd. in Hümmerich, "Quellen und Untersuchungen," 108.

90. *Newe zeittung, von dem lande*, sig. Aiii r.

91. For a summary of earlier concerns about curiosity, see Zacher, *Curiosity and Pilgrimage*, chap. 2; Nevins, "Literature of Curiosity," 4–6.

92. Brant, *Narrenschiff*, fol. XXXVIr. This theme is further developed (although without the direct reference to the new islands) in Johann Geiler von Kaisersberg's oft-reprinted Latin version of the *Narrenschiff: Navicula sive speculum fatuorum*, sig. Zr. A German translation of Kaisersberg's work was also published (also entitled *Narrenschiff*), with the relevant passage on fol. CLXXXIIIr.

93. On the religious basis for the value of curiosity and wonder, see Nevins, "Literature of Curiosity," 9.

94. Schedel, *Liber chronicarum*, Blat XIv.

95. Ruchamer, *Newe vnbekanthe landte*, sig. ai v.

96. Simon Schwartz, dedication letter, BSB Cgm. 935, fol. 2v–3r.

97. Friedman describes such ecumenical attitudes for the medieval period (*Monstrous Races*, 59).

98. Franck, *Weltbuch*, sig. aiv v. For Franck's "positive cultural comparison," see Carina Lee Johnson, "Negotiating the Exotic," 53–54; for the importance of curiosity to Franck, see Müller, "Alte Wissensformen und neue Erfahrungen," 175.

99. Münster, *Cosmographia*, dcccxvii–dcccxviii.

100. Daston and Park, *Wonders and the Order of Nature*, 11.

101. Nevins, "Literature of Curiosity," 13–14.

102. "Vorrede an den Leser," in Castanheda, *Von erfindung Calecut*, sig.)(3v–)(4v.

103. "Vorrede," in *Chronica*, sig. aii r.

104. Betuleius and Diether, dedication letter, in Cortes, *Von dem Newen Hispanien*, sig. ii v. Betuleius and Diether's ignorance of Cortes's disobedience and rebellion indicates how dependent German commentators were on these travel narratives for their understanding of the discoveries.

105. Herr, dedication letter, in Herr, *Die New Welt*, fol. *iii r–*iiii v.

106. Ibid., fol. *iiii r.

107. d'Anghiera, *De Rebus et Insulis Noviter Repertis* (1524), fol. IIIIr. Along with a few exhortations for German Lutherans to imitate the faithfulness of the new converts to the Catholic Church (see n. 108), these asides consti-

tute the main points of intersection between the Reformation debate and the travel accounts in these early years.

108. The comparison between the simple Indians and the luxury-loving Germans is found in Herr, dedication letter, in Herr, *Die New Welt,* sig. *v r. See also the "Interpres" of the *Bottschafft des groszmechtigsten Konigs David,* sig. fiij v–fiv v, which used both the report of Prester John and the subsequent brief account of conversion activities in Mexico to argue that the pope was gaining many more followers than the ones he was losing in Germany, thereby equating believers at home with believers abroad.

109. See Pagden, *Fall of Natural Man.*

110. Münster, *Cosmographia,* ccix. One noticeable difference between early descriptions of the native inhabitants of the Caribbean and those of the Germanic tribes concerns the sexual honor of the women.

111. Leitch, "'Better than the Prodigies,'" chap. 2.

112. Chaplin, *Subject Matter,* 96; Kupperman, *Indians and English,* chap. 3.

113. While the word "barbarian" appears in reprinted or translated texts, such as those of d'Anghiera, German commentators used words such as "inhabitants" to refer to native peoples. See Campbell, *Wonder and Science,* 45, for Thevet's comparisons between native Americans and early European inhabitants.

114. *De Exequiis Caroli V,* sig. Kiii v.

115. Peter Apian judiciously chose to mention Charles's role in bringing Christianity to the natives in the Latin version of the *Astronomicum Caesareum,* where he describes the "Iucatan" as an island "auspiciis diuis CAROLI inuenta ad Christianae fidei sanctimoniam conuersa" (fol. LIIIIv), while omitting this reference in the German version: "Jucatan ain Insel im Spanischen mehr gegen Nidergang gelegen" (sig. Diii v).

116. "Vorrede an den Leser," sig.)(5v–)(6r.

117. Dedication letter, in Feyerabend, *Ander theil dieses Weltbuchs von Schiffahrten,* sig.)(ii v. Feyerabend does rejoice that Peru was discovered by Christians, but for the very crucial reason that this would strengthen their hand against the Turks (sig.)(iii v–)(iiii r.)

118. Daston and Park, *Wonders and the Order of Nature,* chap. 5.

119. This analysis slightly reframes Pagden's insight that "colonization . . . forced the 'savage' and the 'barbarian,' and with them the problem of the intelligibility of other worlds, fully upon the European consciousness" (*European Encounters with the New World,* 13). I would argue that it was colonization that invented the problem of the savage and the barbarian.

120. Handwritten commercial and diplomatic dispatches were always more immediate and accurate sources of news than were printed accounts. See Pieper, *Vermittlung einer neuen Welt.*

121. For the completed translations, see BSB Cgm. 935, 936, 937, 951.

122. Two translations of texts not otherwise available in German are found in the Bayerische Staatsbibliothek, both by Hieronymus Seitz of Augsburg, dated 1530: (1) a translation of Duarte Barbosa's text, with additional material (BSB Cgm. 934); and (2) a translation of the second, third, and fourth of Cortes's letters from Mexico, along with reports from Pedro de Alvarado and Diego Godoy (BSB Cgm 952). These texts were published as a group in Toledo (1525) and Valencia (1526), before being included in Ramusio's collection. See Parks, "Contents and Sources," 29–30.

123. An appendix in Cortes, *Von dem Newen Hispanien,* is attributed to Oviedo, and the second part is in fact his letter recounting Orellana's discovery of the Amazon. However, the first part of the appendix, also attributed to Oviedo, is comprised of abbreviated versions of some of Philipp von Hutten's letters. Both of these sources were added by the translators of this 1550 Augsburg edition, apparently received from high-ranking attendees of the 1548 Diet of Augsburg. See *Von dem Newen Hispanien,* fol LIr; Menninger, *Macht der Augenzeugen,* 65–66. Konrad Peutinger seems to have been the source for a German translation of the first few paragraphs of Oviedo's *De la natural hystoria de las Indias* (Toledo, 1526), now among the Pirckheimer papers (no. 137) in the Stadtbibliothek, Nürnberg. A note states that this is a copy of a document originally found in Peutinger's *Nachlass.*

124. The absence of these last three texts is all the more noticeable because they flew off the presses in the neighboring Netherlands (Schmidt, *Innocence Abroad,* 27–28). It is of course important, as Künast has stressed, not to assume that a text had to be published in Germany in order to be known and read there (*"Getruckt zu Augspurg,"* 18–19). However, a glance at a few book inventories and the sources mentioned and consulted by the wide range of German commentators discussed in this and subsequent chapters reveals that material published elsewhere was not widely read, nor were its contents familiar to many (if any) Germans. The library inventory of Hieronymus Imhoff (1571), while frustratingly listing two unspecified "Cosmographia," does identify the "Cosmographia Munsteri," but contains no entries for travel narratives (GNM, Imhoff-Archiv, Fasc. 41/3b). See also the library inventory of Gabriel Muffel, compiled in 1570, which likewise just lists a "Cosmograuia Munsteri" (GNM, Imhoff-Archiv, Fasc. II/41a), and that of Paulus Behaim (StadtAN, FA Behaim, EII/II, Nr. 613/I), which lists the ubiquitous Münster, as well as a book on the Turks and Muscovites and Sleidanus's chronicle. The library catalog of Hans Sachs, compiled in 1562, lists some old favorites—St. Brendan, the *Nuremberg Chronicle,* Varthema, and Franck's *Weltbuch*—but no identifiable travel literature of non-German origin. See Goedeke, "Büchersammlung des Hans Sachs," 1–6.

125. These examples are taken from Zárate's *History of the Discovery and Conquest of Peru,* published six times before 1580. See the facsimile of the English translation (1581), pp. 15 (*quippu*), 40 (human sacrifice), 46 (the In-

can highway system), and 81 (the death of Atahualpa). Dietrich Briesemeister attributes the decline in interest between the conquest of Mexico and that of Peru to the European crises of the Reformation and Turkish threats, but this suggestion does not explain why currently existing travel accounts were steadily reprinted, nor why publishers were unwilling to invest in new texts that were clearly popular in Italy and the Netherlands, despite wars and religious upheavals in these regions ("Frühe Berichte," 253). Brief accounts of the Peruvian conquest did circulate; see *Copey etlicher brieff, so auß Hispania kummen seindt; Newe zeytung aus Hispanien und Italien.*

2. PLOTTING THE DISCOVERIES: THE COSMOGRAPHIES

1. Waldseemüller and Ringmann, *Cosmographiae introductio,* sig. Aiii v. All references to this work are taken from the 1966 Readex reprint of the Apr. 25, 1507, edition, corresponding to entry 507/10, in Alden, *European Americana,* 11. This edition begins new pagination with the *Four Voyages* text.

2. While Renaissance writers consistently distinguished between mathematical geography and descriptive geography, the nomenclature was somewhat less stable. Following the highly influential *Cosmographicus liber* of Peter Apian, I will use "cosmography" consistently in this chapter to refer to a mathematically based system for measuring the earth.

3. For a discussion of the attribution of this text, see Christine R. Johnson, "Renaissance German Cosmographers," 10–11.

4. The legends, like most of the elements on the *Mercarthen,* were taken from Martin Waldseemüller's 1516 *Carta Marina.* The *Mercarthen* and the *Carta Marina* are reproduced in Shirley, *Mapping of the World,* plates 53 and 43.

5. Fries, *Uslegung der Mercarthen.*

6. Ibid., fol. iii r. All references are to the 1525 edition.

7. The terms are Grafton's (*New Worlds, Ancient Texts,* 5).

8. Zerubavel, *Terra Cognita,* 7–8. See also Chaplin, *Subject Matter,* 17.

9. O'Gorman, *Invention of America,* 128.

10. Relaño, *Shaping of Africa,* 40.

11. See, e.g., Vivanti, "Humanisten und die geographischen Entdeckungen," 283; Berrera-Osorio, "Local Herbs, Global Medicines," 164.

12. Grafton, *New Worlds, Ancient Texts,* 10. For more on the malleability of the classical tradition, see Romm, "New World and 'Novos Orbes,'"; Wuttke, "Humanismus in den deutschsprachigen Ländern."

13. Among the many discussions, see Harley, "Maps, Knowledge, and Power."

14. Some of the many examples include Raman, *Framing "India,"* chap. 3; Klein, *Maps and the Writing of Space,* 92; Schmidt, "Mapping an Empire"; Koch, "Ruling the World."

15. The most striking example of the ideological use of maps is the "four continents' image," in which Europe is portrayed as technologically advanced and civilized, while Asia, Africa, and America are portrayed with varying degrees of natural wealth and barbaric savagery. Such maps are discussed in Gillies, *Shakespeare and the Geography of Difference*, 179–82, with an example on plate 16; Mignolo, *Darker Side of the Renaissance*, 273–81, with an example in fig. 6.11.

16. Boelhower, "Inventing America," 211.

17. The one notable exception is Edwards, "How to Read an Early Modern Map," which, however, concentrates on the deployment of tropes of mathematical certainty, rather than on the creation of these tropes.

18. The *quadrivium* consisted of astronomy, arithmetic, geometry, and music.

19. Apian, *Cosmographicus liber*, Col. 1.

20. The circles were divided into two groups: the "major circles," which divide the globe into two equal parts, and the "minor circles," which circle the globe without dividing it symmetrically.

There are six major circles. Two (*meridian* and *horizon*) are dependent on the viewer's position. The *equator* is the line that the sun's rays strike at a perpendicular angle twice a year on the equinoxes, when day and night are of equal length on all parts of the globe. The *ecliptic* lies at an angle to the equator and traces the sun's yearly path across the earth's surface through the zodiac, a series of twelve stellar constellations (from Aries to Pisces). The ecliptic crosses the equator in Aries and Libra, for the sun is in those signs when its rays are perpendicular to the equator, and it reaches its furthest extent from the equator when the sun is in Cancer and Capricorn. The *colures* are two meridians drawn through both the Arctic and the Antarctic poles, perpendicular to the equator and to each other. One crosses the equator at the points parallel to the signs of Capricorn and Cancer on the ecliptic, the other at the points where the ecliptic crosses the equator. The *horizon* is the hemisphere drawn with a desired position at the center. For an observer at one of the poles, therefore, the horizon would be the equator.

There are four minor circles. The *Tropic of Cancer* is the furthest northward extent of the sun's path and sits 23½° north of the equator. The *Tropic of Capricorn* is the furthest southward extent of the sun's path and sits 23½° south of the equator. The distance of the *Arctic Circle* and the *Antarctic Circle* from the North Pole and the South Pole, respectively, is described by the variation between the equatorial poles and the ecliptical ones.

21. The length of each day along the same line of latitude is precisely the same, and references to latitude were often couched in terms of the length of the longest day of the year. All points along the same line of longitude, meanwhile, experience noon (the point at which the sun reaches its highest point

above the horizon) at the same instant (hence the other name for these lines: meridians). The interval between two lines of longitude can be established by determining the time of a celestial event observable in both places, such as a solar eclipse, relative to local noon. The difference in time would establish longitudinal variation.

22. The armillary sphere shown in figure 1 indicates the equator, the Arctic and Antarctic Circles, the Tropics of Cancer and Capricorn, the horizon, and the two colures. The armillary sphere was simply one of a number of visual aids used by cosmographers; texts featured numerous diagrams illustrating cosmographical concepts. For the importance of visual diagrams in these texts, see Broecke, "Use of Visual Media in Renaissance Cosmography," 131–50.

23. Klaus A. Vogel, "Neue Horizonte der Kosmographie," 77–85.

24. Regiomontanus's teacher at the University of Vienna, Georg Peuerbach, was one of a series of prominent scholars on the faculty, including Peuerbach's predecessor, Johann Gmunden, and Collimitus (Georg Tannstetter). For the reputation of the University of Vienna astronomers, see Rose, *Italian Renaissance of Mathematics,* 91–92. For Peuerbach and Regiomontanus specifically, see Evans, *History and Practice of Ancient Astronomy,* 401–3. Other noted University of Vienna graduates include Joachim Vadianus and Johann Honter.

25. Regiomontanus planned a complete publishing program, including Ptolemy's *Geography* and *Almagest,* Proclus, Euclid, Archimedes, Apollonius's *Conica,* and Hero's *Pneumatica.* Regiomontanus died a few years after arriving in Nuremberg, however, and so completed only a small portion of his printing program. A student, Bernhard Walther, continued his observations of the heavens, and a later cosmographer, Johann Schöner, continued his publishing program. See Rose, *Italian Renaissance of Mathematics,* 104–9.

26. An exchange between the Nuremberg merchant Stephan Gabler and the Lisbon publisher Valentin Fernandes illustrates the division of labor. While Fernandes offered to send Gabler all the latest information from India, he asked in return for an astrolabe; for a copy of Pierre d'Ailly's (Petrus de elyaco) *Imago Mundi;* and, most significantly, for Gabler to check with a learned man about a new and corrected edition of Ptolemy. See GNM, Reichsstadt Nürnberg, XI (Handel u. Industrie), 1d, "Schreiben des Valentin Fernandez in Lissabon an Stephan Gabler, Kaufmann zu Nurnberg, Lissabon, den 26. Juni 1510."

27. For the institutional boost humanism gave astronomy, see Westman, "Astronomer's Role," 120; for mathematics generally, see Rose, *Italian Renaissance of Mathematics,* 292.

28. Certain aspects of Ptolemy's thought had been transmitted to the medieval audience, with much of the impetus for the continued investigation

stemming from Arab initative and influence (Durand, *Vienna-Klosterneuburg Map Corpus*).

29. For the history of this initial, risky publication, see Tedeschi, "Publish and Perish." In the sixteenth century German publishers turned Ptolemy's *Geography* into a thriving business. For a complete listing, see the bibliography.

30. For a full consideration of whether the maps were part of the original Ptolemaic corpus, see Berggren and Jones, "Introduction."

31. For a complete listing of Mela and Proclus Diadochus editions, see the bibliography.

32. On Pliny and his Renaissance commentators, see Eastwood, "Plinian Astronomy." For Renaissance Strabo editions, see the bibliography.

33. Claudius Ptolemaeus, *Opere . . . Nova translatio . . . Joanne Vernero . . . interpreti.*

34. For patterns in editing and commenting on ancient works, see Lattis, *Between Copernicus and Galileo,* 42–43.

35. See the preface in Cochlaeus, *Cosmographia Pomponii Mele,* sig. Ai v. For similiar defenses of the uses of cosmography, see Ptolemaeus, *Geographia universalis,* 158.

36. Waldseemüller, *Der welt kugel,* sig. Aii r.

37. This problem was not, of course, unique to Germany. See Flavio's concerns about matching ancient names with modern places in Italy (e.g., *Italy Illuminated,* 229–31).

38. Gerald Strauss, *Sixteenth Century Germany,* 10.

39. For Copernicus's views on the mathematical certainty of cosmography, see Westman, "Astronomer's Role," 109. For the certainty of cosmography compared to the uncertainty of geography, see Vadianus, *Pomponii Melae de orbis situ* (1557), fol. a3v–a4r.

40. The quote continues, "For its kind of proof proceeds by indisputable methods, namely arithmetic and geometry" (*Ptolemy's Almagest,* 36).

41. Hieronymus Gemusaeus's dedicatory letter, in Regiomantus and Peuerbach, *Epitome,* sig. a2v.

42. For the importance of astrology to medicine, see Siraisi, *Medieval and Early Renaissance Medicine,* 67–68, 135–36 (for "critical days").

43. See, e.g., *Natürlicher kunst der Astronomei;* Apian, *Ein kunstlich Instrument oder Sonnen vr.*

44. For an introduction and translation of the text, see Thorndike, *"Sphere" of Sacrobosco.* Philip Apian was still lecturing from the *Sphere* in 1560 (Christoph Schöner, *Mathematik und Astronomie,* 369).

45. Apian, *Cosmographiae Introductio.* The *Cosmographicus liber* itself circulated widely in Europe, after being annotated by the Louvain professor of mathematics Gemma Frisius. Most of the editions with additions by Frisius were published in Antwerp. However, the Heirs of A. Birckmann did publish

one edition of the annotated *Cosmographia* in 1574; Glareanus, *De geographia,* reprinted numerous times over the next twenty years; Peucer, *De dimensione terrae;* and Eisenmenger (Siderocrates), *Libellus geographicus.* Other texts written as introductory guides to the material include Cochlaeus's edition of Pomponius Mela; Rithaymer, *De Orbis Terrarum Situ Compendium;* Honter, *Rudimentorum cosmographiae libri duo,* which was transformed into verse form and reissued first as *Rudimenta cosmographica* and then as *Rudimentorum cosmographicorum . . . libri iii,* with numerous further editions through 1580; Neander, *Elementa sphaericae doctrinae.* For further information, see the bibliography.

46. Fischer, *Der "Deutsche Ptolemäus."*

47. See, e.g., Münster's discussion of the earth's circumference: "I don't know if you will believe me in these matters that I am going to write about the size of the Earth, if you don't have particular instruction in the noble art of mathematics. But it is enough for me, that among the learned there is no doubt in this matter." Münster then deigns to provide a quick version of the derivation, which seems out of place in one sense, given his prior assertion, but which fits perfectly with the cosmographical program as, indeed, the proof depends on mathematics. The result is a precise answer (5,400 German miles) to the (in fact highly debated) question of the earth's circumference. Although he explains the meaning of the Tropics, the only information Münster provides about the derivation of the Arctic and Antarctic Circles is that it is "too difficult for the common man to comprehend here" (*Cosmographia* [1545], v, ix).

48. Also see Waldseemüller, *Globus mundi,* and its German counterpart, published that same year, *Der welt kugel;* Apian, *Isagoge in typum cosmographicum,* and *Declaratio: et usus typi cosmographici Mappa mundi;* Fries, *Uslegung der Mercarthen,* with its Latin counterpart, *Hydrographiae, hoc est, Charta marinae;* Johann Schöner, *Luculentissima quaedam terrae totius descriptio, Appendices . . . in opusculum Globi astriferi, De nuper sub Castiliae ac Portugalliae regibus . . . repertis insulis ac regionibus* (intended to accompany the author's terrestrial globe showing Magellan's voyage), and *Opusculum geographicum* (produced to accompany another terrestrial globe). On Johann Schöner and globes, see Schultheiss, "Der fränkische Humanist," 17–18.

49. For the resiliency of Ptolemaic authority, see Dilke and Dilke, "Ptolemy's Geography and the New World," 277.

50. Edgerton, "From Mental Matrix to Mappamundi," 13, 36.

51. The exact number of degrees shown varied slightly from edition to edition. The first printed Ptolemaic map (Bologna, 1477) extended in the southern hemisphere only to the Tropic of Capricorn.

52. Lestringant, *Mapping the Renaissance World,* 8.

53. Grafton, *New Worlds, Ancient Texts,* 51, 54.

54. Ptolemaeus, *Clavdivs Ptolemaevs Cosmographia* (Ulm 1482), sig. h2r.

55. See, e.g., Johann Schöner, *Luculentissima quaedam terrae totius descriptio,* fol. Ir.

56. For a summary of Pirckheimer's (occasionally speculative) method, see Gerald Strauss, *Sixteenth Century Germany,* 39–40.

57. *De admirandis* is now considered a spurious composition of Aristotle (*Complete Works,* 2: 1292–93).

58. Pirckheimer, *Germaniae ex Variis Scriptoribus perbrevis explicatio* (1532), sig. D7v.

59. Sebastian Franck was the only one inelegant enough to point this out (*Weltbuch,* sig. aiii v).

60. Cf. Pagden, *European Encounters with the New World,* 94; Hooykaas, *Impact of the Voyages of Discovery,* 4–5.

61. Beginning in 1425, manuscript maps of Scandinavia began to appear, a tradition solidified by the maps of the Danish cartographer Claudius Clavus, which began to appear in the last third of the fifteenth century. Modern maps supplied by Donnus Nicolaus Germanus also formed part of the manuscript tradition, serving as the basis for the *tabulae modernae* in the 1482 Ulm edition of Ptolemy's *Geography* (Dilke and Dilke, "Ptolemy's Geography and the New World," 266–67).

62. A similar pattern occurs in the editions of Ptolemy edited by Sebastian Münster. Of the twenty-one new maps included by Münster, seventeen are of Europe, including five maps depicting various portions of the Rhine landscape. The remaining maps depict Farthest India, Africa, the New Islands, and the world.

63. Cochlaeus's addenda to Pomponius Mela, e.g., include six pages of updated information on Nuremberg (*Cosmographia Pomponii Mela,* sig. Hiiii v–I r).

64. Brant, *Narrenschiff,* fol. LXXXIIIIv.

65. Glareanus, *De geographia,* fol. 35r–v. All references are to the 1528 edition.

66. Waldseemüller and Ringmann, *Cosmographiae introductio,* sig. Aiii v–Aiiii r. See also Apian, *Cosmographiae Introductio,* Cap. XIIII.

67. The ancient climates began with Meroe (16°27′) and ended with Borysthenes (48°32′).

68. In a 1494 edition of Sacrobosco's *De Sphaera,* twenty-four climates in the northern hemisphere are named, the twenty-fourth being "vltimum Pilappen landt" (Leipzig: Martin Landsberg, 1494, sig. Gi r).

69. Apian, *Cosmographicus liber,* Col. 13.

70. Waldseemüller and Ringmann, *Cosmographiae introductio,* sig. C r.

71. Johann Schöner, *Luculentissima quaedam terrae totius descriptio,* fol. 39v.

72. Apian, *Cosmographicus liber,* Cols. 102–4.

73. Dryander, *Novi Annuli Astronomici,* sig. Fiii v.

74. Eisenmenger, *Libellus geographicus,* fol. 27v–28r.

75. Peucer, *De dimensione terrae* (1579), 139, 147.

76. The five zones were introduced in classical Greece by Parmenides and given eternal life by Aristotle (Aujac, Harley, and Woodward, "Foundations of Theoretical Cartography," 145).

77. Waldseemüller and Ringmann, *Cosmographiae introductio,* sig. Biii r–v.

78. Cochlaeus, *Cosmographia Pomponii Mele,* sig. Fi r.

79. I take the term "philosophical present" from Grafton, *New Worlds, Ancient Texts,* 16. For an early example of this technique, see Piccolomini's "De Asia" (esp. chaps. 1, 2, 5). Piccolomini discusses the diverse opinions of the ancients on such questions as the shape of the inhabited earth, its circumnavigability, and the habitality of the torrid zone (Pius II, *Asiae Europaeque elegantiss. descriptio,* 3–5, 8–9).

80. See, e.g., Cochlaeus, *Cosmographia Pomponii Mele,* sig. Fi r; Rithaymer, *De Orbis Terrarum Situ Compendium,* 34.

81. Tannstetter, *De natura locorum* (1515), fol. XIIIr.

82. There was also a medieval tradition of waffling on the inhabitability of the torrid zone. See Relaño, *Shaping of Africa,* 26–27.

83. Vadianus, *Pomponii Melae de orbis situ,* fol. 6r–10r. (All references are to the 1518 edition, unless otherwise stated.)

84. Augustine, *City of God,* 711. See also McCready, "Isidore, the Antipodeans and the Shape of the Earth." 109.

85. Moretti, "Other World and the 'Antipodes,'" 266.

86. As the following explication shows, the Perioecis, the Antoecis, and the Antipodes have been removed from their original locations as part of the Cratesian system of the four large landmasses, separated by oceanic bands, of which the *oikumene* of the ancients was only one. For the basics of the Cratesian system, see Relaño, *Shaping of Africa,* 25.

87. If one were now as interested in the permutations as some of the sixteenth-century cosmographers obviously were, one could point out, as they did, that one's Perioecis would be the Antipodes of one's Antoecis. But that would be overkill. See Vadianus, *Pomponii Melae de orbis situ,* fol. 5r.

88. Ibid., fol. 125v.

89. Stoeffler, [*I*]*n Procli Diadochi . . . commentarius,* fol. 14v. See also Waldseemüller and Ringmann, *Cosmographiae introductio,* sig. B iii v. See also the edition of Sacrobosco's *Sphere* that was annotated by Johannes Glogouienses (entitled *Introductorium compendiosum in tractatum sphere*), which likewise uses the Portuguese voyages to a place "which they call a new world" to bolster the arguments of Ptolemy (sig. Fi v).

90. Tannstetter, *De natura locorum* (1515), fol. XVIIr.

91. Vadianus, *Pomponii Melae de orbis situ,* fol. 5r. This technique also allowed commentators to evade the problem that the gospel, which was supposed to have reached the ends of the earth, had not reached the would-be Antipodes, as scholars including Zacharius Lilius (Florence, 1496) pointed out. Vadianus insists here that it had indeed reached "Antipodes," without needing to reveal that, if the gospel had not reached the New World, it had not reached the Antipodes of all Old World populations. For Lilius's argument, see Klaus A. Vogel, "Sphaera terrae," 414. For more on Vadianus's approach to the Antipodes question, see Klaus A. Vogel, "Amerigo Vespucci und die Humanisten in Wien," 77–103. Vadianus, as well as others, argued that the problem lay not in Augustine's reasoning, but in his use of the false geographical system of Macrobius and Cicero, which had been contradicted "no[n]nullis antiquoru[m], nedum nauigationibus nostrae memoriae," as Juan Luis Vives put it in his commentary on *City of God* (*De Civitate Dei Libri XXII* [Basel: Ambrosius and Aurelius Froben, 1570], 883). See also Stoeffler, [*I*]*n Procli Diadochi . . . commentarius,* fol. 51r–v.

92. This argument seems to hold as well for the replacement of Aristotle's view of earth and water as two spheres in eccentric relationship with the concept of the terraqueous globe, closely associated with Ptolemy but confirmed by the Iberian expeditions. This change is thus another example of resolution rather than revolution. For the Renaissance discussion of this issue, see Klaus A. Vogel, "Sphaera terrae," chap. 5.

93. For several examples of the application of these terms to the newly discovered territories, see Klaus A. Vogel, "Amerigo Vespucci und die Humanisten in Wien," 73–75.

94. Peucer, *De dimensione terrae* (1550), sig. D vi v. See also Vadianus, *Pomponii Melae de orbis situ,* fol. 128r.

95. Stoeffler, [*I*]*n Procli Diadochi . . . commentarius,* fol. 49v.

96. Apian, *Cosmographiae Introductio,* Cap. XX. Of course, people in the other regions of the earth can also be defined by their shadows. The Periscii are those for whom the shadow falls in a complete circle (i.e., those who live in the polar regions, where the sun stays above the horizon for an entire twenty-four-hour period). The Amphistii are those for whom the noon shadow falls both north and south, depending on the time of the year (i.e., those who live between the Tropics). For Ptolemy's use of these terms, see Evans, *History and Practice of Ancient Astronomy,* 62.

97. Waldseemüller, *Der welt kugel,* sig. B iv r–v. In the Latin version of the same text, the list of witnesses consists of those "who have traveled to India, Taprobana, Calicut and the Nile in Egypt, from whence spices are brought to us" (*Globus mundi,* sig. Ci v).

98. Neander, *Elementa sphaericae doctrinae,* 64.

99. For some indication of the imprecisions in both observation and calculation, see Evans, *History and Practice of Ancient Astronomy*. The calculation of longitude was especially difficult, since it required an eclipse (or other equally rare celestial event) to be visible and recorded at a known as well as a new location. Other methods were developed that did not require waiting for a measurable celestial phenomenon, such as the lunar-distance method and the transportation of a timepiece from one location to the other. However, these methods were not practical, given the inadequacies of knowledge and technology, and cosmographers continued to explain the determination of longitude through the older method (Pogo, "Gemma Frisius," 469–506).

100. Some of these distortions were most likely also caused by the different map-projection techniques used: Apian's world map is "onion shaped," while Münster's is oval. Variations within the coordinate listings themselves, even for Europe, while smaller, are still readily apparent if the texts are compared, as in Gallois's appendices to his *Geographes Allemands*.

101. Johann Schöner, *Luculentissima quaedam terrae totius descriptio*, fol. 6r–v.

102. For more on such instruments, see Broecke, "Use of Visual Media in Renaissance Cosmography," 140–42. Sebastian Münster also included such instruments in his *Erklerung des newen Instruments der Sunnen*.

103. For the growing use of machines and instruments to allow nonspecialists to solve astronomical problems without calculations, see Moran, "Princes, Machines and the Valuation of Precision," 211–13.

104. Apian, *Astronomicum Caesearum*, sig. AIIIr. Less grandiose texts also included simple instruments to aid in predictions; see, e.g., Rößlin, *Kalender mit allen Astronomischen haltungen*.

105. Even if the exact indexes varied, the sense of engagement with and control over the text would remain. This held true even for non-European readers: one of the examples Fries gave in his *Hydrographiae* deliberately flipped the situation around, touting the ability of a merchant from "the furthest parts of India" to find the location of Cologne using his book and map (sig. Bv).

106. Glareanus, *De geographia*, fol. 23r. Johannes Stoeffler was even more specific, telling readers to obtain the necessary information from Ptolemy and demonstrating the technique using an African city from the *Geography*, book 4, chap. 1 (*Cosmographiae*, sig. Biii v–Biv r).

107. Ptolemaeus, *Geographiae opus novissima*, Tabula Moderna Secunde Porcionis Aphrice.

108. For the various techniques used by Fries in his *Mercarthen* of 1525, see Hildegard Binder Johnson, *Carta Marina*, 60–61.

109. Peucer, *De dimensione terrae* (1579), 54–55.

110. Glareanus, *De geographia*, fol. 16v.

111. Qtd. in Ravenstein, *Martin Behaim*, 71. The translation *simpel = sinwel (rund)* is suggested in Jahn, *Raumkonzepte in der Frühen Neuzeit*, 155.

112. Turnbull, "Cartography and Science," 9–10. However, Ptolemaic cosmography and practical navigation did share a considerable number of basic assumptions (see Law, "On the Methods of Long-Distance Control," 246–50). Therefore, navigation manuals such as Medina's *Arte de Navegar* and Enciso's *Suma de Geographia* described and relied on the Ptolemaic universe, e.g., explaining topics such as the calculation of latitude and longitude, solar elevation, and eclipse measurements. On the continuing conflict between pilots and cosmographers over the most practical and useful means of representing the earth's surface, see Sandman, "Mirroring the World."

113. Fries, *Uslegung der Mercarthen*, fol. iii r.

114. Apian, *Cosmographia . . . per Gemmam Frisium . . . ob omnibus vindicata mendis*, Col. 53.

115. The ships attacked by sea monsters on the world map in a 1538 Basel edition of Solinus are the exceptions which prove the rule (*Rerum Toto Orbe Memorabilium*, map following p. 150). The glosses on Solinus's text (p. 147), meanwhile, discuss the Portuguese voyages around the Cape of Good Hope without mentioning such dangers.

116. See also the analysis in Relaño, *Shaping of Africa*, 122; Padrón, *Spacious Word*, 83–84.

117. See also Kiening, "'Erfahrung' und 'Vermessung' der Welt."

118. Waldseemüller and Ringmann, *Cosmographiae introductio*, sig. A iiii r.

119. Vespucci, *Von der new gefunnden Region* (1506), sig. A ii v.

120. Vadianus, *Pomponii Melae de orbis situ* (1552), 11.

121. Staden, *Warhafftig Historia*, sig. A iv v–B r. Dryander's background in mathematics as well as medicine made the comparison with cosmographical truths particularly natural (Westman, "Astronomer's Role," 119). For Grynaeus's argument in the preface to *Novus Orbis regionum* about the importance of mathematics in this context, see Pendergrass, "Simon Grynaeus and the Mariners."

122. For the interaction of the different types of information, see Kiening, "'Erfahrung' und 'Vermessung' der Welt," 19–23.

123. Johann Schöner, *Luculentissima quaedam terrae totius descriptio*, fol. 59v. The original number of bridges was actually twelve thousand (Polo, *Travels*, 214).

124. Apian, *Cosmographicus liber*, Col. 94. The designation "lac en konikreich" also appears on Behaim's globe. Ravenstein identifies this name with the place referred to in various versions of Marco Polo as "lach, loac, and lar" (*Martin Behaim*, 85). See Polo, *Travels*, 277–79.

125. See, e.g., Hieronymus Münzer's "Letter to King John of Portugal," 394.

126. Pliny was in fact relying on dubious evidence for this assertion (Romm, *Edges of the Earth in Ancient Thought,* 122).

127. Apian, *Cosmographiae Introductio,* Cap. XXVIII. See also Behaim's remarks on the Portuguese exploration of Africa, qtd. in Ravenstein, *Martin Behaim,* 71.

128. Ptolemaeus, *Geographia universalis,* 187.

129. Apian, *Isagoge in typum cosmographicum seu mappam mundi,* sig. Ai r. For other diagrams centered on Africa, see Waldseemüller, *Der welt kugel,* sig. Ai r; Apian, *Cosmographicus liber,* title page; Honter, *Rudimentorvm Cosmographiae,* 65; Fries, *Hydrographiae,* sig. Ai r; Johann Schöner, *Luculentissima quaedam terrae totius descriptio,* second title page; Cochlaeus, *Meteorologia Aristotelis,* Fo. LXv; Rithaymer, *De Orbis Terrarum Situ Compendium,* sig. aiiii v.

130. This conceit was also used by one of his presumed sources, the world map of Henricus Martellus.

131. Fries, *Carta Marina.*

132. Gregor Reisch, *Margarita philosophica* (1503), inset between sig. o vii v and sig. o viii r.

133. See, e.g., Brotton, *Trading Territories,* 26; Milanesi, "Arsarot oder Anian?"; Neuber, *Fremde Welt im europäischen Horizont,* 43.

134. For a reminder that America's insular status remained tentative until the eighteenth century, see Reichert, "Erfindung Amerikas durch die Kartographie," 142.

135. For a discussion of the name "Parias," see Christine R. Johnson, "Renaissance German Cosmographers," 30–31.

136. The best survey on the shifting usage of the name "America" is Klaus A. Vogel, "'America,'" 18–20.

137. Eisenmenger, *Libellus Geographicus,* fol. 20r.

138. Waldseemüller and Ringmann, *Cosmographiae introductio,* sig. Ciii v. For more on this process, see Christine R. Johnson, "Renaissance German Cosmographers," 21–22.

139. See, e.g., Apian, *Cosmographicus liber,* Col. 69; Johann Schöner, *Luculentissima quaedam totius terrae descriptio,* fol. 60r; Neander, *Elementa Sphaericae doctrinae,* 61–62.

140. Waldseemüller and Ringmann, *Cosmographiae introductio,* sig. Ciii v; Neander, *Elementa Sphaericae doctrinae,* 62.

141. Apian, *Cosmographicus liber,* Cols. 56–57. For the definitions of "continent," see Klaus A. Vogel, "'America,'" 17.

142. Klaus A. Vogel, "Amerigo Vespucci und die Humanisten in Wien," 57.

143. Honter, *Rudimentorum Cosmographiae Libri Duo* (1534), 91.

144. Thus, although Rithaymer admitted that whether America was an island or continent was as yet unknown, he still placed the section "De Terris

et Insvlis nuper repertis" at the end of his text, following sections describing the Atlantic islands and the Indian and African islands (*De Orbis Terrarum Situ Compendium*, 111). The difficulties encountered in the integration process when America was *not* considered an island are illustrated by the later work of Johann Schöner. In 1515, he proclaimed America an island, but he later changed his opinion based on Waldseemüller's 1516 *Carta Marina*, insisting instead that the western lands were part of Asia. However, rather than including them as part of the standard recounting of the regions, he discussed them at the beginning and at the end of his section on the three parts of the world, unable to link them precisely with specific parts of Asia (*Opusculum Geographicum*, fol E4v).

145. The quote continues: "Nam et gentes et loca illius terr[a]e / hactenus sunt et ignota et innominata nobis: nec fiunt ad ea loca nauigationes / nisi multis cu[m] periculis: Proinde geographis non sunt cure" (Cochlaeus, *Cosmographia Pomponii Mele*, sig. Fi v–Fii r).

146. Even Cochlaeus took this approach in his next text, an edition of Aristotle's *Meterologia*, in which he made use of the recently discovered "land of Amerigo . . . said to be larger than Europe" in a discussion of the dimensions and shape of the inhabited world (*Meteorologia Aristotelis*, fol. LXIIv).

3. ACCOUNTING FOR THE DISCOVERIES: THE COMMERCIAL CORRESPONDENCE

1. GNM, Imhoff-Archiv, Fasc. 28, Nr. 17, Fasc. 29, Nr. 7; see also Fasc. 28, Nr. 29. The possibility of a member's, as opposed to an employee's, being sent even to Lisbon is specifically excluded in the 1527 contract among the members of the Imhoff firm (Fasc. 29, Nr. 12, fol. 3r).

2. StadtAN, Libris Literarum (LL), B14/I, Nr. 45, fol. 38v.

3. Poovey, *History of the Modern Fact*, 41–65. These fictions included money of account, the "bank" to which money was owed or loaned, and the pretense that the recorded price actually reflected the cash value of the goods in inventory.

4. Ibid., 4.

5. Ghillany, *Geschichte des Seefahrers Ritter Martin Behaim*, globe facsimile.

6. Ruchamer, *Newe vnbekanthe landte*, sig. gii r.

7. The phrase is from Graziano, "Columbus and the Invention of Discovery," 27.

8. Frey has shown how the gold of India, with its paradisiacal implications, was progressively depicted as more and more accessible ("Montis auri pollicens," 11).

9. Dharampal-Frick, "'Irdisches Paradies,'" 84–85.

10. Hulme, "Tales of Distinction," 159.

11. Montrose, "Work of Gender," 24–25; see also Campbell, "Carnal Knowledge," 11.

12. Braunstein, "Wirtschaftliche Beziehungen zwischen Nürnberg und Italien," 387–95; Weitnauer, *Venezianischer Handel der Fugger*, 90–106.

13. Kellenbenz, *Rise of the European Economy*, 76–78.

14. Ibid., 82.

15. Großhaupt, "Bartholomäus Welser," 77–87; Schultheiss, "Geld und Finanzgeschäfte Nürnberger Bürger," 100–101.

16. Schaper, *Hirschvogel von Nürnberg*, 164.

17. Schultheiss, "Geld und Finanzgeschäfte Nürnberger Bürger," 106; Strieder, "Wirtschaftliches Gesicht des Zeitalters der Fugger," 6.

18. Ehrenberg, *Zeitalter der Fugger*, 1: 90–91; Strieder, "Wirtschaftliches Gesicht des Zeitalters der Fugger," 5.

19. Pölnitz, *Jakob Fugger*, 1: 34–35.

20. For the eclipse of the Hansa from the fifteenth century through the end of the sixteenth century (when the shift in trade routes and the Dutch Revolt produced favorable circumstances, particularly for the city of Hamburg), see Kellenbenz, "Phasen des Hanseatisch-Nordeuropäischen Südamerikahandels," 87–95. For the limited staple trade between the Hansa and Portugal in the sixteenth century, see Pohle, *Deutschland und die überseeische Expansion Portugals*, 268–72.

21. Tom Scott, *Society and Economy in Germany*, 126–29; Walter, "Nürnberg, Augsburg und Lateinamerika," 47.

22. In addition to being related to the Welser factor Lucas Rem, Wilhelm had served as a Fugger factor in Milan (Werner, "Repräsentanten der Augsburger Fugger und Nürnberger Imhoff als Urheber," 11).

23. StadtAA, Chroniken, Nr. 5, Chronik von Wilhelm Rem 1077–1511, fol. 309v.

24. StadtAA, Chroniken, Nr. 14, *Annales de Vetustate Originis* of Achilles Pirminius Gasser, manuscript copy with dedication dated 1571, 1: 745.

25. Pohle, *Deutschland und die überseeische Expansion Portugals*, 97. German firms were represented in Portugal in the late fifteenth century as well (Großhaupt, "Commercial Relations," 362).

26. The contributions to the total of 36,000 cruzados were as follows: Augsburg companies: Welser-Vöhlin—20,000, Fugger—4,000, Höchstetter—4,000, Gossembrot—3,000; Nuremberg companies: Imhoff—3,000, Hirschvogel—2,000 (Pohle, *Deutschland und die überseeische Expansion Portugals*, 102). The attempt to plug in to the new sea route had apparently begun even earlier, when four German firms in Genoa agreed in the spring of 1501 to work together toward this goal (Schulte, *Geschichte der Grossen Ravensburger Handelsgesellschaft*, 1: 277–78).

27. Pohle, *Deutschland und die überseeische Expansion Portugals,* 255. The Antwerp office was closed in 1549 in order to entice merchants back to Portugal (257). As some items, particularly precious stones, continued to be traded in Lisbon, some firms continued to have agents there.

28. The Fuggers contributed 10,000 ducats and the Welsers 2,000 (Haebler, "Fugger und der spanische Gewürzhandel," 36). A few German merchants contributed small amounts to the privately run expedition of Sebastian Cabot, which also sought a westward passage to the Spice Islands (Kellenbenz, "Role of the Great Upper German Families," 50).

29. Schaper, *Hirschvogel von Nürnberg,* 230; Otte, "Jacob und Hans Cromberger und Lazarus Nürnberger."

30. Großhaupt, "Bartholomäus Welser," 207. The Welsers briefly owned a sugar mill in the Canary Islands until 1513, when they sold it to two Cologne merchants (Großhaupt, "Commercial Relations," 385–87). For the potential Venezuela held for the Welser trading networks (not realized during the firm's tenure), see Denzer, "Welser in Venezuela," 290–91. The Fuggers considered a similar colonization contract for a portion of the west coast of South America, and there are hints that they sent out at least one ship to establish their presence there, but nothing more came of this enterprise (Kellenbenz, "Role of the Great Upper German Families," 55–58). See also Simmer, *Gold und Sklaven,* 67–68.

31. Munro, "Monetary Origins of the 'Price Revolution,'" 14–15.

32. Ehrenberg, *Zeitalter der Fugger,* 2: 14; Kellenbenz, *Fugger in Spanien und Portugal,* 1: 67–122; Großhaupt, "Welser als Bankiers."

33. Pohle, *Deutschland und die überseeische Expansion Portugals,* 157–65.

34. SuStBA, 4°Cod. H 13, in Greiff, "Tagebuch des Lucas Rem," 8.

35. The Welsers did contribute to a Portuguese entrepreneur's outfitting of three ships for the fleet of Tristão da Cunha, which sailed in 1506. The Welsers' contribution of 3,430 cruzados, however, represented a minimal, passive investment. Due to transport costs induced by a shipwreck on the route home, the voyage, according to the Welser factor Lucas Rem, resulted in a slight loss (Pohle, *Deutschland und die überseeische Expansion Portugals,* 103).

36. Otte, "Die Welser in Santo Domingo," 476. The German firms' advantageous position when negotiating for access is shown by the fact that three German merchants were able to obtain permission to sail to the Spanish Indies before being legally eligible for such permits.

37. Haebler, "Fugger und der spanische Gewürzhandel," 33–34; Kellenbenz, "Role of the Great Upper German Families," 49–50.

38. The initial (1528) grant was given to Hieronymus Sailer and Heinrich Ehinger, then resident in Spain; in 1530 this document was revised to grant the same rights retroactively to the firm of Bartholom Welser. Scholars have disagreed on whether the Welsers were the intended recipients from the be-

ginning. See Haebler, "Welser und Ehinger in Venezuela," 66–86; Panhorst, *Deutschland und Amerika*, 96–97; Großhaupt, "Bartholomäus Welser," 234. While documents relating to this question are scarce, the latest, most definitive answer, from Götz Simmer, indicates that they were acting under orders from the Welser firm (*Gold und Sklaven*, 68–69).

39. Großhaupt, "Venezuela-Vertrag der Welser," 11–13.

40. Haebler, *Die überseeischen Unternehmungen der Welser*, 52–59; Großhaupt, "Venezuela-Vertrag der Welser," 1.

41. Pohle, *Deutschland und die überseeische Expansion Portugals*, 175.

42. E. Daenell, "Geldgeschäft Karls V.," 138–39.

43. See, e.g., FA 44.1, 84/122 letter, Sept. 16, 1552; FA 2.2.45, entry for 1555.

44. Brotton, *Trading Territories*, 129.

45. A discussion of this text, as well as a complete transcription, is found in Müller, *Welthandelsbräuche*. The authorship and intended readership of this manuscript are disputed. See Müller, *Welthandelsbräuche*, 9–10; Werner, "Repräsentanten der Augsburger Fugger und Nürnberger Imhoff als Urheber." Undisputed, however, are its German origin and its purpose as a compilation of all then-current trading practices.

46. Müller, *Welthandelsbräuche*, 202.

47. GNM (Bibliothek), Nr. 2910, fol. 28r. See also the listing in Lazarus Nürnberger's account, in Krása, Polišenský, and Ratkoš, *Voyages of Discovery*, 58–60.

48. Sprenger, *Merfahrt*.

49. Schaper, "Hirschvogel von Nürnberg und Ihre Faktoren," 184, 189. Nürnberger sailed in 1517, Pock in 1520.

50. For Nürnberger, see Krása, Polišenský, and Ratkoš, *Voyages of Discovery*. For Pock, see StadtAN, FA Behaim, E11/II, Nr. 582, Doc. 14, reprinted, with extensive introductory material, as Georg Pock, "Der Nürnberger Kaufmann Georg Pock."

51. GNM (Bibliothek), Hs 28,884, letter inset between fol. 75v and fol. 76r. The letter is transcribed in Boesch, "Brief des Gabriel Holzschuher."

52. STAN, Reichsstadt Nürnberg, Handschriften Nr. 281, "Der holtschuher vnd holtschuherin puch 1505 Jar dem 9 marci," fol. 34r.

53. StadtAN, Freiherrl. von Tucher'sches Familienarchiv, E29/II, Nr. 47, fol. 76r. The fate of another German, the Welser factor "Hainrich vonn Edl," is recorded in a more businesslike manner in the journal of Sebastian Welser, who noted for the year 1539 that he had lost over 893 Reichsthaler (specifically, R. 893 ß 9 d.2 in gold) because on the way to India vonn Edl "Im briesiell lanndt mit schiff vnd gut pliebenn vnd vonn den selben more[n] erschlag[en] ist gott sey seiner selbenn genedig ame[n]" (STAN, Geuder-Rabensteiner Archiv, Bd. 146, Teil I, fol. 21v).

54. A Nuremburger, Barthel Blümel, represented the interests of Lazarus Nürnberger in Santo Domingo, beginning around 1527. He later traveled on his own to Chile (Walter, "Nürnberg, Augsburg, und Lateinamerika," 56–57). Nürnberger's factors in New Spain were a Hans Henschel from Basel and, later, Markus Hartmann. Eobanus Heuss, son of a Nuremburg humanist, worked on a sugar plantation in Brazil, where he met Hans Staden (Kellenbenz, "Beziehungen Nürnbergs zur Iberischen Halbinsel," 485, 478–79).

55. The boy was a member of the Dalfinger family (StadtAN, Freiherrl. v. Tucher'sches Familienarchiv—Briefarchiv, E29/IV, Fasc. 1, Nr. 11, Doc. 15, letter, Sept. 17, 1533).

56. Müller, *Welthandelsbräuche,* 260.

57. For speculation on the identity of the author of *Copia der Newen Zeytung auß Presillg Landt,* see Kellenbenz, "Role of the Great Upper German Families," 48.

58. *Copia der Newen Zeytung auß Presillg Landt,* sig. Aiii r–v.

59. Ruchamer, *Newe vnbekanthe landte,* sig. eii r.

60. For an overview of these practices, see Favier, *Gold and Spices,* chap. 14.

61. Aspiring merchants usually received a basic education in mathematics (and perhaps other commercial skills) at private schools before serving at a branch office of the firm for hands-on experience. Many of the *Rechnungsbücher* discussed in this section were written for use in private mathematics courses. An excellent bibliographic source is Hoock and Jeannin, *Ars Mercatoria.*

62. For an explanation and translation of one such text, the *Treviso Arithmetic* of 1478, see Swetz, *Capitalism and Arithmetic.* The different types of problems are discussed in Kurt Vogel, "Überholte arithmetische kaufmännische Praktiken."

63. While the double-entry system, particularly its checks and balances, tightened accounting practices and called for the regular tallying of profit and loss, I am not arguing that it had a transformative effect on mercantile practices, as some scholars of early capitalism have argued. For a critique of this position, see Yamey, "Scientific Bookkeeping." Instead, the Italian method was simply the most advanced and highly touted form of self-referential accounting calculations.

64. This expertise, of course, was not confined to Germans. The author of a Portuguese manual even called for his techniques to be applied overseas: "I am printing this arithmetic because it is a thing so necessary in Portugal for transactions with the merchants of India, Persia, Arabia, Ethiopia, and other places discovered by us" (Swetz, *Capitalism and Arithmetic,* 25).

65. Long, *Openness, Secrecy, Authorship,* chaps. 6–7; Rowland, "Abacus and Humanism," 701. The standard work on mercantile contributions to

early modern mathematics is Van Egmond, "Commercial Revolution and the Beginnings of Western Mathematics."

66. Apian, *Newe vnnd wolgegründte vnderweysung aller Kauffmanß Rechnung* (seven editions appeared before 1580); Frisius, *Arithmeticae Practicae Methodus Facilis.* When Frisius's text was reprinted by M. Cholinus in Cologne (1571), new appendices were added on astronomical and calendrical calculation, combining practical arithmetic with practical astronomy.

67. This formulation is in essence a more matter-of-fact version of the point made by Edgerton ("From Mental Matrix to Mappamundi") and Rowland ("Abacus and Humanism") that the mathematical gaze rendered the world ordered, harmonious, and manipulable, which appealed to humanist elites, artists, and merchants. This view of the world required the belief that the mathematical order reflected the natural order, a leap of faith Rowland attributes to Neoplatonic philosophy. As the German texts do not reflect such philosophical underpinnings, I see this faith as rooted in the way the mathematical systems were organized and explained.

68. This point is fully developed for double-entry bookkeeping in Poovey, *History of the Modern Fact,* 55.

69. Gotlieb, *Teutsch verstendig Buchhalten,* sig. Aiii r.

70. See also Poovey, *History of the Modern Fact,* 59–60.

71. Transcribed in Weitnauer, *Venezianischer Handel der Fugger,* 177.

72. Hans Pock, *New Rechenbüchlein auff der Linien vnd Federn,* sig. Fvi v.

73. Prakash, *European Commercial Enterprise,* 3.

74. Müller, *Welthandelsbräuche,* 175, 186.

75. Ibid., 203–4.

76. Ibid., 204–5.

77. StadtAA, Stadtgerichtsakten, Nr. 105, fol. 136r, 146r.

78. Ruchamer, *Newe vnbekanthe landte,* sig. biiii r–v.

79. Müller, *Welthandelsbräuche,* 260.

80. The new weight was sixteen ounces (ibid., 260).

81. Ibid., 290–91.

82. Ibid., 297.

83. Ibid., 298.

84. Kellenbenz, *Das Meder'sche Handelsbuch,* 246.

85. Ibid., 241.

86. Ibid., 182–85.

87. Ibid., 179–80.

88. Simmer, *Gold und Sklaven,* 46.

89. The use of German miners in the overseas territories extended to the silver mines in Mexico and the Portuguese enterprises in Angola. See Werner, "Europäisches Kapital in ibero-amerikanischen Montanunternehmungen," 36–49.

90. Werner, "Kupferhüttenwerk des Hans Tetzel," 315. See also Werner, "Zur Geschichte Tetzelscher Hammerwerke," 216. For the Spanish perspective on Tetzel's experience, see Berrera-Osorio, *Experiencing Nature*, 65–67.

91. For the company contract, see StadtAN, Tetzel-Archiv, E22/I, Doc. U 56.

92. Although the industrial application of this amalgamation technique was developed in the New World, the basic chemistry was already known to alchemists and German miners, including one elusive German, "maestro Lorenzo," who was originally supposed to accompany Medina to New Spain. The history of the amalgamation process and a description of the technique are provided in Berrera-Osorio, *Experiencing Nature*, 68–71.

93. Kellenbenz, *Fugger in Spanien und Portugal*, 1: 381; for the document, see 3: 590.

94. David C. Goodman, *Power and Penury*, 196.

95. GNM (Archiv), Behaim-Archiv, Nr. 29e, Doc. 18, letter from Nuremburg, May 18, 1549.

96. Boesch, "Brief des Gabriel Holzschuher," 159.

97. Schulte, *Geschichte der Grossen Ravensburger Handelsgesellschaft*, 3: 274.

98. GNM (Archiv), Behaim-Archiv, Nr. 29g, Doc. 12. For additional letters mentioning ships from India, see Nr. 29g, Doc. 32; for additional reports on ships from the Spanish colonies, see Nr. 29h-1561, Doc. 6.

99. Kellenbenz, *Fugger in Spanien und Portugal*, 3: 583.

100. For the home office's interest in such details, see also the consideration Bartholomew Welser, in a letter to his Spanish factor, gives the flow of precious metals to Spain from the New World: "Letter to Bartholomew May, February 1547," in Welser, "Zur Geschichte der Welser in Venezuela," 341.

101. StadtAN, Freiherrl. v. Tucher'sches Familienarchiv—Briefarchiv, E29/IV, Fasc. III, Nr. 11, 44r–47v, quote on fol. 47v.

102. Ibid., E29/IV, Fasc. I, Nr. 15, Doc. 17, letter dated Feb. 1, 1552.

103. Müller, *Welthandelsbräuche*, 205.

104. StadtAA, Chronik von Wilhelm Rem, 1077–1511, fol. 313r. The essentials of the entry for 1502, but not the one for 1499, are repeated in the later chronicle of Clemens Sender. See StadtAA, Chroniken, Nr. 8, Chronik von Clemens Sender von Launigen bis 1536, fol. 305r.

105. Soden and Knaake, *Christoph Scheurl's Briefbuch*, 41.

106. Wake, "Changing Pattern of Europe's Pepper and Spice Imports."

107. For a comparison of "Calic°" spices and "vᵃ" spices, see, e.g., the unsigned letter (in the handwriting of Endres Imhoff) to Paulus (I.) Behaim, sent from Antwerp, Mar. 23, 1555, GNM, Behaim-Archiv, Nr. 29g, Doc. 7.

108. Kellenbenz, *Fugger in Spanien und Portugal*, 3: 436.

109. See, e.g., Schulte, *Geschichte der Grossen Ravensburger Handelsgesellschaft*, 3: 449.

110. I am indebted to Maria Snyder for this reference.

111. *Fortunatus* (1554), fol. 12r.

112. Ibid., fol. 19v.

113. Günther, *Fortunatus*, 83. The names "Lumbet" and "Thobar" almost certainly come from Mandeville's *Travels*, although I have not been able to locate the particular spelling. In the 1480 Augsburg edition of Anton Sorg, the forest is called "tambor" (*Jean de Mandeville. Reisen*, 110). Fortunatus also explicitly recommends Mandeville's text for those who want to know more about the wondrous land of India (83).

114. *Fortunatus* (1554), fol. 44v–45r. The accessibility of the land, as well as its specificity, is also stressed in the later version. The earlier one refers the reader to Mandeville for more information about the wonders of the East, before launching into an explanation of why more Germans had not reached this land (its distance from Europe, the difficulty of the journey, insufficient motivation). The failure to travel, as discussed in chap. 1, is thus prominent in the description of the land of pepper. This discussion, of course, is absent from the later version (Günther, *Fortunatus*, 83).

115. *Fortunatus* (1554), fol. 43v.

116. Ibid., fol. 48v.

117. StadtAA, Chronik von Wilhelm Rem 1077–1511, inset page between fol. 317v and fol. 318r. The most likely source of this information, Rem's kinsman Lucas Rem, who was the Welser factor in Lisbon at the time, recorded in his journal that the profit was 150 percent (Greiff, "Tagebuch des Lucas Rem," 8).

118. Between the years 1499 and 1528, the profits of the Imhoff firm of Nuremberg ranged between 1 and 15½ percent (Jahnel, "Die Imhoff," 121).

119. Kellenbenz, *Fugger in Spanien und Portugal*, 1: 420. See also Haebler, "Fugger und der spanische Gewürzhandel," 38.

120. Thus, as early as 1534, Lazarus Spengler of Nuremberg wrote to a certain Vitus Dietrich of the discovery of Peru, concentrating entirely on its wealth (Stadtbibl. N., Cent. V. App 34k (Spengleriana), Fasc. 16, Nr. 28).

121. References in the historiography to the "fairy-tale wealth" (märchenhaften Reichtum) of Peru are thus justified only if the fairy tale in mind was of the *Fortunatus* type. The quote is from Schmitt, "Des Reichsritters Philipp von Hutten Suche nach dem goldenen Glück," 61.

122. BHSA, Kurbayern Äusseres Archiv, Nr. 4291, fol. 193v. For another report on a specific shipment of gold, see Nr. 4291, fol. 149r.

123. Renate Pieper has also noted that correspondence about precious-metal shipments, which often depended on rumors circulating in Spain, could report wildly varying numbers for the amounts expected or arrived in

Spain (*Vermittlung einer neuen Welt,* 221). Even so, a number, however much based on guesswork and gossip, was still a crucial part of the report.

124. HAB, 130. Helmst., fol. 293r. The note on the exchange rate was apparently added later. A separate report, fol. 294v, also mentions gold arriving from Peru. The latest precious metal shipments from Peru also featured regularly in Christoph Scheurl's reports to Duke George of Saxony, because of their implications for the fiscal and military policy of Charles V. See letters 243, 255, and 264 in Soden and Knaacke, *Christoph Scheurl's Briefbuch,* 155, 182, 203–4.

125. This element of calculation applies as well to the Aztec treasure sent by Cortes to Charles and displayed in Brussels. Albrecht Dürer's expressions of wonder upon viewing these objects are often cited, but in the midst of this marveling, Dürer notes the objects' worth in much more concrete terms: "Diese Ding sind alle köstlich gewesen, dass man sie beschätzt um hundertausend Gulden wert" ("Tagebuch der niederländischen Reise," 48).

126. Strieder, *Aus Antwerpener Notariatsarchiven,* 79–83. In that same year another group of Antwerp merchants hired Bernhard Schoutert, a native of Olpe, to go to Peru at their expense and collect all the gold, silver, and other treasures he could find (how he was to do this is not specified) and bring them back to his employers (ibid., 341).

127. A full recounting of this story is found in Ohlau, "Neue Quellen zur Familiengeschichte der Spengler," 244–52, quote on p. 247. Most of the letters on which this article is based can be found at the BHSA, RKG 12024. Ohlau believes that the term "Baru" refers to an island by that name off the coast of Columbia. I think it at least equally likely that the reference is to "Peru," given the date the enterprise was conceived (1535) and the usual variations in spelling all foreign words were subjected to in their transcription into German.

128. Ibid., 249.

129. They were not the only Germans interested in this region; Ulrich Schmidel would participate in its exploration, and a ship financed by Jakob Welser and Sebastian Neidhart carrying crafted metal goods ("Nuremberger wares") accompanied Pedro de Mendoza's expedition to this region in 1536 (Kellenbenz, *Das Meder'sche Handelsbuch,* 78).

130. BHSA, RKG 12024, Nr. 28.

131. Ohlau, "Neue Quellen zur Familiengeschichte der Spengler," 249.

132. For the merchant rationality behind the Venezuela enterprise, see Simmer, *Gold und Sklaven,* 274–75.

133. For detailed discussions of the conflicts and communications within the firm, based on the limited evidence available, see Schmitt, "Beitrag der Hutten-Papiere"; Denzer, "Welser in Venezuela"; Simmer, *Gold und Sklaven,* 273–75. Despite some differences in interpretation, all conclude that the firm's leaders must have known about and supported the conquistadoral policy, although they would have had little control over how it was carried out.

134. Philipp von Hutten, "Tagebuch von 1533–1538 und Briefe," 86.

135. Ibid., 90. As Simmer relates, Cabo de la Vela was a missed opportunity for the Welser colony, as it lay arguably within the borders of Venezuela, yet was given fiscal and administrative independence from both Venezuela and Santa Marta through the efforts of pearl-fishing entrepreneurs, many of whom had emigrated from the nearby island of Cubagua (*Gold und Sklaven*, 446–53).

136. While I agree with Eberhard Schmitt that this pursuit of the "rich land" was a viable and rational course to pursue, I believe that the discovery of Peru marked a watershed and that the discovery of an El Dorado was probably not the Welsers' goal from the beginning, as Schmitt suggests in *Konquista als Konzernpolitik* (17). Simmer argues that finding the rich province had become the overriding goal by the 1531–33 military campaign of the governor Ambrosius Dalfinger, who was following indications he had discovered after arriving in the colony (*Gold und Sklaven*, 743–44). However important local information was, the discovery of Peru made such ideas consistently plausible, even to those in Europe whose support was necessary to sustain these enterprises.

4. TOO RICH FOR GERMAN BLOOD? THE SPICE TRADE AS AN ECONOMIC, MORAL, AND MEDICAL THREAT

1. Hutten, *De Guaiaci Medicina*, sig. h r. A German translation was also published: *Von der wunderbarlichen artzney des holtz Guaiacum genant*.

2. The "French Disease" (*morbus gallicus*), or "Great Pox," has been identified as veneral syphilis, but for the reasons outlined by Arrizabalaga, Henderson, and French (*Great Pox*, 18), I will refer to it with the names used by contemporaries.

3. Weber, "Queu du Roi, Roi des Queux," 154; Montanari, *Culture of Food*, 63. For the use of spices as medicine, see below.

4. Jardine, *Worldly Goods*.

5. For example, Jardine's consideration of the usury prohibition and the *Monopolstreit* focuses on the weakening and eventual dissolution of such barriers to commerce. See ibid., 327–29, 343–46, 371–73. For the different context of seventeenth-century Dutch hand-wringing over the corrupting influence of America, see Schmidt, *Innocence Abroad*, 260–91. Of the New World imports, Schmidt points to tobacco as a lightning rod of concern, a point widely documented throughout Europe. A brief survey of antitobacco sentiment can also be found in Grafton, *New Worlds, Ancient Texts*, 169–76 (see esp. the chapter on medicine, written with Nancy Siraisi). Because tobacco became a widespread consumer good only in the early seventeenth century, I do not analyze it in this chapter.

6. See, e.g., Guerra, "Drugs from the Indies," 29–30.

7. See, e.g., Stannard, "Dioscorides and Renaissance Materia Medica," 13; Finan, *Maize in the Great Herbals*, 180.

8. See, e.g., Sauer, "Changing Perception and Exploitation of New World Plants," 815–23.

9. Norton, "New World of Goods."

10. While my use of this term primarily denotes theologians, their analysis did not differ substantially from that of commentators on Roman and canon law; medieval scholars were thus generally consistent on the issues discussed below. See Baldwin, "Medieval Theories of the Just Price"; Langholm, *Legacy of Scholasticism in Economic Thought,* 95–96. Because the classical tradition of distrust for commerce revivified by humanists lacked the specificity of law-based commentary, it was less important in determining the terms of the debate. See Willibald Pirckheimer's edition of Plutarch's *De vitanda usura* (Nuremberg: F. Peypus, 1515).

11. Höffner, *Wirtschaftsethik und Monopole,* 74.

12. Ibid., 73.

13. Nider, *On the Contracts of Merchants,* 31. Nider was a Dominican friar and eventual professor at the University of Vienna. *De Contractibus Mercatorum* was written at the beginning of the fifteenth century. See Shuman, introduction to *On the Contracts of Merchants,* vii–viii.

14. Ibid., 37.

15. Höffner, *Wirtschaftsethik und Monopole,* 75.

16. Mertens, *Im Kampf gegen die Monopole,* 12.

17. For the history of the usury prohibition, see Noonan, *Scholastic Analysis of Usury.* For specific examples, see Nider, *On the Contracts of Merchants,* 51–54.

18. In general, scholastics did not seem to take possible defaults on loans into account, so the merchant could not even justify his profit by pointing to the risk of default (Noonan, *Scholastic Analysis of Usury,* 80–81, 132).

19. For the negative reputation of merchants even among the chroniclers of Augsburg, see Häberlein, "'Die Tag und Nacht auff Fürkauff trachten.'"

20. Brant, *Narrenschiff,* fol. CXXVr.

21. Hunt and Murray, *History of Business in Medieval Europe,* 70.

22. Baxandall, *Limewood Sculptors of Renaissance Germany,* 107. The craft guilds of Cologne included a demand that the merchant companies be investigated in their 1525 articles of grievance (Tom Scott, *Society and Economy in Germany,* 208).

23. For the limited participation in capital markets, see Mathis, *Deutsche Wirtschaft im 16. Jahrhundert,* 80–82.

24. The vast majority of the south German firms' working capital came from family members, relatives, and employees. Even if they reached outside this circle, their search for capital was limited to areas in which they also had business interests (Häberlein, *Brüder, Freunde und Betrüger,* 244–45).

25. Shuman, introduction, viii.

26. Cuppener, *Ein schons buchlein czu deutsch.*

27. Luther, *Von Kauffshandlung vnd Wucher,* sig. Aii v–Aiv r.

28. For more on this contract and the disputation, see Noonan, *Scholastic Analysis of Usury,* 208.

29. For the Fuggers' involvement in this debate, see Pölnitz, *Jakob Fugger,* 2: 313–17; Pölnitz, "Beziehungen des Johannes Eck zum Augsburger Kapital."

30. Mertens, *Im Kampf gegen die Monopole,* 7–9.

31. Nider, *On the Contracts of Merchants,* 18.

32. The city of Augsburg was the only member of the Diet that consistently argued against limitations on corporations and defended their current practices (Mertens, *Im Kampf gegen die Monopole,* 40).

33. Roll, *Zweite Reichsregiment.* The Reichsregiment eventually collapsed due to lack of funding and conflicts with members of the estates.

34. See, e.g., the complaints of the Imperial Knights (an estate not given an official role in the Diet) about the undue influence of the *Gesellschaften:* "Beschwerdeschrift der . . . Ritterschaft an die Stände," in *Deutsche Reichstagsakten, Jüngere Reihe,* 3: 725.

35. The suggestion that the Reichsregiment be funded was first made by the small committee charged with determining its salaries and upkeep and incorporated into legislation in the 1523 *Reichstagsabschied.* See "Gutachten des kleinen Ausschusses über die Kosten der Unterhaltung von Regiment und Kammergericht," in *Deutsche Reichstagsakten, Jüngere Reihe,* 2: 408–9; "Abschied des Reichstags," in *Deutsche Reichstagsakten, Jüngere Reihe,* 3: 744–45.

36. Mertens, *Im Kampf gegen die Monopole,* 20.

37. Qtd. in ibid., 16–17.

38. The press of other business, especially responding to the new teachings of Martin Luther, prevented the Diet from promulgating the *Polizeiordnung* in its *Reichstagsabschied.* Instead, it passed responsibility for this matter over to the interim government established at the Diet, the Reichsregiment.

39. "Entwurf einer Polizeiordnung," in *Deutsche Reichstagsakten, Jüngere Reihe,* 2: 352–53.

40. Ibid., 2: 351. Usury had been handled in an earlier, separate chapter (2: 345–46).

41. Ibid., 2: 352–53.

42. Rumors like the one reported by Hans von der Planitz, a representative to the Diet for the elector of Saxony, did not help the merchants' cause: "Drei geselschafter zu Augspurgk sollen abermals zu Lisewona in Portugall einen kauf gethan haben, daran sie 1 ½ hundert tausent gulden zu gewin haben sollen das muss alles der gemeine man bezalen" (*Des Kursächsischen Rathes Hans von der Planitz. Berichte,* 626).

43. Entwurf einer Polizeiordnung," 353–54.

44. Ibid., 354.

45. "Ratschlag des kleinen Ausschusses," in *Deutsche Reichstagsakten, Jüngere Reihe,* 3: 575–76.

46. The political delicacy of the situation with metals comes forth in one of the modifications suggested by the large committee to the 1521 *Polizeiordnung,* developed by the small committee. With a specific reference to the experience of George, Duke of Saxony, the large committee pointed out the necessity of granting exclusive contracts in the mining industry to obtain the necessary capital to exploit this natural resource ("Gutachten des großen Ausschusses," in *Deutsche Reichstagsakten, Jüngere Reihe,* 2: 360–61).

47. "Ratschlag des kleinen Ausschusses," 576–77.

48. Ibid., 590–91. By the next Diet (in 1524 in Nuremberg), a list of suggested maximum prices had indeed been established. See "Proposition, die von Statthalter und Regiment den Ständen . . . vorgelegt wurde," in *Deutsche Reichstagsakten, Jüngere Reihe,* 4: 281–84.

49. See chap. 5 for an examination of the corporations' political manueverings.

50. For example, the committee charged with considering monopolies at the 1530 Augsburg Diet repeated at essential points either the *Polizeiordnung* of 1521 or the *Ratschlag* of 1523. For the future course of the *Monopolstreit,* see Mertens, *Im Kampf gegen die Monopole,* 88–113.

51. This case is specifically cited in "Ratschlag des kleinen Ausschusses," 574–75.

52. Ibid., 576.

53. Ibid., 580.

54. Ibid., 580.

55. Ibid., 588–89.

56. The incomplete eclipse of Venice is evident in the price lists publicized by the Diet: e.g., price controls on both "Venetian ginger" and "Calicut ginger" are established ("Proposition . . . bei Eröffnung des Reichstags," 282).

57. An instructive comparison can be made between the specificity of the Diet's complaints during the *Monopolstreit* and the earlier antimerchant proposals made in the *Reformatio* of Emperor Sigismund at the beginning of the fifteenth century, in which the vague understanding of market practices led to equally sweeping (and unrealistic) proposals. The *Reformatio* was printed as part of Johann Bämler's collection *Chronik von allen Kaisern, Königen, und Päpsten,* in sections entitled "Von der kauffleüt ordnung" and "Von den grossen geselschafften."

58. For the unease (not universally shared) with things Italian, see Baxandall, *Limewood Sculptors,* 139–41; for blaming the Italians for sexual sins, see Sieber-Lehmann, *Spätmittelalterlicher Nationalismus,* 296.

59. "Entwurf einer Polizeiordnung," 335.

60. Ibid., 336–37.

61. In the first proposal (1521), all goods brought into or taken out of the empire would be subject to the tariff (*Reichszoll*) ("Gutachten des kleinen Ausschusses," 2: 408–9). For the exemptions, see "Ordnung eines allgemeinen Reichszolls," in *Deutsche Reichstagsakten, Jüngere Reihe*, 3: 625, which was promulgated during the second Nuremberg Diet.

62. See, e.g., the 1530 Jörg Breu broadsheet analyzed in Cuneo, "Constructing the Boundaries of Community."

63. Luther, *Von Kauffshandlung vnd wucher*, sig. Ciii r, Diii v.

64. Ibid., sig. Aii v.

65. Ulrich von Hutten, "Anschawenden," fol. xii v.

66. Ulrich von Hutten, "Praedones," fol. 22v.

67. For the influence of the classical tradition on anxieties about luxury, commerce, and expansion in the English case, see Fitzmaurice, *Humanism and America*.

68. Ulrich von Hutten, "Praedones," fol. 22v–23r.

69. Ulrich von Hutten, *Dialogus oder ein gesprech/Febris/genant*, sig. Avi r.

70. This poem was added to a later edition of *Feber* (Ulrich von Hutten, *Gespraechbüchlin herr Vlrichs von Hutten. Feber das Erst* [1521], sig. biiii v).

71. Stannard, "Dioscorides and Renaissance Materia Medica," 7; Goltz, *Mittelalterliche Pharmazie und Medizin*, 73–76; McVaugh, "Medieval Theory of Compound Medicines." In focusing on the most recognizable of the spices from India and the Near East, I have necessarily omitted nonvegetable ingredients (e.g., the famous viper's flesh that was the basis for theriac).

72. Reeds, *Botany in Medieval and Renaissance Universities*, 41–47.

73. As Alix Cooper argues, the indigenous/exotic debate would prove useful in many different contexts into the eighteenth century (*Inventing the Indigenous*, chap. 1).

74. On these texts, see Ogilvie, *Science of Describing*, 36–37; Arber, *Herbals, Their Origin and Evolution*, chap. 4. For the earlier tradition of herbals, see Chrisman, *Lay Culture, Learned Culture*, 127.

75. Arber, *Herbals, Their Origin and Evolution*, chap. 4; Baader, "Mittelalter und Neuzeit im Werk von Otto Brunfels," 190–94; Stübler, *Leonhart Fuchs: Leben und Werk*; Kusukawa, "Leonhart Fuchs."

76. For details on the herbals' publishing history, see the bibliography. For Bock's additions after the first edition, see Hoppe, *Kräuterbuch des Hieronymus Bock*, 44–47. (All references are to the 1546 edition [cited as *Kreuter Buch*], unless otherwise stated.)

77. The illustrations were reproduced in many later herbals. See Sprague, "Herbal of Leonhart Fuchs," 548.

78. Leonhart Fuchs, *New Kreüterbuch*. In an attempt to take full advantage of the effort and expense involved in creating the original woodcuts, the printer also put out Latin and German octavo versions, which included the

images of the plants and their names, but none of the surrounding textual material (see *Läbliche abbildung und contrafaytung aller kreüter; Primi de stirpium historia commentariorum*).

79. In addition to these authors, a number of other German naturalists studied plants during this period, most notably Euricius Cordus, Valerius Cordus, and Konrad Gesner. For a survey of their activities, see Ogilvie, *Science of Describing*. They participated in the revival of both the classical and the empirical botany described here, but did not produce complete herbals.

80. Hence the importance of the officially regulated, cumulative process for testing New World "balsam" (Berrera-Osorio, "Local Herbs, Global Medicines"). See also Siraisi, *Medieval and Early Renaissance Medicine*, 54.

81. The importance of text-based learning separated physicians and trained apothecaries from empirics, including non-university-trained surgeons. The botanists emphasized these differences in their writing, claiming that they were making this knowledge available to lay audiences to defend against illegitimate practioners, such as peddlers, old women, and Jews. For the different ranks of the medical hierarchy, see Hammond, "Origins of Civic Health Care," 77–82; Findlen, *Possessing Nature*, 261–72. For disparagement of empirics, see Bock, *Kreuter Buch*, sig. aiiii r; Brunfels, *Contrafayt Kreüterbuch*, sig. aiii r. The botanists therefore did not challenge the physicians' claim to expertise, and indeed established different relationships with their learned versus their lay audiences. The Latin texts were presented for the experts in the field, whose professional status was demonstrated through their careful perusal of the correct names of plants and the ancient uses for them. The German texts, on the other hand, walked a fine line, claiming to present authorized knowledge while at the same time insisting that the authority itself remained elsewhere. See Schenda, "'Gemeiner Mann' und sein medikales Verhalten"; Chrisman, *Lay Culture, Learned Culture*, 179–81.

82. The search for a true original text was also necessitated by the increasingly apparent mistakes in the versions then available. The formative debate on the flaws in the extant ancient texts was that over the errors in Pliny's *Natural History*, conducted by several Italian humanists in the last decade of the fifteenth century. A detailed discussion of this dispute can be found in Ogilvie, *Science of Describing*, 121–32. See also Carrara, "Epistemological Problems in Giovanni Mainardi's Commentary."

83. The Arabic authors were not without their defenders (e.g., the doctor and cartographer Lorenz Fries), who praised their medical and teaching, if not their linguistic, ability (Schipperges, *Ideologie und Historiographie des Arabismus*, 20).

84. *De Materia Medica* was known in the Middle Ages through an alphabetized Latin text, but excerpts also circulated widely through the writings of Avicenna and Serapion. In the fifteenth century Italian humanists began to examine the manuscript tradition anew, and the first Greek edition was pub-

lished in Venice in 1499. In 1516 two new Latin translations were published, one by the Italian Ermolao Barbaro (Venice) and one by the Frenchman Jean Ruel (Paris) (Reeds, "Renaissance Humanism and Botany," 525). The Ruel edition was published in Frankfurt under the title *De medicinali materia libri sex . . . per Gualtherum H. Ryff.* A German translation was produced that same decade: *Kreutter Buch des Hochberümpten Pedanii Dioscoridis Anazarbei.*

85. See also Schmitz, "Arzneimittelbegriff der Renaissance," 11.

86. Brunfels, *Contrafayt Kreüterbuch,* fol. biiii r.

87. See, e.g., Bock's difficulties in fixing the local plant *Erdrauch* (*Kreuter Buch,* fol. xliv). See also his discussion of "Wurmkraut/Wellsamen" and its relation to the Mediterranean plants described by Dioscorides and Pliny (fol. cxxviii r). Fuchs also acknowledged that not every plant would have an entry in the ancient texts (Kusukawa, "Leonhart Fuchs," 413).

88. Plant identification was made even more difficult by the fact that no illustrations accompanied the manuscript transmission of the classical texts. Several species were also apparently so well known to his first-century CE audience that Dioscorides considered any description superfluous. For the "confusio nominum," see Dilg, "Pflanzenkunde im Humanismus," 116.

89. See, e.g., Reeds, "Renaissance Humanism and Botany," 540; Dilg, "Botanische Kommentarliteratur in Italien," 227; Stannard, "Dioscorides and Renaissance Materia Medica," 14.

90. For this argument about plants as made in Fuchs's herbal, see Kusukawa, "Leonhart Fuchs," 416.

91. As Hammond argues, the position of the Augsburg Collegium Medicum was strengthened because it was called on to resolve disputes about health matters in the city ("Origins of Civic Health Care," 254).

92. Bock, e.g., regularly explains that he does not "yet" have enough information, so he will wait until he is "better informed." See *Kreuter Buch,* "Von S. Johans blumen," fol. liiii v, "Von Schüsselblumen," fol. lxxvii r–v, and "Von Heiden Ysop," fol. lxxxv r.

93. It is therefore not clear why Bock included the "Brustbeerlin" (Chinese date/jujube) in Part III of the *Kreuter Buch,* since he was unable to include a picture and admitted he had never seen one (fol. xxxii v–xxxiii r).

94. This was not true of earlier herbals, which included extensive chapters devoted to tropical spices, occasionally noting their origin in "India" and quoting both Arabic (Serapion, Avicenna) and classical (Galen, Dioscorides) authors as to their medicinal uses. See, e.g., the Latin *Herbarius,* Part III, chap. xiii (*cinamomum*), chap. xvii (*garioffili*), chap. xxii (*nux muscata*), chap. xxiii (*piper*), chap. xxviii (*zinciber*); *Hortus sanitas, deutsch,* chap. cxiii, sig. gviv (*cinamomum*), chap. cc, sig. nvr (*gariofilus*), chap. cclxxxiii, sig. siir (*nux muscata*), chap. cccxxix, sig. vviir (*piper*), chap. ccccxxxiiii, sig. Ciiir (*zinziber*). For Discorides's original discussion of tropical spices, see *De medicinali materia,* book I (chaps. V, XIII), book II (chaps. CLI, CLII).

95. For connections between local botanical investigations and those of New World plants, see Lowood, "New World and the European Catalog of Nature," 297.

96. Fuchs, *De historia stirpium,* sig. α4r.

97. All of Fuchs's chapters featured full-page folio woodcuts of the plants described, and Brunfels also limited his project to plants then available to illustrators. For their comments on the illustrations, see Fuchs, *De historia stirpium,* sig. ∝6r; Brunfels, *Contrafayt Kreüterbuch,* sig. aiii v. See also Kusukawa, "Leonhart Fuchs." Initially, Bock resisted adding pictures to his herbal, because certain ancient authors such as Pliny and Galen had disparaged the use of images to convey knowledge. After the 1539 edition, however, all subsequent editions were fully illustrated (with a justification by Bock referring to a different set of classical precedents). See Reeds, "Renaissance Humanism and Botany," 530–31. For the informal botanical networks crucial to the spread of seeds and specimens across Europe, see Ogilvie, *Science of Describing,* 151–64; Reeds, *Botany in Medieval and Renaissance Universities,* 106–8.

98. Thus, they are never introduced as simply "new" or "unknown"; the only illustration presented without any scientific discussion is a local plant simply labeled "Ein vnbekant Waldtkraut" (Brunfels, *Contrafayt Kreüterbuch,* CXI).

99. This list is slightly modified from that provided by Riddle, *Dioscorides on Pharmacy and Medicine,* 25.

100. The allure of reconstituting (proven) remedies explains the attention and prestige given to the search for authentic theriac, Galen's "royal antidote of antidotes" (Palmer, "Pharmacy in the Republic of Venice," 108). For the recovery of ancient medicines in general, see Findlen, *Possessing Nature,* chap. 6.

101. Arrizabalaga, Henderson, and French, *Great Pox,* 95 (italics in original).

102. Ibid., 114.

103. See, e.g., the entry for "Schwelcken," in Bock, *Kreuter Buch,* Part III, fol. xxv v.

104. Ibid., fol. cccl v.

105. Leonhart Fuchs, *De historia stirpium,* 731.

106. Bock, *Kreuter Buch,* fol. ccxxxv v–ccxxxvi r. Otto Brunfels disputed the identification in his *Contrafayt Kreüterbuch,* CCCXXI. Oakes Ames identifies "Welsch Bonen" with the kidney bean, originally indigenous to (probably) Brazil (*Economic Annuals and Human Cultures,* 60). See also Bock's discussion of the origin of "Türkisch Korn" (*Kreuter Buch,* fol. ccxlviii v).

107. The incorporation of new arrivals into classical nomenclature could in fact secure them a more prominent place within the pharmacological discussion. Because maize (*Türkisch Korn*) was associated with the ancient plant

Milium Indicum, it is discussed in Ruel's edition of Dioscorides's *De Materia Medica . . . per Gualtherum H. Ryff* (134). See also Ruel's discussion of guaiacum under the heading of ebony, which includes a long description of the treatment for *morbo gallico*, independent of its connection with a Dioscoridean category (*De natura stirpium*, 120–22).

108. See Riddle, *Dioscorides on Pharmacy and Medicine*, 169–74.

109. Fuchs, *De historia stirpium*, 731.

110. Bock, *Kreuter Buch*, fol. ccxxxvi r. For another example, see Leonhart Fuchs's discussion of *Siliquastrus* (*De historia stirpium*, 735).

111. Brunfels, *Contrafayt Kreüterbuch*, CCCXXI.

112. Fuchs, *De historia stirpium*, 824.

113. Bock, *Kreuter Buch*, fol. ccxlix r.

114. Ibid., fol. cccl v.

115. Brunfels, *Contrafayt Kreüterbuch*, XIX.

116. Bock, *Kreuter Buch*, fol. ccxlix r.

117. Fuchs, *De historia stirpium*, 824.

118. Bock, *Kreuter Buch*, fol. ccxlix r.

119. Fuchs, *De historia stirpium*, 702. For the New World origin of the "Turkish Cucumber," see Whitaker, "American Origin of the Cultivated Cucurbits," 102.

120. Bock, *Kreuter Buch*, fol. ccxxxv v.

121. Ibid. fol. ccxlviii v.

122. Ibid., fol. cccli r–v.

123. Cf. Jean Ruel's book of simples, *De natura stirpium*, which included numerous tropical spices.

124. In addition to its stand-alone publication, this text was also printed (without the original preface) as a supplement to the 1577 and 1580 editions of Bock's *Kreuter Buch*, under the title *Item von den vier Elementen*. . . . All references to this work are to the 1550 edition.

125. Bock, *Kreuter Buch*, fol. xxv r.

126. Ibid., fol. ccxci v. For attempts to transplant saffron from Spain and Italy, see Amman, "Deutsch-spanische Wirtschaftsbeziehungen," 146.

127. Brunfels, *Contrafayt Kreüterbuch*, CXVII.

128. Fuchs published a book on the proper compounding of drugs, with descriptions of such necessary ingredients as pepper, ginger, and cardamom, as part of *Methodus Seu Ratio Compendiaria* (*De Usitata . . . componendorum miscendorumque medicamentorum ratione*).

129. Their fierce attacks on the corrupting influence of the Arabic authors did not, however, keep them from citing these authors (although Fuchs was more scrupulous in this matter). See Baader, "Medizinische Theorie und Praxis," 209–10.

130. Brunfels, *Herbarium vivae eicones*, 6.

131. This preface, dated 1551, first appeared in the 1552 edition of the herbal. All references to it are from the 1560 edition of Bock's herbal, referred to as *KreüterBuch.* For the above quote, see *KreüterBuch,* sig. avi v.

132. Arrizabalaga, Henderson, and French, *Great Pox,* 258.

133. Brunfels, *Contrafayt Kreüterbuch,* sig. bii v.

134. Bock, *De historia stirpium . . . quae in Germania nostra nascuntur,* sig. di v.

135. Bock, *New Kreutter Buch, das andere Buch* (1539), sig. lv v–lvi r.

136. Fuchs, *De historia stirpium,* sig. α6r.

137. Bock, *Kreuter Buch,* sig. aiiii v.

138. Brunfels, *Contrafayt Kreüterbuch,* CCXCI.

139. Bock, *Teütsche Speiszkammer,* sig. Aiii v–Aiiii r.

140. Ibid., fol. cvii v. For the widespread critique of luxurious banquets, see Albala, *Eating Right in the Renaissance,* 206–8.

141. Brunfels, *Contrafayt Kreüterbuch,* sig. biii v.

142. Bock, *KreüterBuch,* sig. avi r–v.

143. Bartels, "Drogenhandel und Apothekenrechtliche Beziehungen," 51–53.

144. *Römischer Keyserlicher Maiestat Ordnung und Reformation,* StadtAA, Literalien (1530 Aug.–Dec.), sig. Ciii v.

145. Bock, *Teütsche Speiszkammer,* fol. cvi v–cvii v. Other warnings can be found in the chapters on *Pfefferwurtz* (fol. xcv r) and ginger (fol. xciii v). The *Kreuter Buch* also hints that unscrupulous apothecaries substituted mouse droppings for pepper (fol. clix v).

146. Bock, *Teütsche Speiszkammer,* fol. xcii v.

147. Sebizius, introduction, fol. 5r.

148. Guaiacum, as a foreign import, was not described in the herbals of Brunfels, Bock, or Fuchs. Lonicer, however, devoted a chapter to it (*Kreuterbuch,* fol. LXXVIIIv).

149. The best introduction to this debate is Arrizabalaga, Henderson, and French, *Great Pox.*

150. Most doctors, however, regarded both guaiacum and mercury as valid treatments, to be used according to the state of the patient and the disease (Stein, *Behandlung der Franzosenkrankheit,* 91–92).

151. As Hutten explicitly acknowledged in a letter to Pirckheimer, "For this I first have Christ to thank, then the Fuchers or whoever they are who have brought us a medicine against the destructive disease" (qtd. in Benedek, "Influence of Ulrich von Hutten's Medical Descriptions," 359).

152. Ulrich von Hutten, *De Guaiaci Medicina,* sig. dii v–diii r. See also Johannes Grünpeck's comments about the failure of exotic remedies, qtd. in Quétel, *History of Syphilis,* 18.

153. In fact, Brunfels cites Hutten's remarks about his grandfather's es-chewal of foreign spices and fine clothing in his herbal (*Herbarium vivae*

eicones, 15). The two also shared a commitment to the Reformation, which brought them into personal contact (Chrisman, *Lay Culture, Learned Culture,* 174).

154. Ulrich von Hutten, *De Guaiaci Medicina,* sig. c r.

155. Ibid., sig. diii r. While in this passage Hutten may seem to be disparaging all of academic medicine, in other parts of this text and others, he takes care to praise specific doctors, to quote ancient medical authors, and in fact complain about healers who did not take the patient-centered approach espoused by academic medicine.

156. Absent from this portrayal of Indian health practices (and from the general discussion of the guaiacum remedy in Renaissance Germany) is the characterization noted by other scholars of the French disease as the result of the grotesque appetites and numerous vices of Native Americans. See Chaplin, *Subject Matter,* 217; Grafton, *New Worlds, Ancient Texts,* 182, 186.

157. Ulrich von Hutten, *De Guaiaci Medicina,* sig. giii v.

158. Ibid., sig. dii v.

159. Ibid., sig. b r.

160. For a discusssion of these concerns in Paracelsus's *Herbarius,* see Cooper, *Inventing the Indigenous,* chap. 1.

161. Paracelsus, "Von Blatern . . . der Franzosen," 420. Karl-Heinz Weimann first identified the "Cardinal" as Matthäus Lang in "Paracelus und Kardinal Matthäus Lang als Gegner," 195. For an important reevaluation of the impetus behind Paracelsus's attack, see Toellner, "Matthäus Kardinal Lang von Wellenburg und Paracelsus." Hutten also alleged a collusion involving doctors and merchants; in this case, doctors would acknowledge the wood worked, but only under their supervision, thus receiving a portion of the profits merchants would reap from continued trade (*De Guaiaci Medicina,* sig. diiii v).

162. Paracelsus, *Von der Frantzoesischen kranckheit,* sig. Eiiii v.

163. Paracelsus, "Von Blatern . . . der Franzosen," 312.

164. Pölnitz, the leading Fugger historian, flatly denied this historiographical commonplace (*Die Fugger,* 2nd ed., 288–89). See also Stein, *Behandlung der Franzosenkrankheit,* 168–71.

165. Franck, *Weltbuch,* sig. aii r.

166. Vadianus, *Epitome Trium Terrae Partium,* 58. Pliny also cited luxury as a stimulus to travel (*Natural History,* 2: 227).

167. Kaisersberg, *Navicula sive speculum fatuorum,* sig. Zii r. A later German translation also contains these connections: Kaisersberg, *[N]arenschiff,* fol. CLXXXIVr.

168. Dedication letter to the City Council of Schwäbisch Hall, in Feyerabend, *Ander theil dieses Weltbuchs,* sig.)(iiii v.

169. For another instance in which the discoveries were immediately connected to questionable practices in the spice trade, see StadtAA, *Annales de*

Vetustate Originis of Achilles Pirminius Gasser, manuscript copy with dedication dated 1571, 1: 746.

170. Münster, *Cosmographei* (1556), lxxxviii. The charges are taken from Giovio's *Libellus de Legatione . . . Moschoviae ad Clementem VII,* also included as part of *Die New Welt* (169r–v). The Italian Giovio obviously had a particular stake in denigrating Portuguese trading practices, but none of the commercial rivalry is mentioned here.

5. THE SORROWS OF YOUNG WELSER: THE COMMERCIAL CORRESPONDENCE

1. SuStBA, 2°Cod. Aug. 382a.

2. Pohle, *Deutschland und die überseeische Expansion Portugals,* 266–68. On the Welser disengagement in particular, see Hildebrandt, "Niedergang der Augsburg Welser-Firma," 275.

3. Qtd. in Pagden, *European Encounters with the New World,* 39.

4. Schmidt, *Innocence Abroad,* 290.

5. Colonial and frontier inhabitants of course experienced unfamiliar forms of these challenges, but I am arguing that the true source of their frustrations was the contrast with the earlier idealized images of alterity promoted to attract settlement. The eventual social transformations made possible by the development of creole society were the long-term result of the interactions of different populations after the conquest.

6. Based on Fugger's draft response to this attempt, it appears that Maximilian tried to increase the pressure on his chosen creditors by leveling many of the charges that would appear later in the *Monopolstreit,* directing them, even at this early date, against the spice trade. Fugger's response can be found in FA 2.1.12½, "Rechtfertigung der Fugger gegen den Plan Maxim. I. eine Reichssteuer auf die Gesellschaft zu erheben, circa 1507."

7. Ibid., fol. 1v.

8. StadtAA, Literalien (1509), "Copia der schrift an ku. Mt., 1507?," unpaginated.

9. For the possibility of French intrusion, see Konrad Peutinger, "Ein Gutachten Conrad Peutingers in Sachen der Handelsgesellschaften," 191.

10. StadtAA, Kaufmannschaft und Handel, Fasc. IV 24/20, "1530: Supplication d. St. Augsburg an Kais. Mt. der Monopolien halber (Vnnderricht vnd anerzeigung)," fol. 17v.

11. Ibid., fol. 19v.

12. "1530: Supplication d. St. Augsburg," fol. 4r.

13. "1530: Supplication d. St. Augsburg (Vnnderricht)," fol. 8r–v; Konrad Peutinger, "Ein Gutachten Conrad Peutingers in Sachen der Handelsgesellschaften," 192.

14. "1530: Supplication d. St. Augsburg," fol. 1v.

15. "1530: Supplication d. St. Augsburg (Vnnderricht)," fol. 11r.

16. Konrad Peutinger, "Rechtsauskunft über den Monopolbegriff, 1522/23," in "Conrad Peutingers Gutachten zur Monopolfrage," 8.

17. Konrad Peutinger, "Kurze Denkschrift Konrad Peutingers zur Frage der Monopole und Handelsgesellschaften," in "Conrad Peutingers Gutachten zur Monopolfrage," 15.

18. Konrad Peutinger, "Rechtsauskunft über den Monopolbegriff," 11. For a later version of this argument, in which only fine spices are considered luxuries, see Mertens, *Im Kampf gegen die Monopole,* 90. Peutinger therefore also had to argue that gold and silver were luxuries ("Kurze Denkschrift Konrad Peutingers," 15).

19. This confiscation enabled the king to control the supply and hence the price of pepper (Pohle, *Deutschland und die überseeische Expansion Portugals,* 154 n.623). Pohle (p. 159) mentions only sugar as part of the agreement, but Fugger's "Rechtfertigung" suggests that cash payments were offered as well.

20. "Rechtfertigung der Fugger," fol. 1r.

21. Ibid., fol. 3v.

22. "1530: Supplication d. St. Augsburg (Vnnderricht)," fol. 3r, 5r.

23. Ibid., fol. 15v–16r.

24. "1530: Supplication d. St. Augsburg," fol. 5r–v.

25. "1530: Supplication d. St. Augsburg (Vnnderricht)," fol. 3r.

26. The predominance of the strategy of direct appeal is evident in the relatively low-key efforts made to defend those south German merchants who were in fact charged by the imperial fiscal with monopolistic practices, the Imhoffs and the Welsers. When threatened with the prescribed penalty of confiscation of all goods and exile, the firms did not mount extraordinary defenses to these particular claims. For an example of the initial documents sent by the fiscal, the official in charge of initiating the legal proceedings, see GNM, Imhoff-Archiv, Fasc. 29, Nr. 9, Docs. 1–2 (the Imhoffs' initial response is Doc. 3).

27. The emperor was also responsible for quashing suggestions of an imperial toll (Mertens, *Im Kampf gegen die Monopole,* 64–65).

28. Ibid., 80–85.

29. The interventions of the emperor were in fact virtually ignored by the Diet, which continued to propose decrees and demand action against the *Gesellschaften.* However, as imperial officials were under obligation to obey imperial edicts as well, no further action at the imperial level was possible against specific infractions. For the *Monopolstreit*'s changing nature, see ibid., 114.

30. The Fugger factors in Spain therefore believed it necessary to include in their reports updates on royal policy toward merchants and their holdings, as well their fears that the king would "dissimulate." See, e.g., the letter from Cristoff Raiser, Apr. 17, 1558, FA Handel 2.5.12, Fasc. "Korrespondenz des Gemeinen Spanischen Handels 1550–1577–1625."

31. SuStA, 2° Cod. Aug 198, *Cronica alter und neuer Geschichten durch Wilhelm Rem (Fortsetzung)*, fol. 85v.

32. There are numerous examples of the misdeeds of factors who remained in Europe. For problems with the Lisbon factory, see Schaper, *Hirschvogel von Nürnberg*, 221; Pohle, *Deutschland und die überseeische Expansion Portugals*, 142.

33. The documents pertaining to the suit of Pock's heirs are found at StadtAN, Libris Literarum, B14/I, Nr. 43, fol. 70v–72v, 182r–183r. A separate, later proceeding involved the claims of Pock's illegitimate son Hans for a 500–gulden inheritance from his father's estate; this matter was not settled until 1569 (in favor of Hans Pock's heirs) (Schaper, *Hirschvogel von Nürnberg*, 273).

34. StadtAA, Kaufmannschaft und Handel, Fasc. IV 24/11, "Christoph Herwart in Handelsverbindungen mit Lienhart Hirschvogel in Nürnberg."

35. Ibid.

36. Thus the charges filed in the city court, now found at StadtAA, Stadt-gerichtsakten, Klagsachen 105, "Vrt[ei]lbrieff, herrn hans Welsers [et]c. von Jorg Herwart Zu[m] Lizabona," fol. 10r. This information was confirmed through the account book that Hans Welser eventually produced.

37. As he claimed: ibid., fol. 25r.

38. "Missue N°6," in "Vrt[ei]lbrieff, herrn hans Welsers," fol. 114r–v.

39. "Instrument N°2," in "Vrt[ei]lbrieff, herrn hans Welsers," fol. 106v–109r.

40. "Missiue N°5," in "Vrt[ei]lbrieff, herrn hans Welsers," fol. 112r–v.

41. "Missue N°6," "Vrt[ei]lbrieff, herrn hans Welsers," fol. 114v.

42. "Missiue N°9," in "Vrt[ei]lbrieff, herrn hans Welsers," 127v.

43. Ibid. The lines of ownership were further tangled by the subsequent deaths of both Schwetzer and Imhoff; see "Missiue N°7," in "Vrt[ei]lbrieff, herrn hans Welsers," 117r–120v.

44. "Missiue N°9," 127r–128v. The suit is continued in StadtAA, Stadt-gerichtsakten, Nr. 189. In 1565 the court dismissed the charges against the heirs of Hans Welser, although the last-dated document in the file is an appeal filed by the Herwart lawyer against the dismissal ("Georg Herwart Zue Lysabona Contra Herrn Hannsen Wellser, 1556–1566," 175).

45. "Missiue N°9," 129v.

46. For an account of the suit, see Kellenbenz, *Fugger in Spanien und Portugal,* 1: 418–23.

47. See ibid., 1: 133–35, for examples of the extensive means of accomodating debt repayments to the royal schedule.

48. Pölnitz, *Die Fugger,* 256.

49. GNM, Behaim-Archiv, Nr. 29h—1561, Doc. 6.

50. Lynch, *Spain 1516–1598,* 199. See also Haebler, "Finanzdecrete Philipp's II. und die Fugger."

51. One such report was entitled "Relacion wass die flotas der indias von nueba Sp[ani]a tierra firme Sto. Domingo vnd Honduras bringen" (BHSA, Kasten schwarz, Nr. 6730, fol. 90r–v).

52. For the Fuggers, see Pölnitz, *Die Fugger,* chap. 15; Ehrenberg, *Zeitalter der Fugger,* 1: 170–71. For the last Hirschvogel (Endres II, d. 1550), see Schaper, *Hirschvogel von Nürnberg,* 286–90.

53. Hildebrandt, "Effects of Empire," 70–72.

54. Jahnel, "Die Imhoff," 195; Pölnitz and Kellenbenz, *Anton Fugger,* 3: part 2, 429–32.

55. Tom Scott, *Society and Economy in Germany,* 130–31; Kellenbenz, *Rise of the European Economy,* 151.

56. The classic account of the Welser enterprise, Haebler's *Die überseeischen Unternehmungen der Welser,* has now been superseded by Großhaupt, "Bartholomäus Welser," and the definitive account by Simmer, *Gold und Sklaven.*

57. For the amounts expended and received by the Welser firm, see Simmer, *Gold und Sklaven,* 704–17.

58. For the realism of the search for El Dorado, see Schmitt, "Beitrag der Hutten-Papiere," 205–6.

59. For an exact recounting of the booty won in this campaign, see Simmer, *Gold und Sklaven,* 307–8.

60. Ibid., 362–63.

61. As Simmer argues, this was most likely an attempt to remove the case to Spain, a more favorable venue for Federmann (ibid., 376).

62. Ibid., 370–82.

63. Ibid., 403–4.

64. Ibid., 649.

65. Ibid., 688–89.

66. For the reasons of state in this instance, see ibid., 691, 731; for the Welsers' waning influence with the Spanish Crown, see ibid., 734.

67. "Brief Bartholomae Welsers vom Febr. 1543 an Franz Davila," in Welser, "Zur Geschichte der Welser in Venezuela," 335–36. Simmer regards these comments as a tactic designed to discourage Davila from continuing to seek payment of Federmann's debts from the Welsers (*Gold und Sklaven,* 382), but they also reflect the attitude displayed by Welser's arrest of Federmann and therefore should not be seen as merely opportunistic.

68. "Brief Jakob Rembolds dd . . . 1543 an Franz Davila," in Welser, "Zur Geschichte der Welser in Venezuela," 337.

69. Since the amount won in the plundering of New Granada was relatively modest, this statement probably reflects both the needs of the moment and the exaggerated expectations of wealth raised by reports from the New World—not only from Peru, but also from this new conquest (Simmer, *Gold und Sklaven,* 365).

70. On the transmission of the news to Germany, see ibid., 597–98.

71. Philipp von Hutten, "Tagebuch von 1533–1538 und Briefe," 114.

72. Ibid., 109. Specifically mentioned in this correspondence were gold, silver, and precious stones, indicating that the families expected not only the remaining military equipment but also the results of successful plundering campaigns. In reality, Hutten and Welser possessed only horses, weapons, and a few Indian slaves (Simmer, *Gold und Sklaven*, 601, 563).

73. See the letter from Gabriel Holzschuher quoted in chap. 3.

74. Rott's history and scheme are described in Hildebrandt, "Wirtschaftsentwicklung und Konzentration," 34–40.

75. Ibid., 38.

76. Ibid., 39–40.

77. Haebler, "Konrad Rott und die Thüringische Gesellschaft," 192. This fact had been noted in 1575 by the Fugger factor in Portugal, who, when offered the contract on the European distribution of pepper, suggested caution on the grounds that, while he was sure that the promised amounts of pepper would arrive, he was not sure they could sell that much at the proposed price. See StadtAA, Kaufmannschaft und Handel, Nr. 28 (Conrad Roth 1576), 26.

78. The "will" is found at StadtAA, Literalien, 31.3. 1580 (1579–1580: Falliment des Conrad Roth), fol. 12r–21r.

79. Hildebrandt, "Wirtschaftsentwicklung und Konzentration," 43.

80. *Gesprech, so Pasquinus mit dem Marphorio . . . gehabt.* I was only able to consult a partial version of this document, a transcription at BSB, Cgm. 3991, "Des Pasquino und des Marforio Gespräch," fol. 3rff.

81. "Falliment des Conrad Roths," fol. 13r.

82. Hildebrandt, "Wirtschaftsentwicklung und Konzentration," 37.

83. "Falliment des Conrad Roths," fol. 13v.

84. This attitude is evident as well in some of the initial proceedings surrounding the bankruptcy; several references are made to the hoped-for return of the ship from India, which is the only possibility cited for improving the situation. See StadtAA, Schuld-, Klag-, und Appellationsakten, Teil 2, Karton XXII, Nr. 162, "Konkurz von Konrad Roth, 1580," fol. 6r, 14v.

85. "Des Pasquino und des Marforio Gespräch," fol. 22r.

86. Qtd. in Haebler, "Konrad Rott und die Thüringische Gesellschaft," 177–78.

6. CONCLUSION

1. Bacon, *New Organon*, 69.

2. For an example of the cycle of expectation and repression, see Clendinnen, *Ambivalent Conquests*. For a European example of the dissonance between elite proscriptions and folk beliefs, see Behringer, *Shaman of Oberstdorf.*

3. This distance from the actual events and expeditions produced significantly flawed understandings of the technical and historical aspects of the discoveries (Alexander, *Geometrical Landscapes*, 79). For more on Bacon's rhetoric, see Poovey, *History of the Modern Fact*, 10–11.

4. Findlen, *Possessing Nature*, 27.

5. The images are described and discussed in Schmidt, *Innocence Abroad*, 131–38. By 1700 this emphasis on "exoticism" had become a conscious representational strategy for Dutch publishers (Schmidt, "Inventing Exoticism").

6. Greenblatt, *Marvelous Possessions*, 19. See also Daston and Park, *Wonders and the Order of Nature*, 137.

7. Kiening, "Ordnung der Fremde," 78.

8. This triad is taken from the organizing principles of the inventory of Rudolf II's *Kunst- and Wunderkammer* (Bredekamp, *Lure of Antiquity*, 34).

9. For the inclusion of extra-European artifacts in these collections, see Shelton, "Cabinets of Transgression"; Tudela and Gschwend, "Luxury Goods for Royal Collectors"; Seelig, "Exotica in der Münchener Kunstkammer der bayerischen Wittelsbacher."

10. For real and imagined examples of such architecture, see Bredekamp, *Lure of Antiquity*, figs. 26, 28, 29.

11. For the inclusion of American exotica in the medieval category of the marvelous, see Shelton, "Cabinets of Transgression," 201.

12. Kaufmann, *Mastery of Nature*, chap. 7.

13. Qtd. in Bredekamp, *Lure of Antiquity*, 64. For more on both of these topics, see Kaufmann, *Mastery of Nature*, 185–94.

14. The quote is from Findlen, *Possessing Nature*, 71.

15. Neuber, *Fremde Welt im europäischen Horizont*, 307.

16. Findlen, "Inventing Nature," 301–7.

17. Kaufmann, *Mastery of Nature*, 184–94. See also Rowland, "Abacus and Humanism," for the importance of Neoplatonism in the understanding and control of nature in Renaissance Italy.

18. This idea is also the premise behind Steven Shapin's treatment of skepticism, which he argues is "the attempted calibration of one dubiously trustworthy source by others assumed to be trustworthy" (*Social History of Truth*, 21). Michel de Montaigne's skepticism reveals this dynamic at work, as he bases his famous question "What do I know?" on the things that he did know, including specific details about the nature and natives of the New World ("Apology for Raymond Sebond").

19. Poovey, *History of the Modern Fact*, xii. Merchant accounting is the focus of Poovey's discussion, but astronomy (p. 4) and herbals (p. 5) are also cited.

20. Both the *Geography* and the *Atlas* were conceived as part of the same publishing program, which also included a Christian account of the creation

of the world (Van der Krogt, "Gerhard Mercators Atlas," 30). In his preface to the *Geography,* furthermore, Mercator placed himself within the tradition of humanist translators of this text, beginning with d'Angelo, and worked to establish his version as definitive (*Tabulae Geographicae Claudii Ptolemaei,* "Praefatio," 2r(?)–(?)2v). A decisive break with the humanist tradition seems to have occurred by 1695, when Mercator's Ptolemy maps were issued, without accompanying text or even an index, but with updated cartouches to meet current tastes (Van der Krogt, "Gerhard Mercators Atlas," 31).

21. Ortelius, *Theatrum Orbis Terrarum.* While many of Ortelius's maps contain latitude and longitude markings, many (usually regional ones) do not. In the edition of Mercator's *Atlas* I consulted, on the other hand, only a regional map (Hiberniae V. Tabula) and four small maps of British isles (Angliae VII. Tabula) lack such coordinates, but in the former case the introductory page gives the coordinates for the principal city in the region, while in the latter case it gives latitude and longitude coordinates for each of the islands as a whole. This volume, M: Cb 2° 19 in the Herzog August Bibliothek, is listed in the catalog as "Duisburg, 1585," but fits the description of the 1595 edition provided in Van der Krogt, "Gerhard Mercators Atlas," 33.

22. Or at least he could start to. The *Atlas* was incomplete at Mercator's death. For the addition of maps to the *Atlas,* see Van der Krogt, "Gerhard Mercators Atlas," 33–36.

23. These techniques included, of course, triangulation and other survey measurements, as well as fixing position through astronomical measurement.

Bibliography

MANUSCRIPTS

Bayerische Staatsbibliothek (BSB), Munich
    Cgm:
        934–37
        951–52
        3991
Bayerisches Hauptstaatsarchiv (BHSA), Munich
    Reichskammergerichtsakten (RKG):
        12024
    Kasten schwarz:
        Nr. 6730
    Kurbayern Äusseres Archiv:
        Nr. 4291
    Regensburger Testamente:
        Fasc. 80, Carton 26
Fugger Archiv (FA), Dillinger an der Donau
        2.1.12½
        2.2.45
        2.5.12
        44.1
Germanisches Nationalmuseum (GNM), Nuremberg
    (Archiv):
        Behaim Archiv

Imhoff Archiv
Reichsstadt Nürnberg: XI (Handel und Industrie)
(Bibliothek):
Hs 28,884
Nr. 2908
Nr. 2910
Herzog-August-Bibliothek (HAB), Wolfenbüttel
130. Helmst.
Staats- und Stadtbibliothek Augsburg (SuStBA), Augsburg
2° Cod. Aug. 198
4° Cod. H 13
(Peutinger Nachlaß):
2° Cod. Aug. 382a°
2° Cod. Aug. 402
Staatsarchiv Nürnberg (STAN), Nuremberg
Reichsstadt Nürnberg, Handschriften Nr. 281
Geuder-Rabensteiner Archiv, Bd. 146
Stadtarchiv Augsburg (StadtAA), Augsburg
Chroniken:
Nr. 5
Nr. 8
Nr. 14
Kaufmannschaft und Handel
Literalien:
1509
1580 (1570–80: Falliment des Conrad Roth)
Stadtgerichtsakten:
Nr. 105
Nr. 189
Schuld-, Klag-, und Appellationsakten:
Teil 2, Karton XXII, Nr. 162
Stadtarchiv Nürnberg (StadtAN), Nuremberg
Familien-Archiv Behaim
Tetzel-Archiv
Freiherrl. von Tucher'sches Familienarchiv
Freiherrl. von Tucher'sches Familienarchiv—Briefarchiv
Libris Literarum:
Nr. 45
Nr. 43
Stadtbibliothek Nürnberg (Stadtbibl. N.), Nuremberg
Pirckheimer Papiere
Cent. V. App 34k (Spengleriana)

PUBLISHED WORKS

Acosta, José de. *Natural and Moral History of the Indies.* Ed. Jane E. Mangan. Trans. Frances M. López-Morillas. Durham, NC, 2002.

Albala, Ken. *Eating Right in the Renaissance.* Berkeley and Los Angeles, 2002.

Alden, John, ed. *European Americana: A Chronological Guide to Works Printed in Europe Relating to the Americas, 1493–1776.* Vol. 1, *1493–1600.* New York, 1980.

Alexander, Amir R. *Geometrical Landscapes: The Voyages of Discovery and the Transformation of Mathematical Practice.* Stanford, 2002.

America: Das frühe Bild der Neuen Welt (Ausstellung der Bayerischen Staatsbibliothek München). Ed. Hans Wolf. Munich, 1992.

Ames, Oakes. *Economic Annuals and Human Cultures.* Cambridge, 1939.

Amman, Hektor. "Deutsch-spanische Wirtschaftsbeziehungen bis zum Ende des 15. Jahrhunderts." In Kellenbenz, *Fremde Kaufleute auf der Iberischen Halbinsel,* 132–55.

Anderson, Benedict. *Imagined Communities: Reflections on the Origin and Spread of Nationalism.* London, 1983.

Angliara, Juan de. *Die schiffung mitt dem Lanndt der Gulden Insel.* Augsburg: J. Nadler, 1520?.

Apian, Peter. *Astronomicum Caesareum.* Ingolstadt: P. Apian, 1540.

———. *Astronomicum Cäsareum: Eine Gründtliche außlegung des Buchs Astronomici Cäsarei.* Ingolstadt: P. Apian, 1540.

———. *Cosmographiae Introductio.* Ingolstadt: G. & P. Apianus, 1529 [1533].

———. *Cosmographia . . . per Gemmam Frisium . . . ob omnibus vindicata mendis.* Cologne: Heirs of A. Birckmann, 1574.

———. *Cosmographicus liber.* Landshut: Johann Weissenburger, 1524.

———. *Declaratio: et usus typi cosmographici Mappa mundi.* Regensburg: P. Kohl, 1522.

———. *Ein kunstlich Instrument oder Sonnen vr.* Landshut: J. Weissenburger, 1524.

———. *Eyn Newe vnnd wolgegründte vnderweysung aller Kauffmanß Rechnung.* Ingolstadt: G. Apian, 1527.

———. *Isagoge in typum cosmographicum seu mappam mundi.* Landshut: J. Weissenburger, 1521?.

Arber, Agnes. *Herbals, Their Origin and Evolution: A Chapter in the History of Botany, 1470–1670.* Cambridge, 1912.

Aristotle. *The Complete Works of Aristotle: The Revised Oxford Translation.* Ed. Jonathan Barnes. 2 vols. Princeton, 1984.

Arrizabalaga, Jon, John Henderson, and Roger French. *The Great Pox: The French Disease in Renaissance Europe.* New Haven, 1997.

Aubin, Jean, ed. *La Découverte, le Portugal, et l'Europe*. Paris, 1990.

Augustine, Saint. *The City of God against the Pagans*. Ed. and trans. R. W. Dyson. Cambridge, 1998.

Aujac, Germaine, J. B. Harley, and David Woodward. "The Foundations of Theoretical Cartography in Archaic and Classical Greece." In Harley and Woodward, *The History of Cartography*, 1: 130–47.

Baader, Gerhard. "Die Antikerezeption in der Entwicklung der medizinischen Wissenschaft während der Renaissance." In Schmitz and Keil, *Humanismus und Medizin*, 51–66.

———. "Medizinische Theorie und Praxis zwischen Arabismus und Renaissancehumanismus." In *Der Humanismus und die oberen Fakultäten*, ed. Gundolf Keil, Bernd Möller, and Winfried Trusen, 185–213. Weinheim, 1987.

———. "Mittelalter und Neuzeit im Werk von Otto Brunfels." *Medizinhistorisches Journal* 13, nos. 1–2 (1978): 186–203.

Bacon, Francis. *The New Organon*. Ed. Lisa Jardine and Michael Silverthorne. Cambridge, 2000.

Baldwin, John. "The Medieval Theories of the Just Price: Romanists, Canonists, and Theologians in the Twelfth and Thirteenth Centuries." In *Pre-Capitalist Economic Thought: Three Modern Interpretations*. New York, 1972.

Bämler, Johann. *Chronik von allen Kaisern, Königen, und Päpsten*. Augsburg: n.p., 1476.

Bartels, Karl Heinz. "Drogenhandel und Apothekenrechtliche Beziehungen zwischen Venedig und Nürnberg." Ph.D. dissertation, Universität Marburg, 1964.

Baxandall, Michael. *The Limewood Sculptors of Renaissance Germany*. New Haven, 1980.

Bayerische Staatsbibliothek, ed. *Verzeichnis der im deutschen Sprachbereich erschienenen Drucke des XVI. Jahrhunderts*. 25 vols. Stuttgart, 1983–2000.

Behringer, Wolfgang. *Shaman of Oberstdorf: Chonrad Stoeckhlin and the Phantoms of the Night*. Trans. H. C. Erik Midelfort. Charlottesville, VA, 1998.

Bellorum Christianorum principium contra Saracenos. Basel: H. Petri, 1533.

Benedek, Thomas G. "The Influence of Ulrich von Hutten's Medical Descriptions and Metaphorical Use of Medicine." *Bulletin of the History of Medicine* 66, no. 3 (1992): 355–75.

Berggren, J. Lennart, and Alexander Jones. "Introduction." In *Ptolemy's Geography: An Annotated Translation of the Theoretical Chapters*, 3–54. Princeton, 2000.

Berrera-Osorio, Antonio. *Experiencing Nature: The Spanish American Empire and the Early Scientific Revolution*. Austin, 2006.

———. "Local Herbs, Global Medicines: Commerce, Knowledge, and Commodities in Spanish America." In Smith and Findlen, *Merchants and Marvels*, 163–81.

Bezzel, Irmgard. "News from Portugal in 1506 and 1507, as printed by Johann Weissenburger in Nuremberg." In *The German Book, 1450–1750: Studies Presented to David L. Paisey in his Retirement,* ed. John L. Flood and William A. Kelly, 31–44. London, 1995.

Biagioli, Mario. "The Social Status of Italian Mathematicians, 1450–1600." *History of Science* 27, no. 1 (1989): 41–95.

Binotti, Lucia. "Cultural Identity and the Ideologies of Translation in Sixteenth-Century Europe: Italian Prologues to Spanish Chronicles of the New World." *History of European Ideas* 14, no. 6 (1992): 769–88.

Biondo, Flavio. *Italy Illuminated.* Ed. and trans. Jeffrey A. White. Cambridge, MA, 2005.

Bisaha, Nancy, *Creating East and West: Renaissance Humanists and the Ottoman Turks.* Philadelphia, 2004.

Bock, Hieronymus. *De historia stirpium, maxime earum, quae in Germani nostra nascuntur.* Strassburg: W. Rihel, 1552.

———. *Kreuter Buch. Darin Vnderscheid/Wuerckung vnd Namen der Kreüter.* Strassburg: W. Rihel, 1546.

———. *Kreuter Buch. Darinn Vnderscheidt/Namen vnnd Wuerckung der Kreuter.* Strassburg: W. Rihel, 1551.

———. *KreuterBuch. Darinn Vnderscheidt/Nammen vnnd Wuerckung der Kreutter.* Strassburg: J. Rihel, 1556.

———. *Kreüter Buch. Darinn Vnderscheidt/Namen vnd Wuerckung der Kreüter.* Strassburg: J. Rihel, 1560.

———. *Kreutterbuch darin vnderscheidt Namen vnnd wuerckung der kreutter.* Strassburg: J. Rihel, 1572.

———. *Kreütterbuch, darin underscheidt Nammen und Würckung der Kreütter.* Strassburg: J. Rihel, 1577.

———. *Kreuetterbuch. Darin vnderscheidt Nammen vnd Wuerckung der Kreütter.* Strassburg: J. Rihel, 1580.

———. *New Kreütter Buch von underscheydt, würckung und namen der kreütter, so in teutschen landen wachsen.* Strassburg: W. Rihel, 1539.

———. *Teütsche Speiszkammer.* Strassburg: Wendel Rihel, 1550. Reprint, 1555.

Boelhower, William. "Inventing America: The Culture of the Map." *Revue Français d'Études Américaines* 36 (April 1988): 211–23.

Boemus, Joannes. *Omnium Gentium Mores Leges et Ritus.* Augsburg: Sigismund Grimm and Marcus Wirsung, 1520.

Boesch, Hans. "Ein Brief Gabriel Holzschuher aus Indien vom Januar 1580." *Anzeiger für Kunde der Deutschen Vorzeit* 30, no. 6 (1883): 153–60; 30, no. 7 (1883): 185–89.

Böhme, Max. *Die Grossen Reisesammlungen des 16. Jahrhunderts und ihre Bedeutung.* 1904. Reprint, Amsterdam, 1962.

Bonorand, Conradin. "Hieronymus Sailer aus St. Gallen, Schwiegersohn des Augsburger Grosskaufherrn Bartholomaeus Welser, und seine Tätigkeit im Lichte seines Briefwechsels mit Vadian." *Zwingliana* 20 (1993): 103–25.

Borchardt, Frank L. *German Antiquity in Renaissance Myth.* Baltimore, 1971.

Borm, Wolfgang. *Incunabula Guelferbytana: Blockbücher und Wiegendrucke der Herzog August Bibliothek Wolfenbüttel.* Wiesbaden, 1990.

Borowka-Clausberg, Beate. *Balthasar Sprenger und der frühneuzeitliche Reisebericht.* Munich, 1999.

Bottschafft des Groszmechtigsten Konigs Dauid/aus dem grossen vnd hohen Morenland/den man gemeinlich nennt Priester Johann/an Babst Clemens den Siebenden. Dresden: Wolffgang Stoeckel, 1533.

Boucher, Philip P. *Cannibal Encounters: Europeans and Island Caribs, 1492–1763.* Baltimore, 1992.

Brant, Sebastian. *Doctor Brants Narrenschiff.* Basel: N. Lamparter, 1509.

———. Introduction to *Layen Spiegel: Von rechtmäßigen ordnungen in Burgerlichen vnd peinlichen regimenten,* by Uldaricus Tenngler. Augsburg: H. Otmar, 1509.

Braunstein, Philippe. "Wirtschaftliche Beziehungen zwischen Nürnberg und Italien im Spätmittelalter." In *Beiträge zur Wirtschaftsgeschichte Nürnbergs,* 1: 377–406. Nuremberg, 1967.

Bredekamp, Horst. *The Lure of Antiquity and the Cult of the Machine: The Kunstkammer and the Evolution of Nature, Art and Technology.* Trans. Allison Brown. Princeton, 1995.

Briesemeister, Dietrich. "Frühe Berichte über die spanischen Eroberungen in deutschen Übersetzungen des 16. Jahrhunderts." In *Der eroberte Kontinent: Historische Realität, Rechtfertigung und literarische Darstellung der Kolonisation Amerikas,* ed. Karl Kohut, 246–59. Frankurt a.M, 1991.

Broecke, Steven Vanden. "The Use of Visual Media in Renaissance Cosmography: The *Cosmography* of Peter Apian and Gemma Frisius." *Paedagogica Historica* 36, no. 1 (2000): 131–50.

Brotton, Jerry. *Trading Territories: Mapping the Early Modern World.* London, 1997.

Brunfels, Otto. *Contrafayt Kreüterbuch.* Strassburg: J. Schott, 1532.

———. *Herbarum vivae eiconeb.* Strassburg: J. Schott, 1530.

———. *Herbarium vivae eicones.* Strassburg: J. Schott, 1532. Rev. and exp. ed., 1537.

———. *Kreuterbuch contrafayt.* Strassburg: J. Schott, 1534. Reprint, *Kreüterbuch contrafeyt,* Strassburg: J. Schott, 1539–40.

———. *Kreuterbuch Contrafeyt.* Frankfurt a.M.: H. Guelfferich, 1546.

Burkhardt, Johannes, ed. *Augsburger Handelshäuser im Wandel des historischen Urteils.* Berlin, 1996.

Campbell, Mary B. "Carnal Knowledge: Fracastoro's *De Syphilis* and the Discovery of the New World." In *Crossing Cultures: Essays in the Displacement of Western Civilization,* ed. Daniel Segal, 3–32. Tucson, 1992.

———. *The Witness and the Other World: Exotic European Travel Writing.* Ithaca, 1988.

———. *Wonder and Science: Imagining Worlds in Early Modern Europe.* Ithaca, 1999.

Carion, Johann. *Chronicorum libri tres . . . Hermanno Bonno interprete.* Basel: Matthias Herscher, 1552.

Carrara, Daniela Mugnai. "Epistemological Problems in Giovanni Mainardi's Commentary on Galen's *Ars Parva.*" In *Natural Particulars: Nature and the Disciplines in Renaissance Europe,* ed. Anthony Grafton and Nancy Siraisi, 251–73. Cambridge, MA, 1999.

Cary, George. *The Medieval Alexander.* Cambridge, 1956.

Castanheda, Fernão Lopes de. *Warhafftige vnd volkomen Historia/Von erfindung Calecut vnd anderer Königreich/Landen vnd Inseln/in Indien/vnd dem Indianischen Meer gelegen.* Augsburg?: n.p., 1565. Also published in Feyerabend, *Ander theil dieses Weltbuchs.*

Certeau, Michel de. *The Writing of History.* Trans. Tom Conley. New York, 1988.

Chaplin, Joyce E. *Subject Matter: Technology, the Body, and Science on the Anglo-American Fronter, 1500–1676.* Cambridge, MA, 2001.

Chiappelli, Fredi, ed. *First Images of America: The Impact of the New World on the Old.* 2 vols. Berkeley and Los Angeles, 1976.

Chrisman, Miriam Usher. *Lay Culture, Learned Culture: Books and Social Change in Strasbourg, 1480–1599.* New Haven, 1982.

Chronica, Beschreibung, und gemeyne anzeyge vonn aller Welt herkommen. Frankfurt a.M.: C. Egenolff, 1535.

Clendinnen, Inga. *Ambivalent Conquests: Maya and Spaniard in Yucatan, 1517–1570.* Cambridge, 1987.

Cochlaeus, Johann, ed. *Cosmographia Pomponii Mele.* Nuremberg: J. Weissenburger, 1512.

———, ed. *Meteorologia Aristotelis.* Nuremberg: F. Peypus, 1512.

Colin, Susi. *Das Bild des Indianers im 16. Jahrhundert.* Idstein, 1988.

———. "The Wild Man and the Indian in Early 16th Century Book Illustration." In *Indians and Europe: An Interdisciplinary Collection of Essays,* ed. Christian F. Feest, 5–36. Aachen, 1987.

Columbus, Christopher. *De insulis inventis Epistola.* Basel: J. Wolff, 1493. Also published in Verardi, *In laudem,* and *Bellorum Christianorum.*

———. *Eyn schön hübsch lesen von etlichen insslen.* Strassburg: B. Kistler, 1497.

Cooper, Alix. *Inventing the Indigenous: Local Knowledge and Natural History in Early Modern Europe.* Cambridge, 2007.

Copia der Newen Zeytung auß Presillg Landt. Nuremberg: H. Höltzel, 1514?. Reprint, Augsburg: E. Oeglin, 1514? (additional counterfeit edition).

Copey etlicher brieff, so auß Hispania kummen seindt. Augsburg?: n.p., 1535.

Cortes, Hernan. *De nova maris Oceani Hyspania narratio . . . Tertia . . . in nova maris Oceani Hyspania generalis praefecti preclara narratio.* Nuremberg: F. Peypus, 1524. Reprint, *De insulis nuper inventis . . . cum alio quodam Petri Martyris,* Cologne: Melchior von Neuss for A. Berckmann, 1532.

———. *Von dem Newen Hispanien, so im meer gegen Nidergang.* Augsburg: P. Ulhart, 1550.

Cosgrove, Denis. *The Palladian Landscape: Geographical Change and Its Cultural Representations in Sixteenth-Century Italy.* University Park, PA, 1993.

Cuneo, Pia F. "Constructing the Boundaries of Community: Nationalism, Protestantism, and Economics in a Sixteenth-Century Broadsheet." In *Infinite Boundaries: Order, Disorder and Reorder in Early Modern German Culture,* ed. Max Reinhart, 171–85. Kirksville, MO, 1998.

Cuppener, Cristofer. *Ein schons buchlein czu deutsch doraus ein itzlicher mensche . . . lernen mag was wucher und wucherische hendel vortilget.* Leipzig: Melchior Lotter, 1508.

Daenell, E. "Ein Geldgeschäft Karls V. mit einem Augsburger Kaufmann." *Zeitschrift des historischen Vereins für Schwaben und Neuburg* 37 (1911): 138–39.

d'Anghiera, Peter Martyr. *De nuper sub D. Carolo repertis insulis . . . enchiridion.* Basel: A. Petri, 1521.

———. *De rebus, et insulis noviter repertis.* Nuremberg: F. Peypus, 1524.

———. *De rebus oceanicis.* Basel: J. Bebel, 1533. Reprint, Cologne: G. Calenius & Heirs of J. Quentel, 1574.

Dannenfeldt, Karl H. "Wittenberg Botanists during the Sixteenth Century." In *The Social History of the Reformation,* ed. Lawrence P. Buck and Jonathan W. Zophy, 223–48. Columbus, OH, 1972.

Daston, Lorraine, and Katharine Park. *Wonders and the Order of Nature, 1150–1750.* New York, 1998.

Davis, Natalie Zemon. "Sixteenth-Century French Arithmetics on the Business Life." *Journal of the History of Ideas* 21, no. 1 (1960): 18–48.

De Exequiis Caroli V. Maximi Imperatoris. Augsburg: P. Ulhart, 1559.

Den rechten weg ausz zu faren von Liszbona gen Kallakuth von meyl zu meyl. Nuremberg: J. Weissenburger, 1508.

Denzer, Jörg. "Die Welser in Venezuela—Das Scheitern ihrer wirtschaftlichen Ziele." In Häberlein and Burkhardt, *Die Welser,* 285–319.

Deutsche Reichstagsakten, Jüngere Reihe. Vols. 1–4. Gotha: F. Perthes, 1893–1905.

Dharampal-Frick, Gita. "Die Faszination des Exotischen: Deutsche Indien-Berichte der frühen Neuzeit (1500–1750)." In *Die Kenntnis beider "Indien" im frühneuzeitlichen Europa,* ed. Urs Bitterli and Eberhard Schmitt, 93–128. Munich, 1991.

————. *Indien im Spiegel deutscher Quellen der Frühen Neuzeit (1500–1700): Studien zu einer interkulturellen Konstellation.* Tübingen, 1994.

————. " 'Irdisches Paradies' und 'veritable europäisches Schatzkammer': Konturen und Entwicklungen des deutschen Indienbildes im Zeitalter der Entdeckungen." *Pirckheimer Jahrbuch* (1986): 83–107.

Die Mörin. Eyn Schöne Kurtzweilige vnd Liebliche Histori. Worms: Sebastian Wagner, 1538.

Diener, Hermann. "Die 'Camera Papagalli' im Palast des Papstes: Papageien als Hausgenossen der Päpste, Könige und Fürsten des Mittelalters und der Renaissance." *Archiv für Kulturgeschichte* 49, no. 1 (1967): 43–97.

Dilg, Peter. "Die botanische Kommentarliteratur in Italien um 1500 und ihr Einfluß auf Deutschland." In *Der Kommentar in der Renaissance,* ed. August Beck and Otto Herding, 225–52. Boppard, 1975.

————. "Die Pflanzenkunde im Humanismus—der Humanismus in der Pflanzenkunde." In Schmitz and Krafft, *Humanismus und Naturwissenschaften,* 113–34.

Dilke, Oswald A. W., and Margaret S. Dilke. "Ptolemy's *Geography* and the New World." In Williams and Lewis, *Early Images of the Americas,* 263–85.

Dioscorides. *De medicinali materia libri sex . . . per Gualtherum H. Ryff.* Ed. Jean Ruel. Frankfurt a.M.: C. Egenolff, 1543.

————. *Kreutter Buch des Hochberümpten Pedanii Dioscoridis Anazarbei.* Trans. Johann Dantzer. Frankfurt a.M.: C. Jacob, 1546.

Dobat, Klaus. "Leonhart Fuchs (1501–1566): Physician and Pioneer of Modern Botany." In *Leonhart Fuchs: The New Herbal of 1543 (New Kreüterbuch),* 6–23. Cologne, 2001.

Dollinger, Philippe. *Die Hanse.* 5th ed. Stuttgart, 1998.

Donattini, Massimo. "Der geographische Horizont des italienischen Verlagswesens (1493–1560)." In Prosperi and Reinhard, *Neue Welt im Bewusstsein der Italiener und Deutschen,* 69–134.

Dreyer-Eimbcke, Oswald. *Kolumbus: Entdeckungen und Irrtümer in der deutschen Kartographie.* Frankfurt a.M., 1991.

Dryander, Johann. *Novi Annuli Astronomici.* Marburg: E. Cervicornus, 1536.

Durand, Dana Bennett. *The Vienna-Klosterneuburg Map Corpus of the Fifteenth Century: A Study in the Transition from Medieval to Modern Science.* Leiden, 1952.

Dürer, Albrecht. "Tagebuch der niederländischen Reise." In *Albrecht Dürers schriftlicher Nachlass: Familienchronik/Gedenkbuch/Tagebuch der niederlän-*

dischen Reise/Briefe/Reime/Auswahl aus den theoretischen Schriften, ed. Ernst Heidrick, 24–118. Berlin, 1908.

Eastwood, B. S. "Plinian Astronomy in the Middle Ages and Renaissance." In *Science in the Early Roman Empire: Pliny the Elder, His Sources and Influence,* ed. Roger French and Frank Greenaway, 197–235. Totowa, NJ, 1986.

Edgerton, Samuel. "From Mental Matrix to *Mappamundi* to Christian Empire: The Heritage of Ptolemaic Cartography in the Renaissance." In *Art and Cartography: Six Historical Essays,* ed. David Woodward, 10–50. Chicago, 1987.

Edwards, Jess. "How to Read an Early Modern Map: Between the Particular and the General, the Material and the Abstract, Words and Mathematics." *Early Modern Literary Studies* 9, no. 1 (2003): 6.1–58 (http://purl.oclc .org/emls/09–1/edwamaps.html).

Ehlers, Joachim, ed. *Ansätze und Diskontinuität deutscher Nationsbildung im Mittelalter.* Sigmaringen, 1989.

Ehrenberg, Richard. *Das Zeitalter der Fugger: Geldkapital und Creditverkehr im 16. Jahrhundert.* 2 vols. Jena, 1896.

Ein auszug ettlicher sendbrieff dem . . . Fürsten und Herren Herren Carl Römischen und Hyspanischen König. Nuremberg: F. Peypus, 1520.

Eine schöne newe zeytung so Kayserlich Mayestet auß India yetz newlich zükommen seind. Augsburg: M. Ramminger, 1522.

Ein missif oder sendbrieff newer zeytung/betreffendt ein fryd/ . . . Newe Zeyttung von einer wunderlichen Insel welche . . . durch des Königs von Portugal Schyffart ist gefunden worden. N.p.: n. p., 1533.

Eisenmenger, Samuel [Siderocrates]. *Libellus geographicus, locorum numerandi intervalla rationem in lineis rectis & sphaericis complectens.* Tübingen: Widow of U. Morhart, 1563.

Elliott, J. H. "Final Reflections: The Old World and the New Revisited." In Kupperman, *America in European Consciousness,* 391–408.

———. *The Old World and the New, 1492–1650.* Cambridge, 1970.

———. "Renaissance Europe and America: A Blunted Impact?" In Chiappelli, *First Images of America,* 1: 11–23.

Elsner, John, and Roger Cardinal, eds. *The Cultures of Collecting.* London, 1994.

Estes, J. Worth. "The European Reception of the First Drugs of the New World." *Pharmacy in History* 37, no. 1 (1995): 3–23.

Evans, James. *The History and Practice of Ancient Astronomy.* Oxford, 1998.

Falk, Tilman. "Frühe Rezeption der Neuen Welt in der graphischen Kunst." In *Humanismus und Neue Welt,* ed. Wolfgang Reinhard, 37–64. Weinheim, 1987.

Favier, Jean. *Gold and Spices: The Rise of Commerce in the Middle Ages.* Trans. Caroline Higgitt. New York, 1998.

Federmann, Nicolas. *Indianische historia*. Hagenau: S. Bund, 1557.

Feyerabend, Sigmund, ed. *Ander theil dieses Weltbuchs von Schifffahrten*. Frankfurt a.M.: Martin Lechler for Sigmund Feyerabend & Simon Hüter, 1567.

———, ed. *Erst theil dieses Weltbuchs*. Frankfurt a.M.: Martin Lechler for Sigmund Feyerabend & Simon Hüter, 1567.

Finan, John J. *Maize in the Great Herbals*. Waltham, MA, 1950.

Findlen, Paula. "Inventing Nature: Commerce, Art, and Science in the Early Modern Cabinet of Curiosities." In Smith and Findlen, *Merchants and Marvels*, 297–323.

———. *Possessing Nature: Museums, Collecting, and Scientific Culture in Early Modern Italy*. Berkeley and Los Angeles, 1994.

Fischer, Jos., ed. *Der "Deutsche Ptolemäus" aus dem Ende des XV. Jahrhunderts (um 1490) in Faksimiledruck*. Strassburg, 1910.

Fischer, J., and F. v. Wieser. *Die Weltkarten Waldseemüllers (Ilacomilius) 1507 und 1516*. Innsbruck, 1903.

Fitzmaurice, Andrew. *Humanism and America: An Intellectual History of English Colonisation, 1500–1625*. Cambridge, 2003.

Flint, Valerie I. J. *The Imaginative Landscape of Christopher Columbus*. Princeton, 1992.

Florkin, M., ed. *Materia Medica in the XVIth Century*. Oxford, 1966.

Fortunatus/Vonn seinem Seckel/vnnd Wünschhütlein. Frankfurt a.M.: Hermann Gülfferich, 1554.

Franck, Sebastian. *Warhafftige Beschreibunge aller theil der Welt*. Frankfurt a.M.: M. Lechler for S. Feyerabend & S. Hüter, 1567.

———. *Weltbuch: spiegel und bildtniss des gantzen erdtbodens*. Tübingen: U. Morhart, 1534. Reprint, Ulm: Hans Varnier der Ältere, 1542. Reprint, Frankfurt: n.p., 1542.

Frey, Winfried. "Montis auri pollicens: Mittelalterliche Weltanschauung und die Entdeckung Amerikas." *Germanisch-romanische Monatsschrift* 68, no.1 (1987): 1–18.

Friedman, John Block. *The Monstrous Races in Medieval Art and Thought*. Cambridge, 1981.

Fries, Lorenz. *Carta Marina Universalis 1530*. Munich: n.p., n.d.

———. *Hydrographiae, hoc est, Charta marinae totiusque orbis . . . descriptio*. Strassburg: J. Grüninger, 1530.

———. *Unterweisung und ußlegung der Cartha marina*. Strassburg: J. Grüninger, 1530.

———. *Uslegung der Mercarthen*. Strassburg: J. Grüninger, 1525. Rev. ed., 1527.

Frisius, Gemma. *Arithmeticae Practicae Methodus Facilis*. Wittenberg: Georg Rhau, 1544.

————. *Arithmeticae Practicae Methodus Facilis . . . Huc Accesserunt Iacobi Peletarii Cenomani annotationes.* Cologne: M. Cholinus, 1571.

Frübis, Hildegard. *Die Wirklichkeit des Fremden: Die Darstellung der Neuen Welt im 16. Jahrhundert.* Berlin, 1995.

Fuchs, Barbara. *Mimesis and Empire: The New World, Islam, and European Identities.* Cambridge, 2001.

Fuchs, Leonhart. *De historia stirpium.* Basel: M. Isengrin, 1542.

————. *De Usitata huius temporis componendorum miscendorumque medicamentorum ratione Libri quatuor.* In *Methodus Seu Ratio Compendiaria.* Basel: J. Oporinus, 1555.

————. *Läbliche abbildung und contrafaytung aller kreüter.* Basel: M. Isengrin, 1545.

————. *New Kreüterbuch.* Basel: M. Isengrin, 1543.

————. *Primi de stirpium historia commentariorum tomu vivae imagines.* Basel: M. Isengrin, 1545. Reprint, 1549.

Fuller, Mary C. *Voyages in Print: English Travel to America, 1576–1624.* Cambridge, 1995.

Gallois, Lucien. *Les Geographes Allemands de la Renaissance.* 1890. Reprint, Amsterdam, 1963.

Geiger, Ludwig. "Münster, Sebastian M." In *Allgemeine Deutsche Biographie,* 23: 30–33. Munich, 1886.

Genette, Gérard. *Paratexts: Thresholds of Interpretation.* Trans. Jane E. Lewis. Cambridge, 1997.

Gerbi, Antonello. *Nature in the New World: From Christopher Columbus to Gonzalo Fernández de Oviedo.* Trans. Jeremy Moyle. Pittsburgh, 1985.

Ghetel, H., trans. *Nye vnbekande lande unde ein nye Werldt in korter vergangener tyd gefunden.* Nuremberg: G. Stuchs, 1508.

Ghillany, F. W. *Geschichte des Seefahrers Ritter Martin Behaim nach den ältesten vorhandenen Urkunden bearbeitet.* Nuremberg, 1853.

Gier, Helmut, and Johannes Janota, eds. *Augsburger Buchdruck und Verlagswesen: Von den Anfängen bis zur Gegenwart.* Wiesbaden, 1997.

Giesecke, Michael. "Die typographische Konstruktion der 'Neuen Welt.'" In Wenzel, *Gutenberg und die Neue Welt,* 15–32.

Gillies, John. *Shakespeare and the Geography of Difference.* Cambridge, 1994.

Glareanus, Henricus. *De geographia liber unus.* Basel: J. Faber, 1527. Reprint, 1528.

————. *De geographia liber unus.* Freiburg i. Br.: J. Faber, 1530. Reprint, 1533, 1536, 1539.

————. *De geographia liber unus.* Freiburg i. Br.: S. M. Graf, 1543. Reprint, 1551.

Goedeke, Karl. "Die Büchersammlung des Hans Sachs." *Archiv für Litteraturgeschichte* 7 (1878): 1–6.

Goes, Damião a, *Glaubhafftige zeyttung vnd bericht/des Kriegs . . . zwischen dem Künig auß Portugall/vnd dem Türckischen Kaiser/in India.* Augsburg: P. Ulhart, n.d.

Goltz, Dietlinde. *Mittelalterliche Pharmazie und Medizin: Dargestellt an Geschichte und Inhalt des "Antidotarium Nicolai," Mit einem Nachdruck der Druckfassung von 1471.* Stuttgart, 1976.

Goodman, David C. *Power and Penury: Government, Technology and Science in Philip II's Spain.* Cambridge, 1988.

Goodman, Jennifer. *Chivalry and Exploration, 1298–1630.* Woodbridge, U.K., 1998.

Gotlieb, Johann. *Ein Teutsch verstendig Buchhalten für Herren oder Geselschaffter inhalt wellischem proceß.* Nuremberg: F. Peypus, 1531.

Gottlieb, Gunther. *Europa in der Defensive: Die Spiegelung von Vergangenheit und Gegenwart in frühneuzeitlichen Herodotübersetzungen.* Braunschweig, 2002.

Graf-Stuhlhofer, Franz. *Humanismus zwischen Hof und Universität: Georg Tannstetter (Collimitius) und sein wissenschaftliches Umfeld im Wien des frühen 16. Jahrhunderts.* Wien, 1996.

Grafton, Anthony. *New Worlds, Ancient Texts: The Power of Tradition and the Shock of Discovery.* Cambridge, MA, 1992.

Graziano, Frank. "Columbus and the Invention of Discovery." *Encounters* 4 (Autumn 1990): 26–29.

Greenblatt, Stephen. *Marvelous Possessions: The Wonder of the New World.* Chicago, 1991.

Greiff, B., ed. "Briefe und Berichte über die frühesten Reisen nach Amerika und Ostindien aus den Jahren 1497 bis 1506 aus Dr. Conrad Peutingers Nachlaß." *Sechsundzwanzigster Jahres-Bericht des historischen Kreis-Vereins im Regierungsbezirke von Schwaben und Neuburg für das Jahre 1860.* Augsburg, 1861.

———, ed. "Tagebuch des Lucas Rem aus den Jahren 1494–1541. Ein Beitrag zur Handelsgeschichte der Stadt Augsburg." *Sechsundzwanzigster Jahres-Bericht des historischen Kreis-Vereins im Regierungsbezirke von Schwaben und Neuburg für das Jahre 1860.* Augsburg, 1861.

Großhaupt, Walter. "Bartholomäus Welser: Charakteristik seiner Unternehmungen in Spanien und Übersee." Ph.D. dissertation, Universität Graz, 1987.

———. "Commercial Relations between Portugal and the Merchants of Augsburg and Nuremberg." In Aubin, *La Découverte,* 359–97.

———. "Der Venezuela-Vertrag der Welser." *Scripta Mercaturae* 24, nos. 1–2 (1990): 1–35.

———. "Die Welser als Bankiers der spanischen Krone." *Scripta Mercaturae* 21, nos. 1–2 (1987): 158–88.

Grössing, Helmuth. *Humanistische Naturwissenschaft: Zur Geschichte der Wiener mathematischen Schulen des 15. und 16. Jahrhunderts.* Baden-Baden, 1983.

Guerra, Francisco. "Drugs from the Indies and the Political Economy of the Sixteenth Century." In Florkin, *Materia Medica in the XVIth Century,* 29–54.

Günther, Hans, ed. *Fortunatus. Nach dem Augsburger Druck von 1509.* Halle a.d.S., 1914.

Günther, Siegmund. "Johann Eck als Geograph." *Forschungen zur Kultur- und Literaturgeschichte Bayerns* 2 (1894): 140–62.

Haase, Wolfgang, and Meyer Reinhold, eds. *European Images of the Americas and the Classical Tradition.* Vol. 1, Part 1, *The Classical Tradition and the Americas.* Berlin, 1994.

Häberlein, Mark. *Brüder, Freunde und Betrüger: Soziale Beziehungen, Normen und Konflikte in der Augsburger Kaufmannschaft um die Mitte des 16. Jahrhunderts.* Berlin, 1998.

———. "'Die Tag und Nacht auff Fürkauff trachten.' Augsburger Großkaufleute des 16. und beginnenden 17. Jahrhunderts in der Beurteilung ihrer Zeitgenossen und Mitbürger." In Burkhardt, *Augsburger Handelshäuser im Wandel des historischen Urteils,* 46–68.

———. "Monster und Missionare: Die außereuropäische Welt in Augsburger Drucken der frühen Neuzeit." In Gier and Janota, *Augsburger Buchdruck und Verlagswesen,* 353–80.

Häberlein, Mark, and Johannes Burkhardt, eds. *Die Welser: Neue Forschungen zur Geschichte und Kultur des oberdeutschen Handelhauses.* Berlin, 2002.

Hadden, Richard W. *On the Shoulders of Merchants: Exchange and the Mathematical Conception of Nature in Early Modern Europe.* Albany, 1994.

Hadfield, Andrew. *Literature, Travel, and Colonial Writing in the English Renaissance, 1545–1625.* Oxford, 1998.

Haebler, Konrad. "Die Finanzdecrete Philipp's II. und die Fugger." *Deutsche Zeitschrift für Geschichtswissenschaft* 11 (1894): 276–300.

———. "Die Fugger und der spanische Gewürzhandel." *Zeitschrift des historischen Vereins für Schwaben und Neuburg* 19 (1892): 25–44.

———. *Die überseeischen Unternehmungen der Welser und ihrer Gesellschafter.* Leipzig, 1903.

———. "Konrad Rott und die Thüringische Gesellschaft." *Neues Archiv für Sächsische Geschichte und Altertumskunde* 16 (1895): 177–218.

———. "Welser und Ehinger in Venezuela." *Zeitschrift des historischen Vereins für Schwaben und Neuburg* 21 (1894): 66–86.

Hair, P. E. H. "Early Sources on Guinea." *History in Africa* 21 (1994): 87–126.

Hamann, Günther. "Kartographisches und wirkliches Weltbild in der Renaissancezeit. Zum wechselseitigen Verhältnis von Theorie und Praxis im

Zeitalter der großen Entdeckungsfahrten." In Schmitz and Krafft, *Humanismus und Naturwissenschaften,* 155–79.

Hammond, Mitchell Love. "The Origins of Civic Health Care in Early Modern Germany." Ph.D. dissertation, University of Virginia, 2000.

Harbsmeier, Michael. *Wilde Völkerkunde: Andere Welten in deutschen Reiseberichten der Frühen Neuzeit.* Frankfurt a.M., 1994.

Harley, J. B. "Maps, Knowledge and Power." In *The Iconography of Landscape: Essays on the Symbolic Representation, Design and Use of Past Environments,* ed. Denis Cosgrove and Stephen Daniels, 277–312. Cambridge, 1988.

Harley, J. B., and David Woodward, eds. *The History of Cartography.* Vol. 1, *Cartography in Prehistoric, Ancient, and Medieval Europe and the Mediterranean.* Chicago, 1987.

Hart, Jonathan. *Representing the New World: The English and French Uses of the Example of Spain.* New York, 2000.

Hartog, François. *The Mirror of Herodotus: The Representation of the Other in the Writing of History.* Trans. Janet Lloyd. Berkeley and Los Angeles, 1988.

Herbarius. Mainz: Peter Schöffer, 1484? (IG 1297).

Herodotus. *Herodoti Halicarnassei Historiographi Libri Novem.* Cologne: E. Cervicornus with M. Gottfried Hittorp, 1537.

———. *[V]on dem Persier/vnd vilen andern kriegen vnd geschichten.* Trans. Hieronymus Boner. Augsburg: H. Steiner, 1535.

Herr, Michael, trans. *Die New Welt, der landschaften unnd Insulen, so bis hie her allen Altwelt besschryben unbekant.* Strassburg: G. Ulricher, 1534.

Higgins, Iain Macleod. *Writing East: The "Travels" of Sir John Mandeville.* Philadelphia, 1997.

Hildebrandt, Reinhard. "Der Niedergang des Augsburg Welser-Firma (1560–1614)." In Häberlein and Burkhardt, *Die Welser,* 265–81.

———. "The Effects of Empire: Changes in the European Economy after Charles V." In *Industry and Finance in Early Modern History: Essays Presented to George Hammersley on the Occasion of his 74th Birthday,* ed. Ian Blanchard, Anthony Goodman, and Jennifer Newman, 58–75. Stuttgart, 1992.

———. "Wirtschaftsentwicklung und Konzentration im 16. Jahrhundert: Konrad Rot und die Finanzierungsprobleme seines interkontinentalen Handels." *Scripta Mercaturae* 1 (1970): 25–50.

Hirsch, Rudolf. *Printing, Selling and Reading, 1450–1550.* Wiesbaden, 1967.

Hodgen, Margaret T. *Early Anthropology in the Sixteenth and Seventeenth Centuries.* Philadelphia, 1964.

Hodorowich, Liz. "Armchair Travelers and the Venetian Discovery of the New World." *Sixteenth Century Journal* 36, no. 4 (2005): 1039–62.

Höffner, Joseph. *Wirtschaftsethik und Monopole im fünfzehnten und sechzehnten Jahrhundert.* Jena, 1941.

Honter, Johann. *De cosmographia rudimentis*. In *De sphaera liber i*, by Proclus Diadochus. Basel: S. Henricpetri, 1561.

———. *Rudimenta cosmographica*. Zurich: C. Froschauer, 1546. Reprint, 1548.

———. *Rudimentorum cosmographiae libri duo*. Basel: H. Petri, 1534.

———. *Rudimentorum cosmographicorum . . . libri iii*. Zurich: C. Froschauer, 1548. Reprint, 1549, 1552, 1558, 1564, 1565, 1570, 1573, 1575, 1578.

———. *Rudimentorum cosmographicorum*. Rostock: J. Stoeckelmann & A. Gutterwitz, 1572.

Hoock, Jochen, and Pierre Jeannin. *Ars Mercatoria: Handbücher und Traktate für den Gebrauch des Kaufmanns, 1470–1820*. 6 vols. Paderborn, 1991.

Hooykaas, R. *The Impact of the Voyages of Discovery on Portuguese Humanist Literature*. Coimbra, 1970.

Hoppe, Brigitte. *Das Kräuterbuch des Hieronymus Bock: Wissenschaftshistorische Untersuchung*. Stuttgart, 1969.

Hortus sanitas, deutsch. Basel: Michael Furter, ca. 1486. (IG 1397).

Hulme, Peter. "Tales of Distinction: European Ethnography and the Caribbean." In Schwartz, *Implicit Understandings*, 157–97.

Hümmerich, Franz. "Quellen und Untersuchungen zur Fahrt der ersten Deutschen nach dem portugiesischen Indien 1505/06." *Abhandlungen der Königlich Bayerischen Akademie der Wissenschaften, Philosophisch-philologische und historische Klasse* 30, no. 3 (1918): 104–26.

Hunt, Edwin S., and James M. Murray. *A History of Business in Medieval Europe, 1200–1550*. Cambridge, 1999.

Hutten, Philipp von. "Tagebuch von 1533–1538 und Briefe." Ed. Johann Georg Meusel. *Historisch-litterarisches Magazin* 1 (1785): 51–119.

Hutten, Ulrich von. *De Guaiaci Medicina et Morbo Gallico Liber Unus*. Mainz: Johann Schöffer, 1519.

———. *Dialogus oder ein gesprech/Febris/genant*. Mainz: Johann Schöffer, 1519.

———. "Die Anschawenden." In *Gesprächbüchlin herr Vlrichs von Hutten*. Strassburg: Johann Schott, 1521.

———. *Gesprächbüchlin herr Vlrichs von Hutten*. Mainz: Johann Schöffer, 1519.

———. "Praedones." In *Dialogi Huttenici noui, perquam festiui*. Strassburg: Johann Schott, 1521?

———. *Voder wunderbarlichen artzney des holtz Guaiacum genant*. Trans. Thomas Murner. Strassburg: J. Grüninger, 1519.

Huttich, Johann, trans. *Novus Orbis regionum ac insularum veteribus incogni-tarum*. Basel: J. Herwagen, 1532.

Isenmann, Eberhard. "Kaiser, Reich und deutsche Nation am Ausgang des 15. Jahrhunderts." In Ehlers, *Ansätze und Diskontinuität deutscher Nationsbildung im Mittelalter*, 145–246.

Islam, Syed Manzurul. *The Ethics of Travel: From Marco Polo to Kafka.* Manchester, 1996.

Israel, Jonathan, *Dutch Primacy in World Trade, 1585–1740.* Oxford, 1989.

Jahn, Bernhard. *Raumkonzepte in der Frühen Neuzeit: Zur Konstruktion von Wirklichkeit in Pilgerberichten, Amerikareisebeschreibungen und Prosaerzählungen.* Frankfurt a.M., 1993.

Jahnel, Helga. "Die Imhoff: Eine Nürnberger Patrizier- und Großkaufmannsfamilie." Ph.D. dissertation, Universität Würzburg, 1950.

Jardine, Lisa. *Worldly Goods: A New History of the Renaissance.* New York, 1996.

Joachimsen, Paul. *Geschichtsauffassung und Geschichtsschreibung in Deutschland unter dem Einfluss des Humanismus.* 1910. Reprint, Aalen, 1968.

John III of Portugal. *Serenissimi atque invictissimi portugalliae & Algarbiorum Regis Literae. . . super insigni victoria.* Strassburg: Kraft Müller, 1536.

Johnson, Carina Lee. "Negotiating the Exotic: Aztec and Ottoman Culture in Habsburg Europe, 1500–1590." Ph.D. dissertation, University of California–Berkeley, 2000.

Johnson, Christine R. "Bringing the World Home: Germany and the Age of Discovery, 1492–1580." Ph.D. dissertation, Johns Hopkins University, 2001.

———. "Renaissance German Cosmographers and the Naming of America." *Past and Present* 191 (May 2006): 3–43.

Johnson, Hildegard Binder. *Carta Marina: World Geography in Strassburg, 1525.* Minneapolis, 1963.

Jütte, Robert. *Ärzte, Heiler und Patienten: Medizinischer Alltag in der frühen Neuzeit.* Munich, 1991.

Kaisersberg, Johann Geiler von. *[N]arenschiff.* Strassburg: J. Grüninger, 1520.

———. *Navicula sive speculum fatuorum prestantissimi sacrarum literarium.* Strassburg: M. Schürer, 1510.

Kästner, Hannes. "Der Arzt und die Kosmographie: Beobachtungen über Aufnahme und Vermittlung neuer geographischer Kenntnisse in der deutschen Frührenaissance und der Reformationszeit." In *Literatur und Laienbildung im Spätmittelalter und in der Reformationszeit,* ed. Ludger Grenzmann and Karl Stackmann, 504–31. Stuttgart, 1984.

———. *Fortunatus—Peregrinator mundi: Welterfahrung und Selbsterkenntnis im ersten deutschen Prosaroman der Neuzeit.* Freiburg i. Br., 1990.

Kaufmann, Thomas DaCosta. "From Treasury to Museum: The Collections of the Austrian Habsburgs." In Elsner and Cardinal, *The Cultures of Collecting,* 137–54.

———. *The Mastery of Nature: Aspects of Art, Science, and Humanism in the Renaissance.* Princeton, 1993.

Kelchner, Ernst, and Richard Wülcker, eds. *Mess-Memorial des Frankfurter Buchhändlers Michel Harder Fastenmesse 1569.* Frankfurt a.M., 1873.

Kellenbenz, Hermann. "Briefe über Pfeffer und Kupfer." In *Geschichte, Wirtschaft, Gesellschaft: Festschrift für Clemens Bauer zum 75. Geburtstag*, ed. Erich Hassinger, J. Heinz Müller, and Hugo Otto, 205–27. Berlin, 1974.

————, ed. *Das Meder'sche Handelsbuch und die Welser'schen Nachträge*. Wiesbaden, 1974.

————. "Die Beziehungen Nürnbergs zur Iberischen Halbinsel, besonders im 15. und in der ersten Hälfte des 16. Jahrhunderts." In *Beiträge zur Wirtschaftsgeschichte Nürnbergs*, 1: 456–93. Nuremberg, 1967.

————. *Die Fugger in Spanien und Portugal bis 1560: Ein Großunternehmen des 16. Jahrhunderts*. 3 vols. Munich, 1990.

————, ed. *Fremde Kaufleute auf der Iberischen Halbinsel*. Cologne, 1970.

————. "Phasen des hanseatisch-nordeuropäischen Südamerikahandels," *Hansische Geschichtsblätter* 78 (1960): 87–120.

————. *The Rise of the European Economy: An Economic History of Continental Europe from the Fifteenth to the Eighteenth Century*. Ed. and rev. Gerhard Benecke. New York, 1976.

————. "The Role of the Great Upper German Families in Financing the Discoveries." *Terrae Incognitae* 10 (1978): 45–59.

Kiening, Christian. *Das wilde Subjekt: Kleine Poetik der Neuen Welt*. Göttingen, 2006.

————. " 'Erfahrung' und 'Vermessung' der Welt in der frühen Neuzeit." In *Text—Bild—Karte: Kartographie der Vormoderne*, ed. Jürg Glauser and Christian Kiening, 221–51. Freiburg, 2007.

————. "Ordnung der Fremde: Brasilien und die theoretische Neugierde im 16. Jahrhundert." In *Curiositas: Welterfahrung und ästhetische Neugierde in Mittelalter und früher Neuzeit*, ed. Klaus Krüger, 59–109. Göttingen, 2002.

Klein, Bernhard. *Maps and the Writing of Space in Early Modern England and Ireland*. Basingstoke, Hampshire, 2001.

Knelfelkamp, Ulrich, and Hans-Joachim König. *Die Neuen Welten in alten Büchern: Entdeckung und Eroberung in frühen deutschen Schrift- und Bildzeugnissen*. Bamberg, 1988.

Koch, Mark. "Ruling the World: The Cartographic Gaze in Elizabethan Accounts of the New World." *Early Modern Literary Studies*, special issue 3, 4, no. 2 (1998): 11.1–39 (http://purl.oclc.org/emls/04–2/kochruli.htm).

Kohl, Karl-Heinz. "Über einige der frühesten graphischen Darstellungen der Bewohner der Neuen Welt in der europäischen Kunst." *Jahrbuch für Ästhetik* 1 (1985): 307–34.

König, Erich, ed. *Konrad Peutingers Briefwechsel*. Munich, 1923.

König, Hans-Joachim. "Vielfalt der Kulturen oder europäisches Muster? Amerika und Indios in frühen deutschen Schriftzeugnissen." In Prosperi and Reinhard, *Neue Welt im Bewusstsein der Italiener und Deutschen,* 175–213.

Krása, Miloslav, Josef Polišenský, and Peter Ratkoš, eds. *The Voyages of Discovery in the Bratislava Manuscript Lyc. 515/8 (Codex Bratislavensis).* Prague, 1986.

Krieger, Leonard. "Germany." In *National Consciousness, History, and Political Culture in Early-Modern Europe,* ed. Orest Ranum, 67–97. Baltimore, 1975.

Künast, Hans-Jörg. *"Getruckt zu Augspurg": Buchdruck und Buchhandel in Augsburg zwischen 1468 und 1555.* Tübingen, 1997.

Kupperman, Karen Ordahl, ed. *America in European Consciousness, 1493–1750.* Chapel Hill, 1995.

———. *Indians and English: Facing Off in Early America.* Ithaca, 2000.

Kusukawa, Sachiko. "Leonhart Fuchs on the Importance of Pictures." *Journal of the History of Ideas* 58, no. 3 (1997): 403–27.

Lach, Donald F. *Asia in the Making of Europe.* Vol. 1, book 1, *The Century of Discovery.* Chicago, 1965.

Langholm, Odd. *The Legacy of Scholasticism in Economic Thought: Antecedents of Choice and Power.* Cambridge, 1998.

Larner, John. *Marco Polo and the Discovery of the World.* New Haven, 1999.

Lattis, James M. *Between Copernicus and Galileo: Christoph Clavius and the Collapse of Ptolemaic Cosmology.* Chicago, 1994.

Law, John. "On the Methods of Long-Distance Control: Vessels, Navigation and the Portuguese Route to India," In *Power, Action and Belief: A New Sociology of Knowledge?* ed. John Law, 234–63. London, 1986.

Leitch, Stephanie. " 'Better than the Prodigies': The Prints of Hans Burgkmair, Jörg Breu, and the Marvels of the New World." Ph.D. dissertation, University of Chicago, 2005.

Lestringant, Frank. *Mapping the Renaissance World: The Geographical Imagination in the Age of Discovery.* Trans. David Fausett. Cambridge, 1994.

Long, Pamela O. *Openness, Secrecy, Authorship: Technical Arts and the Culture of Knowledge from Antiquity to the Renaissance.* Baltimore, 2001.

Lonicer, Adam. *Kreuterbuch/Kunstliche Conterfeytunge der Bäume . . . Gewürtze . . . vnd derselben Gestalt/natürlich Krafft vnd Wirckung.* Frankfurt a.M.: C. Egenolff, 1578.

Lowood, Henry. "The New World and the European Catalog of Nature." In Kupperman, *America in European Consciousness,* 295–323.

Lucidarius. *Eyn newer M. Elucidarius/Von allerhandt geschöpffen Gottes.* Strassburg: Jacob Cammerlander, 1535?

Luther, Martin. *Von Kauffshandlung vnd Wucher.* Wittenberg: Hans Lufft, 1524.

Lynch, John. *Spain, 1516–1598: From Nation State to World Empire.* Oxford, 1991.

MacCormack, Sabine. *Religion in the Andes: Vision and Imagination in Early Colonial Peru.* Princeton, 1991.

Mack, Hans-Hubertus. *Humanistische Geisteshaltung und Bildungsbemühungen: Am Beispiel von Heinrich Loriti Glarean (1488–1563).* Bad Heilbrunn, 1992.

Madrignano, Arcangelo. *Itinerarium Portugallensium e Lusitania in Indiam inde in occidentem et demum ad aquilonem.* Milan: J. A. Scinzenzeler, 1508?

Mancall, Peter C. "The Age of Discovery." *Reviews in American History* 26, no. 1 (1998): 26–53.

Mandeville, Sir John. *Incipit Itinerarius Johannes de Montevilla a terra Anglie in partes Jherosolimitanas, et in ulteriores transmarinas.* Cologne: Kornelius de Zierikzee, ca. 1500.

——. *Jean de Mandeville. Reisen. Reprint der Erstdrucke der deutschen Übersetzungen des Michel Velser (Augsburg, bei Anton Sorg, 1480) und des Otto von Diemeringen (Basel, bei Bernhard Richel, 1480/81).* Ed. Ernst Bremer and Klaus Ridder. Hildesheim, 1991.

——. *Von der erfärüng des strengen Ritters johannes von montaville.* Trans. Otto von Diemeringen. Strassburg: J. Knoblauch, 1507.

Manuel I of Portugal. *Ein abschrifft eines santbriefes so . . . dem Bapst Julio dem andern gesandt ist . . . von wunderbarlichen raysen vnd schieffarten.* Nuremberg: Johann Stuchs, 1508.

——. *Epistola potenissimi ac invictissimi Emanuelis regis Portugalie . . . De victoriis habitis in India et Malacha.* Erfurt: Mattheus Maler, 1513. Reprint, Nuremberg: J. Stuchs, 1513.

——. *Geschichte kurtzlich durch die von Portugalien in India, Morenland und andern erdtrich.* Nuremberg: J. Weissenburger, 1507.

——. *Gesta proxime per Portugalenses in India, Ethiopia et aliis orientalibus terris.* Nuremberg: J. Weissenburger, 1507. Reprint, Cologne: Johann von Landen, 1507.

——. *Taprobane Insule Orientalis Ethiopie acquisitio.* Strassburg: Johann Knobloch d. Ä., 1507.

Mason, Peter. *Deconstructing America: Representations of the Other.* London, 1990.

Mathis, Franz. *Die deutsche Wirtschaft im 16. Jahrhundert.* Munich, 1992.

McCready, William D. "Isidore, the Antipodeans and the Shape of the Earth." *Isis* 87, no. 1 (1996): 108–27.

McDonald, Mark P. "Burgkmair's Woodcut Frieze of the Natives of Africa and India." *Print Quarterly* 20, no. 3 (2003): 227–44.

McVaugh, Michael Rogers. "The Medieval Theory of Compound Medicines." Ph.D. dissertation, Princeton University, 1965.

Meadow, Mark A. "Merchants and Marvels: Hans Jacob Fugger and the Origins of the Wunderkammer." In Smith and Findlen, *Merchants and Marvels*, 182–200.

Medina, Pedro de. *L'Art de Naviguer (1554): A Facsimile Reproduction*. Delmar, NY, 1992.

Menninger, Annerose. *Die Macht der Augenzeugen: Neue Welt und Kannibalen-Mythos, 1492–1600*. Stuttgart, 1995.

Menzhausen, Joachim. "Elector Augustus's *Kunstkammer:* An Analysis of the Inventory of 1587." In *The Origins of Museums: The Cabinet of Curiosities in Sixteenth- and Seventeenth-Century Europe*, ed. Oliver Impey and Arthur Macgregor, 69–75. Oxford, 1985.

Mercator, Gerhard. *Atlas, sive Cosmographicae meditationes*. Düsseldorf: A. Buys, 1595.

———. *Tabulae Geographicae Cl. Ptolemaei ad mentem autoris restitute emendatae*. Cologne: Kempen, 1578.

Mertens, Bernd. *Im Kampf gegen die Monopole: Reichstagsverhandlungen und Monopolprozesse im frühen 16. Jahrhundert*. Tübingen, 1996.

Mignolo, Walter D. *The Darker Side of the Renaissance: Literacy, Territoriality, and Colonization*. Ann Arbor, 1995.

Milanesi, Marica. "Asarot oder Anian? Identität und Unterscheidung zwischen Asien und der Neuen Welt in der Kartographie des 16. Jahrhunderts (1500–1570)." In Prosperi and Reinhard, *Neue Welt im Bewusstsein der Italiener und Deutschen*, 15–68.

Montaigne, Michel de. "Apology for Raymond Sebond." In *The Complete Essays of Montaigne*, trans. Donald M. Frame, 318–457. Stanford, 1958.

Montanari, Massimo. *The Culture of Food*. Trans. Carl Ipsen. Oxford, 1994.

Montrose, Louis. "The Work of Gender in the Discourse of Discovery." *Representations* 33 (Winter 1991): 1–41.

Moran, Bruce T. "Princes, Machines and the Valuation of Precision in the 16th Century." *Sudhoffs Archiv* 61, no. 3 (1977): 209–28.

Moretti, Gabriella. "The Other World and the 'Antipodes': The Myth of the Unknown Countries between Antiquity and Renaissance." In Haase and Reinhold, *European Images of the Americas and the Classical Tradition*, 241–84.

Morison, Samuel Eliot. *The European Discovery of America*. Vol. 2, *The Southern Voyages*, A.D. *1492–1616*. New York, 1974.

Müller, Jan-Dirk. "Alte Wissensformen und neue Erfahrungen: Amerika in Sebastian Franck's *Weltbuch*." In Wenzel, *Gutenberg und die Neue Welt*, 171–93.

———. "Augsburger Drucker von Prosaromanen, 1470 bis 1600." In Gier and Janota, *Augsburger Buchdruck und Verlagswesen*, 337–52.

Müller, Karl Otto. *Welthandelsbräuche (1480–1540)*. Stuttgart, 1934.

Munro, John H. "The Monetary Origins of the 'Price Revolution': South German Silver Mining, Merchant Banking, and Venetian Commerce, 1470–1540." In *Global Connections and Monetary History, 1470–1800*, ed. Dennis O. Flynn, Arturo Giráldez, and Richard von Glahn, 1–34. Burlington, VT, 2003.

Münster, Sebastian. *Cosmographei: Beschreibung aller Lender*. Basel: H. Petri, 1550. Rev. eds., 1553, 1556, 1558, 1561, 1564, 1567, 1569, 1574, 1578.

———. *Cosmographia: Beschreibung aller Lender*. Basel: H. Petri, 1544. Rev. ed., Basel: H. Petri, 1545, 1548.

———. *Cosmographiae universalis lib. vi.* Basel: H. Petri, 1550. Reprint, 1552, 1554, 1559, 1572.

———. *Erklerung des newen Instruments der Sunnen*. Oppenheim: Jacob Kobel, 1528.

Münzer, Hieronymus. "Hieronymus Münzer's Bericht über die Entdeckung der Guinea." Ed. Friedrich Kunstmann. *Abhandlungen der III. Classe der königlichen Akademie der Wissenschaften*, Abtheilung II, 7: 291–362.

———. Letter to King John of Portugal. In *The Discovery of North America: A Critical Documentary and Historic Investigation*, ed. Henry Harrisse, 393–95. London, 1892.

Natürlicher kunst der Astronomei/Des weitberumpten M. Johannen Künigspergers. Strassburg: C. Egenolph for Paul Götz, 1529.

Neander, Michael. *Elementa sphaericae doctrinae, seu De primo motu*. Basel: Johann Oporinus, 1561.

Neuber, Wolfgang. *Fremde Welt im europäischen Horizont: Zur Topik der deutschen Amerika-Reiseberichte der Frühen Neuzeit*. Berlin, 1991.

———. " 'Garriebat philomena': Die erste Kolumbus-Reise und ihre narrative Tradierung in Deutschland bis zum Jahr 1600." In *Columbus zwischen zwei Welten: Historische und literarische Wertungen aus fünf Jahrhunderten*, ed. Titus Heydenreich, 125–42. Frankfurt a.M., 1992.

———. "Verdeckte Theologie: Sebastian Brant und die Südamerikaberichte der Frühzeit." In *Der Umgang mit dem Fremden: Beiträge zur Literatur aus und über Lateinamerika*, ed. Titus Heydenreich, 9–29. Munich, 1986.

Neukomm, Titus. "Brief eines Lindauers aus Venezuela vom Jahre 1535." Ed. Franz Jötze. *Forschungen zur Geschichte Bayerns* 15 (1907): 271–78.

Nevins, Mark David. "The Literature of Curiosity: Geographical and Exploration Writings in Early Northern Europe." Ph.D. dissertation, Harvard University, 1993.

Newe zeittung, von dem lande, das die Sponier funden haben ym 1521 iare genant Jucatan. Augsburg?: n.p., 1522?.

Newe zeytung aus Hispanien und Italien, mense Februario, 1534. Nuremberg?: n.p., 1534.

Nider, Johannes. *On the Contracts of Merchants.* Ed. Ronald B. Shuman. Trans. Charles H. Reeves. Norman, OK, 1966.

Nobles, Gregory H. "Straight Lines and Stability: Mapping the Political Order of the Anglo-American Frontier." *Journal of American History* 80, no. 1 (1993): 9–35.

Noonan, John T., Jr. *The Scholastic Analysis of Usury.* Cambridge, MA, 1957.

Norton, Marcia Susan. "New World of Goods: A History of Tobacco and Chocolate in the Spanish Empire, 1492–1700." Ph.D. dissertation, University of California–Berkeley, 2000.

Nutton, Vivian. "Greek Science in the Sixteenth-Century Renaissance." In *Renaissance and Revolution: Humanists, Scholars, Craftsmen and Natural Philosophers in Early Modern Europe,* ed. J. V. Field and Frank A. J. L. James, 15–28. Cambridge, 1993.

Ogilvie, Brian W. *The Science of Describing: Natural History in Renaissance Europe.* Chicago, 2006.

O'Gorman, Edmundo. *The Invention of America: An Inquiry into the Historical Nature of the New World and the Meaning of Its History.* Bloomington, IN, 1961.

Ohlau, Jürgen U. "Neue Quellen zur Familiengeschichte der Spengler: Lazarus Spengler und seine Söhne." *Mitteilungen des Vereins für Geschichte der Stadt Nürnberg* 52 (1963–64): 232–55.

Ortelius, Abraham. *Theatrum Orbis Terrarum.* Antwerp: C. Plantin, 1579.

Otte, Enrique. "Die Welser in Santo Domingo." In *Festschrift für Johannes Vincke,* 2: 475–518. Madrid, 1963.

———. "Jacob und Hans Cromberger und Lazarus Nürnberger, die Begründer des deutschen Amerikahandels." *Mitteilungen des Vereins für Geschichte der Stadt Nürnberg* 52 (1963–64): 129–62.

Padrón, Ricardo. *The Spacious Word: Cartography, Literature, and Empire in Early Modern Spain.* Chicago, 2004.

Pagden, Anthony. *European Encounters with the New World: From Renaissance to Romanticism.* New Haven, 1993.

———. *The Fall of Natural Man: The American Indian and the Origins of Comparative Ethnology.* Cambridge, 1982.

Palencia-Roth, Michael. "The Cannibal Law of 1503." In Williams and Lewis, *Early Images of the Americas,* 21–63.

———. "Enemies of God: Monsters and the Theology of Conquest." In *Monsters, Tricksters, and Sacred Cows: Animal Tales and American Identities,* ed. A. James Arnold, 23–49. Charlottesville, VA, 1996.

Palmer, Richard. "Pharmacy in the Republic of Venice in the Sixteenth Century." In *The Medical Renaissance of the Sixteenth Century,* ed. A. Wear, R. K. French, and I. M. Loine, 100–117. Cambridge, 1985.

Panhorst, Karl H. *Deutschland und Amerika: Ein Rückblick auf das Zeitalter der Entdeckungen und die ersten deutsch-amerikanischen Verbindungen unter besonderer Beachtung der Unternehmungen der Fugger und Welser.* Munich, 1928.

Paracelsus. "Von Blatern, Lähmi, Beulen, Löchern vnd Zitrachten der Franzosen vnd ire Gleichen, inhalten zehn schöne Bücher." In *Sämtliche Werke,* ed. Karl Sudhoff and Wilhelm Matthiessen, 6: 301–479. Munich, 1922.

———. *Von der Frantzösischen kranckheit drey Bücher.* Frankfurt a.M.: Hermann Gülfferich, 1553.

Parks, George B. "The Contents and Sources of Ramusio's *Navigationi.*" In *Navigationi et Viaggi: Venice 1563–1606,* by Gian Battista Ramusio, 1: 1–39. Amsterdam, 1970.

Pendergrass, Jan N. "Simon Grynaeus and the Mariners of *Novus Orbis* (1532)." *Medievalia et Humanistica: Studies in Medieval and Renaissance Culture,* n.s. 19 (1993): 27–45.

Perrone, Egidio. "The Young Book-keeper of the Fugger Company and the Propagation of Double-Entry Book-keeping after Pacioli in the Sixteenth Century." In *Convegno internationzionale straordinario per celebrare Fra' Luca Pacioli,* 231–37. Venice, 1995.

Peucer, Kasper. *De dimensione terrae, et fontibus doctrinae longitudinis et latitudinis locorum.* Wittenberg: Heirs of P. Seitz, 1550.

———. *De dimensione terrae et geometrice numerandis.* Wittenberg: J. Krafft, 1554. Reprint, Wittenberg: J. Lufft, 1579.

Peutinger, Christoph. "Ein Geldgeschäft Bartholomae Welser's und Gesellschaft." Ed. J. M. Freiherr von Welser. *Zeitschrift des Historischen Vereins für Schwaben und Neuburg* 1 (1874): 139–51.

Peutinger, Konrad. "Conrad Peutingers Gutachten zur Monopolfrage: Eine Untersuchung zur Wandlung der Wirtschaftsanschauungen im Zeitalter der Reformation." Ed. Clemens Bauer. *Archiv für Reformationsgeschichte* 45 (1954): 1–43.

———. "Ein Gutachten Conrad Peutingers in Sachen der Handelsgesellschaften, Ende 1522." *Zeitschrift des historischen Vereins für Schwaben und Neuburg* 2 (1895): 188–216.

Phillips, Seymour. "The Outer World of the European Middle Ages." In Schwartz, *Implicit Understandings,* 23–63.

Pieper, Renate. *Die Vermittlung einer neuen Welt: Amerika im Nachrichtennetz des Habsburgischen Imperiums, 1493–1598.* Mainz, 2000.

Pirckheimer, Willibald. *Germania et variis scriptoribus per brevis explicatio.* Nuremberg: J. Petreius, 1530. Rev. ed., 1532.

———. *Germania et variis scriptoribus per brevis explicatio.* Augsburg: H. Steiner, 1530. Reprint, Frankfurt a.M.: C. Egenolff, 1532; Wittenberg: n.p., 1571.

Pius II, Pope. *Asiae Europaque elegatiss. descriptio.* Cologne: Cervicornus, 1531.

Planitz, Hans von der. *Des Kursächsischen Rathes Hans von der Planitz. Berichte aus dem Reichsregiment in Nürnberg 1521–1523.* Ed. Ernst Wülcker. Leipzig, 1899.

Pliny the Elder. *Bücher vnd schrifften/von der Natur/art vnd eigentschafft der Creaturen oder Geschöpffe Gottes.* Frankfurt a.M.: Peter Schmidt for Sigmund Feyerabend and Simon Hüter, 1565.

———. *Natural History.* Trans. H. Rackham. 10 vols. London, 1938–63.

———. *Naturalis Historiae Opus.* Cologne: E. Cervicornus, 1523.

———. *Natürlicher History Fünff Bücher.* Trans. Heinrich von Eppendorff. Strassburg: Hans Schott, 1543.

Pock, Georg. "Der Nürnberger Kaufmann Georg Pock in Portugiesisch-Indien und im Edelsteinland Vijayanagara." Ed. Hedwig Kömmerling-Fitzler. *Mitteilungen des Vereins für Geschichte der Stadt Nürnberg* 55 (1967–68): 137–84.

Pock, Hans. *Ein new Rechenbüchlein auff der Linien vnd Federn . . . auff allen kauffmanschlag/zu gewinn vnd verlust.* Nuremberg: Valentin Neuber, 1549.

Pogo, Alexander. "Gemma Frisius, His Method of Determining Differences of Longitude by Transporting Timepieces (1530), and His Treatise on Triangulation (1533)." *Isis* 22, no. 2 (1935): 469–506.

Pohl, Frederick. *Amerigo Vespucci: Pilot Major.* New York, 1944.

Pohle, Jürgen. *Deutschland und die überseeische Expansion Portugals im 15. und 16. Jahrhundert.* Munich, 2000.

Pölnitz, Götz Freiherr von, and Hermann Kellenbenz. *Anton Fugger.* 3 vols. Tübingen, 1958–86.

———. "Die Beziehungen des Johannes Eck zum Augsburger Kapital." *Historisches Jahrbuch* 60 (1940): 685–706.

———. *Die Fugger.* 2nd ed. Frankfurt a.M., 1960.

———. *Jakob Fugger: Kaiser, Kirche und Kapital in der oberdeutchen Renaissance.* 2 vols. Tübingen, 1949–51.

Polo, Marco. *The Travels.* Trans. Ronald Latham. New York, 1958.

Poovey, Mary. *A History of the Modern Fact: Problems of Knowledge in the Sciences of Wealth and Society.* Chicago, 1998.

Prakash, Om. *European Commercial Enterprise in Pre-colonial India.* Cambridge, 1998.

Proclus Diadochus. *Procli Diadochi Sphera Astronomiam.* Leipzig: Martin Landsberg, ca. 1500.

Prosperi, Adriano, and Wolfgang Reinhard, eds. *Neue Welt im Bewusstsein der Italiener und Deutschen des 16. Jahrhunderts.* Berlin, 1993.

Ptolemaeus, Claudius. *Clavdivs Ptolemaevs Cosmographia. Ulm 1482.* Ed. R. Skelton. Amsterdam, 1963.

———. *Geographiae opus novissima.* Strassburg: J. Schott, 1513.

———. *Geographia universalis, vetus et nova complectens . . . libros viii.* Ed. and trans. Sebastian Münster. Basel: H. Petri, 1540. Reprint, 1542, 1545, 1552.

———. *Geographicae enarrationis libri octo.* Ed. and trans. Willibald Pirckheimer. Strassburg: J. Grüninger for J. Kolberger at Nuremberg, 1525.

———. *Libri VIII de Geographia e Graeco denuo traducti.* Cologne: Joannes Ruremundamus, 1540.

———. *Opere . . . Nova translatio . . . Joanne Vernero . . . interpreti.* Nuremberg: H. Stuchs, 1514.

———. *Opus Geographiae noviter castigatum et emaculatum.* Strassburg: J. Grüninger, 1522.

———. *Ptolemaeus auctis restitutus . . . cum tabulis veteribus ac novis.* Strassburg: J. Schott, 1520.

———. *Ptolemy's Almagest.* Trans. G. J. Toomer. New York, 1984.

Quétel, Claude. *History of Syphilis.* Trans. Judith Braddock and Brian Pike. Cambridge, 1990.

Ralegh, Walter. *The Discoverie of the Large, Rich, and Bewtiful Empyre of Guiana.* Ed. Neil L. Whitehead. Norman, OK, 1997.

Raman, Shankar. *Framing "India": The Colonial Imaginary in Early Modern Culture.* Stanford, 2002.

Randles, W. G. L. "Classical Models of World Geography and their Transformation Following the Discovery of America." In Haase and Reinhold, *European Images of the Americas and the Classical Tradition,* 5–76.

Ravenstein, E. G. *Martin Behaim: His Life and His Globe.* London, 1908.

Reeds, Karen Meier. *Botany in Medieval and Renaissance Universities.* New York, 1991.

———. "Renaissance Humanism and Botany." *Annals of Science* 33, no. 6 (1976): 519–42.

Regiomontanus, Johann, and George Peurbach. *Epitome, in Cl. Ptolemaei Magnam compositionem.* Basel: H. Petri, 1543.

Reichert, Folker E. "Die Erfindung Amerikas durch die Kartographie." *Archiv für Kulturgeschichte* 78, no. 1 (1996): 115–43.

———. "Ludovico de Varthema und sein Itinerar." Introduction to *Reisen im Orient: Ludovico de Varthema,* ed. and trans. Folker Reichert, 7–31. Sigmaringen, 1996.

Reisch, Gregor. *Margarita philosophica.* Freiburg i. Br.: J. Schott, 1503.

———. *Margarita philosophica.* Strassburg: J. Schott, 1504.

Relaño, Francesc. *The Shaping of Africa: Cosmographic Discourse and Cartographic Science in Late Medieval and Early Modern Europe.* Hampshire, 2002.

Riddle, John M. *Dioscorides on Pharmacy and Medicine.* Austin, 1985.

Riesen, Adam. *Rechnung auff der linihen vnd federn in zal/maß/vnd gewicht auff allerley handierung.* Erfurt: Mathes Maler, 1525.

Rithaymer, Georgius. *De Orbis Terrarum Situ Compendium.* Nuremberg: Johann Petreius, 1538.

Roll, Christine. *Das Zweite Reichsregiment, 1521–1530.* Cologne, 1996.

Romeo, Rosario. *Le scoperte americane nella coscienza italiana del cinquecento.* Milan, 1954.

Romm, James S. *The Edges of the Earth in Ancient Thought: Geography, Exploration and Fiction.* Princeton, 1992.

———. "New World and 'Novos Orbes': Seneca in the Renaissance Debate over Ancient Knowledge of the Americas." In Haase and Reinhold, *European Images of the Americas and the Classical Tradition,* 77–116.

Rose, Paul Lawrence. *The Italian Renaissance of Mathematics: Studies on Humanists and Mathematicians from Petrarch to Galileo.* Geneva, 1975.

Rößlin, Eucharius. *Kalender mit allen Astronomischen haltungen.* Frankfurt a.M.: Christian Egenolph, 1533.

Rowland, Ingrid D. "Abacus and Humanism." *Renaissance Quarterly* 48, no. 4 (1995): 695–727.

Rubiés, Joan-Pau. "Futility in the New World: Narratives of Travel in Sixteenth-Century America." In *Voyages and Visions: Towards a Cultural History of Travel,* ed. Jaś Elsner and Joan-Pau Rubiés, 74–100. London, 1999.

———. "New Worlds and Renaissance Ethnology." *History and Anthropology* 6, nos. 2–3 (1993): 157–97.

———. *Travel and Ethnology in the Renaissance: South India through European Eyes, 1250–1625.* Cambridge, 2000.

Ruchamer, Jobst, trans. *Newe vnbekanthe landte.* Nuremberg: G. Stuchs, 1508.

Ruel, Jean. *De natura stirpium libri tres.* Basel: Froben, 1537.

Ruland, Harold L. "A Survey of the Double-Page Maps in Thirty-Five Editions of the *Cosmographia Universalis,* 1544–1628, of Sebastian Münster and in His Editions of Ptolemy's *Geographia,* 1540–1552." *Imago Mundi* 16 (1962): 84–97.

Russel, Paul A. "Syphilis, God's Scourge or Nature's Vengeance? The German Printed Response to a Public Problem in the Early Sixteenth Century." *Archiv für Reformationsgeschichte* 80 (1989): 286–307.

Ryan, Michael T. "Assimilating New Worlds in the Sixteenth and Seventeenth Centuries." *Comparative Studies in Society and History* 23, no. 4 (1981): 519–38.

Ryan, Simon. *The Cartographic Eye: How Explorers Saw Australia.* Cambridge, 1996.

Sacrobosco, Johann. *Introductorium compendiosum in tractatum sphere.* Ed. Johannes Glogouienses. Strassburg: H. Grau for J. Knoblauch, 1518.

———. *Libellus de sphaera.* Wittenberg: n.p., 1538.

———. *Opus sphaericum.* Cologne: Sons of H. Quetel, 1505. Reprint, 1508.

———. *Sphaera mundi.* Leipzig: M. Landsberg or C. Kachelofen, ca. 1502.

Said, Edward W. *Orientalism.* New York, 1979.

Sandman, Alison. "Mirroring the World: Sea Charts, Navigation, and Territorial Claims in Sixteenth-Century Spain." In Smith and Findlen, *Merchants and Marvels,* 83–108.

Sankt Brandans Seefahrt: Faksimiledruck der Originalausgabe, Augsburg um 1476. Ed. Elisabeth Geck. Wiesbaden, 1969.

Santos Lopes, Marília dos. *Afrika: Eine neue Welt im deutschen Schriften des 16. und 17. Jahrhunderts.* Stuttgart, 1992.

Sauer, Jonathan D. "Changing Perception and Exploitation of New World Plants in Europe, 1492–1800." In Chiappelli, *First Images of America,* 2: 813–32.

Scales, Len. "Late Medieval Germany: An Under-Stated Nation?" In *Power and the Nation in European History,* ed. Len Scales and Oliver Zimmer, 166–91. Cambridge, 2005.

Schaper, Christa. "Die Hirschvogel von Nürnberg und ihre Faktoren in Lissabon und Sevilla." In Kellenbenz, *Fremde Kaufleute auf der Iberischen Halbinsel,* 176–99.

———. *Die Hirschvogel von Nürnberg und ihr Handelshaus.* Nuremberg, 1973.

Schedel, Hartmann. *Liber chronicarum. German.* Nuremberg: A. Koberger, 1493.

Schenda, Rudolf. "Der 'gemeine Mann' und sein medikales Verhalten im 16. und 17. Jahrhundert." In *Pharmazie und der gemeine Mann: Hausarznei und Apotheke in deutschen Schriften der frühen Neuzeit,* 2nd ed., 9–20. Wolfenbüttel, 1988.

Schipperges, Heinrich. *Ideologie und Historiographie des Arabismus.* Wiesbaden, 1961.

Schlosser, Julius von. *Die Kunst- und Wunderkammern der Spätrenaissance: Ein Beitrag zur Geschichte des Sammelwesens.* 2nd ed. Braunschweig, 1978.

Schmidel, Ulrich. *Neuwe Welt: Das ist, Warhafftige Beschreibunge aller schönen Historien von erfindung viler unbekanten Königreichen.* Frankfurt a.M.: Martin Lechler for Sigmund Feyerabend and Simon Hüter, 1567. Also published in Feyerabend, *Ander theil dieses Weltbuchs.*

Schmidt, Benjamin. *Innocence Abroad: The Dutch Imagination and the New World, 1570–1670.* Cambridge, 2001.

———. "Inventing Exoticism: The Project of Dutch Geography and the Marketing of the World, circa 1700." In Smith and Findlen, *Merchants and Marvels,* 347–69.

———. "Mapping an Empire: Cartographic and Colonial Rivalry in Seventeenth-Century Dutch and English North America." *William and Mary Quarterly,* 3rd ser., 54, no. 3 (1997): 549–78.

Schmitt, Eberhard. "Der Beitrag der Hutten-Papiere zur Beurteilung des Venezuela-Unternehmens der Welser-Kompanie im 16. Jahrhundert." In Burkhardt, *Augsburger Handelshäuser im Wandel des historischen Urteils,* 191–209.

———. "Des Reichsritters Philipp von Hutten Suche nach dem goldenen Glück der Neuen Welt. Zur Erstveröffentlichung des ältesten bekannten Briefs eines Deutschen aus der Neuen Welt." *Periplus: Jahrbuch für aussereuropäische Geschichte* 2 (1992): 56–71.

———. *Konquista als Konzernpolitik: Die Welser-Stathalterschaft über Venezuela 1528–1556.* Bamberg, 1992.

Schmitz, Rudolf. "Der Arzneimittelbegriff der Renaissance." In Schmitz and Keil, *Humanismus und Medizin,* 1–22. Weinheim, 1984.

Schmitz, Rudolf, and Gundolf Keil, eds. *Humanismus und Medizin.* Weinheim, 1980.

Schnell, Rüdiger. "Deutsche Literatur und deutsches Nationalbewußtsein in Spätmittelalter und Früher Neuzeit." In Ehlers, *Ansätze und Diskontinuität deutscher Nationsbildung im Mittelalter,* 247–319.

Schöner, Christoph. *Mathematik und Astronomie an der Universität Ingolstadt im 15. und 16. Jahrhundert.* Berlin, 1994.

Schöner, Johann. *Appendices . . . in opusculum Globi astriferi nuper ad eodem editum.* Nuremberg: H. Stuchs, 1518.

———. *De nuper sub Castiliae ac Portugalliae regibus . . . repertis insulis ac regionibus.* Timiripae [Cologne?]: E. Cervicornus?, 1523.

———. *Luculentissima quaedam terrae totius descripto.* Nuremberg: H. Stuchs, 1515.

———. *Opusculum geographicum.* Nuremberg: P. Petreius, 1533. Reprint, in *Opera mathematica,* Nuremberg: J. vom Berg & V. Neuber, 1551.

Schulte, Aloys. *Geschichte der Grossen Ravensburger Handelsgesellschaft, 1380–1530.* 3 vols. Stuttgart, 1923.

Schultheiss, Werner. "Der fränkische Humanist Johannes Schöner und Amerika." *Frankische Blätter für Geschichtsforschung und Heimatpflege* 1, no. 5 (1949): 17–18.

———. "Geld und Finanzgeschäfte Nürnberger Bürger vom 13.–17. Jahrhundert." In *Beiträge zur Wirtschaftsgeschichte Nürnbergs,* 1: 49–116. Nuremberg, 1967.

Schwartz, Stuart B., ed. *Implicit Understandings: Observing, Reporting, and*

Reflecting on the Encounters between Europeans and Other Peoples in the Early Modern Era. Cambridge, 1994.

Scott, Joan W. "Experience." In *Feminists Theorize the Political,* ed. Judith Butler and Joan W. Scott, 22–40. New York, 1992.

Scott, Tom. *Society and Economy in Germany, 1300–1600.* New York, 2002.

Sebizius, Melchior. Introduction to *Siben Buecher von dem Feldbau/vnd vollkommmener bestellung eynes ordenlichen Mayerhofs oder Landguts.* Strassburg: B. Jobin, 1579.

Seelig, Lorenz. "Exotica in der Münchener Kunstkammer des bayerischen Wittelsbacher." In Trnek and Haag, *Exotica,* 145–61.

Shapin, Steven. *A Social History of Truth: Civility and Science in Seventeenth-Century England.* Chicago, 1994.

Shelton, Anthony Alan. "Cabinets of Transgression: Renaissance Collections and the Incorporation of the New World." In Elsner and Cardinal, *The Cultures of Collecting,* 177–203.

Shirley, Rodney W. *The Mapping of the World: Early Printed World Maps, 1471–1700.* London, 1983.

Shuman, Ronald B. Introduction to *On the Contracts of Merchants,* by Johannes Nider, vii–x. Norman, OK, 1966.

Sieber-Lehmann, Claudius. *Spätmittelalterlicher Nationalismus: Die Burgunderkriege am Oberrhein und in der Eidgenossenschaft.* Göttingen, 1995.

Silver, Larry. "Germanic Patriotism in the Age of Dürer." In *Dürer and his Culture,* ed. Dagmar Eichberger and Charles Zika, 38–68. Cambridge, 1998.

Simmer, Götz. *Gold und Sklaven: Die Provinz Venezuela während der Welser-Verwaltung (1528–1556).* Berlin, 2000.

Siraisi, Nancy G. *Medieval and Early Renaissance Medicine: An Introduction to Knowledge and Practice.* Chicago, 1990.

Slessarev, Vsevolod. *Prester John: The Letter and the Legend.* Minneapolis, 1959.

Slights, William W. E. *Managing Readers: Printed Marginalia in English Renaissance Books.* Ann Arbor, 2001.

Smith, Pamela H., and Paula Findlen, eds. *Merchants and Marvels: Commerce, Science and Art in Early Modern Europe.* New York, 2002.

Smith, Stefan Halikowski. "A Question of Quality: The Commercial Contest between Portuguese Atlantic Spices and Their Venetian Levantine Equivalents during the Sixteenth Century." *Itinerario* 26, no. 2 (2002): 45–63.

Soden, Franz Freiherr von, and J. K. F. Knaake, eds. *Christoph Scheurl's Briefbuch, ein Beitrag zur Geschichte der Reformation und ihrer Zeit.* Potsdam, 1867.

Solinus, C. Julius. *[D]e Memorabilibus Mundi.* Speyer: Konrad Hirst, 1512.

————. *Rerum Toto Orbe Memorabilium.* Basel: M. Isengrin and H. Petri, 1538.

Spitz, Lewis. "The Course of German Humanism." In *Itinerarium Italicum: The Profile of the Italian Renaissance in the Mirror of Its European Transformations,* ed. Heiko Oberman and Thomas Brady, 371–436. Leiden, 1975.

Sprague, T. A. "The Herbal of Leonhart Fuchs." *Journal of the Linnean Society* 48 (1931): 545–642.

Sprenger, Balthasar. *Die Merfart vnd erfarung nüwer Schiffung vnd Wege zu viln onerkanten Inseln vnd Künigreichen.* N.p.: n.p., 1509. Also published in Hümmerich, "Quellen und Untersuchungen."

Staden, Hans. *Warhafftig Historia unnd beschreibung einer Landschafft.* Frankfurt a.M.: W. Han, 1557. Reprint, *Warhafftige Historia.*

————. *Warhaftige Historia und beschreibung eyner Landtschafft der Welden, Nacketen, Grimmingen Menschfresser.* Marburg: A. Kolbe, 1557. Reprint, *Varhaftige beschreibung eyner Landschafft.* Also published in Feyerabend, *Ander theil dieses Weltbuchs.*

Stadtwald, Kurt. *Roman Popes and German Patriots: Antipapalism in the Politics of the German Humanist Movement from Gregor Heimburg to Martin Luther.* Geneva, 1996.

Stagl, Justin. *A History of Curiosity: The Theory of Travel, 1550–1800.* Chur, 1995.

Stannard, Jerry. "Dioscorides and Renaissance Materia Medica." In Florkin, *Materia Medica in the XVIth Century,* 1–21.

Stauber, Richard. *Die Schedelsche Bibliothek: Ein Beitrag zur Geschichte der Ausbreitung der italienischen Renaissance, des deutschen Humanismus und der medizinischen Literatur.* Freiburg i. Br., 1908.

Stein, Claudia. *Die Behandlung der Franzosenkrankheit in der Frühen Neuzeit am Beispiel Augsburgs.* Stuttgart, 2003.

Stoeffler, Johannes. *Cosmographicae Aliquot descriptiones.* Marburg: E. Cervicornus, 1537.

————. *[I]n Procli Diadochi . . . Sphaeram mundi . . . commentarius.* Tübingen: Ulrich Morhart, 1534.

Strabo. *De Situ Orbis Libri XVII.* Basel: H. Petri, 1549.

————. *Geographicorum Lib. XVII.* Basel: Johan Walder, 1539.

Strauss, Gerald. *Sixteenth Century Germany: Its Topography and Topographers.* Madison, 1959.

Strauss, Walter L. *The Complete Drawings of Albrecht Dürer.* 6 vols. New York, 1974.

Strieder, Jacob. *Aus Antwerpener Notariatsachiven: Quellen zur Deutschen Wirtschaftsgeschichte des 16. Jahrhunderts.* 1930. Reprint, Wiesbaden, 1962.

————. "Das wirtschaftliche Gesicht des Zeitalters der Fugger." In *Das reiche Augsburg: Ausgewählte Aufsätze Jakob Strieders zur Augsburger und süddeutschen Wirtschaftsgeschichte des 15. und 16. Jahrhunderts,* ed. Heinz Friedrich Deininger, 3–49. Munich, 1938.

Stübler, Eberhard. *Leonhart Fuchs: Leben und Werk.* Munich, 1928.

Surius, Laurentius. *Kurtze Chronik oder Beschreibung der vornembsten händeln vnd geschichten.* Trans. Heinrich Fabricius. Cologne: Gerwinus Calenius and the Heirs of Johann Quentel, 1568.

Svejokovský, František. "Three Centuries of America in Czech Literature, 1508–1818." In *East Central European Perceptions of Early America,* ed. Béla Király and George Barany, 33–55. Lisse, 1977.

Swetz, Frank J. *Capitalism and Arithmetic: The New Math of the 15th Century; Including the Full Text of the "Treviso Arithmetic" of 1478.* Trans. David Eugene Smith. La Salle, IL, 1987.

Talbot, Charles H. "America and the European Drug Trade." In Chiappelli, *First Images of America,* 2: 833–44.

Tannstetter, Georg [Collimitus], ed. *De natura locorum,* by Albertus Magnus. Vienna: n.p., 1514. Reprint, Strassburg: M. Schürer for L. & L. Alantsee, 1515.

Tedeschi, Martha. "Publish and Perish: The Career of Lienhart Holle in Ulm." In *Printing the Written Word: The Social History of Books, circa 1450–1520,* ed. Sandra Hindman, 41–67. Ithaca, 1991.

Thorndike, Lynn. *The "Sphere" of Sacrobosco and Its Commentators.* Chicago, 1949.

Todorov, Tzvetan. *The Conquest of America: The Question of the Other.* Trans. Richard Howard. New York, 1984.

Toellner, R. "Matthäus Kardinal Lang von Wellenburg und Paracelsus: Zur Polemik der Paracelsus gegen Kardinal Lang und die Fugger." In *Aktuelle Probleme aus der Geschichte der Medizin,* ed. R. Blaser and H. Buess, 489–97. Basel, 1966.

Transylvanus, Maximilianus. *De Moluccis insulis, itemque aliis pluribus mirandis, quae novissima Castellanorum navigatio suscepta nuper invenit.* Cologne: E. Cervicornus, 1523.

Trnek, Helmut, and Sabine Haag, eds. *Exotica: Portugals Entdeckungen im Spiegel fürstlicher Kunst- und Wunderkammern der Renaissance.* Mainz, 2001.

Tudela, Almudena Pérez de, and Annemaire Jordan Gschwend. "Luxury Goods for Royal Collectors: Exotica, Princely Gifts and Rare Animals Exchanged between the Iberian Courts and Central Europe in the Renaissance (1560–1612)." In Trnek and Haag, *Exotica,* 1–127.

Turnbull, David. "Cartography and Science in Early Modern Europe: Mapping the Construction of Knowledge Spaces." *Imago Mundi* 48 (1996): 5–24.

Tzanaki, Rosemary. *Mandeville's Medieval Audiences: A Study on the Reception of the "Book" of Sir John Mandeville (1371–1550).* Hampshire, 2003.

Vadianus, Joachim [Joachim von Watt]. *Epitome trium terrae partium, Asia, Africae et Europae.* Zurich: C. Froschauer, 1534. Reprint, 1546, 1548, ca. 1550.

———, ed. *Pomponii Melae de orbis situ libri tres.* Vienna: L & L. Alantsee, 1518. Reprint, Basel: A. Cratander, 1522, 1557, 1564.

Van der Krogt, Peter. "Gerhard Mercators Atlas." In *Vierhundert Jahre Mercator, Vierhundert Jahre Atlas: "Die ganze Welt zwischen zwei Buchdeckeln," Eine Geschichte der Atlanten,* ed. Hans Wolff, 30–39. Weissenhorn (Bayern), 1995.

Van Egmond, Warren. "The Commercial Revolution and the Beginnings of Western Mathematics in Renaissance Florence, 1300–1500." Ph.D. dissertation, Indiana University, 1976.

Varthema, Ludovico de. *Die Ritterlich und lobwirdig rayß.* Augsburg: Hans Miller, 1515. Reprint, Delmar, NY, 1992.

Verardi, Carlo. *In laudem . . . Fer. Hisp. regis.* Basel: J. Bergmann, 1494.

Vergil, Polydore. *On Discovery.* Trans. and ed. Brian P. Copenhaver. Cambridge, MA, 2002.

Vespucci, Amerigo. *Be [De] ora antarctica per regem Portugallie pridem inventa.* Strassburg: M. Hupfuff, 1505.

———. *Das sind die new gefunden menschen oder volcker.* Nuremberg: G. Stuchs, 1505–6.

———. *Dise figur anzaight uns das volck und insel.* Augsburg: H. Froschauer, 1505–6 (2 versions).

———. *Diß büchlein saget wie die . . . her Fernandus K. zü Castilien und herr Emanuel K. zü Portugal haben das weyte mör ersüchet unnd funden vil Insulen unnd ein Nüwe Welt.* Strassburg: J. Grüninger, 1509.

———. *Epistola Albericij. De novo mundo.* Rostock: H. Barkhusen, 1505.

———. *Mundus Novus.* Augsburg: J. Otmar, 1504 (2 versions).

———. *Mundus Novus.* Cologne: J. Landen, 1505.

———. *Mundus Novus.* Nuremberg: n.p., 1505.

———. *Van den nygen Insulen und landen.* Magdeburg: J. Winter, 1506.

———. *Von den nawen Insulen unnd Landen.* Leipzig: W. Müller [Stöckel], 1505.

———. *Von den newen Insulen und landen.* Leipzig: M. Landsberg, 1506 (2 versions).

———. *Von den nüwen Insulen und landen.* Strassburg: M. Hupfuff, 1505.

———. *Von der neü gefunden Region.* Basel: M. Furter, 1505.

———. *Von der neüwen gefunden Region.* Munich: J. Schobser, 1505.

———. *Von der neuw gefunden Region.* Augsburg: J. Schönsperger, ca. 1505.

———. *Von der new gefunnden Region.* Nuremberg: W. Huber, 1506.

Vigneras, Louis-André. "Saint Thomas, Apostle of America." *Hispanic American Historical Review* 57, no. 1 (1977): 82–90.

Vivanti, Corrado. "Die Humanisten und die geographischen Entdeckungen." In Prosperi and Reinhard, *Neue Welt im Bewusstsein der Italiener und Deutschen,* 273–90.

Vogel, Klaus A. "'America': Begriff, geographische Konzeption und frühe Entdeckungsgeschichte in der Perspektive der deutschen Humanisten." In *Von der Weltkarte zum Kuriositätenkabinett: Amerika im deutschen Humanismus und Barock,* ed. Karl Kohut, 11–43. Frankfurt a.M., 1995.

———. "Amerigo Vespucci und die Humanisten in Wien. Die Rezeption der geographischen Entdeckungen und der Streit zwischen Joachim Vadian und Johannes Camers über die Irrtümer der Klassiker." *Pirckheimer Jahrbuch* (1992): 53–104.

———. "Cultural Variety in a Renaissance Perspective: Johannes Boemus on 'The Manners, Laws and Customs of All People' (1520)." In *Shifting Cultures: Interaction and Discourse in the Expansion of Europe,* ed. Henriette Bugge and Joan-Pau Rubiés, 17–34. Münster, 1995.

———. "L'écho des découvertes dans la littérature géographique allemande de la première moitié du XVIe siècle." In Aubin, *La Découverte,* 295–308.

———. "Neue Horizonte der Kosmographie: Die kosmographischen Bücherlisten Hartmann Schedels (um 1498) und Konrad Peutingers (1523)." *Anzeiger des Germanischen Nationalmuseums* (1991): 77–85.

———. "Sphaera terrae: Das mittelalterliche Bild der Erde und die kosmographische Revolution." Ph.D. dissertation, Universität Göttingen, 1995.

Vogel, Kurt. "Überholte arithmetische kaufmännische Praktiken aus dem Mittelalter." In *Beiträge zur Geschichte der Arithmetik,* 67–87. Munich, 1978.

Wagner, Sabine. "Von 'neüwen inseln' und 'canibales': Zur Columbus- und Anghiera-Rezeption bei Sebastian Münster." In *Columbus zwischen zwei Welten: Historische und literarische Wertungen aus fünf Jahrhunderten,* ed. Titus Heydenreich, 107–24. Frankfurt a.M., 1992.

Wake, C. H. H. "The Changing Pattern of Europe's Pepper and Spice Imports, ca. 1400–1700." *Journal of European Economic History* 8, no. 2 (1979): 361–403.

Waldseemüller, Martin. *Der welt kugel.* Strassburg: J. Grüninger, 1509.

———. *Globus mundi. Declaratio sive descriptio mundi et totius orbis terrarum.* Strassburg: J. Grüninger, 1509.

Waldseemüller, Martin, and Matthias Ringmann. *Cosmographiae introductio.* St. Die: G. Lud, 1507 (4 editions). Reprint, Strassburg: J. Grüninger, 1509.

———. *Cosmographiae Introductio and the English translation of Joseph Fischer and Franz von Wieser.* New York, 1907. Reprint, 1966.

Walter, Rolf. "Nürnberg, Augsburg und Lateinamerika im 16. Jahrhundert—Die Begegnung zweier Welten." *Pirckheimer Jahrbuch* (1986): 45–82.

Weber, A. S. "Queu du Roi, Roi des Queux: Taillevent and the Profession of Medieval Cooking." In *Food and Eating in Medieval Europe,* ed. Martha Carlin and Joel T. Rosenthal, 145–57. London, 1998.

Weimann, Karl-Heinz. "Paracelsus und Kardinal Matthäus Lang als Gegner im Guajak-Streit." *Sudhoffs-Archiv* 45 (1961): 193–200.

Weitnauer, Alfred. *Venezianischer Handel der Fugger: Nach der Musterbuchhaltung des Matthäus Schwarz.* Munich, 1931.

Welser, Joh. Mich. Ant. von, ed. "Zur Geschichte der Welser in Venezuela." *Zeitschrift des Historischen Vereins für Schwaben und Neuburg* 1 (1874): 334–41.

Wenzel, Horst, ed. *Gutenberg und die Neue Welt.* Munich, 1994.

Werner, Theodor Gustav. "Das Kupferhüttenwerk des Hans Tetzel aus Nürnberg auf Kuba und seine Finanzierung durch europäisches Finanzkapital (1545–1571)." *Vierteljahrschrift für Sozial- und Wirtschaftsgeschichte* 48, no. 4 (1961): 289–329; 48, no. 4 (1961): 444–502.

———. "Europäisches Kapital in ibero-amerikanischen Montanunternehmungen des 16. Jahrhunderts." *Vierteljahrschrift für Sozial- und Wirtschaftsgeschichte* 48, no. 1 (1961): 18–55.

———. "Repräsentanten der Augsburger Fugger und Nürnberger Imhoff als Urheber der wichtigsten Handschriften des Paumgartner-Archivs über Welthandelsbräuche im Spätmittelalter und am Beginn der Neuzeit." *Vierteljahrschrift für Sozial- und Wirtschaftsgeschichte* 52, no. 1 (1965): 1–41.

———. "Zur Geschichte Tetzelscher Hammerwerke bei Nürnberg und des Kupferhüttenwerks Hans Tetzels auf Kuba." *Mitteilungen des Vereins für Geschichte der Stadt Nürnberg* 55 (1967–68): 214–25.

Westman, Robert S. "The Astronomer's Role in the Sixteenth Century: A Preliminary Study." *History of Science* 18, no. 2 (1980): 105–47.

Whitaker, Thomas W. "American Origin of the Cultivated Cucurbits." *Annals of the Missouri Botanical Garden* 34, no. 2 (1947): 101–11.

Williams, Jerry M., and Robert E. Lewis, eds. *Early Images of the Americas: Transfer and Invention.* Tucson, 1993.

Woodward, David. "Medieval *Mappaemundi.*" In Harley and Woodward, *The History of Cartography,* 1: 286–370.

Wuttke, Dieter. "Humanismus in den deutschsprachigen Ländern und Entdeckungsgeschichte, 1493–1534." *Pirckheimer Jahrbuch* (1992): 9–52.

Yamey, B. S. "Scientific Bookkeeping and the Rise of Capitalism." *Economic History Review,* 2nd ser., 1, nos. 2–3 (1949): 99–113.

Zacher, Christian K. *Curiosity and Pilgrimage: The Literature of Discovery in Fourteenth-Century England.* Baltimore, 1976.

Zamora, Margarita. *Reading Columbus.* Berkeley and Los Angeles, 1993.

Zárate, Augustin de. *A History of the Discovery and Conquest of Peru.* 1581. Reprint, London, 1933.

Zerubavel, Eviatar. *Terra Cognita: The Mental Discovery of America.* New Brunswick, NJ, 1992.

Zeydel, Edwin H. "Sebastian Brant and the Discovery of America." *Journal of English and Germanic Philology* 42 (1943): 410–11.

Ziegler, Jacob. *Iacobi Ziegleri . . . in C. Plinii de Naturali Historia Librum Secundum commentarius . . . Item, Georgii Collimitii, et Ioachimi Vadiani, in eundem secundum Plinii scholia quaedam.* Basel: H. Petri, 1531.

Index

Italicized page numbers refer to illustrations.